DAILY LIGHT
IN THE GOOD NEWS BIBLE

Daily Light

IN THE GOOD NEWS BIBLE

Compiled by Geoffrey Baskett

Collins

Marshall Pickering

First published in Great Britain in 1990 by Marshall Pickering

Marshall Pickering is an imprint of
the Collins Religious Division,
part of the Collins Publishing Group,
8 Grafton Street, London W1X 3LA

ISBN 0 551 02040 7

Text set in Times by Avocet Robinson, Buckingham

Printed in Great Britain by
Cox & Wyman Ltd, Reading, Berks

I am the light of the world.
Whoever follows me will have
the light of life and will
never walk in darkness.

– John 8:12

FOREWORD

This remarkable book of devotions contains two sections of Bible Readings for each day—Morning and Evening. This arrangement of Scripture selections is truly "Daily Light on the Daily Path".

The Scripture passages for each morning and evening revolve around a single theme. In one year you will have read portions from Genesis to Revelation. We commend this heartily for your daily reading.

Keep this book by your side, morning and evening. In the Bible are to be found "everything we need to live a truly religious life" (2 Peter 1:3).

The regular reading of the Word of God is important to our daily growth in the meaning and power of the Christian life. In times like these it is well to be grounded in a Book that is a lamp to our feet, and a light to our path (Psalm 119:105).

Billy Graham

THE STORY OF DAILY LIGHT

The origin of Daily Light is so closely bound up with the family of Bagster and the publishing firm of that name, that the proper background of the compilation of this most popular of all daily devotional books must necessarily include some account of Samuel Bagster, his antecedents and life.

Samuel Bagster was born on December 26, 1772, the second son of George and Mary Bagster of a Lyme Regis, Dorsetshire, family. Samuel Bagster's father, George Bagster, was a member of the congregation which assembled for worship under the pastorship of Dr Andrew Gifford, a Baptist minister, notable antiquarian and assistant librarian at the British Museum. It was at these prayer meetings that George Bagster met his friend Mr John Birch, whose daughter, Eunice Birch, became Samuel Bagster's wife.

When Samuel Bagster was seven years of age, his father sent him to school with the Rev. John Ryland, a Baptist minister who was the father of the well-known Dr Ryland, of Bristol. From his parents and from Rev. John Ryland, Samuel Bagster learned the precepts and practice of a devout Christian which sustained him throughout his life and which in turn he passed on to his children.

Samuel Bagster was indentured to a bookseller in the Strand and on completion of his apprenticeship he opened his own bookshop at No. 81 Strand, London, on April 19, 1794, when twenty-one years of age. As one might expect from a high-principled and religious-minded man, he made it a rule that he would never sell any book which might be considered questionable in taste or subject. An attitude of mind by no means common in those days.

Samuel Bagster and Eunice Birch were married at the Parish Church of St Giles in the Field on December 19, 1797. She was a brave woman of high principles and steadfast faith, a real helpmeet to her husband throughout their long married life. She died the day before her hundredth birthday on August 22, 1877, a few months after she had been honoured by a personal visit from Queen Victoria, who, it is said, knelt at Mrs Bagster's bedside to receive the blessing of this, her revered and venerable subject.

Samuel and Eunice Bagster were blessed with twelve children, and it was Jonathan, their tenth child, who was mainly responsible for the idea and for the method by which DAILY LIGHT was compiled. He was the Editor-in-Chief, and his daughter Ann was his chief assistant.

The practice of corporate daily worship had always been followed in the family, and it was the daily text that Jonathan Bagster selected that the family, joined together in prayer, were asked to illustrate by further applicable texts. The resultant Scripture quotations were then carefully considered, discussed and arranged by common consent of all those present, after which the manuscript would be laid aside for prayer and meditation to see if there would be any guidance for its further improvement. Sometimes it was weeks before it was felt that the reading for a particular day could not be improved and then that page would be sent to the printer to be set in type. Later it would be read and corrected and all the references would be verified. Each day for over two years the readings were compiled, corrected and improved in this way until the whole book was ready for publication in two volumes, one of the Morning readings and the other of the Evening readings.

Robert Bagster, one of Jonathan's sons, who as a lad

was present with the family at these daily prayers, wrote these words many years after: "Few are able to appreciate the heart-searching care with which every text was selected, the days, nay the weeks, of changes, alterations and improvements, until at last each page was passed on to the printer. It has been said that each page was prayed over. This is true enough, but far less than the fact that portions were left over for weeks to see if any further guidance came. So this book stands to-day quite unrivalled, with not one word altered since those devoted people put it forth to the world. It has struck me as a wonderful thought that hundreds of thousands of Christians throughout the world, to its remotest corners, are each day reading the same page with its message of comfort and help."

The truth of this last statement is amply borne out by the many letters that are still received which tell of the help that DAILY LIGHT has been, and still is, to the Missionaries from the frozen wastes of Canada and Alaska to the steaming heat of the jungles of Assam, Burma and tropical Africa and every climate between these extremes.

Thus the spirit of God-fearing devotion, passed down through successive generations, bears fruit which increases year by year and spreads to the very ends of the earth. The parable of the grain of mustard seed was never so aptly illustrated as by the story of DAILY LIGHT.

In 1970 Samuel Bagster Ltd. was incorporated with Marshall Morgan & Scott, whose successor, Marshall Pickering, is now part of the Religious Division of the Colins Publishing Group.

The one thing I do, however, is to forget what is behind me . . . so I run straight towards the goal in order to win the prize, which is God's call through Christ Jesus to the life above.[1]

Father! You have given them to me, and I want them to be with me where I am, so that they may see my glory, the glory you gave me; for you loved me before the world was made.[2]—I am still full of confidence, because I know whom I have trusted, and I am sure that he is able to keep safe until that Day what he has entrusted to me.[3]—God, who began this good work in you, will carry it on until it is finished on the Day of Christ Jesus.[4]

You know that many runners take part in a race, but only one of them wins the prize. Run, then in such a way as to win the prize. Every athlete in training submits to strict discipline, in order to be crowned with a wreath that will not last; but we do it for one that will last for ever[5]—Let us rid ourselves of everything that gets in the way, and of the sin which holds on to us so tightly, and let us run with determination the race that lies before us. Let us keep our eyes fixed on Jesus, on whom our faith depends from beginning to end.[6]

[1]PHIL. 3.13, 14. [2]John 17.24.—[3]2 Tim. 1.12.—[4]Phil. 1.6. [5]1 Cor. 9.24, 25.—[6]Heb. 12.1, 2.

Evening

The LORD himself will lead you and be with you. He will not fail you or abandon you, so do not lose courage or be afraid.[1]

If you do not go with us, don't make us leave this place.[2]—LORD, I know that no one is the master of his own destiny; no person has control over his own life.[3]

The LORD guides a man in the way he should go and protects those who please him. If they fall, they will not stay down, because the LORD will help them up.[4]

I always stay close to you, and you hold me by the hand. You guide me with your instruction and at the end you will receive me with honour.[5]—I am certain that nothing can separate us from his love: neither death nor life, neither angels nor other heavenly rulers or powers, neither the present nor the future, neither the world above nor the world below—there is nothing in all creation that will ever be able to separate us from the love of God which is ours through Christ Jesus our Lord.[6]

[1]DEUT. 31.8. [2]Exod. 33.15.—[3]Jer. 10.23. [4]Ps. 37.23, 24. [5]Ps. 73.23, 24.—[6]Rom. 8.38, 39.

Morning

***Sing a new song to the Lord.*[1]**

Shout for joy to God our defender; sing praise to the God of Jacob! Start the music and beat the tambourines; play pleasant music on the harps and the lyres.[2]—He taught me to sing a new song, a song of praise to our God. Many who see this will take warning and will put their trust in the Lord.[3]

Remember that I have commanded you to be determined and confident! Don't be afraid or discouraged, for I, the Lord your God, am with you wherever you go.[4]—The joy that the Lord gives you will make you strong.[5]—Paul . . . thanked God and was greatly encouraged.[6]

You know that the time has come for you to wake up from your sleep. For the moment when we will be saved is closer now than it was when we first believed. The night is nearly over, day is almost here. Let us stop doing the things that belong to the dark, and let us take up weapons for fighting in the light. Let us conduct ourselves properly, as people who live in the light of day—no orgies or drunkenness, no immorality or indecency, no fighting or jealousy. But take up the weapons of the Lord Jesus Christ, and stop paying attention to your sinful nature and satisfying its desires.[7]

[1]ISA. 42.10. [2]Ps. 81.1, 2.—[3]Ps. 40.3. [4]Josh. 1.9.—[5]Neh. 8.10.—[6]Acts 28.15. [7]Rom. 13.11–14.

Evening

***Receive my prayer as incense, my uplifted hands as an evening sacrifice.*[1]**

Make an altar out of acacia wood, for burning incense. Put this altar outside the curtain which hangs in front of the Covenant Box. That is the place where I will meet you. Every morning when Aaron comes to get the lamps ready, he is to burn sweet-smelling incense on it. He must do the same when he lights the lamps in the evening. This offering of incense is to continue without interruption for all time to come.[2]

[Jesus] is able, now and always, to save those who come to God through him, because he lives for ever to plead with God for them.[3]—The smoke of the burning incense went up with the prayers of God's people from the hands of the angel standing before God.[4]

Come as living stones, and let yourselves be used in building the spiritual temple, where you will serve as holy priests to offer spiritual and acceptable sacrifices to God through Jesus Christ.[5]

Pray at all times.[6]

[1]PS. 141.2. [2]Ex. 30:1, 6–8. [3]Heb. 7.25.—[4]Rev. 8.4. [5]1 Pet. 2.5. [6]1 Thess. 5.17.

He led them by a straight road to a city where they could live.[1]

He found them wandering through the desert, a desolate, wind-swept wilderness. He protected them and cared for them, as he would protect himself. Like an eagle teaching its young to fly, catching them safely on its spreading wings, the LORD kept Israel from falling. The LORD alone led his people without the help of a foreign god.[2]—I am your God and will take care of you until you are old and your hair is grey. I made you and will care for you; I will give you help and rescue you.[3]

He gives me new strength. He guides me in the right paths, as he has promised. Even if I go through the deepest darkness, I will not be afraid, LORD, for you are with me. Your shepherd's rod and staff protect me.[4]

I will always guide you and satisfy you with good things. I will keep you strong and well. You will be like a garden that has plenty of water, like a spring of water that never runs dry.[5]—This God is our God for ever and ever; he will lead us for all time to come.[6]—He is the greatest teacher of all.[7]

[1]PS. 107.7. [2]Deut. 32.10–12.—[3]Isa. 46.4. [4]Ps. 23.3, 4. [5]Isa. 58.11.—[6]Ps. 48.14.—[7]Job 36.22.

Evening

Jesus asked him, "What do you want me to do for you?" "Sir," he answered, "I want to see again."[1]

Open my eyes, so that I may see the wonderful truths in your law.[2]—Then he opened their minds to understand the Scriptures.[3]

The Helper, the Holy Spirit, whom the Father will send in my name, will teach you everything and make you remember all that I have told you.[4]—Every good gift and every perfect present comes from heaven; it comes down from God, the Creator of the heavenly lights, who does not change or cause darkness by turning.[5]

I ask the God of our Lord Jesus Christ, the glorious Father, to give you the Spirit, who will make you wise and reveal God to you, so that you will know him. I ask that your minds may be opened to see his light, so that you will know what is the hope to which he has called you, how rich are the wonderful blessings he promises his people, and how very great is his power at work in us who believe. This power working in us is the same as the mighty strength which he used when he raised Christ from death and seated him at his right hand in the heavenly world.[6]

[1]LUKE 18.41. [2]Ps. 119.18.—[3]Luke 24.45. [4]John 14.26.—[5]Jas 1.17. [6]Eph. 1.17–20.

***You have not yet entered the land that the LORD your God is giving you, where you can live in peace.*[1]**

There is no safety here any more.[2]—There still remains for God's people a rest like God's resting on the seventh day.[3]—This hope . . . is safe and sure, and goes through the curtain of the heavenly temple into the inner sanctuary. On our behalf Jesus has gone in there before us, and has become a high priest for ever.[4]

There are many rooms in my Father's house, and I am going to prepare a place for you. I would not tell you this if it were not so. And after I go and prepare a place for you, I will come back and take you to myself, so that you will be where I am.[5]—I want very much to leave this life and be with Christ, which is a far better thing.[6]

He will wipe away all tears from their eyes. There will be no more death, no more grief or crying or pain. The old things have disappeared.[7]—In the grave wicked men stop their evil, and tired workmen find rest at last.[8]

Store up riches for yourselves in heaven, where moths and rust cannot destroy, and robbers cannot break in and steal. For your heart will always be where your riches are.[9]—Set your hearts on the things that are in heaven . . . Keep your minds fixed on things there, not on things here on earth.[10]

[1]DEUT. 12.9. [2]Mic. 2.10.—[3]Heb. 4.9.—[4]Heb. 6.19, 20. [5]John 14.2, 3.—[6]Phil. 1.23. [7]Rev. 21.4.—[8]Job 3.17. [9]Matt. 6.20, 21.—[10]Col. 3.1, 2.

Evening

***Where, Death, is your victory? Where, Death, is your power to hurt?*[1]**

Death gets its power to hurt from sin.[2]—He has appeared once and for all, to remove sin through the sacrifice of himself. Everyone must die once, and after that be judged by God. In the same manner Christ also was offered in sacrifice once to take away the sins of many. He will appear a second time, not to deal with sin, but to save those who are waiting for him.[3]

Since the children, as he calls them, are people of flesh and blood, Jesus himself became like them and shared their human nature. He did this so that through his death he might destroy the Devil, who has the power over death, and in this way set free those who were slaves all their lives because of their fear of death.[4]

The time is here for me to leave this life. I have done my best in the race, I have run the full distance, and I have kept the faith. And now there is waiting for me the victory prize of being put right with God.[5]

[1]1 COR. 15.55. [2]1 Cor. 15.56.—[3]Heb. 9.26–28. [4]Heb. 2.14, 15. [5]2 Tim. 4.6–8.

We who believe, then, do receive that rest which God promised.[1]

They . . . will not give up their sinning.[2]—I see a different law at work in my body—a law that fights against the law which my mind approves of. It makes me a prisoner to the law of sin which is at work in my body. What an unhappy man I am! Who will rescue me from this body that is taking me to death?[3]

Come to me, all of you who are tired from carrying heavy loads, and I will give you rest.[4]—Now that we have been put right with God through faith, we have peace with God through our Lord Jesus Christ. He has brought us by faith into this experience of God's grace, in which we now live. And so we boast of the hope we have of sharing God's glory![5]

Whoever receives that rest which God promised will rest from his own work.[6]—I no longer have a righteousness of my own, the kind that is gained by obeying the Law. I now have the righteousness that is given through faith in Christ, the righteousness that comes from God and is based on faith.[7]—He offered rest and comfort to all of you, but you refused to listen to him.[8]

[1]HEB. 4.3. [2]Jer. 9.5.—[3]Rom. 7.23, 24. [4]Matt. 11.28.—[5]Rom. 5.1, 2. [6]Heb. 4.10.—[7]Phil. 3.9.—[8]Isa. 28.12.

Evening

Lord, place a guard at my mouth, a sentry at the door of my lips.[1]

If you kept a record of our sins, who could escape being condemned?[2]—They made him so bitter that he spoke without stopping to think.[3]

It is not what goes into a person's mouth that makes him ritually unclean; rather, what comes out of it makes him unclean.[4]

Thoughtless words can wound as deeply as any sword, but wisely spoken words can heal. A lie has a short life, but truth lives on for ever.[5]—No one has ever been able to tame the tongue. It is evil and uncontrollable, full of deadly poison. Words of thanksgiving and cursing pour out from the same mouth. My brothers, this should not happen![6]

Now you must get rid of all these things: anger, passion, and hateful feelings. No insults or obscene talk must ever come from your lips. Do not lie to one another, for you have taken off the old self with its habits.[7]—God wants you to be holy and completely free from sexual immorality.[8]—They have never been known to tell lies.[9]

[1]PS. 141.3. [2]Ps. 130.3.—[3]Ps. 106.33. [4]Matt. 15.11. [5]Prov. 12.18, 19.—[6]Jas 3.8, 10. [7]Col. 3.8, 9.—[8]1 Thess. 4.3.—[9]Rev. 14.5.

***Lord* our God, may your blessings be with us. Give us success in all we do![1]**

You became famous in every nation for your perfect beauty, because I was the one who made you so lovely.[2]—All of us, then, reflect the glory of the Lord with uncovered faces; and that same glory, coming from the Lord, who is the Spirit, transforms us into his likeness in an ever greater degree of glory.[3]

Happy are those who obey the LORD, who live by his commands. Your work will provide for your needs; you will be happy and prosperous.[4]—Ask the LORD to bless your plans, and you will be successful in carrying them out.[5]

Keep on working with fear and trembling to complete your salvation, because God is always at work in you to make you willing and able to obey his own purpose.[6]—May our Lord Jesus Christ himself and God our Father, who loved us and in his grace gave us unfailing courage and a firm hope, encourage you and strengthen you to always do and say what is good.[7]

[1]PS. 90.17. [2]Ezek. 16.14.—[3]2 Cor. 3.18. [4]Ps. 128.1, 2.—[5]Prov. 16.3. [6]Phil. 2.12, 13.—[7]2 Thess. 2.16, 17.

Evening

The apostles returned and met with Jesus, and told him all they had done and taught.[1]

Some friends are more loyal than brothers.[2]—The LORD would speak with Moses face to face, just as a man speaks with a friend.[3]—You are my friends if you do what I command you. I do not call you servants any longer, because a servant does not know what his master is doing. Instead, I call you friends, because I have told you everything I have heard from my Father.[4]

When you have done all you have been told to do, say, "We are ordinary servants; we have only done our duty."[5]

The Spirit that God has given you does not make you slaves and cause you to be afraid; instead, the Spirit makes you God's children, and by the Spirit's power we cry out to God, "Father!"[6]

Don't worry about anything, but in all your prayers ask God for what you need, always asking him with a thankful heart.[7]—The LORD is pleased when good men pray.[8]

[1]MARK 6.30. [2]Prov. 18.24.—[3]Exod. 33.11.—[4]John 15.14, 15. [5]Luke 17.10. [6]Rom. 8.15. [7]Phil. 4.6.—[8]Prov. 15.8.

I pray you, O God, remember to my credit everything that I have done.[1]

The LORD [said] . . . "I remember how faithful you were when you were young, how you loved me when we were first married; you followed me through the desert."[2]—I will honour the covenant I made with you when you were young, and I will make a covenant with you that will last for ever.[3]—I will show my concern for you and keep my promise to bring you back home. I alone know the plans I have for you, plans to bring you prosperity and not disaster, plans to bring about the future you hope for.[4]

As high as the heavens are above the earth, so high are my ways and thoughts above yours.[5]—I would turn to God and present my case to him. We cannot understand the great things he does, and to his miracles there is no end.[6]—You have done many things for us, O LORD our God; there is no one like you! You have made many wonderful plans for us. I could never speak of them all—their number is so great![7]

[1]NEH. 5.19. [2]Jer. 2.2.—[3]Ezek. 16.60.—[4]Jer. 29.10, 11. [5]Isa. 55.9.—[6]Job 5.8, 9.—[7]Ps. 40.5.

Evening

I will always be with you; I will never abandon you.[1]

The LORD kept every one of the promises that he had made to the people of Israel.[2]—God is not like men, who lie; he is not a human who changes his mind. Whatever he promises, he does.[3]

Remember that the LORD your God is the only God and that he is faithful. He will keep his covenant and show his constant love to a thousand generations of those who love him and obey his commands.[4]—He never forgets his covenant.[5]

Can a woman forget her own baby and not love the child she bore? Even if a mother should forget her child, I will never forget you . . . I have written your name on the palms of my hands.[6]

The LORD your God is with you; his power gives you victory. The LORD will take delight in you, and in his love he will give you new life. He will sing and be joyful over you, as joyful as people at a festival.[7]

[1]JOSH. 1.5. [2]Josh. 21.45.—[3]Num. 23.19. [4]Deut. 7.9.—[5]Ps. 111.5. [6]Isa. 49.15, 16. [7]Zeph. 3.17, 18.

***Those who know you, LORD, will trust you; you do not abandon anyone who comes to you.*[1]**

The LORD is like a strong tower, where the righteous can go and be safe.[2]—God is my saviour; I will trust him and not be afraid. The LORD gives me power and strength; he is my saviour.[3]

I am an old man now; I have lived a long time, but I have never seen a good man abandoned by the LORD or his children begging for food.[4]—For the LORD loves what is right and does not abandon his faithful people. He protects them for ever, but the descendants of the wicked will be driven out.[5]—The LORD has made a solemn promise, and he will not abandon you, for he has decided to make you his own people.[6]—From such terrible dangers of death he saved us, and will save us; and we have placed our hope in him that he will save us again.[7]

Be satisfied with what you have. For God has said, "I will never leave you; I will never abandon you." Let us be bold, then, and say, "The Lord is my helper, I will not be afraid. What can anyone do to me?"[8]

[1]PS. 9.10. [2]Prov. 18.10.—[3]Isa. 12.2. [4]Ps. 37.25.—[5]Ps. 37.28.—[6]1 Sam. 12.22.—[7]2 Cor. 1.10. [8]Heb. 13.5, 6.

Evening

***They have never been known to tell lies; they are faultless.*[1]**

No sin will be found in Israel and no wickedness in Judah, because I will forgive those people whose lives I have spared.[2]—There is no other god like you, O LORD; you forgive the sins of your people who have survived. You do not stay angry for ever, but you take pleasure in showing us your constant love. You will be merciful to us once again. You will trample our sins underfoot and send them to the bottom of the sea![3]

God . . . decided that through Jesus Christ he would make us his sons . . . let us praise God for his glorious grace, for the free gift he gave us in his dear Son![4]—But now, by means of the physical death of his Son, God has made you his friends, in order to bring you, holy, pure, and faultless, into his presence.[5]

To him who is able to keep you from falling, and to bring you faultless and joyful before his glorious presence—to the only God our Saviour, through Jesus Christ our Lord, be glory, majesty, might, and authority, from all ages past, and now, and for ever and ever! Amen.[6]

[1]REV. 14.5. [2]Jer. 50.20.—[3]Mic. 7.18, 19. [4]Eph. 1.5, 6.—[5]Col. 1.22. [6]Jude 24, 25.

You have warned those who show you reverence, so that they might escape destruction.[1]

The LORD is my Banner.[2]—From east to west everyone will fear him and his great power. He will come like a rushing river, like a strong wind.[3]

Then we will shout for joy over your victory and celebrate your triumph by praising our God.[4]—The LORD has shown that we are in the right. Let's go and tell the people in Jerusalem what the LORD our God has done.[5]—In all these things we have complete victory through him who loved us![6]—Thanks be to God who gives us the victory through our Lord Jesus Christ![7]—Jesus is the one who leads them to salvation.[8]

Finally, build up your strength in union with the Lord and by means of his mighty power.[9]—Serve me as a brave and loyal soldier, and fight the LORD's battles.[10]—Don't be discouraged, any of you. Do the work, for I am with you . . . do not be afraid.[11]—Take a good look at the fields; the crops are now ripe and ready to be harvested![12]—Just a little while longer, and he who is coming will come; he will not delay.[13]

[1]PS. 60.4. [2]Exod. 17.15.—[3]Isa. 59.19. [4]Ps. 20.5.—[5]Jer. 51.10.—[6]Rom. 8.37.—[7]1 Cor. 15.57.—[8]Heb. 2.10. [9]Eph. 6.10.—[10]1 Sam. 18.17.—[11]Hag. 2.4, 5.—[12]John 4.35.—[13]Heb. 10.37.

Evening

Just one* [*thing*] *is needed.[1]

There are many who pray: "Give us more blessings, O LORD. Look on us with kindness!" But the joy that you have given me is more than they will ever have with all their corn and wine.[2]

As a deer longs for a stream of cool water, so I long for you, O God. I thirst for you, the living God.[3]—O God, you are my God, and I long for you. My whole being desires you; like a dry, worn-out, and waterless land, my soul is thirsty for you.[4]

"I am the bread of life," Jesus told them. "He who comes to me will never be hungry; he who believes in me will never be thirsty." "Sir . . . give us this bread always."[5]—Mary . . . sat down at the feet of the Lord and listened to his teaching.[6]—I have asked the LORD for one thing; one thing only do I want: to live in the LORD's house all my life, to marvel there at his goodness, and to ask for his guidance.[7]

[1]LUKE 10.42. [2]Ps. 4.6, 7. [3]Ps. 42.1, 2.—[4]Ps. 63.1. [5]John 6.35, 34.—[6]Luke 10.39.—[7]Ps. 27.4.

Morning

***May the God who gives us peace make you holy in every way and keep your whole being—spirit, soul, and body—free from every fault at the coming of our Lord Jesus Christ.*[1]**

Christ loved the church and gave his life for it . . . in order to present the church to himself in all its beauty—pure and faultless, without spot or wrinkle or any other imperfection.[2]—So we preach Christ to everyone. With all possible wisdom we warn and teach them in order to bring each one into God's presence as a mature individual in union with Christ.[3]

God's peace, which is far beyond human understanding, will keep your hearts and minds safe in union with Christ Jesus.[4]—The peace that Christ gives is to guide you in the decisions you make; for it is to this peace that God has called you together in the one body.[5]

May our Lord Jesus Christ himself and God our Father, who loved us and in his grace gave us unfailing courage and a firm hope, encourage you and strengthen you to always do and say what is good.[6]—He will also keep you firm to the end, so that you will be faultless on the Day of our Lord Jesus Christ.[7]

[1]1 THESS. 5.23. [2]Eph. 5.25, 27.—[3]Col. 1.28. [4]Phil. 4.7.—[5]Col. 3.15. [6]2 Thess. 2.16, 17.—[7]1 Cor. 1.8.

Evening

***But can you, O God, really live on earth among men and women?*[1]**

The people must make a sacred tent for me, so that I may live among them.[2]—There I will meet the people of Israel, and the dazzling light of my presence will make the place holy. I will live among the people of Israel, and I will be their God.[3]

He goes up to the heights, taking many captives with him; he receives gifts from rebellious men. The LORD God will live there.[4]

We are the temple of the living God! As God himself has said, "I will make my home with my people and live among them; I will be their God, and they shall be my people."[5]—Your body is the temple of the Holy Spirit, who lives in you.[6]—In union with him you too are being built together with all the others into a place where God lives through his Spirit.[7]

When I place my Temple there to be among them for ever, then the nations will know that I, the LORD, have chosen Israel to be my own people.[8]

[1]2 CHR. 6.18. [2]Exod. 25.8.—[3]Exod. 29.43, 45. [4]Ps. 68.18. [5]2 Cor. 6.16.— [6]1 Cor. 6.19.—[7]Eph. 2.22. [8]Ezek. 37.28.

O God, it is right for us to praise you in Zion and keep our promises to you.[1]

There is for us only one God, the Father, who is the Creator of all things and for whom we live; and there is only one Lord, Jesus Christ, through whom all things were created and through whom we live.[2]—So that all will honour the Son in the same way as they honour the Father. Whoever does not honour the Son does not honour the Father who sent him.[3]—Let us, then, always offer praise to God as our sacrifice through Jesus, which is the offering presented by lips that confess him as Lord.[4]—Giving thanks is the sacrifice that honours me, and I will surely save all who obey me.[5]

After this I looked, and there was an enormous crowd—no one could count all the people! They were from every race, tribe, nation, and language, and they stood in front of the throne and of the Lamb, dressed in white robes and holding palm branches in their hands. They called out in a loud voice: "Salvation comes from our God, who sits on the throne, and from the Lamb!" They worshipped God, saying, "Amen! Praise, glory, wisdom, thanksgiving, honour, power, and might belong to our God for ever and ever! Amen!"[6]

[1]PS. 65.1. [2]1 Cor. 8.6.—[3]John 5.23.—[4]Heb. 13.15.—[5]Ps. 50.23. [6]Rev. 7.9–12.

Evening

He keeps me from the grave and blesses me with love and mercy.[1]

The one who will rescue them is strong—his name is the LORD Almighty.[2]—I will not save this people from the world of the dead or rescue them from the power of death. Bring on your plagues, death! Bring on your destruction, world of the dead![3]

Since the children, as he calls them, are people of flesh and blood, Jesus himself became like them and shared their human nature. He did this so that through his death he might destroy the Devil, who has the power over death, and in this way set free those who were slaves all their lives because of their fear of death.[4]

Whoever believes in the Son has eternal life; whoever disobeys the Son will not have life, but will remain under God's punishment.[5]

For you have died, and your life is hidden with Christ in God. Your real life is Christ and when he appears, then you too will appear with him and share his glory![6]—When he comes on that Day to receive glory from all his people and honour from all who believe.[7]

[1]PS. 103.4. [2]Jer. 50.34.—[3]Hos. 13.14. [4]Heb. 2.14, 15. [5]John 3.36. [6]Col. 3.3, 4.—[7]2 Thess. 1.10.

God our Saviour, through Jesus Christ.[1]

God has brought you into union with Christ Jesus, and God has made Christ to be our wisdom. By him we are put right with God; we become God's holy people and are set free.[2]—Can you discover the limits and bounds of the greatness and power of God? The sky is no limit for God, but it lies beyond your reach. God knows the world of the dead, but you do not know it.[3]

The wisdom I proclaim is God's secret wisdom, which is hidden from mankind, but which he had already chosen for our glory even before the world was made.[4]—God, who is the Creator of all things, kept his secret hidden through all the past ages, in order that at the present time, by means of the church, the angelic rulers and powers in the heavenly world might learn of his wisdom in all its different forms.[5]

If any of you lacks wisdom, he should pray to God, who will give it to him; because God gives generously and graciously to all.[6]—The wisdom from above is pure first of all; it is also peaceful, gentle, and friendly; it is full of compassion and produces a harvest of good deeds; it is free from prejudice and hypocrisy.[7]

[1]JUDE 25. [2]1 Cor. 1.30.—[3]Job 11.7, 8. [4]1 Cor. 2.7.—[5]Eph. 3.9, 10. [6]Jas 1.5.— [7]Jas 3.17.

Evening

When I lie down to sleep, the hours drag; I toss all night and long for dawn.[1]

"Sentry, how soon will the night be over?" I answer, "Morning is coming."[2]

He who is coming will come; he will not delay.[3]—He is like the sun shining on a cloudless dawn, the sun that makes the grass sparkle after rain.[4]

I am going to prepare a place for you. And after I go and prepare a place for you, I will come back and take you to myself, so that you will be where I am. Do not be worried and upset; do not be afraid. You heard me say to you, "I am leaving, but I will come back to you."[5]

May all your enemies die . . . O LORD, but may your friends shine like the rising sun![6]

All of you are people who belong to the light, who belong to the day. We do not belong to the night or to the darkness.[7]

There will be no night there.[8]

[1]JOB 7.4. [2]Isa. 21.11, 12. [3]Heb. 10.37.—[4]2 Sam. 23.4. [5]John 14.2, 3, 27, 28. [6]Judg. 5.31. [7]1 Thess. 5.5. [8]Rev. 21.25.

You, Lord, give perfect peace to those who keep their purpose firm and put their trust in you.[1]

Leave your troubles with the LORD, and he will defend you; he never lets honest men be defeated.[2]—God is my saviour; I will trust him and not be afraid. The LORD gives me power and strength; he is my saviour.[3]

Why are you so frightened? How little faith you have![4]—Don't worry about anything, but in all your prayers ask God for what you need, always asking him with a thankful heart. And God's peace, which is far beyond human understanding, will keep your hearts and minds safe in union with Christ Jesus.[5]—Come back and quietly trust in me. Then you will be strong and secure.[6]

Because everyone will do what is right, there will be peace and security for ever.[7]—Peace is what I leave with you; it is my own peace that I give you. I do not give it as the world does. Do not be worried and upset; do not be afraid.[8]—Grace and peace be yours from God, who is, who was, and who is to come.[9]

[1]ISA. 26.3. [2]Ps. 55.22.—[3]Isa. 12.2. [4]Matt. 8.26.—[5]Phil. 4.6, 7.—[6]Isa. 30.15. [7]Isa 32.17.—[8]John 14.27.—[9]Rev. 1.4.

Evening

If you become angry, do not let your anger lead you into sin, and do not stay angry all day.[1]

If your brother sins against you, go to him and show him his fault. But do it privately, just between yourselves. If he listens to you, you have won your brother back. . . . "Lord, if my brother keeps on sinning against me, how many times do I have to forgive him? Seven times?" "No, not seven times," answered Jesus, "but seventy times seven."[2]

When you stand and pray, forgive anything you may have against anyone, so that your Father in heaven will forgive the wrongs you have done.[3]

You are the people of God; he loved you and chose you for his own. So then, you must clothe yourselves with compassion, kindness, humility, gentleness, and patience. Be tolerant with one another and forgive one another whenever any of you has a complaint against someone else. You must forgive one another just as the Lord has forgiven you.[4]—Be kind and tender-hearted to one another, and forgive one another, as God has forgiven you through Christ.[5]

[1]EPH. 4.26. [2]Matt. 18.15, 21, 22. [3]Mark 11.25. [4]Col. 3.12, 13.—[5]Eph. 4.32.

The Father . . . is greater than I.[1]

When you pray, say this: Father: may your holy name be honoured.[2]—My Father and their Father, my God and their God.[3]

I love the Father; that is why I do everything as he commands me.[4]—The words that I have spoken to you do not come from me. The Father, who remains in me, does his own work.[5]

The Father loves his Son and has put everything in his power.[6]—For you gave him authority over all mankind, so that he might give eternal life to all those you gave him.[7]

"Lord, show us the Father; that is all we need." Jesus answered, "For a long time I have been with you all; yet you do not know me, Philip? Whoever has seen me has seen the Father. Why, then, do you say, 'Show us the Father'? Do you not believe that I am in the Father and the Father is in me?"[8]—The Father and I are one.[9]—I love you just as the Father loves me; remain in my love. If you obey my commands, you will remain in my love, just as I have obeyed my Father's commands and remain in his love.[10]

[1]JOHN 14.28. [2]Luke 11.2.—[3]John 20.17. [4]John 14.31.—[5]John 14.10. [6]John 3.35.—[7]John 17.2. [8]John 14.8–10.—[9]John 10.30.—[10]John 15.9, 10.

Evening

Her offspring will crush your head, and you will bite their heel.[1]

Many people were shocked when they saw him; he was so disfigured that he hardly looked human.[2]—Because of our sins he was wounded, beaten because of the evil we did. We are healed by the punishment he suffered, made whole by the blows he received.[3]

This is your hour to act, when the power of darkness rules.[4]—You have authority over me only because it was given to you by God.[5]

The Son of God appeared for this very reason, to destroy what the Devil had done.[6]—Jesus . . . drove out many demons. He would not let the demons say anything, because they knew who he was.[7]

I have been given all authority in heaven and on earth.[8]—Believers . . . will drive out demons in my name.[9]

God, our source of peace, will soon crush Satan under your feet.[10]

[1]GEN. 3.15. [2]Isa. 52.14.—[3]Isa. 53.5. [4]Luke 22.53.—[5]John 19.11. [6]1 John 3.8.—[7]Mark 1.34. [8]Matt. 28.18.—[9]Mark 16.17. [10]Rom. 16.20.

I lie defeated in the dust; revive me, as you have promised.[1]

You have been raised to life with Christ, so set your hearts on the things that are in heaven, where Christ sits on his throne at the right-hand side of God. Keep your minds fixed on things there, not on things here on earth. For you have died, and your life is hidden with Christ in God.[2]—We, however, are citizens of heaven, and we eagerly wait for our Saviour, the Lord Jesus Christ, to come from heaven. He will change our weak mortal bodies and make them like his own glorious body, using that power by which he is able to bring all things under his rule.[3]

For what our human nature wants is opposed to what the Spirit wants, and what the Spirit wants is opposed to what our human nature wants. These two are enemies, and this means that you cannot do what you want to do.[4]—So then, my brothers, we have an obligation, but it is not to live as our human nature wants us to. For if you live according to your human nature, you are going to die; but if by the Spirit you put to death your sinful actions, you will live.[5]—I appeal to you, my friends, as strangers and refugees in this world! Do not give in to bodily passions, which are always at war against the soul.[6]

[1]PS. 119.25. [2]Col. 3.1–3.—[3]Phil. 3.20, 21. [4]Gal. 5.17.—[5]Rom. 8.12, 13.—[6]1 Pet. 2.11.

Evening

The amount of faith that God has given you.[1]

[He] is weak in faith.[2]—His faith filled him with power, and he gave praise to God.[3]

How little faith you have! Why did you doubt?[4]—You are a woman of great faith! What you want will be done for you.[5]

"Do you believe that I can heal you?" "Yes, Sir!" they answered . . . "Let it happen, then, just as you believe!"[6]

Make our faith greater.[7]—Keep on building yourselves up on your most sacred faith.[8]—Keep your roots deep in him, build your lives on him, and become stronger in your faith, as you were taught.[9]—It is God himself who makes us, together with you, sure of our life in union with Christ.[10]—But after you have suffered for a little while, the God of all grace, who calls you to share his eternal glory in union with Christ, will himself perfect you and give you firmness, strength, and a sure foundation.[11]

We who are strong in the faith ought to help the weak to carry their burdens. We should not please ourselves.[12]—Let us stop judging one another. Instead, you should decide never to do anything that would make your brother stumble or fall into sin.[13]

[1]ROM. 12.3. [2]Rom. 14.1.—[3]Rom. 4.20. [4]Matt. 14.31.—[5]Matt. 15.28. [6]Matt. 9.28, 29. [7]Luke 17.5.—[8]Jude 20.—[9]Col. 2.7.—[10]2 Cor. 1.21.—[11]1 Pet. 5.10. [12]Rom. 15.1.—[13]Rom. 14.13.

Morning

It was by God's own decision that the Son has in himself the full nature of God.[1]

The Father loves his Son and has put everything in his power.[2]—God raised him to the highest place above and gave him the name that is greater than any other name. And so, in honour of the name of Jesus all beings in heaven, on earth, and in the world below will fall on their knees, and all will openly proclaim that Jesus Christ is Lord, to the glory of God the Father.[3]—Christ rules there above all heavenly rulers, authorities, powers, and lords; he has a title superior to all titles of authority in this world and in the next.[4]—For through him God created everything in heaven and on earth, the seen and the unseen things, including spiritual powers, lords, rulers, and authorities. God created the whole universe through him and for him.[5]

Christ died and rose to life in order to be the Lord of the living and of the dead.[6]—You have been given full life in union with Him. He is supreme over every spiritual ruler and authority.[7]—Out of the fullness of his grace he has blessed us all, giving us one blessing after another.[8]

[1]COL. 1.19. [2]John 3.35.—[3]Phil. 2.9–11.—[4]Eph. 1.21.—[5]Col. 1.16. [6]Rom. 14.9.—[7]Col. 2.10.—[8]John 1.16.

Evening

Write, then, the things you see, both the things that are now and the things that will happen afterwards.[1]

Men were under the control of the Holy Spirit as they spoke the message that came from God.[2]—What we have seen and heard we announce to you also, so that you will join with us in the fellowship that we have with the Father and with his Son Jesus Christ.[3]

Look at my hands and my feet, and see that it is I myself. Feel me, and you will know, for a ghost doesn't have flesh and bones, as you can see I have. He said this and showed them his hands and his feet.[4]—The one who saw this happen has spoken of it, so that you also may believe. What he said is true, and he knows that he speaks the truth.[5]

We have not depended on made-up stories in the making known to you the mighty coming of our Lord Jesus Christ. With our own eyes we saw his greatness.[6]—Your faith, then, does not rest on human wisdom but on God's power.[7]

[1]REV. 1.19. [2]2 Pet. 1.21.—[3]1 John 1.3. [4]Luke 24.39, 40.—[5]John 19.35. [6]2 Pet. 1.16.—[7]1 Cor. 2.5.

You save my life from all danger; you forgive all my sins.[1]

God showed his love for us by sending his only Son into the world, so that we might have life through him. This is what love is: it is not that we have loved God, but that he loved us and sent his Son to be the means by which our sins are forgiven.[2]

There is no other god like you, O LORD; you forgive the sins of your people who have survived. You do not stay angry for ever, but you take pleasure in showing us your constant love. You will be merciful to us once again. You will trample our sins underfoot and send them to the bottom of the sea![3]—I cried to you for help, O LORD my God, and you healed me; you kept me from the grave. I was on my way to the depths below, but you restored my life.[4]—When I felt my life slipping away, then, O LORD, I prayed to you, and in your holy Temple you heard me.[5]—I waited patiently for the LORD's help; then he listened to me and heard my cry. He pulled me out of a dangerous pit, out of the deadly quicksand. He set me safely on a rock and made me secure.[6]

[1]ISA. 38.17. [2]1 John 4.9, 10. [3]Mic. 7.18, 19.—[4]Ps. 30. 2, 3.—[5]Jonah 2.7.—[6]Ps. 40.1, 2.

Evening

The things you see.[1]

What we see now is like a dim image in a mirror.[2]—We do not . . . see man ruling over all things now.[3]

So we are even more confident of the message proclaimed by the prophets. You will do well to pay attention to it, because it is like a lamp shining in a dark place until the Day dawns and the light of the morning star shines in your hearts.[4]—Your word is a lamp to guide me and a light for my path.[5]

But remember, my friends, what you were told in the past by the apostles of our Lord Jesus Christ. They said to you, "When the last days come, people will appear who will mock you, people who follow their own godless desires."[6]—The Spirit says clearly that some people will abandon the faith in later times; they will obey lying spirits and follow the teachings of demons.[7]

My children, the end is near![8]—The night is nearly over, day is almost here. Let us stop doing the things that belong to the dark, and let us take up weapons for fighting in the light.[9]

[1]REV. 1.19. [2]1 Cor. 13.12.—[3]Heb. 2.8. [4]2 Pet. 1.19.—[5]Ps. 119.105. [6]Jude 17, 18.—[7]1 Tim. 4.1. [8]1 John 2.18.—[9]Rom. 13.12.

The one who was to come.[1]

Jesus . . . was made lower than the angels . . . now crowned with glory and honour because of the death he suffered.[2]—Christ . . . died for everyone.[3]—Just as all people were made sinners as the result of the disobedience of one man, in the same way they will all be put right with God as the result of the obedience of the one man.[4]

The first man, Adam, was created a living being; but the last Adam is the life-giving Spirit. It is not the spiritual that comes first, but the physical, and then the spiritual.[5]—God said, "And now we will make human beings; they will be like us and resemble us. They will have power over the fish, the birds, and all animals, domestic and wild, large and small." So God created human beings, making them to be like himself.[6]—In these last days [God] has spoken to us through his Son . . . He reflects the brightness of God's glory and is the exact likeness of God's own being.[7]—You gave him authority over all mankind.[8]

The first Adam, made of earth, came from the earth; the second Adam came from heaven. Those who belong to the earth are like the one who was made of earth; those who are of heaven are like the one who came from heaven.[9]

[1]ROM. 5.14. [2]Heb. 2.9.—[3]2 Cor. 5.14.—[4]Rom. 5.19. [5]1 Cor. 15.45, 46.—[6]Gen. 1.26, 27.—[7]Heb. 1.1–3.—[8]John 17.2. [9]1 Cor. 15.47, 48.

Evening

The things that will happen afterwards.[1]

The scripture says, "What no one ever saw or heard, what no one ever thought could happen, is the very thing God prepared for those who love him." But it was to us that God made known his secret by means of his Spirit.[2]—The Spirit . . . who reveals the truth about God . . . will tell you of things to come.[3]

Look, he is coming on the clouds: Everyone will see him, including those who pierced him. All peoples on earth will mourn over him. So shall it be![4]

Our brothers, we want you to know the truth about those who have died, so that you will not be sad, as those are who have no hope. We believe that Jesus died and rose again, and so we believe that God will take back with Jesus those who have died believing in him. There will be the shout of command, the archangel's voice, the sound of God's trumpet, and the Lord himself will come down from heaven. Those who have died believing in Christ will rise to life first; then we who are living at that time will be gathered up along with them in the clouds to meet the Lord in the air. And so we will always be with the Lord.[5]

[1]REV. 1.19. [2]1 Cor. 2.9, 10.—[3]John 16.13. [4]Rev. 1.7. [5]1 Thess. 4.13, 14, 16, 17.

With all humility and many tears I did my work as the Lord's servant.[1]

If one of you wants to be great, he must be the servant of the rest; and if one of you wants to be first, he must be your slave—like the Son of Man, who did not come to be served, but to serve and to give his life to redeem many people.[2]

If someone thinks he is somebody when really he is nobody, he is only deceiving himself.[3]—Because of God's gracious gift to me I say to every one of you: Do not think of yourself more highly than you should. Instead, be modest in your thinking, and judge yourself according to the amount of faith that God has given you.[4]—When you have done all you have been told to do, say, "We are ordinary servants; we have only done our duty."[5]

We are proud that our conscience assures us that our lives in this world . . . have been ruled by God-given frankness and sincerity, by the power of God's grace and not by human wisdom.[6]—We who have this spiritual treasure are like common clay pots, in order to show that the supreme power belongs to God, not to us.[7]

[1]ACTS 20.19. [2]Matt. 20.26–28. [3]Gal. 6.3.—[4]Rom. 12.3.—[5]Luke 17.10. [6]2 Cor. 1.12.—[7]2 Cor. 4.7.

Evening

. . . each of us going his own way.[1]

Noah . . . was the first man to plant a vineyard . . . he became drunk.[2]—[Abram] . . . said to his wife Sarai . . . "Tell them that you are my sister; then because of you they will let me live and treat me well."[3]—Isaac said to Jacob . . . "Your voice sounds like Jacob's voice, but your arms feel like Esau's arms . . . Are you really Esau?" "I am," he [Jacob] answered.[4]—Moses . . . spoke without stopping to think.[5]—The men of Israel accepted some food from them, but did not consult the LORD. Joshua made a treaty of friendship with the people.[6]—David had done what pleased [the LORD] and had never disobeyed any of his commands, except in the case of Uriah the Hittite.[7]

What a record all of these have won by their faith![8]—But by the free gift of God's grace all are put right with him through Christ Jesus, who sets them free.[9]—The LORD made the punishment fall on him, the punishment all of us deserved.[10]

I want you to know that I am not doing all this for your sake. I want you to feel the shame and disgrace of what you are doing. I, the Sovereign LORD, have spoken.[11]

[1]ISA. 53.6. [2]Gen. 9.20, 21.—[3]Gen. 12.11, 13.—[4]Gen. 27.21, 24.—[5]Ps. 106.32, 33.—[6]Josh. 9.14, 15.—[7]1 Kgs. 15.5. [8]Heb. 11.39.—[9]Rom. 3.24.—[10]Isa. 53.6. [11]Ezek. 36.32.

He will be called, "Wonderful . . ."[1]

The Word became a human being and, full of grace and truth, lived among us. We saw his glory, the glory which he received as the Father's only Son.[2]—Your name and your commands are supreme.[3]

He will be called Immanuel, which means "God is with us".[4]—You will name him Jesus—because he will save his people from their sins.[5]

All will honour the Son in the same way as they honour the Father.[6]—For this reason God raised him to the highest place above and gave him the name that is greater than any other name.[7]—Christ rules there above all heavenly rulers, authorities, powers, and lords; he has a title superior to all titles of authority in this world and in the next. God put all things under Christ's feet.[8]—He had a name written on him, but no one except himself knows what it is . . . "King of kings and Lord of lords."[9]

God's power is so great that we cannot come near him.[10]—Who is he, if you know? Who is his son?[11]

[1]ISA. 9.6. [2]John 1.14.—[3]Ps. 138.2. [4]Matt. 1.23.—[5]Matt. 1.21. [6]John 5.23.—[7]Phil. 2.9.—[8]Eph. 1.21, 22.—[9]Rev. 19.12, 16. [10]Job 37.23.—[11]Prov. 30.4.

Evening

Jacob's descendants he chose for himself.[1]

You belong to Christ, and Christ belongs to God.[2]—I belong to my lover, and he desires me.[3]—My lover is mine.[4]—The Son of God . . . loved me and gave his life for me.[5]

You do not belong to yourselves but to God; he bought you for a price. So use your bodies for God's glory.[6]—You are the people he rescued from Egypt, that blazing furnace. He brought you out to make you his own people, as you are today.[7]

We are partners working together for God, and you are God's field.[8]—But Christ is faithful as the Son in charge of God's house. We are his house if we keep up our courage and our confidence in what we hope for.[9]—Living stones . . . holy priests.[10]

"They will be My people," says the LORD Almighty. "On the day when I act, they will be my very own."[11]—"All I have is yours, and all you have is mine; and my glory is shown through them."[12]—The wonderful blessings he promises his people.[13]

[1]DEUT. 32.9. [2]1 Cor. 3.23.—[3]S. of S. 7.10.—[4]S. of S. 2.16.—[5]Gal. 2.20.—[6]1 Cor. 6.19, 20.—[7]Deut. 4.20. [8]1 Cor. 3.9.—[9]Heb. 3.6.—[10]1 Pet. 2.5. [11]Mal. 3.17.—[12]John 17.10.—[13]Eph. 1.18.

***He prunes every branch that does bear fruit, so that it will be clean and bear more fruit.*[1]**

He will be like a strong soap, like a fire that refines metal. He will come to judge like one who refines and purifies silver. As a metal-worker refines silver and gold, so the LORD's messenger will purify the priests, so that they will bring to the LORD the right kind of offerings.[2]

We also boast of our troubles, because we know that trouble produces endurance, endurance brings God's approval, and his approval creates hope. This hope does not disappoint us, for God has poured out his love into our hearts by means of the Holy Spirit, who is God's gift to us.[3]—Endure what you suffer as being a father's punishment; your suffering shows that God is treating you as his sons. Was there ever a son who was not punished by his father? If you are not punished, as all his sons are, it means you are not real sons. When we are punished, it seems to us at the time something to make us sad, not glad. Later, however, those who have been disciplined by such punishment reap the peaceful reward of a righteous life. Lift up your tired hands, then, and strengthen your trembling knees![4]

[1]JOHN 15.2. [2]Mal. 3.2, 3. [3]Rom. 5.3–5.—[4]Heb. 12.7, 8, 11, 12.

Evening

***Proud people are the ones who are happy.*[1]**

I am the high and holy God, who lives for ever. I live in a high and holy place, but I also live with people who are humble and repentant, so that I can restore their confidence and hope.[2]

It is better to be humble and stay poor than to be one of the arrogant and get a share of their loot.[3]—Happy are those who know they are spiritually poor; the Kingdom of heaven belongs to them![4]

There are seven things that the LORD hates . . . a proud look . . .[5]—The LORD hates everyone who is arrogant.[6]

Examine me, O God, and know my mind; test me, and discover my thoughts. Find out if there is any evil in me and guide me in the everlasting way.[7]

May God our Father and the Lord Jesus Christ give you grace and peace. I thank my God for you every time I think of you; and every time I pray for you all, I pray with joy.[8]—Happy are those who are humble; they will receive what God has promised![9]

[1]MAL. 3.15. [2]Isa. 57.15. [3]Prov. 16.19.—[4]Matt. 5.3. [5]Prov. 6.16, 17.—[6]Prov. 16.5. [7]Ps. 139. 23, 24. [8]Phil. 1.2–4.—[9]Matt. 5.5.

Morning

This God is our God for ever and ever; he will lead us for all time to come.[1]

LORD, you are my God; I will honour you and praise your name. You have done amazing things; you have faithfully carried out the plans you made long ago.[2]—You, LORD, are all I have, and you give me all I need; my future is in your hands.[3]

He gives me new strength. He guides me in the right paths, as he has promised. Even if I go through the deepest darkness, I will not be afraid, LORD, for you are with me. Your shepherd's rod and staff protect me.[4]—I always stay close to you, and you hold me by the hand. You guide me with your instruction and at the end you will receive me with honour. What else have I in heaven but you? Since I have you, what else could I want on earth? My mind and my body may grow weak, but God is my strength; he is all I ever need.[5]—We are glad because of him; we trust in his holy name.[6]—You will do everything you have promised; LORD, your love is eternal. Complete the work that you have begun.[7]

[1]PS. 48.14. [2]Isa. 25.1.—[3]Ps. 16.5. [4]Ps. 23.3, 4.—[5]Ps. 73.23–26.—[6]Ps. 33.21.—[7]Ps. 138.8.

Evening

Whenever I am anxious and worried, you comfort me and make me glad.[1]

In despair and far from home I call to you! Take me to a safe refuge.[2]

LORD, rescue me from all this trouble.[3]—Leave your troubles with the LORD, and he will defend you; he never lets honest men be defeated.[4]

I am very young and don't know how to rule.[5]—If any of you lacks wisdom, he should pray to God, who will give it to him; because God gives generously and graciously to all.[6]

Who, then, is capable of such a task?[7]—I know that good does not live in me—that is, in my human nature.[8]—My grace is all you need, for my power is greatest when you are weak.[9]

Courage, my son! Your sins are forgiven. Courage, my daughter! Your faith has made you well.[10]

My soul will feast and be satisfied . . . As I lie in bed, I remember you; all night long I think of you, because you have always been my help.[11]

[1]PS. 94.19. [2]Ps. 61.2. [3]Isa. 38.14.—[4]Ps. 55.22. [5]1 Kgs. 3.7.—[6]Jas 1.5. [7]2 Cor. 2.16.—[8]Rom. 7.18.—[9]2 Cor. 12.9. [10]Matt. 9.2, 22. [11]Ps. 63.5, 6.

This hope does not disappoint us.[1]

I am the LORD; no one who waits for my help will be disappointed.[2]—I will bless the person who puts his trust in me.[3]—You, LORD, give perfect peace to those who keep their purpose firm and put their trust in you. Trust in the LORD for ever; he will always protect us.[4]—I depend on God alone; I put my hope in him. He alone protects and saves me; he is my defender, and I shall never be defeated.[5]—I am still full of confidence, because I know whom I have trusted.[6]

To those who were to receive what he promised, God wanted to make it very clear that he would never change his purpose; so he added his vow to the promise. There are these two things, then, that cannot change and about which God cannot lie. So we who have found safety with him are greatly encouraged to hold firmly to the hope placed before us. We have this hope as an anchor for our lives. It is safe and sure, and goes through the curtain of the heavenly temple into the inner sanctuary. On our behalf Jesus has gone in there before us.[7]

[1]ROM. 5.5. [2]Isa. 49.23.—[3]Jer. 17.7.—[4]Isa. 26.3, 4.—[5]Ps. 62.5, 6.—[6]2 Tim. 1.12. [7]Heb. 6.17–20.

Evening

Persecuted . . . preaching about the cross of Christ.[1]

If anyone wants to come with me, he must forget self, carry his cross, and follow me.[2]

Don't you know that to be the world's friend means to be God's enemy? Whoever wants to be the world's friend makes himself God's enemy.[3]—We must pass through many troubles to enter the Kingdom of God.[4]

Whoever believes in him will not be disappointed.[5]—This stone is of great value for you that believe; but for those who do not believe: "The stone which the builders rejected as worthless turned out to be the most important of all." . . . "the stone that will make people stumble, the rock that will make them fall."[6]

I will boast only about the cross of our Lord Jesus Christ; for by means of his cross the world is dead to me, and I am dead to the world.[7]—I have been put to death with Christ on his cross.[8]—Those who belong to Christ Jesus have put to death their human nature with all its passions and desires.[9]

If we continue to endure, we shall also rule with him. If we deny him, he also will deny us.[10]

[1]GAL. 5.11. [2]Matt. 16.24. [3]Jas 4.4.—[4]Acts 14.22. [5]Rom. 9.33.—[6]1 Pet. 2.7, 8. [7]Gal. 6.14.—[8]Gal. 2.19.—[9]Gal. 5.24. [10]2 Tim. 2.12.

The Lord is coming soon.[1]

There will be the shout of command, the archangel's voice, the sound of God's trumpet, and the Lord himself will come down from heaven. Those who have died believing in Christ will rise to life first; then we who are living at that time will be gathered up along with them in the clouds to meet the Lord in the air. And so we will always be with the Lord. So then, encourage one another with these words.[2]—He who gives his testimony to all this says, "Yes indeed! I am coming soon!" So be it. Come, Lord Jesus![3]

My friends, as you wait for that Day, do your best to be pure and faultless in God's sight and to be at peace with him.[4]—Avoid every kind of evil. May the God who gives us peace make you holy in every way and keep your whole being—spirit, soul, and body—free from every fault at the coming of our Lord Jesus Christ. He who calls you will do it, because he is faithful.[5]

Be patient. Keep your hopes high, for the day of the Lord's coming is near.[6]

[1]PHIL. 4.5. [2]1 Thess. 4.16–18.—[3]Rev. 22.20. [4]2 Pet. 3.14.—[5]1 Thess. 5.22–24. [6]Jas 5.8.

Evening

The very best of the vines.[1]

My friend has a vineyard on a very fertile hill. He dug the soil and cleared it of stones; he planted the finest vines . . . he waited for the grapes to ripen, but every grape was sour.[2]—I planted you like a choice vine from the very best seed. But look what you have become! You are like a rotten, worthless vine.[3]

What human nature does is quite plain. It shows itself in immoral, filthy, and indecent actions . . . [People] are envious, get drunk, have orgies, and do other things like these. But the Spirit produces love, joy, peace, patience, kindness, goodness, faithfulness, humility, and self-control.[4]

I am the real vine, and my Father is the gardener. He breaks off every branch in me that does not bear fruit, and he prunes every branch that does bear fruit, so that it will be clean and bear more fruit. Remain united to me, and I will remain united to you. My Father's glory is shown by your bearing much fruit; and in this way you become my disciples.[5]

[1]GEN. 49.11. [2]Isa. 5.1, 2.—[3]Jer. 2.21. [4]Gal. 5.19, 21–23. [5]John 15.1, 2, 4, 8.

God puts people right through their faith in Jesus Christ. God does this to all who believe in Christ.[1]

Christ was without sin, but for our sake God made him share our sin in order that in union with him we might share the righteousness of God.[2]—By becoming a curse for us Christ has redeemed us from the curse that the Law brings.[3]—God has brought you into union with Christ Jesus, and God has made Christ to be our wisdom. By him we are put right with God; we become God's holy people and are set free.[4]—He saved us. It was not because of any good deeds that we ourselves had done, but because of his own mercy that he saved us, through the Holy Spirit, who gives us new birth and new life by washing us. God poured out the Holy Spirit abundantly on us through Jesus Christ our Saviour.[5]

I reckon everything as complete loss for the sake of what is so much more valuable, the knowledge of Christ Jesus my Lord. For his sake I have thrown everything away; I consider it all as mere refuse, so that I may gain Christ and be completely united with him. I no longer have a righteousness of my own, the kind that is gained by obeying the Law. I now have the righteousness that is given through faith in Christ, the righteousness that comes from God and is based on faith.[6]

[1]ROM. 3.22. [2]2 Cor. 5.21.—[3]Gal. 3.13.—[4]1 Cor. 1.30.—[5]Titus 3.5, 6. [6]Phil. 3.8, 9.

Evening

The Spirit makes you God's children, and by the Spirit's power we cry out to God, "Father! My Father!"[1]

Jesus . . . looked up to heaven and said, "Father . . . Holy Father . . . Righteous Father."[2]—"Father," he prayed, "my Father."[3]—To show that you are his sons, God sent the Spirit of his Son into our hearts, the Spirit who cries out, "Father, my Father."[4]—It is through Christ that all of us, Jews and Gentiles, are able to come in the one Spirit into the presence of the Father. So then, you Gentiles are not foreigners or strangers any longer; you are now fellow-citizens with God's people and members of the family of God.[5]

You are our father . . . you, LORD, are our father, the one who has always rescued us.[6]

I will get up and go to my father and say, "Father, I have sinned against God and against you. I am no longer fit to be called your son; treat me as one of your hired workers." So he got up and started back to his father.[7]

Since you are God's dear children, you must try to be like him.[8]

[1]ROM. 8.15. [2]John 17.1, 11, 25.—[3]Mark 14.36.—[4]Gal. 4.6.—[5]Eph. 2.18, 19. [6]Isa. 63.16. [7]Luke 15.18–20. [8]Eph. 5.1.

Morning

Let us, then, go to him outside the camp and share his shame. For there is no permanent city for us here on earth; we are looking for the city which is to come. [1]

My dear friends, do not be surprised at the painful test you are suffering, as though something unusual were happening to you. Rather be glad that you are sharing Christ's sufferings, so that you may be full of joy when his glory is revealed.[2]—As you share in our sufferings, you also share in the help we receive.[3]

Happy are you if you are insulted because you are Christ's folowers; this means that the glorious Spirit, the Spirit of God, is resting on you.[4]

As the apostles left the Council, they were happy, because God had considered them worthy to suffer disgrace for the sake of Jesus.[5]—He [Moses] preferred to suffer with God's people rather than to enjoy sin for a little while. He reckoned that to suffer scorn for the Messiah was worth far more than all the treasures of Egypt, for he kept his eyes on the future reward.[6]

[1]HEB. 13.13, 14. [2]1 Pet. 4.12, 13.—[3]2 Cor. 1.7. [4]1 Pet. 4.14. [5]Acts 5.41.—[6]Heb. 11.25, 26.

Evening

The Lord Jesus Christ . . . will change our weak mortal bodies and make them like his own glorious body. [1]

Above the dome there was something that looked like a throne made of sapphire, and sitting on the throne was a figure that looked like a man. The figure seemed to be shining like bronze in the middle of a fire. It shone all over with a bright light that had in it all the colours of the rainbow. This was the dazzling light which shows the presence of the LORD.[2]

All of us, then, reflect the glory of the Lord with uncovered faces; and that same glory, coming from the Lord, who is the Spirit, transforms us into his likeness in an ever greater degree of glory.[3]—It is not yet clear what we shall become. But we know that when Christ appears, we shall be like him, because we shall see him as he really is.[4]

Never again will they hunger or thirst.[5]—They were . . . singing the song of Moses, the servant of God, and the song of the Lamb.[6]

[1]PHIL. 3.20, 21. [2]Ezek. 1.26–28. [3]2 Cor. 3.18.—[4]1 John 3.2. [5]Rev. 7.16.—[6]Rev. 15.3.

***You know that Christ appeared in order to take away sins, and that there is no sin in him.*[1]**

In these last days [God] has spoken to us through his Son. He reflects the brightness of God's glory and is the exact likeness of God's own being, sustaining the universe with his powerful word. After achieving forgiveness for the sins of mankind, he sat down in Heaven at the right-hand side of God, the Supreme Power.[2]—Christ was without sin, but for our sake God made him share our sin in order that in union with him we might share the righteousness of God.[3]

Spend the rest of your lives here on earth in reverence for him. For you know what was paid to set you free from the worthless manner of life handed down by your ancestors. It was not something that can be destroyed, such as silver or gold; it was the costly sacrifice of Christ, who was like a lamb without defect or flaw. He had been chosen by God before the creation of the world and was revealed in these last days for your sake.[4]—We are ruled by the love of Christ, now that we recognize that one man died for everyone, which means that all share in his death. He died for all, so that those who live should no longer live for themselves, but only for him who died and was raised to life for their sake.[5]

[1]1 JOHN 3.5. [2]Heb. 1.1–3.—[3]2 Cor. 5.21. [4]1 Pet. 1.17–20.—[5]2 Cor. 5.14, 15.

Evening

***I am now giving you the choice between life and death, between God's blessing and God's curse . . . choose life.*[1]**

"I do not want anyone to die," says the Sovereign LORD. "Turn away from your sins and live."[2]

They would not have been guilty of sin if I had not come and spoken to them; as it is, they no longer have any excuse for their sin.[3]

The servant who knows what his master wants him to do, but does not get himself ready and do it, will be punished with a heavy whipping.[4]

For sin pays its wage—death; but God's free gift is eternal life in union with Christ Jesus our Lord.[5]—Whoever believes in the Son has eternal life; whoever disobeys the Son will not have life, but will remain under God's punishment.[6]—Surely you know that when you surrender yourselves as slaves to obey someone, you are in fact the slaves of the master you obey—either of sin, which results in death, or of obedience, which results in being put right with God.[7]

Whoever wants to serve me must follow me, so that my servant will be with me where I am. And my Father will honour anyone who serves me.[8]

[1]DEUT. 30.19. [2]Ezek. 18.32. [3]John 15.22. [4]Luke 12.47. [5]Rom. 6.23.—[6]John 3.36.—[7]Rom. 6.16. [8]John 12.26.

May he always live secure.[1]

And when you are arrested and taken to court, do not worry beforehand about what you are going to say; when the time comes, say whatever is then given to you. For the words you speak will not be yours; they will come from the Holy Spirit.[2]—So do not worry about tomorrow; it will have enough worries of its own. There is no need to add to the troubles each day brings.[3]

The God of Israel . . . gives strength and power to his people.[4]—He strengthens those who are weak and tired.[5]

"My grace is all you need, for my power is greatest when you are weak." I am most happy, then, to be proud of my weaknesses, in order to feel the protection of Christ's power over me. I am content with weaknesses, insults, hardships, persecutions, and difficulties for Christ's sake. For when I am weak, then I am strong.[6]—I have the strength to face all conditions by the power that Christ gives me.[7]—I shall march, march on, with strength![8]

[1]DEUT. 33.25. [2]Mark 13.11.—[3]Matt. 6.34. [4]Ps. 68.35.—[5]Isa. 40.29. [6]2 Cor. 12.9, 10.—[7]Phil. 4.13.—[8]Judg. 5.21.

Evening

Wake up, North Wind. South Wind, blow on my garden; fill the air with fragrance.[1]

When we are punished, it seems to us at the time something to make us sad, not glad. Later, however, those who have been disciplined by such punishment reap the peaceful reward of a righteous life.[2]—The Spirit produces love, joy, peace . . .[3]

He took them away with a cruel wind from the east.[4]

As a father is kind to his children, so the LORD is kind to those who honour him.[5]

Even though our physical being is gradually decaying, yet our spiritual being is renewed day after day. And this small and temporary trouble we suffer will bring us a tremendous and eternal glory, much greater than the trouble. For we fix our attention, not on things that are seen, but on things that are unseen.[6]

Even though he was God's Son, he learnt through his sufferings to be obedient.[7]—We have a High Priest who was tempted in every way that we are, but did not sin.[8]

[1]S. OF S. 4.16. [2]Heb. 12.11.—[3]Gal. 5.22. [4]Isa. 27.8. [5]Ps. 103.13. [6]2 Cor. 4.16–18. [7]Heb. 5.8.—[8]Heb. 4.15.

A God Who Sees.[1]

LORD, you have examined me and you know me. You know everything I do; from far away you understand all my thoughts. You see me, whether I am working or resting; you know all my actions. Even before I speak, you already know what I will say. Your knowledge of me is too deep; it is beyond my understanding.[2]

The LORD sees what happens everywhere; he is watching us, whether we do good or evil.[3]—The LORD sees everything you do. Wherever you go, he is watching.[4]—God knows your hearts. For the things that are considered of great value by man are worth nothing in God's sight.[5]—The LORD keeps close watch over the whole world, to give strength to those whose hearts are loyal to him.[6]

Jesus . . . knew them all. There was no need for anyone to tell him about them, because he himself knew what was in their hearts.[7]—Lord, you know everything; you know that I love you.[8]

[1]GEN. 16.13. [2]Ps. 139. 1–4, 6. [3]Prov. 15.3.—[4]Prov. 5.21.—[5]Luke 16.15.—[6]2 Chrn. 16.9. [7]John 2.24, 25.—[8]John 21.17.

Evening

I will praise you with all my heart, O Lord my God; I will proclaim your greatness for ever.[1]

Giving thanks is the sacrifice that honours me.[2]—How good it is to give thanks to you, O LORD, to sing in your honour, O Most High God, to proclaim your constant love every morning and your faithfulness every night.[3]

Praise the LORD, all living creatures![4]

My brothers, because of God's great mercy to us I appeal to you: Offer yourselves as a living sacrifice to God, dedicated to his service and pleasing to him. This is the true worship that you should offer.[5]—As a sacrifice for sins . . . Jesus also died outside the city, in order to purify the people from sin with his own blood. Let us, then, always offer praise to God as our sacrifice through Jesus, which is the offering presented by lips that confess him as Lord.[6]—In the name of our Lord Jesus Christ, always give thanks for everything to God the Father.[7]

The Lamb who was killed is worthy to receive power, wealth, wisdom, and strength, honour, glory, and praise![8]

[1]PS. 86.12. [2]Ps. 50.23.—[3]Ps. 92.1, 2. [4]Ps. 150.6. [5]Rom. 12.1.—[6]Heb. 13.11, 12, 15.—[7]Eph. 5.20. [8]Rev. 5.12.

Morning

Let us run with determination the race that lies before us. Let us keep our eyes fixed on Jesus, on whom our faith depends from beginning to end. [1]

If anyone wants to come with me, he must forget self, take up his cross every day, and follow me.[2]—None of you can be my disciple unless he gives up everything he has.[3]—Let us stop doing the things that belong to the dark.[4]

Every athlete in training submits to strict discipline. I run straight for the finishing-line; that is why I am like a boxer who does not waste his punches. I harden my body with blows and bring it under complete control, to keep myself from being disqualified after having called others to the contest.[5]—I do not claim that I have already succeeded or have already become perfect. The one thing I do, however, is to forget what is behind me and do my best to reach what is ahead. So I run straight towards the goal in order to win the prize, which is God's call through Christ Jesus to the life above.[6]—Let us try to know the LORD.[7]

[1]HEB. 12.1, 2. [2]Luke 9.23.—[3]Luke 14.33.—[4]Rom. 13.12. [5]1 Cor. 9.25–27.—[6]Phil. 3.12–14.—[7]Hos. 6.3.

Evening

It is best to learn this patience in our youth. [1]

Teach a child how he should live, and he will remember it all his life.[2]

Our human fathers . . . punished us and we respected them. How much more, then, should we submit to our spiritual Father and live! Our human fathers punished us for a short time, as it seemed right to them; but God does it for our own good, so that we may share his holiness.[3]

You punished your people, LORD, and in anguish they prayed to you.[4]—Before you punished me, I used to go wrong, but now I obey your word. My punishment was good for me, because it made me learn your commands.[5]

I alone know the plans I have for you, plans to bring you prosperity and not disaster, plans to bring about the future you hope for.[6]—Humble yourselves, then, under God's mighty hand, so that he will lift you up in his own good time.[7]

[1]LAM. 3.27. [2]Prov. 22.6. [3]Heb. 12.9, 10. [4]Isa. 26.16.—[5]Ps. 119.67, 71. [6]Jer. 29.11.—[7]1 Pet. 5.6.

If you do not drive out the inhabitants of the land, those that are left will be as troublesome as splinters in your eyes and thorns in your sides, and they will fight against you.[1]

Run your best in the race of faith.[2]—The weapons we use in our fight are not the world's weapons but God's powerful weapons, which we use to destroy strongholds. We destroy false arguments; we pull down every proud obstacle that is raised against the knowledge of God; we take every thought captive and make it obey Christ.[3]

We have an obligation, but it is not to live as our human nature wants us to. For if you live according to your human nature, you are going to die; but if by the Spirit you put to death your sinful actions, you will live.[4]

For what our human nature wants is opposed to what the Spirit wants, and what the Spirit wants is opposed to what our human nature wants. These two are enemies, and this means that you cannot do what you want to do.[5]—I see a different law at work in my body—a law that fights against the law which my mind approves of.[6]—In all these things we have complete victory through him who loved us![7]

[1]NUM. 33.55. [2]1 Tim. 6:12.—[3]2 Cor. 10.4, 5. [4]Rom. 8.12, 13. [5]Gal. 5.17.—[6]Rom. 7.23.—[7]Rom. 8.37.

Evening

If a man sins against another man, God can defend him; but who can defend a man who sins against the LORD?[1]

If anyone does sin, we have someone who pleads with the Father on our behalf—Jesus Christ, the righteous one. And Christ himself is the means by which our sins are forgiven.[2]—God offered him, so that by his sacrificial death he should become the means by which people's sins are forgiven through their faith in him. God did this in order to demonstrate that he is righteous. In the past he was patient and overlooked people's sins; but in the present time he deals with their sins, in order to demonstrate his righteousness. In this way God shows that he himself is righteous and that he puts right everyone who believes in Jesus.[3]

In mercy the angel will say, "Release him! He is not to go down to the world of the dead. Here is the ransom to set him free."[4]

In view of all this, what can we say? If God is for us, who can be against us? Who will accuse God's chosen people? God himself declares them not guilty! Who, then, will condemn them? Not Christ Jesus, who died, or rather, who was raised to life and is at the right-hand side of God, pleading with him for us![5]

[1]1 SAM. 2.25. [2]1 John 2.1, 2.—[3]Rom. 3.25, 26. [4]Job 33.24. [5]Rom. 8.31, 33, 34.

You love him, although you have not seen him.[1]

Our life is a matter of faith, not of sight.[2]—We love because God first loved us.[3]—We ourselves know and believe the love which God has for us. God is love, and whoever lives in love lives in union with God and God lives in union with him.[4]—You also became God's people when you heard the true message, the Good News that brought you salvation. You believed in Christ, and God put his stamp of ownership on you by giving you the Holy Spirit he had promised.[5]—God's plan is to make known his secret to his people, this rich and glorious secret which he has for all peoples. And the secret is that Christ is in you, which means that you will share in the glory of God.[6]

If someone says he loves God, but hates his brother, he is a liar. For he cannot love God, whom he has not seen, if he does not love his brother, whom he has seen.[7]

Jesus said to him, "Do you believe because you see me? How happy are those who believe without seeing me!"[8]—Happy are all who go to him for protection.[9]

[1]1 PET. 1.8. [2]2 Cor. 5.7.—[3]1 John 4.19.—[4]1 John 4.16.—[5]Eph. 1.13.—[6]Col. 1.27. [7]1 John 4.20. [8]John 20.29.—[9]Ps. 2.12.

Evening

The Lord Our Salvation.[1]

All of us have been sinful; even our best actions are filthy through and through.[2]

I will praise your power, Sovereign LORD; I will proclaim your goodness, yours alone.[3]—Jerusalem rejoices because of what the LORD has done. She is like a bride dressed for her wedding. God has clothed her with salvation and victory.[4]

Bring the best robe and put it on him.[5]—She has been given clean shining linen to wear. (The linen is the good deeds of God's people.)[6]

I reckon everything as complete loss for the sake of what is so much more valuable, the knowledge of Christ Jesus my Lord . . . that I may gain Christ and be completely united with him. I no longer have a righteousness of my own, the kind that is gained by obeying the Law. I now have the righteousness that is given through faith in Christ, the righteousness that comes from God and is based on faith.[7]

[1]JER. 23.6. [2]Isa. 64.6. [3]Ps. 71.16.—[4]Isa. 61.10. [5]Luke 15.22.—[6]Rev. 19.8. [7]Phil. 3.8, 9.

Keep me from anything evil that might cause me pain.[1]

Why are you sleeping? Get up and pray that you will not fall into temptation.[2]—The spirit is willing, but the flesh is weak.[3]

I ask you, God, to let me have two things before I die: keep me from lying, and let me be neither rich nor poor. So give me only as much food as I need. If I have more, I might say that I do not need you. But if I am poor, I might steal and bring disgrace on my God.[4]

The LORD will protect you from all danger; he will keep you safe.[5]—I will rescue you from the power of wicked and violent men. I, the LORD, have spoken.[6]—No child of God keeps on sinning, for the Son of God keeps him safe, and the Evil One cannot harm him.[7]

Because you have kept my command to endure, I will also keep you safe from the time of trouble which is coming upon the world to test all the people on earth.[8]—The Lord knows how to rescue godly people from their trials.[9]

[1]1 CHRN. 4.10. [2]Luke 22.46.—[3]Matt. 26.41. [4]Prov. 30.7–9. [5]Ps. 121.7.—[6]Jer. 15.21.—[7]1 John 5.18. [8]Rev. 3.10.—[9]2 Pet. 2.9.

Evening

Even among stars there are different kinds of beuaty.[1]

They had been arguing among themselves about who was the greatest. Jesus sat down, called the twelve disciples, and said to them, "Whoever wants to be first must place himself last of all and be the servant of all."[2]—Serve one another; for the scripture says, "God resists the proud, but shows favour to the humble." Humble yourselves, then, under God's mighty hand, so that he will lift you up in his own good time.[3]

The attitude you should have is the one that Christ Jesus had . . . of his own free will he gave up all he had, and took the nature of a servant. He became like man. For this reason God raised him to the highest place above and gave him the name that is greater than any other name. And so, in honour of the name of Jesus all beings in heaven, on earth, and in the world below will fall on their knees.[4]

The wise leaders will shine with all the brightness of the sky. And those who have taught many people to do what is right will shine like the stars for ever.[5]

[1]1 COR. 15.41. [2]Mark 9.34, 35.—[3]1 Pet. 5.5, 6. [4]Phil. 2.5, 7, 9, 10. [5]Dan. 12.3.

Don't be discouraged, any of you. Do the work, for I am with you.[1]

I am the vine, and you are the branches. Whoever remains in me, and I in him, will bear much fruit; for you can do nothing without me.[2]—I have the strength to face all conditions by the power that Christ gives me.[3]—Build up your strength in union with the Lord and by means of his mighty power.[4]—The joy that the LORD gives you will make you strong.[5]

Have courage! You are now hearing the same words the prophets spoke.[6]—Give strength to hands that are tired and to knees that tremble with weakness. Tell everyone who is discouraged, "Be strong and don't be afraid!"[7]—The LORD ordered him, "Go . . . I myself am sending you."[8]

If God is for us, who can be against us?[9]—God in his mercy has given us this work to do, and so we are not discouraged.[10]

Let us not become tired of doing good; for if we do not give up, the time will come when we will reap the harvest.[11]—Thanks be to God who gives us the victory through our Lord Jesus Christ![12]

[1]HAG. 2.4. [2]John 15.5.—[3]Phil. 4.13.—[4]Eph. 6.10.—[5]Neh. 8.10. [6]Zech. 8.9.—[7]Isa. 35. 3, 4.—[8]Judg. 6.14. [9]Rom. 8.31.—[10]2 Cor. 4.1. [11]Gal. 6.9.—[12]1 Cor. 15.57.

Evening

Even darkness is not dark for you.[1]

He watches every step men take. There is no darkness dark enough to hide a sinner from God.[2]—No one can hide where I cannot see him. Do you not know that I am everywhere in heaven and on earth?[3]

You need not fear any dangers at night or sudden attacks during the day or the plagues that strike in the dark or the evils that kill in daylight. You have made the LORD your defender, the Most High your protector, and so no disaster will strike you, no violence will come near your home.[4]—He will not let you fall; your protector is always awake. The LORD will protect you from all danger; he will keep you safe.[5]

Even if I go through the deepest darkness, I will not be afraid, LORD, for you are with me. Your shepherd's rod and staff protect me.[6]

[1]PS. 139.12. [2]Job 34.21, 22.—[3]Jer. 23.24. [4]Ps. 91.5, 6, 9, 10.—[5]Ps. 121.3, 5, 7. [6]Ps. 23.4.

Morning

The Lord has said that his people are never to return there.[1]

They did not keep thinking about the country they had left; if they had, they would have had the chance to return. Instead, it was a better country they longed for, the heavenly country. [Moses] preferred to suffer with God's people rather than to enjoy sin for a little while. He reckoned that to suffer scorn for the Messiah was worth far more than all the treasures of Egypt.[2]—My righteous people, however, will believe and live; but if any of them turns back, I will not be pleased with him. We are not people who turn back and are lost. Instead, we have faith and are saved.[3]—Anyone who starts to plough and then keeps looking back is of no use to the Kingdom of God.[4]

I will boast only about the cross of our Lord Jesus Christ; for by means of his cross the world is dead to me, and I am dead to the world.[5]—The Lord says, "You must leave them and separate yourselves from them. Have nothing to do with what is unclean, and I will accept you."[6]

God, who began this good work in you, will carry it on until it is finished on the Day of Christ Jesus.[7]

[1]DEUT. 17.16. [2]Heb. 11.15, 16, 25, 26.—[3]Heb. 10.38, 39.—[4]Luke 9.62. [5]Gal. 6.14.—[6]2 Cor. 6.17. [7]Phil. 1.6.

Evening

They persecute those whom you have punished; they talk about the sufferings of those you have wounded.[1]

While I was holding back my anger against my people, those nations made the sufferings of my people worse.[2]

My brothers, if someone is caught in any kind of wrongdoing, those of you who are spiritual should set him right; but you must do it in a gentle way. And keep an eye on yourselves, so that you will not be tempted, too.[3]

Whoever turns a sinner back from his wrong way will save that sinner's soul from death and bring about the forgiveness of many sins.[4]—Warn the idle, encourage the timid, help the weak, be patient with everyone.[5]

Stop judging one another. Instead, you should decide never to do anything that would make your brother stumble or fall into sin.[6]—We who are strong in the faith ought to help the weak to carry their burdens. We should not please ourselves.[7]

Love . . . is not happy with evil.[8]—Whoever thinks he is standing firm had better be careful that he does not fall.[9]

[1]PS. 69.26. [2]Zech. 1.15. [3]Gal. 6.1. [4]Jas 5.20.—[5]1 Thess. 5.14. [6]Rom. 14.13.—[7]Rom. 15.1. [8]1 Cor. 13.4, 6.—[9]1 Cor. 10.12.

I have come in order that you might have life—life in all its fullness.[1]

You must not eat the fruit of that tree; if you do, you will die the same day.[2]—She took some of the fruit and ate it. Then she gave some to her husband, and he also ate it.[3]

Sin pays its wage—death; but God's free gift is eternal life in union with Christ Jesus our Lord.[4]—Through the sin of one man death began to rule because of that one man. But how much greater is the result of what was done by the one man, Jesus Christ! All who receive God's abundant grace and are freely put right with him will rule in life through Christ.[5]—Just as death came by means of a man, in the same way the rising from death comes by means of a man. For just as all people die because of their union with Adam, in the same way all will be raised to life because of their union with Christ.[6]—Our Saviour, Christ Jesus . . . has ended the power of death and through the gospel has revealed immortal life.[7]

God has given us eternal life, and this life has its source in his Son. Whoever has the Son has this life; whoever does not have the Son of God does not have life.[8]—God did not send his Son into the world to be its judge, but to be its saviour.[9]

[1]JOHN 10.10. [2]Gen. 2.17.—[3]Gen. 3.6. [4]Rom. 6.23.—[5]Rom. 5.17.—
[6]1 Cor. 15.21, 22.—[7]2 Tim. 1.10. [8]1 John 5.11, 12.—[9]John 3.17.

Evening

All of us must appear before Christ, to be judged by him.[1]

We know that God is right when he judges the people.[2]—When the Son of Man comes as King and all the angels with him, he will sit on his royal throne, and the people of all the nations will be gathered before him. Then he will divide them . . . as a shepherd separates the sheep from the goats.[3]

Then God's people will shine like the sun in their Father's Kingdom.[4]—Who will accuse God's chosen people? God himself declares them not guilty! Who, then, will condemn them? Not Christ Jesus, who died, or rather, who was raised to life and is at the right-hand side of God, pleading with him for us![5]—There is no condemnation now for those who live in union with Christ Jesus.[6]

We are judged and punished by the Lord, so that we shall not be condemned together with the world.[7]

[1]2 COR. 5.10. [2]Rom. 2.2.—[3]Matt. 25.31, 32. [4]Matt. 13.43.—[5]Rom. 8.33, 34.—
[6]Rom. 8.1. [7]1 Cor. 11.32.

Our Lord poured out his abundant grace on me and gave me the faith and love which are ours in union with Christ Jesus.[1]

You know the grace of our Lord Jesus Christ; rich as he was, he made himself poor for your sake, in order to make you rich by means of his poverty.[2]—Where sin increased, God's grace increased much more.[3]

He did this to demonstrate for all time to come the extraordinary greatness of his grace in the love he showed to us in Christ Jesus. For it is by God's grace that you have been saved through faith. It is not the result of your own efforts, but God's gift, so that no one can boast about it.[4]—We know that a person is put right with God only through faith in Jesus Christ, never by doing what the Law requires. We, too, have believed in Christ Jesus in order to be put right with God through our faith in Christ, and not by doing what the Law requires. For no one is put right with God by doing what the Law requires.[5]—He saved us. It was not because of any good deeds that we ourselves had done, but because of his own mercy that he saved us, through the Holy Spirit, who gives us new birth and new life by washing us. God poured out the Holy Spirit abundantly on us through Jesus Christ our Saviour.[6]

[1]1 TIM. 1.14. [2]2 Cor. 8.9.—[3]Rom. 5.20. [4]Eph. 2.7–9.—[5]Gal. 2.16.—[6]Titus 3.5, 6.

Evening

I am the bright morning star.[1]

A king, like a bright star, will arise in that nation.[2]

The night is nearly over, day is almost here. Let us stop doing the things that belong to the dark, and let us take up weapons for fighting in the light.[3]— . . . until the morning breezes blow and the darkness disappears. Return, my darling, like a gazelle, like a stag on the mountains of Bether.[4]

"Sentry, how soon will the night be over?" . . . I answer, "Morning is coming, but night will come again. If you want to ask again, come back and ask."[5]

I am the light of the world.[6]—I will . . . give them the morning star.[7]

Be on watch, be alert, for you do not know when the time will come. It will be like a man who goes away from home on a journey and leaves his servants in charge, after giving to each one his own work to do and after telling the doorkeeper to keep watch. Be on guard, then, because you do not know when the master of the house is coming—it might be in the evening or at midnight or before dawn or at sunrise. If he comes suddenly, he must not find you asleep. What I say to you, then, I say to all: Watch![8]

[1]REV. 22.16. [2]Num. 24.17. [3]Rom. 13.12.—[4]S. of S. 2.17. [5]Isa. 21.11, 12. [6]John 8.12.—[7]Rev. 2.28. [8]Mark 13.33–37.

You will have all you want to eat, and you will give thanks to the LORD your God for the fertile land that he has given you.[1]

Make certain that you do not forget the LORD your God.[2]—When one of them saw that he was healed, he came back, praising God in a loud voice. He threw himself to the ground at Jesus' feet and thanked him. The man was a Samaritan. Jesus said, "There were ten men who were healed; where are the other nine? Why is this foreigner the only one who came back to give thanks to God?"[3]

Everything that God has created is good . . . everything is to be received with a prayer of thanks, because the word of God and the prayer make it acceptable to God.[4]—Whoever will eat anything does so in honour of the Lord, because he gives thanks to God for the food.[5]—It is the LORD's blessing that makes you wealthy. Hard work can make you no richer.[6]

Praise the LORD, my soul! All my being, praise his holy name! Praise the LORD, my soul, and do not forget how kind he is. He forgives all my sins and heals all my diseases. He keeps me from the grave and blesses me with love and mercy.[7]

[1]DEUT. 8.10. [2]Deut. 8.11.—[3]Luke 17.15–18. [4]1 Tim. 4.4, 5.—[5]Rom. 14.6.—[6]Prov. 10.22. [7]Ps. 103.1–4.

Evening

His heart was filled with pity for them.[1]

Jesus Christ is the same yesterday, today, and for ever.[2]—Our High Priest is not one who cannot feel sympathy for our weaknesses . . . we have a High Priest who was tempted in every way that we are, but did not sin.[3]—He is able to be gentle with those who are ignorant and make mistakes.[4]—Then he returned and found the three disciples asleep. He said to Peter, "Simon, are you asleep? Weren't you able to stay awake even for one hour?" . . . "Keep watch, and pray that you will not fall into temptation. The spirit is willing, but the flesh is weak."[5]

As a father is kind to his children, so the LORD is kind to those who honour him. He knows what we are made of; he remembers that we are dust.[6]

You, O Lord, are a merciful and loving God, always patient, always kind and faithful. Turn to me and have mercy on me; strengthen me and save me.[7]

[1]MATT. 14.14. [2]Heb. 13.8.—[3]Heb. 4.15.—[4]Heb. 5.2.—[5]Mark 14.37, 38. [6]Ps. 103.13, 14. [7]Ps. 86.15, 16.

***I do not call you servants any longer, because a servant does not know what his master is doing. Instead, I call you friends, because I have told you everything I heard from my Father.*[1]**

The LORD said to himself, "I will not hide from Abraham what I am going to do."[2]—Jesus answered, "The knowledge about the secrets of the Kingdom of heaven has been given to you, but not to them."[3]—But it was to us that God made known his secret by means of his Spirit. The Spirit searches everything, even the hidden depths of God's purposes.[4]—God's secret wisdom . . . hidden from mankind, but which he had already chosen for our glory even before the world was made.[5]

Happy are those whom you choose, whom you bring to live in your sanctuary. We shall be satisfied with the good things of your house, the blessings of your sacred Temple.[6]—The LORD is the friend of those who obey him and he affirms his covenant with them.[7]—I gave them the message that you gave me, and they received it; they know that it is true that I came from you, and they believe that you sent me.[8]

You are my friends if you do what I command you.'[9]

[1]JOHN 15.15. [2]Gen. 18.17.—[3]Matt. 13.11.—[4]1 Cor. 2.10.—[5]1 Cor. 2.7. [6]Ps. 65.4.—[7]Ps. 25.14.—[8]John 17.8. [9]John 15.14.

Evening

***I will protect and defend you like a wall; you will praise me because I have saved you.*[1]**

The city's wall was built on twelve foundation stones, on which were written the names of the twelve apostles of the Lamb.[2]

You . . . are not foreigners or strangers any longer; you are now fellow-citizens with God's people and members of the family of God. You, too, are built upon the foundation laid by the apostles and prophets, the cornerstone being Christ Jesus himself. He is the one who holds the whole building together and makes it grow into a sacred temple dedicated to the Lord. In union with him you too are being built together with all the others into a place where God lives through his Spirit.[3]—You have found out for yourselves how kind the Lord is. Come to the Lord, the living stone rejected by man as worthless but chosen by God as valuable. Come as living stones, and let yourselves be used in building the spiritual temple, where you will serve as holy priests to offer spiritual and acceptable sacrifices to God through Jesus Christ.[4]

O God, it is right for us to praise you in Zion.[5]

[1]ISA. 60.18. [2]Rev. 21.14. [3]Eph. 2.19–22.—[4]1 Pet. 2.3–5. [5]Ps. 65.1.

Now he is enjoying himself here.[1]

Your days of grief will come to an end. I, the LORD, will be your eternal light, more lasting than the sun and moon.[2]—The Sovereign LORD will destroy death for ever! He will wipe away the tears from everyone's eyes and take away the disgrace his people have suffered throughout the world.[3]—These are the people who have come safely through the terrible persecution. They have washed their robes and made them white with the blood of the Lamb. That is why they stand before God's throne and serve him day and night in his temple. He who sits on the throne will protect them with his presence. Never again will they hunger or thirst; neither sun nor any scorching heat will burn them, because the Lamb, who is in the centre of the throne, will be their shepherd, and he will guide them to springs of life-giving water.[4]—He will wipe away all tears from their eyes. There will be no more death, no more grief or crying or pain. The old things have disappeared.[5]

[1]LUKE 16.25. [2]Isa. 60.20.—[3]Isa. 25.8.—[4]Rev. 7.14–17.—[5]Rev. 21.4.

Evening

Night is coming when no one can work.[1]

Happy are those who . . . die in the service of the Lord! They will enjoy rest from their hard work, because the results of their service go with them.[2]—In the grave wicked men stop their evil, and tired workmen find rest at last.[3]—Samuel said to Saul, "Why have you disturbed me? Why did you make me come back?"[4]

Work hard at whatever you do, because there will be no action, no thought, no knowledge, no wisdom in the world of the dead—and that is where you are going.[5]—The LORD is not praised by the dead, by any who go down to the land of silence.[6]

The hour has come for me to be sacrificed; the time is here for me to leave this life. I have done my best in the race, I have run the full distance, and I have kept the faith. And now there is waiting for me the victory prize of being put right with God, which the Lord, the righteous Judge, will give me on that Day—and not only to me, but to all those who wait with love for him to appear.[7]

There still remains for God's people a rest like God's resting on the seventh day. For whoever receives that rest which God promised will rest from his own work, just as God rested from his.[8]

[1]JOHN 9.4. [2]Rev. 14.13.—[3]Job 3.17.—[4]1 Sam. 28.15. [5]Eccles. 9.10.—[6]Ps. 115.17. [7]2 Tim. 4.6–8. [8]Heb. 4.9.

Your eyes are like a lamp for the body. When your eyes are sound, your whole body is full of light.[1]

Whoever does not have the Spirit cannot receive the gifts that come from God's Spirit. Such a person really does not understand them; they are nonsense to him, because their value can be judged only on a spiritual basis.[2]—Open my eyes, so that I may see the wonderful truths in your law.[3]

I am the light of the world. Whoever follows me will have the light of life and will never walk in darkness.[4]—All of us . . . reflect the glory of the Lord with uncovered faces; and that same glory, coming from the Lord, who is the Spirit, transforms us into his likeness in an ever greater degree of glory.[5]—The God who said, "Out of the darkness the light shall shine!" is the same God who made his light shine in our hearts, to bring us the knowledge of God's glory shining in the face of Christ.[6]

I . . . ask the God of our Lord Jesus Christ, the glorious Father, to give you the Spirit, who will make you wise and reveal God to you, so that you will know him . . . so that you will know what is the hope to which he has called you, how rich are the wonderful blessings he promises his people.[7]

[1]LUKE 11.34. [2]1 Cor. 2.14.—[3]Ps. 119.18. [4]John 8.12.—[5]2 Cor. 3.18.—[6]2 Cor. 4.6. [7]Eph. 1.16–18.

Evening

He struck the rock, and water flowed out in a torrent.[1]

Our ancestors . . . were all under the protection of the cloud, and all passed safely through the Red Sea. In the cloud and in the sea they were all baptized as followers of Moses. All ate the same spiritual bread and drank the same spiritual drink. They drank from the spiritual rock that went with them; and that rock was Christ himself.[2]—One of the soldiers . . . plunged his spear into Jesus' side, and at once blood and water poured out.[3]—Because of our sins he was wounded, beaten because of the evil we did. We are healed by the punishment he suffered, made whole by the blows he received.[4]

Yet you are not willing to come to me in order to have life.[5]—My people have committed two sins: they have turned away from me, the spring of fresh water, and they have dug cisterns, cracked cisterns that can hold no water at all.[6]

Whoever is thirsty should come to me and drink.[7]—Come, whoever is thirsty; accept the water of life as a gift, whoever wants it.[8]

[1]PS. 78.20. [2]1 Cor. 10.1–4.—[3]John 19.34.—[4]Isa. 53.5. [5]John 5.40.—[6]Jer. 2.13. [7]John 7.37.—[8]Rev. 22.17.

Then the people who feared the LORD spoke to one another, and the LORD listened and heard what they said. In his presence, there was written down in a book a record of those who feared the LORD and respected him.[1]

Jesus himself drew near and walked along with them.[2]—Where two or three come together in my name, I am there with them.[3]—All my other fellow-workers, whose names are in God's book of the living.[4]

Christ's message in all its richness must live in your hearts. Teach and instruct each other with all wisdom. Sing psalms, hymns, and sacred songs; sing to God with thanksgiving in your hearts.[5]—In order that none of you be deceived by sin and become stubborn, you must help one another every day, as long as the word "Today" in the scripture applies to us.[6]

You can be sure that on the Judgement Day everyone will have to give account of every useless word he has ever spoken. Your words will be used to judge you—to declare you either innocent or guilty.[7]—Their sentence is written down.[8]

[1]MAL. 3.16. [2]Luke 24.15.—[3]Matt. 18.20.—[4]Phil. 4.3. [5]Col. 3.16.—[6]Heb. 3.13. [7]Matt. 12.36, 37.—[8]Isa. 65.6.

Evening

The cedars of Lebanon get plenty of rain—the LORD's own trees, which he planted.[1]

I will be to the people of Israel like rain in a dry land. They will blossom like flowers; they will be firmly rooted like the trees of Lebanon. They will be alive with new growth, and beautiful like olive trees. They will be fragrant like the cedars of Lebanon.[2]—I will bless the person who puts his trust in me. He is like a tree growing near a stream and sending out roots to the water. It is not afraid when hot weather comes, because its leaves stay green; it has no worries when there is no rain; it keeps on bearing fruit.[3]

I am the LORD. I cut down the tall trees and make the small trees grow tall. I wither up the green trees and make the dry trees become green.[4]

The righteous will flourish like palm trees; they will grow like the cedars of Lebanon. They are like trees planted in the house of the LORD, that flourish in the Temple of our God, that still bear fruit in old age and are always green and strong.[5]

[1]PS. 104.16. [2]Hos. 14.5, 6.—[3]Jer. 17.7, 8. [4]Ezek. 17.24. [5]Ps. 92.12–14.

Morning

"They will be my people," says the LORD Almighty. "On the day when I act, they will be my very own."[1]

I have made you known to those you gave me out of the world. They belonged to you, and you gave them to me. They have obeyed your word. I pray for them. I do not pray for the world but for those you gave me, for they belong to you. All I have is yours, and all you have is mine; and my glory is shown through them. Father! You have given them to me, and I want them to be with me where I am, so that they may see my glory, the glory you gave me; for you loved me before the world was made.[2]

I will come back and take you to myself, so that you will be where I am.[3]—He comes on that Day to receive glory from all his people and honour from all who believe.[4]—We who are living at that time will be gathered up along with them in the clouds to meet the Lord in the air. And so we will always be with the Lord.[5]—You will be like a beautiful crown for the LORD.[6]

[1]MAL. 3.17. [2]John 17.6, 9, 10, 24. [3]John 14.3.—[4]2 Thess. 1.10.—[5]1 Thess. 4.17.—[6]Isa. 62.3.

Evening

Moses requested, "Please, let me see the dazzling light of your presence."[1]

The God who said, "Out of darkness the light shall shine!" is the same God who made his light shine in our hearts, to bring us the knowledge of God's glory shining in the face of Christ.[2]—The Word became a human being and, full of grace and truth, lived among us. We saw his glory, the glory which he received as the Father's only Son. No one has ever seen God. The only Son, who is the same as God and is at the Father's side, he has made him known.[3]

I thirst for you, the living God; when can I go and worship in your presence?[4]—When you said, "Come and worship me," I answered, "I will come, LORD."[5]

All of us, then, reflect the glory of the Lord with uncovered faces; and that same glory, coming from the Lord, who is the Spirit, transforms us into his likeness in an ever greater degree of glory.[6]—Father! You have given them to me, and I want them to be with me where I am, so that they may see my glory, the glory you gave me; for you loved me before the world was made.[7]

[1]EXOD. 33.18. [2]2 Cor. 4.6.—[3]John 1.14, 18. [4]Ps. 42.2.—[5]Ps. 27.8. [6]2 Cor. 3.18.—[7]John 17.24.

Above the dome there was something that looked like a throne made of sapphire, and sitting on the throne was a figure that looked like a man.[1]

The man Christ Jesus.[2]—He became like man and appeared in human likeness.[3]—Since the children, as he calls them, are people of flesh and blood, Jesus himself became like them and shared their human nature. He did this so that through his death he might destroy the Devil, who has the power over death.[4]

I am the living one! I was dead, but now I am alive for ever and ever.[5]—Christ has been raised from death and will never die again—death will no longer rule over him. Because he died, sin has no power over him; and now he lives his life in fellowship with God.[6]—Suppose that you should see the Son of Man go back up to the place where he was before?[7]—He raised Christ from death and seated him at his right side in the heavenly world.[8]—The full content of divine nature lives in Christ, in his humanity.[9]

Though it was in weakness that he was put to death on the cross, it is by God's power that he lives. In union with him we also are weak; but in our relations with you we shall share God's power in his life.[10]

[1]EZEK. 1.26. [2]1 Tim. 2.5.—[3]Phil. 2.7.—[4]Heb. 2.14. [5]Rev. 1.18.—[6]Rom. 6.9, 10.—[7]John 6.62.—[8]Eph. 1.20.—[9]Col. 2.9. [10]2 Cor. 13.4.

Evening

Your promise gave me life.[1]

The first man, Adam, was created a living being; but the last Adam is the life-giving Spirit.[2]

Just as the Father is himself the source of life, in the same way he has made his Son to be the source of life.[3]—I am the resurrection and the life. Whoever believes in me will live, even though he dies; and whoever lives and believes in me will never die.[4]

The Word was the source of life, and this life brought light to mankind. Some . . . did receive him and believed in him; so he gave them the right to become God's children. They did not become God's children by natural means, that is, by being born as the children of a human father; God himself was their Father.[5]

What gives life is God's Spirit; man's power is of no use at all. The words I have spoken to you bring God's life-giving Spirit.[6]—The word of God is alive and active, sharper than any double-edged sword. It cuts all the way through, to where soul and spirit meet . . . It judges the desires and thoughts of man's heart.[7]

[1]PS. 119.50. [2]1 Cor. 15.45. [3]John 5.26.—[4]John 11.25, 26. [5]John 1.4, 12, 13. [6]John 6.63.—[7]Heb. 4.12.

Let it be so for now. For in this way we shall do all that God requires.[1]

I love to do your will, my God! I keep your teaching in my heart.[2]

Do not think that I have come to do away with the Law of Moses and the teachings of the prophets. I have not come to do away with them, but to make their teachings come true. Remember that as long as heaven and earth last, not the least point nor the smallest detail of the Law will be done away with.[3]—The LORD is a God who is eager to save, so he exalted his laws and teachings.[4]—You will be able to enter the Kingdom of heaven only if you are more faithful than the teachers of the Law and the Pharisees in doing what God requires.[5]

What the Law could not do, because human nature was weak, God did. He condemned sin in human nature by sending his own Son, who came with a nature like man's sinful nature, to do away with sin. God did this so that the righteous demands of the Law might be fully satisfied in us who live according to the Spirit, and not according to human nature.[6]—Christ has brought the Law to an end, so that everyone who believes is put right with God.[7]

[1]MATT. 3.15. [2]Ps. 40.8. [3]Matt. 5.17, 18.—[4]Isa. 42.21.—[5]Matt. 5.20. [6]Rom. 8.3, 4.—[7]Rom. 10.4.

Evening

I, the LORD, am all you need.[1]

What else have I in heaven but you? Since I have you, what else could I want on earth? My mind and my body may grow weak, but God is my strength; he is all I ever need.[2]—You, LORD, are all I have, and you give me all I need; my future is in your hands. How wonderful are your gifts to me; how good they are![3]

The LORD is all I have, and so I put my hope in him.[4]

Your commandments are my eternal possession; they are the joy of my heart.[5]

O God, you are my God, and I long for you. My whole being desires you; like a dry, worn-out, and waterless land, my soul is thirsty for you. . . . Because you have always been my help. In the shadow of your wings I sing for joy.[6]

My lover is mine, and I am his.[7]

[1]NUM. 18.20. [2]Ps. 73.25, 26.—[3]Ps. 16.5, 6. [4]Lam. 3.24. [5]Ps. 119.111. [6]Ps. 63.1, 7. [7]S. of S. 2.16.

Can anyone really say that his conscience is clear, that he has got rid of his sin?[1]

The LORD looks down from heaven at mankind to see if there are any who are wise, any who worship him. But they have all gone wrong; they are all equally bad.[2]—Those who obey their human nature cannot please God.[3]

I know that good does not live in me—that is, in my human nature. For even though the desire to do good is in me, I am not able to do it. I don't do the good I want to do; instead, I do the evil that I do not want to do.[4]—All of us have been sinful; even our best actions are filthy through and through.[5]

The whole world is under the power of sin; and so the gift which is promised on the basis of faith in Jesus Christ is given to those who believe.[6]—God was making all mankind his friends through Christ. God did not keep an account of their sins.[7]

If we say that we have no sin, we deceive ourselves, and there is no truth in us. But if we confess our sins to God, he will keep his promise and do what is right: he will forgive us our sins and purify us from all our wrongdoing.[8]

[1]PROV. 20.9. [2]Ps. 14.2, 3.—[3]Rom. 8.8. [4]Rom. 7.18, 19.—[5]Isa. 64.6. [6]Gal. 3.22.—[7]2 Cor. 5.19. [8]1 John 1.8, 9.

Evening

The ocean depths raise their voice, O LORD.[1]

The LORD rules supreme in heaven, greater than the roar of the ocean, more powerful than the waves of the sea.[2]—LORD God Almighty, none is as mighty as you; in all things you are faithful, O LORD. You rule over the powerful sea; you calm its angry waves.[3]

I am the LORD; why don't you fear me? Why don't you tremble before me? I placed the sand as the boundary of the sea, a permanent boundary that it cannot cross.[4]

When you pass through deep waters, I will be with you; your troubles will not overwhelm you.[5]

Peter got out of the boat and started walking on the water to Jesus. But when he noticed the strong wind, he was afraid and started to sink down in the water. "Save me, Lord!" he cried. At once Jesus reached out and grabbed hold of him and said, "How little faith you have! Why did you doubt?"[6]

When I am afraid, O LORD Almighty, I put my trust in you.[7]

[1]PS. 93.3. [2]Ps. 93.4.—[3]Ps. 89.8, 9. [4]Jer. 5.22. [5]Isa. 43.2. [6]Matt. 14.29–31. [7]Ps. 56.3.

There is a fragrance about you; the sound of your name recalls it.[1]

Your life must be controlled by love, just as Christ loved us and gave his life for us as a sweet-smelling offering and sacrifice that pleases God.[2]—This stone is of great value for you that believe.[3]—God raised him to the highest place above and gave him the name that is greater than any other name. And so, in honour of the name of Jesus all beings in heaven, on earth, and in the world below will fall on their knees.[4]—The full content of divine nature lives in Christ, in his humanity.[5]

If you love me, you will obey my commandments.[6]—God has poured out his love into our hearts by means of the Holy Spirit, who is God's gift to us.[7]—The sweet smell of the perfume filled the whole house.[8]—They realized then that they had been companions of Jesus.[9]

O LORD, our Lord, your greatness is seen in all the world! Your praise reaches up to the heavens.[10]—Immanuel . . . God is with us.[11]—He will be called, "Wonderful Counsellor", "Mighty God", "Eternal Father", "Prince of Peace".[12]—The LORD is like a strong tower, where the righteous can go and be safe.[13]

[1]S. OF S. 1.3. [2]Eph. 5.2.—[3]1 Pet. 2.7.—[4]Phil. 2.9, 10.—[5]Col. 2.9. [6]John 14.15.—[7]Rom. 5.5.—[8]John 12.3.—[9]Acts 4.13. [10]Ps. 8.1.—[11]Matt. 1.23.—[12]Isa. 9.6.—[13]Prov. 18.10.

Evening

While we live in this earthly tent, we groan with a feeling of oppression.[1]

O Lord, you know what I long for; you hear all my groans. I am drowning in the flood of my sins; they are a burden too heavy to bear.[2]—What an unhappy man I am! Who will rescue me from this body that is taking me to death?[3]

All of creation groans with pain, like the pain of childbirth. But it is not just creation alone which groans; we who have the Spirit as the first of God's gifts also groan within ourselves, as we wait for God to make us his sons and set our whole being free.[4]—It may now be necessary for you to be sad for a while because of the many kinds of trials you suffer.[5]

I know that I shall soon put off this mortal body.[6]—What is mortal must be changed into what cannot die. So when this takes place, and the mortal has been changed into the immortal, then the scripture will come true: "Death is destroyed; victory is complete!"[7]

[1]2 COR. 5.4. [2]Ps. 38.9, 4.—[3]Rom. 7.24. [4]Rom. 8.22, 23.—[5]1 Pet. 1.6. [6]2 Pet. 1.14.—[7]1 Cor. 15.53, 54.

[He] shall carry [the sacrificed bull] . . . outside the camp to the ritually clean place where the ashes are poured out, and there he shall burn it on a wood fire.

So they took charge of Jesus. He went out, carrying his cross, and came to "The Place of the Skull", as it is called. (In Hebrew it is called "Golgotha".) There they crucified him.[2]—The Jewish High Priest brings the blood of the animals into the Most Holy Place to offer it as a sacrifice for sins; but the bodies of the animals are burnt outside the camp. For this reason Jesus also died outside the city, in order to purify the people from sin with his own blood. Let us, then, go to him outside the camp and share his shame.[3]—To share in his sufferings.[4]

Be glad that you are sharing Christ's sufferings, so that you may be full of joy when his glory is revealed.[5]—This small and temporary trouble we suffer will bring us a tremendous and eternal glory, much greater than the trouble.[6]

[1]LEV. 4.12. [2]John 19.16–18.—[3]Heb. 13.11–13.—[4]Phil. 3.10. [5]1 Pet. 4.13.—[6]2 Cor. 4.17.

Evening

God created human beings, making them to be like himself.[1]

Since we are God's children, we should not suppose that his nature is anything like an image of gold or silver or stone, shaped by the art and skill of man.[2]

God's mercy is so abundant, and his love for us is so great, that while we were spiritually dead in our disobedience he brought us to life with Christ. It is by God's grace that you have been saved. God has made us what we are, and in our union with Christ Jesus he has created us for a life of good deeds, which he has already prepared for us to do.[3]—Those whom God had already chosen he also set apart to become like his Son, so that the Son would be the first among many brothers.[4]

We know that when Christ appears, we shall be like him, because we shall see him as he really is.[5]—When I awake, your presence will fill me with joy.[6]

Whoever wins the victory will receive this from me: I will be his God, and he will be my son.[7]—Since we are his children, we will possess the blessings he keeps for his people, and we will also possess with Christ what God has kept for him.[8]

[1]GEN. 1.27. [2]Acts 17.29. [3]Eph. 2.4, 5, 10.—[4]Rom. 8.29. [5]1 John 3.2.—[6]Ps. 17.15. [7]Rev. 21.7.—[8]Rom. 8.17.

You are my place of safety when trouble comes.[1]

There are many who pray: "Give us more blessings, O LORD. Look on us with kindness!"[2]—Every morning I will sing aloud of your constant love. You have been a refuge for me, a shelter in my time of trouble.[3]

I felt secure and said to myself, "I will never be defeated." You were good to me, LORD; you protected me like a mountain fortress. But then you hid yourself from me, and I was afraid. I called to you, LORD; I begged for your help: "What will you gain from my death? What profit from my going to the grave? Are dead people able to praise you? Can they proclaim your unfailing goodness? Hear me, LORD, and be merciful! Help me, LORD!"[4]

"For one brief moment I left you; with deep love I will take you back. I turned away angry for only a moment, but I will show you my love for ever." So says the LORD who saves you.[5]—You will be sad, but your sadness will turn into gladness.[6]—Tears may flow in the night, but joy comes in the morning.[7]

[1]JER. 17.17. [2]Ps. 4.6.—[3]Ps. 59.16. [4]Ps. 30.6–10. [5]Isa. 54.7, 8.—[6]John 16.20.—[7]Ps. 30.5.

Evening

Adam . . . had a son who was like him.[1]

Nothing clean can ever come from anything as unclean as man.[2]—I have been evil from the day I was born; from the time I was conceived, I have been sinful.[3]

In the past you were spiritually dead because of your disobedience and sins. In our natural condition we, like everyone else, were destined to suffer God's anger.[4]—I am a mortal man, sold as a slave to sin. I do not understand what I do; for I don't do what I would like to do, but instead I do what I hate. I know that good does not live in me—that is, in my human nature. For even though the desire to do good is in me, I am not able to do it.[5]

Sin came into the world through one man . . . all people were made sinners as the result of the disobedience of one man.[6]—God's grace is much greater, and so is his free gift to so many people through the grace of the one man, Jesus Christ.[7]

The law of the Spirit, which brings us life in union with Christ Jesus, has set me free from the law of sin and death.[8]

Thanks be to God who gives us the victory through our Lord Jesus Christ![9]

[1]GEN. 5.3. [2]Job 14.4.—[3]Ps. 51.5. [4]Eph. 2.1, 3.—[5]Rom. 7.14, 15, 18. [6]Rom. 5.12, 19.—[7]Rom. 5.15. [8]Rom. 8.2. [9]1 Cor. 15.57.

***It is the* LORD *who gives wisdom; from him come knowledge and understanding.*[1]**

Trust in the LORD with all your heart. Never rely on what you think you know.[2]—If any of you lacks wisdom, he should pray to God, who will give it to him; because God gives generously and graciously to all.[3]—What seems to be God's foolishness is wiser than human wisdom, and what seems to be God's weakness is stronger than human strength.[4]—I will give you such words and wisdom that none of your enemies will be able to refute or contradict what you say.[5]—God purposely chose what the world considers nonsense in order to shame the wise. This means that no one can boast in God's presence.[6]

The explanation of your teachings gives light and brings wisdom to the ignorant.[7]—I keep your law in my heart, so that I will not sin against you.[8]

They were all well impressed with him and marvelled at the eloquent words that he spoke.[9]—Nobody has ever talked like this man![10]—God has brought you into union with Christ Jesus, and God has made Christ to be our wisdom.[11]

[1]PROV. 2.6. [2]Prov. 3.5.—[3]Jas 1.5.—[4]1 Cor. 1.25.—[5]Luke 21.15.—[6]1 Cor. 1.27, 29. [7]Ps. 119.130.—[8]Ps. 119.11. [9]Luke 4.22.—[10]John 7.46.—[11]1 Cor. 1.30.

Evening

***I decided that the time to save my people had come.*[1]**

You shall set the fiftieth year apart and proclaim freedom to all the inhabitants of the land. During this year all property that has been sold shall be restored to the original owner or his descendants.[2]

Those of our people who have died will live again! Their bodies will come back to life. All those sleeping in their graves will wake up and sing for joy. As the sparkling dew refreshes the earth, so the LORD will revive those who have long been dead.[3]

There will be the shout of command, the archangel's voice, the sound of God's trumpet, and the Lord himself will come down from heaven. Those who have died believing in Christ will rise to life first; then we who are living at that time will be gathered up along with them in the clouds to meet the Lord in the air. And so we will always be with the Lord.[4]

The one who will rescue them is strong—his name is the LORD Almighty.[5]

[1]ISA. 63.4. [2]Lev. 25.10. [3]Isa. 26.19. [4]1 Thess. 4.16, 17. [5]Jer. 50.34.

After a life of suffering, he will again have joy; he will know that he did not suffer in vain.[1]

Jesus . . . said, "It is finished!" Then he bowed his head and died.[2]—Christ was without sin, but for our sake God made him share our sin in order that in union with him we might share the righteousness of God.[3]

They are the people I made for myself, and they will sing my praises![4]—God . . . kept his secret hidden . . . in order that at the present time, by means of the church, the angelic rulers and powers in the heavenly world might learn of his wisdom in all its different forms. God did this according to his eternal purpose, which he achieved through Christ Jesus our Lord.[5]—He did this to demonstrate for all time to come the extraordinary greatness of his grace in the love he showed us in Christ Jesus.[6]

You believed in Christ, and God put his stamp of ownership on you by giving you the Holy Spirit he had promised. The Spirit is the guarantee that we shall receive what God has promised his people, and this assures us that God will give complete freedom to those who are his.[7]

You are the chosen race, the King's priests, the holy nation, God's own people, chosen to proclaim the wonderful acts of God, who called you out of darkness into his own marvellous light.[8]

[1]ISA. 53.11. [2]John 19.30.—[3]2 Cor. 5.21. [4]Isa. 43.21.—[5]Eph. 3.9–11.—[6]Eph. 2.7. [7]Eph. 1.13, 14. [8]1 Pet. 2.9.

Evening

That day in the desert when they put him to the test.[1]

If a person is tempted by such trials, he must not say, "This temptation comes from God." For God cannot be tempted by evil, and he himself tempts no one. But a person is tempted when he is drawn away and trapped by his own evil desire. Then his evil desire conceives and gives birth to sin.[2]

They were filled with craving in the desert and put God to the test.[3]

Jesus returned from the Jordan full of the Holy Spirit and was led by the Spirit into the desert, where he was tempted by the Devil for forty days. In all that time he ate nothing, so that he was hungry when it was over. The Devil said to him, "If you are God's Son, order this stone to turn into bread."[4]

He can help those who are tempted, because he himself was tempted and suffered.[5]—Simon, Simon! Listen! Satan has received permission to test all of you, to separate the good from the bad, as a farmer separates the wheat from the chaff. But I have prayed for you, Simon, that your faith will not fail.[6]

[1]HEB. 3.8. [2]Jas 1.13–15. [3]Ps. 106.14. [4]Luke 4.1–3. [5]Heb. 2.18.—[6]Luke 22.31, 32.

I am the Lord and I make you holy.[1]

I am the LORD your God, and I have set you apart from the other nations. You shall be holy and belong only to me, because I am the LORD and I am holy. I have set you apart from the other nations so that you would belong to me alone.[2]

Those who have been called by God, who live in the love of God the Father.[3]—Dedicate them to yourself by means of the truth; your word is truth.[4]—May the God who gives us peace make you holy in every way and keep your whole being—spirit, soul, and body—free from every fault at the coming of our Lord Jesus Christ.[5]

Jesus . . . died outside the city, in order to purify the people from sin with his own blood.[6]—Our God and Saviour Jesus Christ . . . gave himself for us, to rescue us from all wickedness and to make us a pure people who belong to him alone and are eager to do good.[7]—He purifies people from their sins, and both he and those who are made pure all have the same Father. That is why Jesus is not ashamed to call them his brothers.[8]—For their sake I dedicate myself to you, in order that they, too, may be truly dedicated to you.[9]—You . . . were made a holy people by his Spirit, to obey Jesus Christ and be purified by his blood.[10]

[1]LEV. 20.8. [2]Lev. 20.24, 26. [3]Jude 1.—[4]John 17.17.—[5]1 Thess. 5.23. [6]Heb. 13.12.—[7]Titus 2.13, 14.—[8]Heb. 2.11.—[9]John 17.19.—[10]1 Pet. 1.2.

Evening

Light shines on the righteous, and gladness on the good.[1]

Let those who wept as they sowed their seed, gather the harvest with joy. Those who wept as they went out carrying the seed will come back singing for joy, as they bring in the harvest.[2]

What you sow is a bare seed . . . not the full-bodied plant that will later grow up.[3]

Let us give thanks to the God and Father of our Lord Jesus Christ! Because of his great mercy he gave us new life by raising Jesus Christ from death. This fills us with a living hope. Be glad about this, even though it may now be necessary for you to be sad for a while because of the many kinds of trials you suffer. Their purpose is to prove that your faith is genuine. Even gold, which can be destroyed, is tested by fire; and so your faith, which is much more precious than gold, must also be tested, so that it may endure. Then you will receive praise and glory and honour on the Day when Jesus Christ is revealed.[4]

[1]PS. 97.11. [2]Ps. 126.5, 6. [3]1 Cor. 15.37. [4]1 Pet.1.3, 6, 7.

***Those who have reverence for the* LORD *will learn from him the path they should follow.*[1]**

The eyes are like a lamp for the body. If your eyes are sound, your whole body will be full of light.[2]

Your word is a lamp to guide me and a light for my path.[3]—If you wander off the road to the right or the left, you will hear his voice behind you saying, "Here is the road. Follow it."[4]—The LORD says, "I will teach you the way you should go; I will instruct you and advise you. Don't be stupid like a horse or a mule, which must be controlled with a bit and bridle to make it submit." The wicked will have to suffer, but those who trust in the LORD are protected by his constant love. You that are righteous, be glad and rejoice because of what the Lord has done. You that obey him, shout for joy![5]—With faithfulness and love he leads all who keep his covenant and obey his commands.[6]

LORD, I know that no one is the master of his own destiny; no person has control over his own life.[7]—Teach me your ways, O LORD; make them known to me.[8]

[1]PS. 25.25. [2]Matt. 6.22. [3]Ps. 119.105.—[4]Isa. 30.21.—[5]Ps. 32.8–11.—[6]Ps. 25.10. [7]Jer. 10.23.—[8]Ps. 25.4.

Evening

***You will not be afraid when you go to bed, and you will sleep soundly through the night.*[1]**

Suddenly a strong wind blew up, and the waves began to spill over into the boat, so that it was about to fill with water. Jesus was in the back of the boat, sleeping with his head on a pillow.[2]

Don't worry about anything, but in all your prayers ask God for what you need, always asking him with a thankful heart. And God's peace, which is far beyond human understanding, will keep your hearts and minds safe in union with Christ Jesus.[3]

When I lie down, I go to sleep in peace; you alone, O LORD, keep me perfectly safe.[4]—The LORD provides for those he loves, while they are asleep.[5]

They kept on stoning Stephen as he called out to the Lord, "Lord Jesus, receive my spirit!" He knelt down and cried out in a loud voice, "Lord! Do not remember this sin against them!" He said this and died.[6]—We . . . would much prefer to leave our home in the body and be at home with the Lord.[7]

[1]PROV. 3.24. [2]Mark 4.37, 38. [3]Phil. 4.6, 7. [4]Ps. 4.8.—[5]Ps. 127.2. [6]Acts 7.59, 60.— [7]2 Cor. 5.8.

The sprinkled blood that promises much better things than does the blood of Abel.[1]

There is the Lamb of God, who takes away the sin of the world![2]—The Lamb that was killed.[3]—The blood of bulls and goats can never take away sins. For this reason, when Christ was about to come into the world, he said to God: "You do not want sacrifices and offerings, but you have prepared a body for me." We are all purified from sin by the offering that he made of his own body once and for all.[4]

Then Abel brought the first lamb born to one of his sheep . . . and gave the best parts of it as an offering. The LORD was pleased with Abel and his offering.[5]—Christ loved us and gave his life for us as a sweet-smelling offering and sacrifice that pleases God.[6]

Let us come near to God with a sincere heart and a sure faith, with hearts that have been purified from a guilty conscience and with bodies washed with clean water.[7]—We have . . . complete freedom to go into the Most Holy Place by means of the death of Jesus.[8]

[1]HEB. 12.24. [2]John 1.29.—[3]Rev. 13.8.—[4]Heb. 10.4, 5, 10. [5]Gen. 4.4.—[6]Eph. 5.2. [7]Heb. 10.22.—[8]Heb. 10.19.

Evening

Who has felt the full power of your anger?[1]

At noon the whole country was covered with darkness, which lasted for three hours. At about three o'clock Jesus cried out with a loud shout, "*Eli, Eli, lema sabachthani?*" which means, "My God, my God, why did You abandon me?"[2]—The LORD made the punishment fall on him, the punishment all of us deserved.[3]

There is no condemnation now for those who live in union with Christ Jesus.[4]—Now that we have been put right with God through faith, we have peace with God through our Lord Jesus Christ.[5]—By becoming a curse for us Christ has redeemed us from the curse that the Law brings.[6]

God showed his love for us by sending his only Son into the world, so that we might have life through him. This is what love is: it is not that we have loved God, but that he loved us and sent his Son to be the means by which our sins are forgiven.[7]—God shows that he himself is righteous and that he puts right everyone who believes in Jesus.[8]

[1]PS. 90.11. [2]Matt. 27.45, 46.—[3]Isa. 53.6. [4]Rom. 8.1.—[5]Rom. 5.1.—[6]Gal. 3.13. [7]1 John 4.9, 10.—[8]Rom. 3.26.

The sovereign LORD says, "I will once again let the Israelites ask me for help."[1]

You do not have what you want because you do not ask God for it.[2] Ask, and you will receive; seek, and you will find; knock, and the door will be opened to you. For everyone who asks will receive, and anyone who seeks will find, and the door will be opened to him who knocks.[3]—We have courage in God's presence, because we are sure that he hears us if we ask him for anything that is according to his will. He hears us whenever we ask him; and since we know this is true, we know also that he gives us what we ask from him.[4]—If any of you lacks wisdom, he should pray to God, who will give it to him; because God gives generously and graciously to all.[5]—Open your mouth, and I will feed you.[6]—They should always pray and never become discouraged.[7]

The LORD watches over the righteous and listens to their cries. The righteous call to the LORD, and he listens.[8]—You will ask him in my name; and I do not say that I will ask him on your behalf, for the Father himself loves you. He loves you because you love me. Ask and you will receive, so that your happiness may be complete.[9]

[1]EZEK. 36.37. [2]Jas 4.2. [3]Matt. 7.7, 8.—[4]1 John 5.14, 15.—[5]Jas 1.5.—[6]Ps. 81.10.—[7]Luke 18.1. [8]Ps. 34.15, 17.—[9]John 16.26, 27, 24.

Evening

When God sends us something good, we welcome it. How can we complain when he sends us trouble?[1]

I know that your judgements are righteous, LORD, and that you punished me because you are faithful.[2]—You are our father, LORD. We are like clay, and you are like the potter. You created us.[3]—He is the LORD; he will do whatever seems best to him.[4]

LORD, if I argued my case with you, you would prove to be right. Yet I must question you about matters of justice.[5]

He will come to judge like one who refines and purifies silver.[6]—The Lord corrects everyone he loves, and punishes everyone he accepts as a son.[7]—A pupil should be satisfied to become like his teacher, and a slave like his master.[8]—Even though he was God's Son, he learnt through his sufferings to be obedient.[9]

Be glad that you are sharing Christ's sufferings, so that you may be full of joy when his glory is revealed.[10]—These are the people who have come safely through the terrible persecution. They have washed their robes and made them white with the blood of the Lamb.[11]

[1]JOB 2.10. [2]Ps. 119.75.—[3]Isa. 64.8.—[4]1 Sam. 3.18. [5]Jer. 12.1. [6]Mal. 3.3.—[7]Heb. 12.6.—[8]Matt. 10.25.—[9]Heb. 5.8. [10]1 Pet. 4.13.—[11]Rev. 7.14.

Resist the Devil, and he will run away from you.[1]

From east to west everyone will fear him and his great power.[2]—Jesus answered, "Go away, Satan! The scripture says, 'Worship the Lord your God and serve only him!' " Then the Devil left Jesus; and angels came and helped him.[3]

Build up your strength in union with the Lord and by means of his mighty power. Put on all the armour that God gives you, so that you will be able to stand up against the Devil's evil tricks.[4]—Have nothing to do with the worthless things that people do, things that belong to the darkness. Instead, bring them out to the light.[5]—Keep Satan from getting the upper hand of us; for we know what his plans are.[6]—Be alert, be on the watch! Your enemy, the Devil, roams round like a roaring lion, looking for someone to devour. Be firm in your faith and resist him, because you know that your fellow-believers in all the world are going through the same kind of sufferings.[7]

Who will accuse God's chosen people? God himself declared them not guilty![8]

[1]JAS 4.7. [2]Isa. 59.19.—[3]Matt. 4.10, 11. [4]Eph. 6.10, 11.—[5]Eph. 5.11.—[6]2 Cor. 2.11.—[7]1 Pet. 5.8, 9. [8]Rom. 8.33.

Evening

How I wish I knew where to find him.[1]

All of you that honour the LORD and obey the words of his servant, the path you walk may be dark indeed, but trust in the LORD, rely on your God.[2]

You will seek me, and you will find me because you will seek me with all your heart.[3]—Ask, and you will receive; seek, and you will find; knock and the door will be opened to you. For everyone who asks will receive, and he who seeks will find, and the door will be opened to anyone who knocks.[4]

Join with us in the fellowship that we have with the Father and with his Son Jesus Christ.[5]—In union with Christ Jesus, you who used to be far away have been brought near by the sacrificial death of Christ. It is through Christ that all of us, Jews and Gentiles, are able to come in the one Spirit into the presence of the Father.[6]

If . . . we say that we have fellowship with him, yet at the same time live in the darkness, we are lying.[7]

I will be with you always.[8]—I will never leave you; I will never abandon you.[9]—The Spirit . . . remains with you and is in you.[10]

[1]JOB 23.3. [2]Isa. 50.10. [3]Jer. 29.13.—[4]Luke 11.9, 10. [5]1 John 1.3.—[6]Eph. 2.13, 18. [7]1 John 1.6. [8]Matt. 28.20.—[9]Heb. 13.5.—[10]John 14.17.

Morning

***Let us examine our ways and turn back to the* L*ORD*.**[1]

Examine me and test me, LORD; judge my desires and thoughts.[2]—Sincerity and truth are what you require; fill my mind with your wisdom.[3]—I have considered my conduct, and I promise to follow your instructions. Without delay I hurry to obey your commands.[4]—Everyone should examine himself first, and then eat the bread and drink from the cup.[5]

If we confess our sins to God, he will keep his promise and do what is right: he will forgive us our sins and purify us from all our wrongdoing.[6]—If anyone does sin, we have someone who pleads with the Father on our behalf—Jesus Christ, the righteous one.[7]—We have, then, my brothers, complete freedom to go into the Most Holy Place by means of the death of Jesus. He opened for us a new way, a living way, through the curtain—that is, through his own body. We have a great priest in charge of the house of God. So let us come near to God with a sincere heart and a sure faith, with hearts that have been purified from a guilty conscience and with bodies washed with clean water.[8]

[1]LAM. 3.40. [2]Ps. 26.2.—[3]Ps. 51.6.—[4]Ps. 119.59, 60.—[5]1 Cor. 11.28. [6]1 John 1.9.—[7]1 John 2.1.—[8]Heb. 10.19–22.

Evening

All round the throne there was a rainbow the colour of an emerald.[1]

As a sign of this everlasting covenant which I am making with you and with all living beings, I am putting my bow in the clouds. It will be the sign of my covenant with the world. When the rainbow appears in the clouds, I will see it and remember the everlasting covenant between me and all living beings on earth.[2]—An eternal covenant . . . that will not be broken . . . that will not be changed.[3]—There are these two things, then, that cannot change and about which God cannot lie. So we who have found safety with him are greatly encouraged to hold firmly to the hope placed before us.[4]

We are here to bring the Good News to you: what God promised our ancestors he would do, he has now done for us, who are their descendants, by raising Jesus to life.[5]

Jesus Christ is the same yesterday, today, and for ever.[6]

[1]REV. 4.3. [2]Gen. 9.12, 13, 16.—[3]2 Sam. 23.5.—[4]Heb. 6.18. [5]Acts 13.32, 33. [6]Heb. 13.8.

Think of yourselves as dead, so far as sin is concerned, but living in fellowship with God through Christ Jesus.[1]

Whoever hears my words and believes in him who sent me has eternal life. He will not be judged, but has already passed from death to life.[2]—So far as the Law is concerned, however, I am dead—killed by the Law itself—in order that I might live for God. I have been put to death with Christ on his cross, so that it is no longer I who live, but it is Christ who lives in me. This life that I live now, I live by faith in the Son of God, who loved me and gave his life for me.[3]

Because I live, you also will live.[4]—I give them eternal life, and they shall never die. No one can snatch them away from me. What my Father has given me is greater than everything, and no one can snatch them away from the Father's care. The Father and I are one.[5]

You have been raised to life with Christ, so set your hearts on the things that are in heaven, where Christ sits on his throne at the right-hand side of God. For you have died, and your life is hidden with Christ in God.[6]

[1]ROM. 6.11. [2]John 5.24.—[3]Gal. 2.19, 20. [4]John 14.19.—[5]John 10.28–30. [6]Col. 3.1, 3.

Evening

God . . . will give . . . generously and graciously to all.[1]

He . . . said to her, "Where are they? Is there no one left to condemn you?" "No one, sir," she answered. "Well, then," Jesus said, "I do not condemn you either. Go, but do not sin again."[2]

God's grace is much greater, and so is his free gift to so many people through the grace of the one man, Jesus Christ. After so many sins, comes the undeserved gift of "Not guilty!"[3]

But God's mercy is so abundant, and his love for us is so great, that while we were spiritually dead in our disobedience he brought us to life with Christ. It is by God's grace that you have been saved. In our union with Christ Jesus he raised us up with him to rule with him in the heavenly world. He did this to demonstrate for all time to come the extraordinary greatness of his grace in the love he showed us in Christ Jesus.[4]

God . . . did not even keep back his own Son, but offered him for us all! He gave us his Son—will he not also freely give us all things?[5]

[1]JAS 1.5. [2]John 8.10, 11. [3]Rom. 5.15, 16. [4]Eph. 2.4–7. [5]Rom. 8.32.

Morning

God loved the world so much that he gave his only Son, so that everyone who believes in him may not die but have eternal life.[1]

God . . . through Christ changed us from enemies into his friends and gave us the task of making others his friends also. Our message is that God was making all mankind his friends through Christ. God did not keep an account of their sins, and he has given us the message which tells how he makes them his friends. Here we are, then, speaking for Christ, as though God himself were making his appeal through us. We plead on Christ's behalf: let God change you from enemies into his friends! Christ was without sin, but for our sake God made him share our sin in order that in union with him we might share the righteousness of God.[2]—God is love. And God showed his love for us by sending his only Son into the world, so that we might have life through him. This is what love is: it is not that we have loved God, but that he loved us and sent his Son to be the means by which our sins are forgiven. Dear friends, if this is how God loved us, then we should love one another.[3]

[1]JOHN 3.16. [2]2 Cor. 5.18–21.—[3]1 John 4.8–11.

Evening

The Lord gave us mind and conscience; we cannot hide from ourselves.[1]

"Whichever one of you has committed no sin may throw the first stone at her." When they heard this, they all left, one by one, the older ones first.[2]

"Who told you that you were naked?" God asked. "Did you eat the fruit that I told you not to eat?"[3]

The person who does not do the good he knows he should do is guilty of sin.[4]—If our conscience condemns us, we know that God is greater than our conscience and that he knows everything. And so, my dear friends, if our conscience does not condemn us, we have courage in God's presence.[5]

All foods may be eaten, but it is wrong to eat anything that will cause someone else to fall into sin. Happy is the person who does not feel guilty when he does something he judges is right![6]

Examine me, O God, and know my mind; test me and discover my thoughts. Find out if there is any evil in me and guide me in the everlasting way.[7]

[1]PROV. 20.27. [2]John 8.7, 9. [3]Gen. 3.11. [4]Jas 4.17.—[5]1 John 3.20, 21. [6]Rom. 14.20, 22. [7]Ps. 139.23, 24.

Never boast about tomorrow. You don't know what will happen between now and then.[1]

When the time came for me to show you favour I heard you; when the day arrived for me to save you, I helped you.[2]—The light will be among you a little longer. Continue on your way while you have the light, so that the darkness will not come upon you; for the one who walks in the dark does not know where he is going. Believe in the light, then, while you have it, so that you will be the people of the light.[3]

Work hard at whatever you do, because there will be no action, no thought, no knowledge, no wisdom in the world of the dead—and that is where you are going.[4]

Lucky man! You have all the good things you need for many years. Take life easy, eat, drink, and enjoy yourself! You fool! This very night you will have to give up your life; then who will get all these things you have kept for yourself? This is how it is with those who pile up riches for themselves but are not rich in God's sight.[5]

The world and everything in it that people desire is passing away; but he who does the will of God lives for ever.[6]

[1]PROV. 27.1. [2]2 Cor. 6.2.—[3]John 12.35, 36. [4]Eccles. 9.10. [5]Luke 12.19–21. [6]1 John 2.17.

Evening

You are always the same, and your life never ends.[1]

Before you created the hills or brought the world into being, you were eternally God, and will be God for ever.[2]

I am the LORD, and I do not change. And so you, the descendants of Jacob, are not yet completely lost.[3]—Jesus Christ is the same yesterday, today, and for ever.[4]

Every good gift and every perfect present comes from heaven; it comes down from God, the Creator of the heavenly lights, who does not change or cause darkness by turning.[5]—God does not change his mind about whom he chooses and blesses.[6]

God is not like men, who lie; he is not a human who changes his mind.[7]—The LORD's unfailing love and mercy still continue.[8]

Jesus lives on for ever, and his work as priest does not pass on to someone else. And so he is able, now and always, to save those who come to God through him, because he lives for ever to plead with God for them.[9]—Don't be afraid! I am the first and the last.[10]

[1]PS. 102.27. [2]Ps. 90.2. [3]Mal. 3.6.—[4]Heb. 13.8. [5]Jas 1.17.—[6]Rom. 11.29. [7]Num. 23.19.—[8]Lam. 3.22. [9]Heb. 7.24, 25.—[10]Rev. 1.17.

The Spirit produces love. [1]

God is love, and whoever lives in love lives in union with God and God lives in union with him.[2]—God has poured out his love into our hearts by means of the Holy Spirit, who is God's gift to us.[3]—This stone is of great value for you that believe.[4]—We love because God first loved us.[5]—We are ruled by the love of Christ, now that we recognize that one man died for everyone, which means that all share in his death. He died for all, so that those who live should no longer live for themselves, but only for him who died and was raised to life for their sake.[6]

You yourselves have been taught by God how you should love one another.[7]—My commandment is this: love one another, just as I love you.[8]—Above everything, love one another earnestly, because love covers over many sins.[9]—Your life must be controlled by love, just as Christ loved us and gave his life for us as a sweet-smelling offering and sacrifice that pleases God.[10]

[1]GAL. 5.22. [2]1 John 4.16.—[3]Rom. 5.5.—[4]1 Pet. 2.7.—[5]1 John 4.19.—[6]2 Cor. 5.14, 15. [7]1 Thess. 4.9.—[8]John 15.12.—[9]1 Pet. 4.8.—[10]Eph. 5.2.

Evening

The L*ORD* *is my Banner.* [1]

If God is for us, who can be against us?[2]—The LORD is with me, I will not be afraid; what can anyone do to me?[3]

You have warned those who show you reverence, so that they might escape destruction.[4]

The LORD is my light and my salvation; I will fear no one. Even if a whole army surrounds me, I will not be afraid; even if enemies attack me, I will still trust God.[5]

God himself is our leader.[6]—The LORD Almighty is with us; the God of Jacob is our refuge.[7]

They will fight against the Lamb; but the Lamb . . . will defeat them.[8]

Why do the nations plan rebellion? Why do people make their useless plots? From his throne in heaven the Lord laughs and mocks their feeble plans.[9]—Make your plans! But they will never succeed. Talk as much as you like! But it is all useless, because God is with us.[10]

[1]EXOD. 17.15. [2]Rom. 8.31.—[3]Ps. 118.6. [4]Ps. 60.4. [5]Ps. 27.1, 3. [6]2 Chr. 13.12.—[7]Ps. 46.7. [8]Rev. 17.14. [9]Ps. 2.1, 4.—[10]Isa. 8.10.

God has given me children in the land of my trouble.[1]

Let us give thanks to the God and Father of our Lord Jesus Christ, the merciful Father, the God from whom all help comes! He helps us in all our troubles, so that we are able to help others who have all kinds of troubles, using the same help that we ourselves have received from God. Just as we have a share in Christ's many sufferings, so also through Christ we share in God's great help.[2]

Be glad about this, even though it may now be necessary for you to be sad for a while because of the many kinds of trials you suffer. Their purpose is to prove that your faith is genuine. Even gold . . . is tested by fire; and so your faith, which is much more precious than gold, must also be tested, so that it may endure. Then you will receive praise and glory and honour on the Day when Jesus Christ is revealed.[3]—The Lord stayed with me and gave me strength.[4]

Those who suffer because it is God's will for them, should by their good actions trust themselves completely to their Creator, who always keeps his promises.[5]

[1]GEN. 41.52. [2]2 Cor. 1.3–5. [3]1 Pet. 1.6, 7.—[4]2 Tim. 4.17. [5]1 Pet. 4.19.

Evening

There still remains for God's people a rest.[1]

In the grave wicked men stop their evil, and tired workmen find rest at last. Even prisoners enjoy peace, free from shouts and harsh commands.[2]

Happy are those who from now on die in the service of the Lord! They will enjoy rest from their hard work, because the results of their service go with them.[3]

"Our friend Lazarus has fallen asleep" . . . Jesus meant that Lazarus had died, but they thought he meant natural sleep.[4]

While we live in this earthly tent, we groan with a feeling of oppression.[5]—We who have the Spirit as the first of God's gifts also groan within ourselves, as we wait for God to make us his sons and set our whole being free. For it was by hope that we were saved; but if we see what we hope for, then it is not really hope . . . But if we hope for what we do not see, we wait for it with patience.[6]

[1]HEB. 4.9. [2]Job 3.17, 18. [3]Rev. 14.13. [4]John 11.11, 13. [5]2 Cor. 5.4.—[6]Rom. 8.23–25.

Trust in the LORD with all your heart. Never rely on what you think you know. Remember the LORD in everything you do, and he will show you the right way.[1]

Trust in God at all times, my people. Tell him all your troubles, for he is our refuge.[2]

The LORD says, "I will teach you the way you should go; I will instruct you and advise you. Don't be stupid like a horse or a mule, which must be controlled with a bit and bridle to make it submit." The wicked will have to suffer, but those who trust in the LORD are protected by his constant love.[3]—If you wander off the road to the right or the left, you will hear his voice behind you saying, "Here is the road. Follow it."[4]

If you do not go with us, don't make us leave this place. How will anyone know that you are pleased with your people and with me if you do not go with us? Your presence with us will distinguish us from any other people on earth.[5]

[1]PROV. 3.5, 6. [2]Ps. 62.8. [3]Ps. 32.8–10.—[4]Isa. 30.21. [5]Exod. 33.15, 16.

Evening

The prize, which is God's call through Christ Jesus to the life above.[1]

You will have riches in heaven; . . . come and follow me.[2]—I will . . . give you a great reward.[3]

"Well done, you good and faithful servant!" said his master. "You have been faithful in managing small amounts, so I will put you in charge of large amounts. Come on in and share my happiness!"[4]—They will rule as kings for ever and ever.[5]

You will receive the glorious crown which will never lose its brightness.[6]—The life which God has promised.[7]—The victory prize of being put right with God.[8]—Crowned with a wreath . . . that will last for ever.[9]

Father! You have given them to me, and I want them to be with me where I am, so that they may see my glory, the glory you gave me.[10]—So we will always be with the Lord.[11]

What we suffer at this present time cannot be compared at all with the glory that is going to be revealed to us.[12]

[1]PHIL. 3.14. [2]Matt. 19.21.—[3]Gen. 15.1. [4]Matt. 25.21.—[5]Rev. 22.5. [6]1 Pet. 5.4.—[7]Jas 1.12.—[8]2 Tim. 4.8.—[9]1 Cor. 9.25. [10]John 17.24.—[11]1 Thess. 4.17. [12]Rom. 8.18.

Set your hearts on the things that are in heaven, . . . not on things here on earth.[1]

Do not love the world or anything that belongs to the world. If you love the world, you do not love the Father.[2]—Do not store up riches for yourselves here on earth, where moths and rust destroy, and robbers break in and steal. Instead, store up riches for yourselves in heaven, where moths and rust cannot destroy, and robbers cannot break in and steal. For your heart will always be where your riches are.[3]

Our life is a matter of faith, not of sight.[4]—For this reason we never become discouraged. Even though our physical being is gradually decaying, yet our spiritual being is renewed day after day. And this small and temporary trouble we suffer will bring us a tremendous and eternal glory, much greater than the trouble. For we fix our attention, not on things that are seen, but on things that are unseen. What can be seen lasts only for a time, but what cannot be seen lasts for ever.[5]—The rich blessings that God keeps for his people. He keeps them for you in heaven, where they cannot decay or spoil or fade away.[6]

[1]COL. 3.1, 2. [2]1 John 2.15.—[3]Matt. 6.19–21. [4]2 Cor. 5.7.—[5]2 Cor. 4.16–18.—[6]1 Pet. 1.4.

Evening

He bends his back to carry the load.[1]

Remember the prophets . . . take them as examples of patient endurance under suffering.[2]—All these things happened to them as examples for others, and they were written down as a warning for us. For we live at a time when the end is about to come.[3]

When God sends us something good, we welcome it. How can we complain when he sends us trouble? In spite of everything he suffered, Job said nothing against God.[4]—Aaron remained silent.[5]—He is the LORD; he will do whatever seems best to him.[6]

Leave your troubles with the LORD, and he will defend you.[7]—He endured the suffering that should have been ours, the pain that we should have borne.[8]

Come to me, all of you who are tired from carrying heavy loads, and I will give you rest. Take my yoke and put it on you, and learn from me, because I am gentle and humble in spirit; and you will find rest. For the yoke I will give you is easy, and the load I will put on you is light.[9]

[1]GEN. 49.15. [2]Jas 5.10.—[3]1 Cor. 10.11. [4]Job 2.10.—[5]Lev. 10.3.—[6]1 Sam. 3.18. [7]Ps. 55.22.—[8]Isa. 53.4. [9]Matt. 11.28–30.

Lord, rescue me from all this trouble.[1]

LORD, I look up to you, up to heaven, where you rule. As a servant depends on his master, as a maid depends on her mistress, so we will keep looking to you, O LORD our God, until you have mercy on us.[2]—Hear my cry, O God; listen to my prayer! In despair and far from home I call to you! Take me to a safe refuge, for you are my protector, my strong defence against my enemies. Let me live in your sanctuary all my life; let me find safety under your wings.[3]—The poor and the helpless have fled to you and have been safe in times of trouble. You give them shelter from storms.[4]

Christ himself suffered for you and left you an example, so that you would follow in his steps. He committed no sin, and no one ever heard a lie come from his lips. When he was insulted, he did not answer back with an insult; when he suffered, he did not threaten, but placed his hopes in God, the righteous Judge.[5]

[1]ISA. 38.14. [2]Ps. 123.1, 2.—[3]Ps. 61.1–4.—[4]Isa. 25.4. [5]1 Pet. 2.21–23.

Evening

Run your best in the race of faith.[1]

There were troubles everywhere, quarrels with others, fears in our hearts.[2]—Don't be afraid . . . we have more on our side than they have on theirs.[3]—Build up your strength in union with the Lord and by means of his mighty power.[4]

You are coming against me with sword, spear, and javelin, but I come against you in the name of the LORD Almighty, the God of the Israelite armies, which you have defied.[5]—God is my strong refuge . . . he trains me for battle, so that I can use the strongest bow.[6]—The capacity we have comes from God.[7]

His angel guards those who honour the LORD and rescues them from danger.[8]—Elisha's servant looked up and saw the hillside covered with horses and chariots of fire all around Elisha.[9]

There isn't enough time for me to speak of [all those who] through faith . . . fought whole countries and won. They were weak, but became strong; they were mighty in battle and defeated the armies of foreigners.[10]

[1]1 TIM. 6.12. [2]2 Cor. 7.5.—[3]2 Kgs 6.16.—[4]Eph. 6.10. [5]1 Sam. 17.45.—[6]2 Sam. 22.33, 35.—[7]2 Cor. 3.5. [8]Ps. 34.7.—[9]2 Kgs 6.17. [10]Heb. 11.32–34.

He . . . guards those who are devoted to him.[1]

The LORD . . . always went ahead of you to find a place for you to camp. To show you the way, he went in front of you in a pillar of fire by night and in a pillar of cloud by day.[2]—Like an eagle teaching its young to fly, catching them safely on its spreading wings . . . the LORD alone led his people.[3]—The LORD guides a man in the way he should go and protects those who please him. If they fall, they will not stay down, because the LORD wil help them up.[4]—The good man suffers many troubles, but the LORD saves him from them all.[5]—The righteous are guided and protected by the LORD, but the evil are on the way to their doom.[6]—We know that in all things God works for good with those who love him, those whom he has called according to his purpose.[7]—We have the LORD our God to help us and to fight our battles.[8]

The LORD your God is with you; his power gives you victory. The LORD will take delight in you, and in his love he will give you new life. He will sing and be joyful over you.[9]

[1]PROV. 2.8. [2]Deut. 1.32, 33.—[3]Deut. 32.11, 12.—[4]Ps. 37.23, 24.—[5]Ps. 34.19.—[6]Ps. 1.6.—[7]Rom. 8.28.—[8]2 Chr. 32.8. [9]Zeph. 3.17.

Evening

My God, my God, why did you abandon me?[1]

Because of our sins he was wounded, beaten because of the evil we did. We are healed by the punishment he suffered, made whole by the blows he received . . . the LORD made the punishment fall on him, the punishment all of us deserved . . . he was put to death for the sins of our people . . . The LORD says, "It was my will that he should suffer; his death was a sacrifice to bring forgiveness."[2]

Jesus our Lord . . . because of our sins he was handed over to die.[3]—Christ died for sins once and for all, a good man on behalf of sinners, in order to lead you to God.[4]—Christ himself carried our sins in his body to the cross, so that we might die to sin and live for righteousness. It is by his wounds that you have been healed.[5]

Christ was without sin, but for our sake God made him share our sin in order that in union with him we might share the righteousness of God.[6]

By becoming a curse for us Christ has redeemed us from the curse that the Law brings; for the scripture says, "Anyone who is hanged on a tree is under God's curse."[7]

[1]MATT. 27.46. [2]Isa. 53, 5, 6, 8, 10. [3]Rom. 4.24, 25.—[4]1 Pet. 3.18.—[5]1 Pet. 2.24. [6]2 Cor. 5.21. [7]Gal. 3.13.

Your Creator will be like a husband to you—The LORD Almighty is his name.[1]

There is a deep secret truth revealed in this scripture, which I understand as applying to Christ and the church.[2]

No longer will you be called "Forsaken," . . . your new name will be, "God is Pleased with Her," . . . because the LORD is pleased with you . . . As a groom is delighted with his bride, so your God will delight in you.[3]—He has sent me to comfort all who mourn, to give to those who mourn in Zion joy and gladness instead of grief, a song of praise instead of sorrow.[4]

Jerusalem rejoices because of what the LORD has done. She is like a bride dressed for her wedding. God has clothed her with salvation and victory.[5]

I will make you my wife; I will be true and faithful; I will show you constant love and mercy and make you mine for ever.[6]

Who . . . can separate us from the love of Christ?[7]

[1]ISA. 54.5. [2]Eph. 5.32. [3]Isa. 62.4, 5.—[4]Isa. 61.2, 3. [5]Isa. 61.10. [6]Hos. 2.19. [7]Rom. 8.35.

Evening

I am always in your care.[1]

The LORD . . . protects those who belong to him.[2]—The LORD said to Elijah, "Leave this place and go east and hide yourself near the brook of Cherith, east of the Jordan. The brook will supply you with water to drink, and I have commanded ravens to bring you food there." Then the LORD said to Elijah, "Now go to the town of Zarephath, near Sidon, and stay there. I have commanded a widow who lives there to feed you."[3]

I tell you not to be worried about the food and drink you need in order to stay alive, or about clothes for your body. Your Father in heaven knows that you need all these things.[4]

Trust in the LORD with all your heart. Never rely on what you think you know. Remember the LORD in everything you do, and he will show you the right way.[5]—Leave all your worries with him, because he cares for you.[6]

[1]PS. 31.15. [2]Deut. 33.3.—[3]1 Kgs 17.2–4, 8, 9. [4]Matt. 6.25, 32. [5]Prov. 3.5, 6.—[6]1 Pet. 5.7.

You forgive all my sins.[1]

There is no other God like you, O LORD; you forgive the sins of your people who have survived. You do not stay angry for ever, but you take pleasure in showing us your constant love. You will be merciful to us once again. You will trample our sins underfoot and send them to the bottom of the sea![2]

"For one brief moment I left you; with deep love I will take you back. I turned away angry for only a moment, but I will show you my love for ever." So says the LORD who saves you.[3]—I will forgive their sins and I will no longer remember their wrongs.[4]

Happy are those whose sins are forgiven, whose wrongs are pardoned. Happy is the man whom the LORD does not accuse of doing wrong and who is free from all deceit.[5]—The blood of Jesus, his Son, purifies us from every sin.[6]

[1]ISA. 38.17. [2]Mic.7.18, 19. [3]Isa. 54.7, 8.—[4]Jer. 31.34. [5]Ps. 32.1, 2.—[6]1 John 1.7.

Evening

I am still full of confidence, because I know whom I have trusted, and I am sure that he is able.[1]

Able to do so much more than we can ever ask for, or even think of.[2]

Able to give you more than you need, so that you will always have all you need for yourselves and more than enough for every good cause.[3]

He can help those who are tempted.[4]

Able . . . to save those who come to God through him, because he lives for ever to plead with God for them.[5]

Able to keep you from falling, and to bring you faultless and joyful before his glorious presence.[6]

Able to keep safe until that Day what he has entrusted to me.[7]

He will change our weak mortal bodies and make them like his own glorious body, using that power by which he is able to bring all things under his rule.[8]

"Do you believe that I can heal you?" . . . "Yes, sir!" they answered. "Let it happen, then, just as you believe!"[9]

[1]2 TIM. 1.12. [2]Eph. 3.20. [3]2 Cor. 9.8. [4]Heb. 2.18. [5]Heb. 7.25. [6]Jude 24. [7]2 Tim. 1.12. [8]Phil. 3.21. [9]Matt. 9.28, 29.

God . . . generously gives us everything for our enjoyment.[1]

Make certain that you do not forget the LORD your God; do not fail to obey any of his laws that I am giving you today. When you have all you want to eat and have built good houses to live in . . . make sure that you do not become proud and forget the LORD your God . . . who gives you the power to become rich.[2]

If the LORD does not build the house, the work of the builders is useless; if the LORD does not protect the city, it is useless for the sentries to stand guard. It is useless to work so hard for a living, getting up early and going to bed late. For the LORD provides for those he loves, while they are asleep.[3]—Your people did not conquer the land with their swords; they did not win it by their own power; it was by your power and your strength, by the assurance of your presence, which showed that you loved them.[4]—There are many who pray: "Give us more blessings, O LORD. Look on us with kindness!"[5]

[1]1 TIM. 6.17. [2]Deut. 8.11, 12, 14, 18. [3]Ps. 127.1, 2.—[4]Ps. 44.3.—[5]Ps. 4.6.

Evening

They were singing a new song.[1]

He opened for us a new way, a living way.[2]—It was not because of any good deeds that we ourselves had done, but because of his own mercy that he saved us, through the Holy Spirit, who gives us new birth and new life by washing us. God poured out the Holy Spirit abundantly on us through Jesus Christ our Saviour.[3]—It is by God's grace that you have been saved through faith. It is not the result of your own efforts, but God's gift, so that no one can boast about it.[4]

To you alone, O LORD, to you alone, and not to us, must glory be given.[5]—He loves us, and by his sacrificial death he has freed us from our sins and made us a kingdom of priests to serve his God and Father. To Jesus Christ be the glory and power for ever and ever! Amen.[6]—You were killed, and by your sacrificial death you bought for God people from every tribe, language, nation, and race.[7]—I looked, and there was an enormous crowd—no one could count all the people! They called out in a loud voice: "Salvation comes from our God, who sits on the throne, and from the Lamb!"[8]

[1]REV. 14.3. [2]Heb. 10.20.—[3]Titus 3.5, 6.—[4]Eph. 2.8, 9. [5]Ps. 115.1.—[6]Rev. 1.5, 6.—[7]Rev. 5.9.—[8]Rev. 7.9, 10.

The Lord Provides.[1]

God himself will provide one.[2]

Dont think that the LORD is too weak to save you or too deaf to hear your call for help![3]—The Saviour will come from Zion and remove all wickedness from the descendants of Jacob.[4]

Happy is the man who has the God of Jacob to help him and who depends on the LORD his God.[5]—The LORD watches over those who obey him, those who trust in his constant love. He saves them from death.[6]

With all his abundant wealth through Christ Jesus, my God will supply all your needs.[7]—God has said, "I will never leave you; I will never abandon you." Let us be bold, then, and say, "The Lord is my helper, I will not be afraid. What can anyone do to me?"[8]—The LORD protects and defends me; I trust in him. He gives me help and makes me glad; I praise him with joyful songs.[9]

[1]GEN. 22.14. [2]Gen. 22.8. [3]Isa. 59.1.—[4]Rom. 11.26. [5]Ps. 146.5.—[6]Ps. 33.18, 19. [7]Phil. 4.19.—[8]Heb. 13.5, 6.—[9]Ps. 28.7.

Evening

He feeds his flock among the lilies.[1]

Where two or three come together in my name, I am there with them.[2]—Whoever loves me will obey my teaching. My Father will love him, and my Father and I will come to him and live with him.[3]

If you obey my commands, you will remain in my love, just as I have obeyed my Father's commands and remain in his love.[4]

Let my lover come to his garden and eat the best of its fruits.[5]—I have entered my garden, my sweetheart, my bride. I am gathering my spices and myrrh; I am eating my honey and honeycomb.[6]—The Spirit produces love, joy, peace, patience, kindness, goodness, faithfulness, humility, and self-control.[7]

My Father's glory is shown by your bearing much fruit; and in this way you become my disciples.[8]—He prunes every branch that does bear fruit, so that it will be clean and bear more fruit.[9]—Your lives will be filled with the truly good qualities which only Jesus Christ can produce, for the glory and praise of God.[10]

[1]S. OF S. 2.16. [2]Matt. 18.20.—[3]John 14.23. [4]John 15.10. [5]S. of S. 4.16.— [6]S. of S. 5.1.—[7]Gal. 5.22, 23. [8]John 15.8.—[9]John 15.2.—[10]Phil. 1.11.

May the LORD *bless you and take care of you.*[1]

It is the LORD's blessing that makes you wealthy. Hard work can make you no richer.[2]—You bless those who obey you, LORD; your love protects them like a shield.[3]

He will not let you fall; your protector is always awake. The protector of Israel never dozes or sleeps. The LORD will guard you; he is by your side to protect you. The LORD will protect you from all danger; he will keep you safe. He will protect you as you come and go now and for ever.[4]—I watch over it and water it continually. I guard it night and day so that no one will harm it.[5]

Holy Father! Keep them safe by the power of your name. While I was with them, I kept them safe by the power of your name, the name you gave me. I protected them.[6]

The Lord will rescue me from all evil and take me safely into his heavenly Kingdom. To him be the glory for ever and ever! Amen.[7]

[1]NUM. 6.24. [2]Prov. 10.22.—[3]Ps. 5.12. [4]Ps. 121.3–5, 7, 8.—[5]Isa. 27.3. [6]John 17.11, 12. [7]2 Tim. 4.18.

Evening

Jesus wept.[1]

He endured suffering and pain.[2]—Our High Priest is not one who cannot feel sympathy for our weaknesses.[3]—It was only right that God, who creates and preserves all things, should make Jesus perfect through suffering, in order to bring many sons to share his glory.[4]—Even though he was God's Son, he learnt through his sufferings to be obedient.[5]

I have not rebelled or turned away from him. I bared my back to those who beat me. I did not stop them when they insulted me, when they pulled out the hairs of my beard and spat in my face.[6]

See how much he loved him![7]—It is clear that it is not the angels that he helps. Instead, as the scripture says, "He helps the descendants of Abraham." This means that he had to become like his brothers in every way, in order to be their faithful and merciful High Priest in his service to God, so that the people's sins would be forgiven.[8]

[1]JOHN 11.35. [2]Isa. 53.3.—[3]Heb. 4.15.—[4]Heb. 2.10.—[5]Heb. 5.8. [6]Isa. 50.5, 6. [7]John 11.36.—[8]Heb. 2.16, 17.

Morning

***May the* LORD *be kind and gracious to you; may the* LORD *look on you with favour and give you peace.*[1]**

No one has ever seen God. The only Son, who is the same as God and is at the Father's side, he has made him known.[2]—He reflects the brightness of God's glory and is the exact likeness of God's own being.[3]—They do not believe, because their minds have been kept in the dark by the evil god of this world. He keeps them from seeing the light shining on them, the light that comes from the Good News about the glory of Christ, who is the exact likeness of God.[4]

Look on your servant with kindness; save me in your constant love. I call to you, LORD; don't let me be disgraced.[5]—You were good to me, LORD; you protected me like a mountain fortress. But then you hid yourself from me, and I was afraid.[6]—How happy are the people who worship you with songs, who live in the light of your kindness![7]

The LORD gives strength to his people and blesses them with peace.[8]

Courage! It is I. Don't be afraid![9]

[1]NUM. 6.25, 26. [2]John 1.18.—[3]Heb. 1.3.—[4]2 Cor. 4.4. [5]Ps. 31.16, 17.—[6]Ps. 30.7.—[7]Ps. 89.15. [8]Ps. 29.11. [9]Matt. 14.27.

Evening

***What pleases him.*[1]**

No one can please God without faith.[2]—Those who obey their human nature cannot please God.[3]—The LORD takes pleasure in his people.[4]

God will bless you . . . if you endure the pain of undeserved suffering because you are conscious of his will. If you endure suffering even when you have done right, God will bless you for it.[5]—The ageless beauty of a gentle and quiet spirit, which is of the greatest value in God's sight.[6]

Giving thanks is the sacrifice that honours me, and I will surely save all who obey me.[7]—I will praise God with a song; I will proclaim his greatness by giving him thanks. This will please the LORD more than offering him cattle, more than sacrificing a full-grown bull.[8]

My brothers, because of God's great mercy to us I appeal to you: Offer yourselves as a living sacrifice to God, dedicated to his service and pleasing to him. This is the true worship that you should offer.[9]

[1]1 JOHN 3.22. [2]Heb. 11.6.—[3]Rom. 8.8.—[4]Ps. 149.4. [5]1 Pet. 2.19, 20.—[6]1 Pet. 3.4. [7]Ps. 50.23.—[8]Ps. 69.30, 31. [9]Rom. 12.1.

There is one God, and there is one who brings God and mankind together, the man Christ Jesus.[1]

Since the children . . . are people of flesh and blood, Jesus himself became like them and shared their human nature.[2]

Turn to me now and be saved, people all over the world! I am the only God there is.[3]

We have someone who pleads with the Father on our behalf—Jesus Christ, the righteous one.[4]—In union with Christ Jesus, you who used to be far away have been brought near by the sacrificial death of Christ. Christ himself has brought us peace.[5]—When Christ . . . entered once and for all into the Most Holy Place . . . he took his own blood and obtained eternal salvation for us. For this reason Christ is the one who arranges a new covenant, so that those who have been called by God may receive the eternal blessings that God has promised.[6]—He is able . . . to save those who come to God through him, because he lives for ever to plead with God for them.[7]

[1]1 TIM. 2.5. [2]Heb. 2.14. [3]Isa. 45.22. [4]1 John 2.1.—[5]Eph. 2.13, 14.—[6]Heb. 9.12, 15.—[7]Heb. 7.25.

Evening

My heart is breaking, and so I turn my thoughts to him.[1]

You, LORD, give perfect peace to those who keep their purpose firm and put their trust in you. Trust in the LORD for ever; he will always protect us.[2]

Leave your troubles with the LORD, and he will defend you.[3]—He does not neglect the poor or ignore their suffering; he does not turn away from them, but answers when they call for help.[4]—Is anyone among you in trouble? He should pray.[5]

Do not be worried and upset; do not be afraid.[6]—I tell you not to be worried about the food and drink you need in order to stay alive, or about clothes for your body. Look at the birds: they do not sow seeds, gather a harvest and put it in barns; yet your Father in heaven takes care of them! Aren't you worth much more than birds?[7]—Stop your doubting, and believe![8]—I will be with you always, to the end of the age.[9]

[1]PS. 42.6. [2]Isa. 26.3, 4. [3]Ps. 55.22.—[4]Ps. 22.24.—[5]Jas 5.13. [6]John 14.27.—[7]Matt. 6.25, 26.—[8]John 20.27.—[9]Matt. 28.20.

Morning

Bring credit to the teaching about God our Saviour in all they do.[1]

Your way of life should be as the gospel of Christ requires.[2]—Happy are you if you are insulted because you are Christ's followers. If any of you suffers, it must not be because he is a murderer or a thief or a criminal or a meddler in other people's affairs.[3]—Be innocent and pure as God's perfect children, who live in a world of corrupt and sinful people. You must shine among them like stars lighting up the sky.[4]—Your light must shine before people, so that they will see the good things you do and praise your Father in heaven.[5]

Never let go of loyalty and faithfulness. Tie them round your neck; write them on your heart. If you do this, both God and man will be pleased with you.[6]—My brothers, fill your minds with those things that are good and that deserve praise: things that are true, noble, right, pure, lovely, and honourable.[7]

[1]TITUS 2.10. [2]Phil. 1.27.—[3]1 Pet. 4.14, 15.—[4]Phil. 2.15.—[5]Matt. 5.16. [6]Prov. 3.3, 4.—[7]Phil. 4.8.

Evening

The words I have spoken to you bring God's life-giving Spirit.[1]

By his own will he brought us into being through the word of truth.[2]—The written law brings death, but the Spirit gives life.[3]

Christ loved the church and gave his life for it. He did this to dedicate the church to God by his word, after making it clean by washing it in water, in order to present the church to himself in all its beauty—pure and faultless, without spot or wrinkle or any other imperfection.[4]

How can a young man keep his life pure? By obeying your commands. Your promise gave me life. I keep your law in my heart, so that I will not sin against you. I take pleasure in your laws; your commands I will not forget. I trust in your word. The law that you gave means more to me than all the money in the world. I will never neglect your instructions, because by them you have kept me alive. How sweet is the taste of your instructions—sweeter even than honey! I gain wisdom from your laws, and so I hate all bad conduct.[5]

[1]JOHN 6.63. [2]Jas 1.18.—[3]2 Cor. 3.6. [4]Eph. 5.25, 26, 27. [5]Ps. 119.9, 50, 11, 16, 42, 72, 93, 103, 104.

Perfect through suffering.[1]

"The sorrow in my heart is so great that it almost crushes me. Stay here and keep watch with me." He went a little farther on, threw himself face downwards on the ground, and prayed, "My Father, if it is possible, take this cup of suffering from me! Yet not what I want, but what you want."[2]—In great anguish he prayed even more fervently; his sweat was like drops of blood falling to the ground.[3]

The danger of death was all round me; the horrors of the grave closed in on me; I was filled with fear and anxiety.[4]—Insults have broken my heart, and I am in despair. I had hoped for sympathy, but there was none; for comfort, but I found none.[5]—When I look beside me, I see that there is no one to help me, no one to protect me. No one cares for me.[6]

We despised him and rejected him; he endured suffering and pain. No one would even look at him—we ignored him as if he were nothing.[7]

[1]HEB. 2.10. [2]Matt. 26.38, 39.—[3]Luke 22.44. [4]Ps. 116.3.—[5]Ps. 69.20.—[6]Ps. 142.4. [7]Isa. 53.3.

Evening

I, the* L*ORD*, *made the earth, the sky, the sea, and everything in them.[1]

How clearly the sky reveals God's glory! How plainly it shows what he has done![2]—The LORD created the heavens by his command, the sun, moon, and stars by his spoken word. When he spoke, the world was created; at his command everything appeared.[3]—To the LORD the nations are nothing, no more than a drop of water; the distant islands are as light as dust.[4]

It is by faith that we understand that the universe was created by God's word, so that what can be seen was made out of what cannot be seen.[5]

When I look at the sky, which you have made, at the moon and the stars, which you set in their places—what is man, that you think of him; mere man, that you care for him?[6]

[1]EXOD. 20.11. [2]Ps. 19.1.—[3]Ps. 33.6, 9.—[4]Isa. 40.15. [5]Heb. 11.3. [6]Ps. 8.3, 4.

Morning

You don't even know what your life tomorrow will be! You are like a puff of smoke, which appears for a moment and then disappears.[1]

My days race by, not one of them good. My life passes like the swiftest boat, as fast as an eagle swooping down on a rabbit.[2]—You carry us away like a flood; we last no longer than a dream. We are like weeds that sprout in the morning, that grow and burst into bloom, then dry up and die in the evening.[3]—We are all born weak and helpless. All lead the same short, troubled life. We grow and wither as quickly as flowers.[4]

The world and everything in it that people desire is passing away; but he who does the will of God lives for ever.[5]—They will disappear, but you will remain; they will all wear out like clothes. You will discard them like clothes, and they will vanish. But you are always the same, and your life never ends.[6]—Jesus Christ is the same yesterday, today, and for ever.[7]

[1]JAS 4.14. [2]Job 9.25, 26.—[3]Ps. 90.5, 6.—[4]Job 14.1, 2. [5]1 John 2.17.—[6]Ps. 102.26, 27.—[7]Heb. 13.8.

Evening

I will sing with my spirit, but I will sing also with my mind.[1]

Be filled with the Spirit. Speak to one another with the words of psalms, hymns, and sacred songs; sing . . . to the Lord with praise in your hearts.[2]—Christ's message in all its richness must live in your hearts. Teach and instruct each other with all wisdom. Sing psalms, hymns, and sacred songs; sing to God with thanksgiving in your hearts.[3]

I will always praise the LORD; let all his creatures praise his holy name for ever.[4]

Praise the LORD! It is good to sing praise to our God; it is pleasant and right to praise him. Sing hymns of praise to the LORD; play music on the harp to our God.[5]

I heard a voice from heaven that sounded like a roaring waterfall, like a loud peal of thunder. It sounded like the music made by musicians playing their harps.[6]

[1]1 COR. 14.15. [2]Eph. 5.18, 19.—[3]Col. 3.16. [4]Ps. 145.21. [5]Ps. 147.1, 7. [6]Rev. 14.2.

The man shall put his hand on its head, and it will be accepted as a sacrifice to take away his sins.[1]

For you know what was paid to set you free from the worthless manner of life handed down by your ancestors. It was not something that can be destroyed, such as silver or gold; it was the costly sacrifice of Christ, who was like a lamb without defect or flaw.[2]—Christ himself carried our sins in his body to the cross.[3]

The free gift he gave us in his dear Son![4]

Come as living stones, and let yourselves be used in building the spiritual temple, where you will serve as holy priests to offer spiritual and acceptable sacrifices to God through Jesus Christ.[5]—So then, my brothers, because of God's great mercy to us I appeal to you: Offer yourselves as a living sacrifice to God, dedicated to his service and pleasing to him.[6]

To him who is able to keep you from falling, and to bring you faultless and joyful before his glorious presence—to the only God our Saviour, through Jesus Christ our Lord, be glory, majesty, might, and authority, from all ages past, and now, and for ever and ever![7]

[1]LEV. 1.4. [2]1 Pet. 1.18, 19.—[3]1 Pet. 2.24. [4]Eph. 1.6. [5]1 Pet. 2.5.—[6]Rom. 12.1. [7]Jude 24, 25.

Evening

[*He*] ***was tempted in every way that we are, but did not sin.***[1]

The woman saw how beautiful the tree was and how good its food would be to eat, and she thought how wonderful it would be to become wise. So she took some of the fruit and ate it. Then she gave some to her husband, and he also ate it.[2]

What the sinful self desires, what people see and want, and everything in this world that people are so proud of . . .[3]

Then the Devil came to him and said, "If you are God's Son, order these stones to turn into bread." But Jesus answered, "The scripture says, 'Man cannot live on bread alone, but needs every word that God speaks.' " The Devil . . . showed him all the kingdoms of the world in all their greatness. Then Jesus answered, "Go away, Satan!"[4]

Now he can help those who are tempted, because he himself was tempted and suffered.[5]

Happy is the person who remains faithful under trials.[6]

[1]HEB. 4.15. [2]Gen. 3.6. [3]1 John 2.16. [4]Matt. 4.3, 4, 8, 10. [5]Heb. 2.18. [6]Jas 1.12.

My eyes grew tired from looking to heaven.[1]

I am worn out, O LORD; have pity on me! Give me strength; I am completely exhausted and my whole being is deeply troubled. How long, O LORD, will you wait to help me? Come and save me, LORD; in your mercy rescue me from death.[2]—I am terrified, and the terrors of death crush me. I am gripped by fear and trembling; I am overcome with horror. I wish I had wings, like a dove. I would fly away and find rest.[3]

You need to be patient.[4]

They still had their eyes fixed on the sky as he went away, when two men dressed in white suddenly stood beside them and said, "Galileans, why are you standing there looking up at the sky? This Jesus, who was taken from you into Heaven, will come back in the same way that you saw him go to heaven."[5]—We . . . are citizens of heaven, and we eagerly wait for our Saviour, the Lord Jesus Christ, to come from heaven.[6]—We wait for the blessed Day we hope for, when the glory of our great God and Saviour Jesus Christ will appear.[7]

[1]ISA. 38.14. [2]Ps. 6.2–4.—[3]Ps. 55.4–6. [4]Heb. 10.36. [5]Acts 1.10, 11.—[6]Phil. 3.20.—[7]Titus 2.13.

Evening

His name will be written on their foreheads.[1]

I am the good shepherd . . . I know my sheep.[2]—The solid foundation that God has laid cannot be shaken; and on it are written these words: "The Lord knows those who are his" and "Whoever says that he belongs to the Lord must turn away from wrongdoing."[3]

The LORD is good; he protects his people in times of trouble; he takes care of those who turn to him.[4]—Do not harm the earth, the sea or the trees, until we mark the servants of our God with a seal on their foreheads.[5]

You believed in Christ, and God put his stamp of ownership on you by giving you the Holy Spirit he had promised. The Spirit is the guarantee that we shall receive what God has promised his people.[6]—It is God himself who has set us apart, who has placed his mark of ownership upon us, and who has given us the Holy Spirit in our hearts as the guarantee of all that he has in store for us.[7]

I will write on him the name of my God and the name of the city of my God, the new Jerusalem, which will come down out of heaven from my God. I will also write on him my new name.[8]—The city will be called "The LORD Our Salvation."[9]

[1]REV. 22.4. [2]John 10.14.—[3]2 Tim. 2.19. [4]Nahum 1.7.—[5]Rev. 7.3. [6]Eph. 1.13, 14.—[7]2 Cor. 1.21, 22. [8]Rev. 3.12.—[9]Jer. 33.16.

God chose his Servant and sent him first to you, to bless you by making every one of you turn away from his wicked ways.[1]

Let us give thanks to the God and Father of our Lord Jesus Christ! Because of his great mercy he gave us new life by raising Jesus Christ from death. This fills us with a living hope.[2]

Our great God and Saviour Jesus Christ . . . gave himself for us, to rescue us from all wickedness and to make us a pure people who belong to him alone and are eager to do good.[3]—Be holy in all that you do, just as God who called you is holy. The scripture says, "Be holy because I am holy."[4]

The God and Father of our Lord Jesus Christ . . . has blessed us by giving us every spiritual blessing in the heavenly world.[5]—The full content of divine nature lives in Christ, in his humanity, and you have been given full life in union with him.[6]—Out of the fullness of his grace he has blessed us all, giving us one blessing after another.[7]

God . . . did not even keep back his own Son, but offered him for us all! He gave us his Son—will he not also freely give us all things?[8]

[1]ACTS 3.26. [2]1 Pet. 1.3. [3]Titus 2.13, 14.—[4]1 Pet. 1.15, 16. [5]Eph. 1.3.—[6]Col. 2.9, 10.—[7]John 1.16 [8]Rom. 8.32.

Evening

Strengthen me, as you have promised.[1]

Remember your promise to me, your servant; it has given me hope.[2]—LORD, rescue me from all this trouble.[3]

Heaven and earth will pass away, but my words will never pass away.[4]—Every one of you knows in his heart and soul that the LORD your God has given you all the good things that he promised. Every promise he made has been kept; not one has failed.[5]

"God loves you, so don't let anything worry you or frighten you." When he had said this, I felt even stronger and said, "Sir, tell me what you have to say. You have made me feel better."[6]—Don't be discouraged, any of you. Do the work, for I am with you.[7]—Not by military might or by your own strength, but by my spirit.[8]

Build up your strength in union with the Lord and by means of his mighty power.[9]

[1]PS. 119.28. [2]Ps. 119.49.—[3]Isa. 38.14. [4]Luke 21.33.—[5]Josh. 23.14. [6]Dan. 10.19.—[7]Hag. 2.4.—[8]Zech. 4.6. [9]Eph. 6.10.

The explanation of your teachings gives light and brings wisdom to the ignorant.[1]

The message that we have heard from his Son and announce is this: God is light, and there is no darkness at all in him.[2]—The God who said, "Out of darkness the light shall shine!" is the same God who made his light shine in our hearts, to bring us the knowledge of God's glory shining in the face of Christ.[3]—The Word . . . was the same as God. The Word was the source of life, and this life brought light to mankind.[4]—If we live in the light—just as he is in the light—then we have fellowship with one another, and the blood of Jesus, his Son, purifies us from every sin.[5]

I keep your law in my heart, so that I will not sin against you.[6]—You have been made clean already by the teaching I have given you.[7]

You yourselves used to be in the darkness, but since you have become the Lord's people, you are in the light. So you must live like people who belong to the light.[8]—You are the chosen race, the King's priests, the holy nation, God's own people, chosen to proclaim the wonderful acts of God, who called you out of darkness into his own marvellous light.[9]

[1]PS. 119.130. [2]1 John 1.5.—[3]2 Cor. 4.6.—[4]John 1.1, 4.—[5]1 John 1.7. [6]Ps. 119.11.—[7]John 15.3. [8]Eph. 5.8.—[9]1 Pet. 2.9.

Evening

Noah had no faults.[1]

Only the person who is put right with God through faith shall live.[2]—Noah built an altar to the LORD; he took one of each kind of ritually clean animal and bird, and burnt them whole as a sacrifice on the altar. The odour of the sacrifice pleased the LORD.[3]—The Lamb that was killed.[4]

Now that we have been put right with God through faith, we have peace with God through our Lord Jesus Christ.[5]

No one is put right in God's sight by doing what the Law requires; what the Law does is to make man know that he has sinned. But now God's way of putting people right with himself has been revealed. It has nothing to do with law, even though the Law of Moses and the prophets gave their witness to it. God puts people right through their faith in Jesus Christ. God does this to all who believe in Christ, because there is no difference at all.[6]

We rejoice because of what God has done through our Lord Jesus Christ, who has now made us God's friends.[7]

Who will accuse God's chosen people? God himself declares them not guilty! Those whom God set apart, he called; and those he called, he put right with himself.[8]

[1]GEN. 6.9. [2]Gal. 3.11.—[3]Gen. 8.20, 21.—[4]Rev. 13.8. [5]Rom. 5.1. [6]Rom. 3.20–22. [7]Rom. 5.11. [8]Rom. 8.33, 30.

Wake up, and strengthen what you still have before it dies completely.[1]

The end of all things is near. You must be self-controlled and alert, to be able to pray.[2]—Be alert, be on the watch! Your enemy, the Devil, roams round like a roaring lion, looking for someone to devour.[3]—Be on your guard! Make certain that you do not forget, as long as you live, what you have seen with your own eyes.[4]—My righteous people, however, will believe and live; but if any of them turns back, I will not be pleased with him. We are not people who turn back and are lost. Instead, we have faith and are saved.[5]

What I say to you, then, I say to all: Watch![6]

Do not be afraid—I am with you! I am your God—let nothing terrify you! I will make you strong and help you; I will protect you and save you. I am the LORD your God; I strengthen you.[7]

[1]REV. 3.2. [2]1 Pet. 4.7.—[3]1 Pet. 5.8.—[4]Deut. 4.9.—[5]Heb. 10.38, 39. [6]Mark 13.37. [7]Isa. 41.10, 13.

Evening

Has he stopped loving us?[1]

His love is eternal.[2]—I, the LORD, am not easily angered, and I show great love and faithfulness.[3]—O LORD, you forgive the sins of your people . . . you do not stay angry for ever, but you take pleasure in showing us your constant love. You will be merciful to us once again. You will trample our sins underfoot and send them to the bottom of the sea![4]—It was not because of any good deeds that we ourselves had done, but because of his own mercy that he saved us.[5]

Let us give thanks to the God and Father of our Lord Jesus Christ, the merciful Father, the God from whom all help comes! He helps us in all our troubles, so that we are able to help others who have all kinds of troubles, using the same help that we ourselves have received from God.[6]

He had to become . . . their faithful and merciful High Priest in his service to God, so that the people's sins would be forgiven. And now he can help those who are tempted, because he himself was tempted and suffered.[7]

[1]PS. 77.8. [2]Ps. 136.23.—[3]Num. 14.18.—[4]Mic. 7.18, 19.—[5]Titus 3.5. [6]2 Cor. 1.3, 4. [7]Heb. 2.17, 18.

Lot looked round and saw that the whole Jordan Valley . . . had plenty of water, like the Garden of the LORD . . . before the LORD destroyed the cities of Sodom and Gomorrah. So Lot chose the whole Jordan Valley for himself.[1]

Lot . . . that good man.[2]

Do not deceive yourselves; no one makes a fool of God. A person will reap exactly what he sows.[3]—Remember Lot's wife![4]

Do not try to work together as equals with unbelievers, for it cannot be done. How can right and wrong be partners? How can light and darkness live together? "You must leave them and separate yourselves from them. Have nothing to do with what is unclean . . . says the Lord Almighty."[5]—Have nothing at all to do with such people. You yourselves used to be in the darkness, but since you have become the Lord's people, you are in the light. So you must live like people who belong to the light . . . Try to learn what pleases the Lord. Have nothing to do with the worthless things that people do, things that belong to the darkness. Instead, bring them out to the light.[6]

[1]GEN. 13.10, 11. [2]2 Pet. 2.7, 8. [3]Gal. 6.7.—[4]Luke 17.32. [5]2 Cor. 6.14, 17.—[6]Eph. 5.7, 8, 10, 11.

Evening

Maybe the LORD will be with me, and I will drive them out, just as the LORD said.[1]

God has said, "I will never leave you; I will never abandon you." Let us be bold, then, and say, "The Lord is my helper, I will not be afraid. What can anyone do to me?"[2]—I will praise your power, Sovereign LORD; I will proclaim your goodness, yours alone.[3]

Because everyone will do what is right, there will be peace and security for ever.[4]

Stand ready, with truth as a belt tight round your waist, with righteousness as your breastplate. For we are not fighting against human beings but against the wicked spiritual forces in the heavenly world, the rulers, authorities, and cosmic powers of this dark age. So put on God's armour now! Then when the evil day comes, you will be able to resist the enemy's attacks; and after fighting to the end, you will still hold your ground.[5]—The LORD is with you . . . go with all your great strength.[6]

[1]JOSH. 14.12. [2]Heb. 13.5, 6.—[3]Ps. 71.16. [4]Isa. 32.17. [5]Eph. 6.14, 12, 13.—[6]Judg. 6.12, 14.

Holy, holy, holy, is the LORD God Almighty.[1]

You are enthroned as the Holy One, the one whom Israel praises.[2]—"Do not come any closer. Take off your sandals, because you are standing on holy ground. I am the God of your ancestors, the God of Abraham, Isaac and Jacob." So Moses covered his face, because he was afraid to look at God.[3]—To whom can the holy God be compared? Is there anyone else like him?[4]—I am the LORD your God, the holy God of Israel, who saves you. I alone am the LORD, the only one who can save you.[5]

Be holy in all that you do, just as God who called you is holy. The scripture says, "Be holy because I am holy."[6]—Don't you know that your body is the temple of the Holy Spirit, who lives in you and who was given to you by God? You do not belong to yourselves but to God.[7]—We are the temple of the living God! As God himself has said, "I will make my home with my people and live among them; I will be their God, and they shall be my people."[8]—Do two men start travelling together without arranging to meet?[9]

[1]REV. 4.8. [2]Ps. 22.3.—[3]Exod. 3.5, 6.—[4]Isa. 40.25.—[5]Isa. 43.3, 11. [6]1 Pet. 1.15, 16.—
[7]1 Cor. 6.19.—[8]2 Cor. 6.16.—[9]Amos 3.3.

Evening

They held him back, saying, "Stay with us."[1]

Listen! I stand at the door and knock; if anyone hears my voice and opens the door, I will come into his house and eat with him, and he will eat with me.[2]—Tell me, my love, where will you lead your flock to graze? Where will they rest from the noonday sun? Why should I need to look for you among the flocks of the other shepherds?[3]—I found him. I held him and wouldn't let him go.[4]

Let my lover come to his garden and eat the best of its fruits.[5]—I have entered my garden.[6]—I did not require the people of Israel to look for me in a desolate waste.[7]

I will be with you always, to the end of the age.[8]—I will never leave you; I will never abandon you.[9]—Where two or three come together in my name, I am there with them.[10]—The world will see me no more, but you will see me.[11]

[1]LUKE 24.29. [2]Rev. 3.20.—[3]S. of S. 1.7.—[4]S. of S. 3.4. [5]S. of S. 4.16.—
[6]S. of S. 5.1.—[7]Isa. 45.19. [8]Matt. 28.20.—[9]Heb. 13.5.—[10]Matt. 18.20.—
[11]John 14.19.

Abram put his trust in the Lord, and because of this the Lord was pleased with him and accepted him.[1]

His faith did not leave him, and he did not doubt God's promise; his faith filled him with power, and he gave praise to God. He was absolutely sure that God would be able to do what he had promised. That is why Abraham, through faith, "was accepted as righteous by God." The words . . . were not written for him alone. They were written also for us who are to be accepted as righteous, who believe in him who raised Jesus our Lord from death.[2]

When God promised Abraham and his descendants that the world would belong to him, he did so, not because Abraham obeyed the Law, but because he believed and was accepted as righteous by God.[3]

The person who is put right with God through faith shall live.[4]—Let us hold on firmly to the hope we profess, because we can trust God to keep his promise.[5]—Our God is in heaven; he does whatever he wishes.[6]—There is nothing that God cannot do. How happy you are to believe that the Lord's message to you will come true.[7]

[1]GEN. 15.6. [2]Rom. 4.20–24. [3]Rom 4.13. [4]Rom. 1.17.—[5]Heb. 10.23.—[6]Ps. 115.3.—[7]Luke 1.37, 45.

Evening

God . . . calls you to share in his own Kingdom.[1]

My kingdom does not belong to this world; if my kingdom belonged to this world, my followers would fight . . . No, my kingdom does not belong here![2]—There he now waits until God puts his enemies as a footstool under his feet.[3]

The power to rule over the world belongs now to our Lord and his Messiah, and he will rule for ever and ever![4]—You have made them a kingdom of priests to serve our God, and they shall rule on earth.[5]—Then I saw thrones, and those who sat on them were given the power to judge . . . They came to life and ruled as kings with Christ for a thousand years.[6]—Then God's people will shine like the sun in their Father's Kingdom.[7]—Do not be afraid, little flock, for your Father is pleased to give you the Kingdom.[8]

Just as my Father has given me the right to rule, so I will give you the same right. You will eat and drink at my table in my Kingdom, and you will sit on thrones to rule over the twelve tribes of Israel.[9]

May your Kingdom come.[10]

[1]1 THESS. 2.12. [2]John 18.36.—[3]Heb. 10.13. [4]Rev. 11.15.—[5]Rev. 5.10.—[6]Rev. 20.4.—[7]Matt. 13.43.—[8]Luke 12.32. [9]Luke 22.29, 30. [10]Matt. 6.10.

I will never leave you; I will never abandon you.[1]

Let us be bold, then, and say, "The Lord is my helper, I will not be afraid. What can anyone do to me?"[2]

I will be with you and protect you wherever you go, and I will bring you back to this land. I will not leave you until I have done all that I have promised you.[3]—Be determined and confident. Do not be afraid of them. Your God, the LORD himself, will be with you. He will not fail you or abandon you.[4]

Demas fell in love with this present world and has deserted me. No one stood by me the first time I defended myself; all deserted me. May God not count it against them! But the Lord stayed with me and gave me strength.[5]—My father and mother may abandon me, but the LORD will take care of me.[6]

I will be with you always, to the end of the age.[7]—I am the living one! I was dead, but now I am alive for ever and ever.[8]—When I go, you will not be left all alone; I will come back to you.[9]

[1]HEB. 13.5. [2]Heb. 13.6. [3]Gen. 28.15.—[4]Deut. 31.6. [5]2 Tim. 4.10, 16, 17.— [6]Ps. 27.10. [7]Matt. 28.20.—[8]Rev. 1.18.—[9]John 14.18.

Evening

Master . . . we worked hard all night long and caught nothing. But if you say so, I will let down the nets.[1]

I have been given all authority in heaven and on earth. Go, then, to all peoples everywhere and make them my disciples; baptize them in the name of the Father, the Son, and the Holy Spirit, and teach them to obey everything I have commanded you. And I will be with you always, to the end of the age.[2]

The Kingdom of heaven is like this. Some fishermen throw their net out in the lake and catch all kinds of fish.[3]

I have no right to boast just because I preach the gospel. After all, I am under orders to do so. And how terrible it would be for me if I did not preach the gospel! I become all things to all men, that I may save some of them by whatever means are possible.[4]

Let us not become tired of doing good; for if we do not give up, the time will come when we will reap the harvest.[5]—The word that I speak will not fail to do what I plan for it; it will do everything I send it to do.[6]—The one who sows and the one who waters really do not matter. It is God who matters, because he makes the plant grow.[7]

[1]LUKE 5.5. [2]Matt. 28.18–20. [3]Matt. 13.47. [4]1 Cor. 9.16, 22. [5]Gal. 6.9.— [6]Isa. 55.11.—[7]1 Cor. 3.7.

Morning

The Kingdom of heaven will be like this. Once there was a man who was about to go on a journey; he called his servants and put them in charge of his property. He gave to each one according to his ability. [1]

Surely you know that when you surrender yourselves as slaves to obey someone, you are in fact slaves of the master you obey.[2]

It is one and the same Spirit who does all this; as he wishes, he gives a different gift to each person. The Spirit's presence is shown in some way in each person for the good of all.[3]—Each one, as a good manager of God's different gifts, must use for the good of others the special gift he has received from God.[4]—The one thing required of such a servant is that he be faithful to his master.[5]—Much is required from the person to whom much is given; much more is required from the person to whom much more is given.[6]

Who, then, is capable of such a task?[7]—I have the strength to face all conditions by the power that Christ gives me.[8]

[1]MATT. 25.14, 15. [2]Rom. 6.16. [3]1 Cor. 12.11, 7.—[4]1 Pet. 4.10.—[5]1 Cor. 4.2.—[6]Luke 12.48. [7]2 Cor. 2.16.—[8]Phil. 4.13.

Evening

Share your belongings with your needy fellow-Christians. [1]

David asked, "Is there anyone left of Saul's family? . . . I would like to show him kindness for Jonathan's sake."[2]

Come, you that are blessed by my Father! Come and possess the kingdom which has been prepared for you ever since the creation of the world. I was hungry and you fed me, thirsty and you gave me a drink; I was a stranger and you received me in your homes, naked and you clothed me; I was sick and you took care of me, in prison and you visited me. Whenever you did this for one of the least important of these brothers of mine, you did it for me![3]—Whoever gives even a drink of cold water to one of the least of these my followers . . . will certainly receive a reward.[4]

Do not forget to do good and to help one another, because these are the sacrifices that please God.[5]—God is not unfair. He will not forget the work you did or the love you showed for him in the help you gave and are still giving to your fellow-Christians.[6]

[1]ROM. 12.13. [2]2 Sam. 9.1. [3]Matt. 25.34–36, 40.—[4]Matt. 10.42. [5]Heb. 13.16.—[6]Heb. 6.10.

If you do what is right, you are certain to be rewarded.[1]

After a long time the master of those servants came back and settled accounts with them. The servant who had received five thousand coins came in and handed over the other five thousand. "You gave me five thousand coins, sir," he said. "Look! Here are another five thousand that I have earned." "Well done, you good and faithful servant!" said his master. "You have been faithful in managing small amounts, so I will put you in charge of large amounts. Come on in and share my happiness!"[2]

All of us must appear before Christ, to be judged by him. Each one will receive what he deserves, according to everything he has done, good or bad, in his bodily life.[3]

I have done my best in the race, I have run the full distance, and I have kept the faith. Now there is waiting for me the victory prize of being put right with God, which the Lord, the righteous Judge, will give me on that Day.[4]

I am coming soon. Keep safe what you have, so that no one will rob you of your victory prize.[5]

[1]PROV. 11.18. [2]Matt. 25.19–21. [3]2 Cor. 5.10. [4]2 Tim. 4.7, 8. [5]Rev. 3.11.

Evening

God keeps his promise.[1]

God is not like men, who lie; he is not a human who changes his mind. Whatever he promises, he does; he speaks, and it is done.[2]—The Lord has made a solemn promise and will not take it back.[3]

To those who were to receive what he promised, God wanted to make it very clear that he would never change his purpose; so he added his vow to the promise. There are these two things, then, that cannot change and about which God cannot lie. So we who have found safety with him are greatly encouraged to hold firmly to the hope placed before us.[4]—Those who suffer because it is God's will for them, should by their good actions trust themselves completely to their Creator, who always keeps his promise.[5]

I know whom I have trusted, and I am sure that he is able to keep safe until that Day what he has entrusted to me.[6]—He who calls you will do it, because he is faithful.[7]—It is he who is the "Yes" to all God's promises. This is why through Jesus Christ our "Amen" is said to the glory of God.[8]

[1]1 COR. 10.13. [2]Num. 23.19.—[3]Heb. 7.21. [4]Heb. 6.17, 18.—[5]1 Pet. 4.19. [6]2 Tim. 1.12.—[7]1 Thess. 5.24.—[8]2 Cor. 1.20.

Be determined and confident![1]

The LORD is my light and my salvation; I will fear no one. The LORD protects me from all danger; I will never be afraid.[2]—He strengthens those who are weak and tired. Even those who are young grow weak; young men can fall exhausted. But those who trust in the LORD for help will find their strength renewed. They will rise on wings like eagles; they will run and not get weary; they will walk and not grow weak.[3]—My mind and my body may grow weak, but God is my strength; he is all I ever need.[4]

If God is for us, who can be against us?[5]—The LORD is with me, I will not be afraid; what can anyone do to me?[6]

By your power we defeat our enemies.[7]—In all these things we have complete victory through him who loved us![8]

Now begin the work, and may the LORD be with you.[9]

[1]JOSH. 1.18. [2]Ps. 27.1.—[3]Isa. 40.29–31.—[4]Ps. 73.26. [5]Rom. 8.31.—[6]Ps. 118.6. [7]Ps. 44.5.—[8]Rom. 8.37. [9]1 Chr. 22.16.

Evening

Our friend . . . has fallen asleep.[1]

Our brothers, we want you to know the truth about those who have died, so that you will not be sad, as are those who have no hope. We believe that Jesus died and rose again, and so we believe that God will take back with Jesus those who have died believing in him.[2]

If the dead are not raised, neither has Christ been raised. And if Christ has not been raised, then your faith is a delusion and you are still lost in your sins. It would also mean that the believers in Christ who have died are lost. But the truth is that Christ has been raised from death, as the guarantee that those who sleep in death will also be raised.[3]

When the whole nation had crossed the Jordan, the LORD said to Joshua, . . . "take twelve stones out of the middle of the Jordan, from the very place where the priests were standing . . . These stones will always remind the people of Israel of what happened here."[4]—God has raised this very Jesus from death, and we are all witnesses to this fact.[5]—Witnesses that God had already chosen . . . who ate and drank with him after he rose from death.[6]

[1]JOHN 11.11. [2]1 Thess. 4.13, 14. [3]1 Cor. 15.16–18, 20. [4]Josh. 4.1, 3, 7.—[5]Acts 2.32.—[6]Acts 10.41.

Come, you that are blessed by my Father! Come and possess the kingdom which has been prepared for you ever since the creation of the world.[1]

Do not be afraid, little flock, for your Father is pleased to give you the Kingdom.[2]—God chose the poor people of this world to be rich in faith and to possess the kingdom which he promised to those who love him.[3]—We will also possess with Christ what God has kept for him; for if we share Christ's suffering, we will also share his glory.[4]

The Father himself . . . loves you because you love me.[5]—God is not ashamed for them to call him their God, because he has prepared a city for them.[6]

Whoever wins the victory will receive this from me: I will be his God, and he will be my son.[7]—Now there is waiting for me the victory prize of being put right with God, which the Lord, the righteous Judge, will give me on that Day—and not only to me, but to all those who wait with love for him to appear.[8]—God, who began this good work in you, will carry it on until it is finished on the Day of Christ Jesus.[9]

[1]MATT. 25.34. [2]Luke 12.32.—[3]Jas 2.5.—[4]Rom. 8.17. [5]John 16.27.—[6]Heb. 11.16. [7]Rev. 21.7.—[8]2 Tim. 4.8.—[9]Phil. 1.6.

Evening

Wealth is not permanent. Not even nations last for ever.[1]

All [man] does is for nothing; he gathers wealth, but doesn't know who will get it.[2]—Keep your minds fixed on things [in heaven], not on things here on earth.[3]—Do not store up riches for yourselves here on earth, where moths and rust destroy, and robbers break in and steal. Instead, store up riches for yourselves in heaven . . . For your heart will always be where your riches are.[4]

Every athlete in training submits to strict discipline, in order to be crowned with a wreath that will not last; but we do it for one that will last for ever.[5]—We fix our attention, not on things that are seen, but on things that are unseen.[6]—If you do what is right, you are certain to be rewarded.[7]—Now there is waiting for me the victory prize of being put right with God, which the Lord, the righteous Judge, will give me on that Day—and not only to me, but to all those who wait with love for him to appear.[8]—The glorious crown which will never lose its brightness.[9]

[1]PROV. 27.24. [2]Ps. 39.6.—[3]Col. 3.2.—[4]Matt. 6.19–21. [5]1 Cor. 9.25.—[6]2 Cor. 4.18.—[7]Prov. 11.18.—[8]2 Tim. 4.8.—[9]1 Pet. 5.4.

Isaac . . . went out in the early evening to take a walk in the fields.[1]

May my words and my thoughts be acceptable to you, O LORD, my refuge and my redeemer.[2]

When I look at the sky, which you have made, at the moon and the stars, which you set in their places—what is man, that you think of him; mere man, that you care for him?[3]—How wonderful are the things the LORD does! All who are delighted with them want to understand them.[4]

Happy are those who reject the advice of evil men, who do not follow the example of sinners or join those who have no use for God. Instead, they find joy in obeying the Law of the LORD, and they study it day and night.[5]—Be sure that the book of the Law is always read in your worship. Study it day and night.[6]—My soul will feast and be satisfied, and I will sing glad songs of praise to You. As I lie in bed, I remember you; all night long I think of you.[7]

[1]GEN. 24.62, 63. [2]Ps. 19.14. [3]Ps. 8.3, 4.—[4]Ps. 111.2. [5]Ps. 1.1, 2.—[6]Josh. 1.8.—[7]Ps. 63.5, 6.

Evening

How much longer will you forget me, LORD? For ever? How much longer will you hide yourself from me?[1]

Every good gift and every perfect present comes from heaven; it comes down from God, the Creator of the heavenly lights, who does not change or cause darkness by turning.[2]—But the people of Jerusalem said, "The LORD has abandoned us! He has forgotten us." "Can a woman forget her own baby and not love the child she bore? Even if a mother should forget her child, I will never forget you."[3]

I will never forget you. I have swept your sins away like a cloud.[4]

Jesus loved Martha and her sister and Lazarus. Yet when he received the news that Lazarus was ill, he stayed where he was for two more days.[5]—A woman . . . came to him. "Son of David!" she cried out. "Have mercy on me, sir!" But Jesus did not say a word to her.[6]

Your faith, which is much more precious than gold, must also be tested.[7]

[1]PS. 13.1. [2]Jas 1.17.—[3]Isa. 49.14, 15. [4]Isa. 44.21, 22. [5]John 11.5, 6.—[6]Matt. 15.22, 23. [7]1 Pet. 1.7.

With all his abundant wealth through Christ Jesus, my God will supply all your needs.[1]

Be concerned above everything else with the Kingdom of God and with what he requires of you, and he will provide you with all these other things.[2]—God . . . did not even keep back his own Son, but offered him for us all! He gave us his Son—will he not also freely give us all things?[3]—Everything belongs to you: Paul, Apollos, and Peter; this world, life and death, the present and the future—all these are yours, and you belong to Christ, and Christ belongs to God.[4]—We seem to have nothing, yet we really possess everything.[5]

The LORD is my shepherd; I have everything I need.[6]—The LORD is our protector and glorious king, blessing us with kindness and honour. He does not refuse any good thing to those who do what is right.[7]—God . . . generously gives us everything for our enjoyment.[8]—God is able to give you more than you need, so that you will always have all you need for yourselves and more than enough for every good cause.[9]

[1]PHIL. 4.19. [2]Matt. 6.33.—[3]Rom. 8.32.—[4]1 Cor. 3.21–23.—[5]2 Cor. 6.10. [6]Ps. 23.1.—[7]Ps. 84.11.—[8]1 Tim. 6.17.—[9]2 Cor. 9.8.

Evening

How can light and darkness live together?[1]

People love the darkness rather than the light, because their deeds are evil.[2]—All of you are people who belong to the light, who belong to the day. We do not belong to the night or to the darkness.[3]

The darkness has made him blind.[4]—Your word is a lamp to guide me and a light for my path.[5]

There is violence in every dark corner of the land.[6]—Love comes from God. Whoever loves is a child of God and knows God. Whoever does not love does not know God, for God is love.[7]

The road of the wicked . . . is dark as night. They fall, but cannot see what they have stumbled over. The road the righteous travel is like the sunrise, getting brighter and brighter until daylight has come.[8]

I have come into the world as light, so that everyone who believes in me should not remain in the darkness.[9]

You yourselves used to be in the darkness, but since you have become the Lord's people, you are in the light. So you must live like people who belong to the light.[10]

[1]2 COR. 6.14. [2]John 3.19.—[3]1 Thess. 5.5. [4]1 John 2.11.—[5]Ps. 119.105. [6]Ps. 74.20.— [7]1 John 4.7, 8. [8]Prov. 4.19, 18. [9]John 12.46. [10]Eph. 5.8.

The Spirit produces . . . joy.[1]

Joy which the Holy Spirit gives.[2]—A great and glorious joy which words cannot express.[3]

Although saddened, we are always glad . . . I am running over with joy.[4]—We . . . boast of our troubles.[5]

Jesus, on whom our faith depends from beginning to end . . . because of the joy that was waiting for him . . . thought nothing of the disgrace of dying on the cross.[6]—I have told you this so that my joy may be in you and that your joy may be complete.[7]—Just as we have a share in Christ's many sufferings, so also through Christ we share in God's great help.[8]

May you always be joyful in your union with the Lord. I say it again: rejoice![9]—The joy that the LORD gives you will make you strong.[10]

You will show me the path that leads to life; your presence fills me with joy and brings me pleasure for ever.[11]—The Lamb, who is in the centre of the throne, will be their shepherd, and he will guide them to springs of life-giving water. And God will wipe away every tear from their eyes.[12]

[1]GAL. 5.22. [2]Rom. 14.17.—[3]1 Pet. 1.8. [4]2 Cor. 6.10; 7.4.—[5]Rom. 5.3. [6]Heb. 12.2.—[7]John 15.11.—[8]2 Cor. 1.5. [9]Phil. 4.4.—[10]Neh. 8.10. [11]Ps. 16.11.—[12]Rev. 7.17.

Evening

The LORD is Peace.[1]

You will have a son who will rule in peace, because I will give him peace from all his enemies. His name will be Solomon, because during his reign I will give Israel peace and security.[2]

There is something here greater than Solomon![3]—A child is born to us! A son is given to us! And he will be our ruler. He will be called, "Wonderful Counsellor", "Mighty God", "Eternal Father", "Prince of Peace".[4]—God's people will be free from worries, and their homes peaceful and safe. (But hail will fall on the forests, and the city will be torn down.)[5]

Christ himself has brought us peace.[6]—He will bring peace.[7]

They will fight against the Lamb; but the Lamb . . . will defeat them, because He is Lord of lords and King of kings.[8]

Peace is what I leave with you; it is my own peace that I give you.[9]

[1]JUDG. 6.24. [2]1 Chr. 22.9. [3]Matt. 12.42.—[4]Isa. 9.6.—[5]Isa. 32.18, 19. [6]Eph. 2.14.—[7]Mic. 5.5. [8]Rev. 17.14. [9]John 14.27.

If you are going to turn to the Lord with all your hearts, you must get rid of all the foreign gods and the images of the goddess Astarte. Dedicate yourselves completely to the Lord and worship only him.[1]

My children, keep yourselves safe from false gods![2]—"You must leave them and separate yourselves from them. Have nothing to do with what is unclean, and I will accept you. I will be your father, and you shall be my sons and daughters," says the Lord Almighty.[3]—You cannot serve both God and money.[4]

Do not worship any other god, because I, the LORD, tolerate no rivals.[5]—Serve him with an undivided heart and a willing mind. He knows all our throughts and desires.[6]

Sincerity and truth are what you require; fill my mind with your wisdom.[7]—Man looks at the outward appearance, but I look at the heart.[8]—My dear friends, if our conscience does not condemn us, we have courage in God's presence.[9]

[1]1 SAM. 7.3. [2]1 John 5.21.—[3]2 Cor. 6.17, 18.—[4]Matt. 6.24. [5]Exod. 34.14.—[6]1 Chr. 28.9. [7]Ps. 51.6.—[8]1 Sam. 16.7.—[9]1 John 3.21.

Evening

Will the Son of Man find faith on earth when he comes?[1]

He comes to his own country, but his own people did not receive him.[2]—The Spirit says clearly that some people will abandon the faith in later times.[3]

Preach the message . . . insist upon proclaiming it, (whether the time is right or not) . . . convince, reproach, and encourage, as you teach with all patience. The time will come when people will not listen to sound doctrine, but will follow their own desires and will collect for themselves more and more teachers who will tell them what they are itching to hear. They will turn away from listening to the truth and give their attention to legends.[4]

No one knows . . . when that day or hour will come—neither the angels in heaven, nor the Son; only the Father knows. Be on watch, be alert, for you do not know when the time will come.[5]—How happy are those servants whose master finds them awake and ready when he returns![6]—We wait for the blessed Day we hope for, when the glory of our great God and Saviour Jesus Christ will appear.[7]

[1]LUKE 18.8. [2]John 1.11.—[3]1 Tim. 4.1. [4]2 Tim. 4.2–4. [5]Mark 13.32, 33.—[6]Luke 12.37.—[7]Titus 2.13.

Do not forget one thing, my dear friends! There is no difference in the Lord's sight between one day and a thousand years; to him the two are the same. The Lord is not slow to do what he has promised, as some think.[1]

"My thoughts," says the LORD, "are not like yours, and my ways are different from yours. As high as the heavens are above the earth, so high are my ways and thoughts above yours. My word is like the snow and the rain that come down from the sky to water the earth . . . so also will be the word that I speak—it will not fail to do what I plan for it; it will do everything I send it to do."[2]

God has made all people prisoners of disobedience, so that he might show mercy to them all. How great are God's riches! How deep are his wisdom and knowledge! Who can explain his decisions? Who can understand his ways?[3]

[1]2 PET. 3.8, 9. [2]Isa. 55.8–11. [3]Rom. 11.32, 33.

Evening

You who survived were like a burning stick saved from a fire.[1]

The sinful people of Zion are trembling with fright. They say, "God's judgement is like a fire that burns for ever. Can any of us survive a fire like that?"[2]—We felt that the death sentence had been passed on us. But this happened so that we should rely, not on ourselves, but only on God, who raises the dead. From such terrible dangers of death he saved us, and will save us; and we have placed our hope in him that he will save us again.[3]—Sin pays its wage—death; but God's free gift is eternal life in union with Christ Jesus our Lord.[4]

It is a terrifying thing to fall into the hands of the living God![5]—We know what it means to fear the Lord, and so we try to persuade others.[6]

Insist on proclaiming it (whether the time is right or not).[7]—Save others by snatching them out of the fire.[8]

Give . . . this message from the LORD: "Not by military might or by your own strength, but by my spirit."[9]—God our Saviour, who wants everyone to be saved and to come to know the truth.[10]

[1]AMOS 4.11. [2]Isa. 33.14.—[3]2 Cor. 1.9, 10.—[4]Rom. 6.23. [5]Heb. 10.31.—[6]2 Cor. 5.11. [7]2 Tim. 4.2.—[8]Jude 23. [9]Zech. 4.6.—[10]1 Tim. 2.3, 4.

Don't be afraid! I am the first and the last.[1]

You have not come . . . to what you can feel, to Mount Sinai with its blazing fire, the darkness and the gloom, the storm . . . Instead, you have come to Mount Zion . . . to God, who is the judge of all mankind, and to the spirits of good people made perfect. You have come to Jesus, who arranged the new covenant.[2]—Jesus, on whom our faith depends from beginning to end.[3]—Our High Priest is not one who cannot feel sympathy for our weaknesses. We have a High Priest who was tempted in every way that we are, but did not sin. Let us have confidence, then, and approach God's throne, where there is grace. There we will receive mercy and find grace to help us just when we need it.[4]

The LORD, who rules and protects Israel, the LORD Almighty, has this to say: "I am the first, the last, the only God; there is no other god but me."[5]—"Mighty God", "Eternal Father", "Prince of Peace".[6]

LORD, from the very beginning you are God. You are my God, holy and eternal.[7]—The LORD alone is God; God alone is our defence.[8]

[1]REV. 1.17. [2]Heb. 12.18, 22–24.— [3]Heb. 12.2.—[4]Heb. 4.15, 16. [5]Isa. 44.6.—[6]Isa. 9.6.
[7]Hab. 1.12.—[8]2 Sam. 22.32.

Evening

Take me to a safe refuge.[1]

Don't worry about anything, but in all your prayers ask God for what you need, always asking him with a thankful heart. And God's peace, which is far beyond human understanding, will keep your hearts and minds safe in union with Christ Jesus.[2]

When I am ready to give up, he knows what I should do.[3]—God knows every step I take; if he tests me, he will find me pure.[4]—O Lord, you have always been our home.[5]—The poor and the helpless have fled to you and have been safe in times of trouble. You give them shelter from storms and shade from the burning heat.[6]

God alone is our defence.[7]—They shall never die. No one can snatch them away from me.[8]—Give me strength, as you promised, and I shall live; don't let me be disappointed in my hope![9]—We have this hope as an anchor for our lives. It is safe and sure, and goes through the curtain of the heavenly temple into the inner sanctuary.[10]

[1]PS. 61.2. [2]Phil. 4.6, 7. [3]Ps. 142.3.—[4]Job 23.10.—[5]Ps. 90.1.—[6]Isa. 25.4.
[7]Ps. 18.31.—[8]John 10.28.—[9]Ps. 119.116.—[10]Heb. 6.19.

"Let me go; daylight is coming." "I won't, unless you bless me."[1]

If the enemies of my people want my protection, let them make peace with me. Yes, let them make peace with me.[2]

You are a woman of great faith! What you want will be done for you.[3]—Let it happen, then, just as you believe![4]—When you pray, you must believe and not doubt at all. Whoever doubts is like a wave in the sea that is driven and blown about by the wind. A person like that . . . must not think that he will receive anything from the Lord.[5]

As they came near the village to which they were going, Jesus acted as if he were going farther; but they held him back, saying, "Stay with us." . . . He disappeared from their sight. They said to each other, "Wasn't it like a fire burning in us when he talked to us on the road and explained the Scriptures to us?"[6]—Tell me your plans, so that I may serve you and continue to please you . . . I will go with you, and I will give you victory.[7]

[1]GEN. 32.26. [2]Isa. 27.5. [3]Matt. 15.28.—[4]Matt. 9.29.—[5]Jas 1.6, 7. [6]Luke 24.28, 29, 31, 32.—[7]Exod. 33.13, 14.

Evening

Jesus, on whom our faith depends from beginning to end.[1]

"I am the first and the last," says the Lord God Almighty, who is, who was, and who is to come.[2]—Who was it that made this happen? Who has determined the course of history? I, the LORD, was there at the beginning, and I, the LORD, will be there at the end.[3]

Those . . . who live in the love of God the Father and the protection of Jesus Christ.[4]—May the God who gives us peace make you holy in every way and keep your whole being—spirit, soul, and body—free from every fault at the coming of our Lord Jesus Christ. He who calls you will do it, because he is faithful.[5]—God, who began this good work in you, will carry it on until it is finished on the Day of Christ Jesus.[6]—How can you be so foolish! You began by God's Spirit; do you now want to finish by your own power?[7]—LORD, your love is eternal. Complete the work that you have begun.[8]

God is always at work in you to make you willing and able to obey his own purpose.[9]

[1]HEB. 12.2. [2]Rev. 1.8.—[3]Isa. 41.4. [4]Jude 1.—[5]1 Thess. 5.23, 24.—[6]Phil. 1.6.— [7]Gal. 3.3.—[8]Ps. 138.8. [9]Phil. 2.13.

He lives for ever to plead with God for them.[1]

Who . . . will condemn them? Not Christ Jesus, who died . . . and is . . . pleading with him for us.[2]—Christ did not go into a man-made Holy Place, which was a copy of the real one. He went into heaven itself, where he now appears on our behalf in the presence of God.[3]

If anyone does sin, we have someone who pleads with the Father on our behalf—Jesus Christ, the righteous one.[4]—There is one who brings God and mankind together, the man Christ Jesus.[5]

We have a great High Priest who has gone into the very presence of God—Jesus, the Son of God. Our High Priest is not one who cannot feel sympathy for our weaknesses. On the contrary, we have a High Priest who was tempted in every way that we are, but did not sin. Let us have confidence, then, and approach God's throne, where there is grace. There we will receive mercy and find grace to help us just when we need it.[6]—It is through Christ that all of us . . . are able to come in the one Spirit into the presence of the Father.[7]

[1]HEB. 7.25. [2]Rom. 8.34.—[3]Heb. 9.24. [4]1 John 2.1.—[5]1 Tim. 2.5. [6]Heb. 4.14–16.—[7]Eph. 2.18.

Evening

Those who know you, Lord, will trust you.[1]

He will be called "The Lord Our Salvation."[2]—I will praise your power, Sovereign Lord; I will proclaim your goodness, yours alone.[3]

He will be called "Wonderful Counsellor."[4]—Lord, I know that no one is the master of his own destiny; no person has control over his own life.[5]

"Mighty God," "Eternal Father."[6]—I know whom I have trusted, and I am sure that he is able to keep safe until that Day what he has entrusted to me.[7]

"Prince of Peace."[8]—Christ himself has brought us peace.[9]—Now that we have been put right with God through faith, we have peace with God through our Lord Jesus Christ.[10]

The Lord is like a strong tower, where the righteous can go and be safe.[11]—Those who go to Egypt for help are doomed.[12]—Just as a bird hovers over its nest to protect its young, so I, the Lord Almighty, will protect Jerusalem and defend it.[13]

[1]PS. 9.10. [2]Jer. 23.6.—[3]Ps. 71.16. [4]Isa. 9.6.—[5]Jer. 10.23. [6]Isa. 9.6.—[7]2 Tim. 1.12. [8]Isa. 9.6.—[9]Eph. 2.14.—[10]Rom. 5.1. [11]Prov. 18.10.—[12]Isa. 31.1.—[13]Isa. 31.5.

Although saddened, we are always glad; we seem poor, but we make many people rich; we seem to have nothing, yet we really possess everything.[1]

We boast of the hope we have of sharing God's glory! We also boast of our troubles.[2]—In all our troubles I am still full of courage; I am running over with joy.[3]—You believe in him . . . so you rejoice with a great and glorious joy which words cannot express.[4]

They have been severely tested by the troubles they went through; but their joy was so great that they were extremely generous in their giving, even though they are very poor.[5]—I am less than the least of all God's people; yet God gave me this privilege of taking to the Gentiles the Good News about the infinite riches of Christ, and of making all people see how God's secret plan is to be put into effect. God, who is the Creator of all things, kept his secret hidden through all the past ages.[6]

God chose the poor people of this world to be rich in faith and to possess the kingdom which he promised to those who love him.[7]—God is able to give you more than you need, so that you will always have all you need for yourselves and more than enough for every good cause.[8]

[1]2 COR. 6.10. [2]Rom. 5.2, 3.—[3]2 Cor. 7.4.—[4]1 Pet. 1.8. [5]2 Cor. 8.2.—[6]Eph. 3.8, 9. [7]Jas 2.5.—[8]2 Cor. 9.8.

Evening

The Lord will help them when they are sick and will restore them to health.[1]

It was not an angel, but the Lord himself who saved them. In his love and compassion he rescued them.[2]—Lord, your dear friend is ill.[3]—My grace is all you need, for my power is greatest when you are weak.[4]

I am most happy, then, to be proud of my weaknesses, in order to feel the protection of Christ's power over me.[5]—I have the strength to face all conditions by the power that Christ gives me.[6]

Even though our physical being is gradually decaying, yet our spiritual being is renewed day after day.[7]

In him we live and move and exist.[8]—He strengthens those who are weak and tired. Even those who are young grow weak; young men can fall exhausted. But those who trust in the Lord for help will find their strength renewed.[9]—God has always been your defence; his eternal arms are your support.[10]

[1]PS. 41.3. [2]Isa. 63.9.—[3]John 11.3.—[4]2 Cor. 12.9. [5]2 Cor. 12.9.—[6]Phil. 4.13. [7]2 Cor. 4.16. [8]Acts 17.28.—[9]Isa. 40.29–31.—[10]Deut. 33.27.

In union with Christ you have become rich in all things.[1]

When we were still helpless, Christ died for the wicked at the time that God chose.[2]—God . . . did not even keep back his own Son. . . . will he not also freely give us all things?[3]

The full content of divine nature lives in Christ, in his humanity, and you have been given full life in union with him. He is supreme over every spiritual ruler and authority.[4]

Remain united to me, and I will remain united to you. A branch cannot bear fruit by itself; it can do so only if it remains in the vine. In the same way you cannot bear fruit unless you remain in me. I am the vine, and you are the branches. Whoever remains in me, and I in him, will bear much fruit; for you can do nothing without me.[5]—Even though the desire to do good is in me, I am not able to do it.[6]—Each one of us has received a special gift in proportion to what Christ has given.[7]

If you remain in me and my words remain in you, then you will ask for anything you wish, and you shall have it.[8]—Christ's message in all its richness must live in your hearts.[9]

[1]1 COR. 1.5. [2]Rom. 5.6.—[3]Rom. 8.32. [4]Col. 2.9, 10. [5]John 15.4, 5.—[6]Rom. 7.18.—[7]Eph. 4.7. [8]John 15.7.—[9]Col. 3.16.

Evening

They will see his face.[1]

"Please let me see the dazzling light of your presence." "I will not let you see my face, because no one can see me and stay alive."[2]—No one has ever seen God. The only Son, who is the same as God and is at the Father's side, he has made him known.[3]

Everyone willl see him, including those who pierced him. All peoples on earth will mourn over him.[4]—I look into the future, and I see the nation of Israel. A king, like a bright star, will arise in that nation.[5]

I know there is someone in heaven who will come at last to my defence. Even after my skin is eaten by disease, while still in this body I will see God.[6]—I will see you, because I have done no wrong; and when I awake, your presence will fill me with joy.[7]—When Christ appears, we shall be like him, because we shall see him as he really is.[8]—The Lord himself will come down from heaven. Those who have died believing in Christ will rise to life first; then we who are living at that time will be gathered up along with them in the clouds to meet the Lord in the air.[9]

[1]REV. 22.4. [2]Exod. 33.18, 20.—[3]John 1.18. [4]Rev. 1.7.—[5]Num. 24.17. [6]Job 19.25, 26.—[7]Ps. 17.15.—[8]1 John 3.2.—[9]1 Thess. 4.16, 17.

Do not be afraid—I will save you.[1]

Do not be afraid—you will not be disgraced again; you will not be humiliated. You will forget your unfaithfulness as a young wife, and your desperate loneliness as a widow. Your Creator will be like a husband to you—the LORD Almighty is his name. The holy God of Israel will save you.[2]—I have swept your sins away like a cloud. Come back to me; I am the one who saves you.[3]—It was the costly sacrifice of Christ, who was like a lamb without defect or flaw.[4]

The one who will rescue them is strong—his name is the LORD Almighty. He himself will take up their cause.[5]—What my Father has given me is greater than everything, and no one can snatch them away from the Father's care.[6]

May God our Father and the Lord Jesus Christ give you grace and peace. In order to set us free from this present evil age, Christ gave himself for our sins, in obedience to the will of our God and Father. To God be the glory for ever and ever! Amen.[7]

[1]ISA. 43.1. [2]Isa. 54.4, 5.—[3]Isa. 44.22.—[4]1 Pet. 1.19. [5]Jer. 50.34.—[6]John 10.29. [7]Gal. 1.3–5.

Evening

I will tell of the LORD's unfailing love; I praise him for all he has done for us.[1]

He pulled me out of a dangerous pit, out of the deadly quicksand. He set me safely on a rock and made me secure.[2]—The Son of God . . . loved me and gave his life for me.[3]—He gave us his Son—will he not also freely give us all things?[4]—God has shown us how much he loves us—it was while we were still sinners that Christ died for us![5]

It is God himself . . . who has placed his mark of ownership upon us, and who has given us the Holy Spirit in our hearts as the guarantee of all that he has in store for us.[6]—The Spirit is the guarantee that we shall receive what God has promised his people, and this assures us that God will give complete freedom to those who are his. Let us praise his glory![7]

God's mercy is so abundant, and his love for us is so great, that while we were spiritually dead in our disobedience he brought us to life with Christ. It is by God's grace that you have been saved. In our union with Christ Jesus he raised us up with him to rule with him in the heavenly world.[8]

[1]ISA. 63.7. [2]Ps. 40.2.—[3]Gal. 2.20.—[4]Rom. 8.32.—[5]Rom. 5.8. [6]2 Cor. 1.21, 22.—[7]Eph. 1.14. [8]Eph. 2.4–6.

I am dark but beautiful.[1]

I have been evil from the day I was born; from the time I was conceived, I have been sinful.[2]—"You became famous in every nation for your perfect beauty, because I was the one who made you so lovely." This is what the Sovereign LORD says.[3]

Lord! I am a sinful man![4]—How beautiful you are, my love![5]

I am ashamed of all I have said and repent in dust and ashes.[6]—How beautiful you are, my love; how perfect you are![7]

When I want to do what is good, what is evil is the only choice I have.[8]—Courage, my son! Your sins are forgiven.[9]

I know that good does not live in me—that is, in my human nature.[10]—You have been given full life in union with him.[11]—A mature individual in union with Christ.[12]

You have been purified from sin; you have been dedicated to God; you have been put right with God by the Lord Jesus Christ and by the Spirit of our God.[13]—You are . . . chosen to proclaim the wonderful acts of God, who called you out of darkness into his own marvellous light.[14]

[1]S. OF S. 1.5. [2]Ps. 51.5.—[3]Ezek. 16.14. [4]Luke 5.8.—[5]S. of S. 4.1. [6]Job 42.6.—[7]S. of S. 4.7. [8]Rom. 7.21.—[9]Matt. 9.2. [10]Rom. 7.18.—[11]Col. 2.19.—[12]Col. 1.28. [13]1 Cor. 6.11.—[14]1 Pet. 2.9.

Evening

Everyone who wants to live a godly life in union with Christ Jesus will be persecuted.[1]

I came to set sons against their fathers, daughters against their mothers, daughters-in-law against their mothers-in-law; a man's worst enemies will be the members of his own family.[2]—Whoever wants to be the world's friend makes himself God's enemy.[3]—Do not love the world or anything that belongs to the world. If you love the world, you do not love the Father. Everything that belongs to the world—what the sinful self desires, what people see and want, and everything in this world that people are so proud of—none of this comes from the Father; it all comes from the world.[4]

If the world hates you, just remember that it has hated me first. If you belonged to the world, then the world would love you as its own. But I chose you from this world, and you do not belong to it; that is why the world hates you. No slave is greater than his master.[5]—I gave them your message, and the world hated them, because they do not belong to the world, just as I do not belong to the world.[6]

[1]2 TIM. 3.12. [2]Matt. 10.35, 36.—[3]Jas 4.4.—[4]1 John 2.15, 16. [5]John 15.18–20.—[6]John 17.14.

The more you talk, the more likely you are to sin. If you are wise, you will keep quiet.[1]

My dear brothers! Everyone must be quick to listen, but slow to speak and slow to become angry.[2]—It is better to be patient than powerful. It is better to win control over yourself than over whole cities.[3]—If a person never makes a mistake in what he says, he is perfect and is also able to control his whole being.[4]—Your words will be used to judge you—to declare you either innocent or guilty.[5]—LORD, place a guard at my mouth, a sentry at the door of my lips.[6]

Christ himself suffered for you and left you an example, so that you would follow in his steps. He committed no sin, and no one ever heard a lie come from his lips. When he was insulted, he did not answer back with an insult; when he suffered, he did not threaten, but placed his hopes in God, the righteous Judge.[7]—Think of what he went through; how he put up with so much hatred from sinners! So do not let yourselves become discouraged and give up.[8]

They have never been known to tell lies; they are faultless.[9]

[1]PROV. 10.19. [2]Jas 1.19.—[3]Prov. 16.32.—[4]Jas 3.2.—[5]Matt. 12.37.—[6]Ps. 141.3. [7]1 Pet. 2.21–23.—[8]Heb. 12.3. [9]Rev. 14.5.

Evening

Teach me, LORD, what you want me to do.[1]

I will teach you the way you should go; I will instruct you and advise you.[2]—Because the LORD is righteous and good, he teaches sinners the path they should follow. He leads the humble in the right way and teaches them his will.[3]

I am the gate. Whoever comes in by me will be saved; he will come in and go out and find pasture.[4]

Jesus answered him, "I am the way, the truth, and the life; no one goes to the Father except by me."[5]—We have . . . complete freedom to go into the Most Holy Place by means of the death of Jesus. He opened for us a new way, a living way, through the curtain—that is, through his own body. We have a great priest in charge of the house of God. So let us come near to God with a sincere heart and a sure faith.[6]

Let us try to know the LORD.[7]—With faithfulness and love he leads all who keep his covenant and obey his commands.[8]

[1]PS. 27.11. [2]Ps. 32.8.—[3]Ps. 25.8, 9. [4]John 10.9. [5]John 14.6.—[6]Heb. 10.19–22. [7]Hos. 6.3.—[8]Ps. 25.10.

Morning

***What the Law could not do, because human nature was weak, God did. He condemned sin in human nature by sending his own Son, who came with a nature like man's sinful nature, to do away with sin.*[1]**

The Jewish Law is not a full and faithful model of the real things; it is only a faint outline of the good things to come. The same sacrifices are offered for ever, year after year. If the people worshipping God had really been purified from their sins . . . all sacrifices would stop.[2]—Everyone who believes in him is set free from all the sins from which the Law of Moses could not set you free.[3]

Since the children . . . are people of flesh and blood, Jesus himself became like them and shared their human nature. He did this so that through his death he might destroy the Devil, who has the power over death, and in this way set free those who were slaves all their lives because of their fear of death. For it is clear that it is not the angels that he helps. Instead, as the scripture says, "He helps the descendants of Abraham." This means that he had to become like his brothers in every way.[4]

[1]ROM. 8.3. [2]Heb. 10.1, 2.—[3]Acts 13.39. [4]Heb. 2.14–17.

Evening

***Everyone has sinned and is far away from God's saving presence.*[1]**

There is no one who is righteous . . . no one does what is right, not even one.[2]—There is no one on earth who does what is right all the time and never makes a mistake.[3]—Can anyone be righteous or pure in God's sight?[4]

Let us take care . . . that none of you will be found to have failed to receive that promised rest.[5]

I recognize my faults; I am always conscious of my sins. I have been evil from the day I was born; from the time I was conceived, I have been sinful.[6]

The LORD forgives you; you will not die.[7]—Those he called, he put right with himself, and he shared his glory with them.[8]—All of us . . . reflect the glory of the Lord with uncovered faces; and that same glory, coming from the Lord, who is the Spirit, transforms us into his likeness in an ever greater degree of glory.[9]—You must . . . continue faithful on a firm and sure foundation, and must not allow yourselves to be shaken from the hope you gained when you heard the gospel.[10]

Live the kind of life that pleases God, who calls you to share in his own Kingdom and glory.[11]

[1]ROM. 3.23. [2]Rom. 3.10, 12.—[3]Eccles. 7.20.—[4]Job 25.4. [5]Heb. 4.1. [6]Ps. 51.3, 5. [7]2 Sam. 12.13.—[8]Rom. 8.30.—[9]2 Cor. 3.18.—[10]Col. 1.23. [11]1 Thess. 2.12.

***Honour the* LORD *by making him an offering from the best of all that your land produces.*[1]**

Remember that the person who sows few seeds will have a small crop; the one who sows many seeds will have a large crop.[2]—Every Sunday each of you must put aside some money, in proportion to what he has earned, and save it up.[3]

God is not unfair. He will not forget the work you did or the love you showed for him in the help you gave and are still giving to your fellow-Christians.[4]

My brothers, because of God's great mercy to us I appeal to you: Offer yourselves as a living sacrifice to God, dedicated to his service and pleasing to him. This is the true worship that you should offer.[5]—We are ruled by the love of Christ, now that we recognize that one man died for everyone, which means that all share in his death. He died for all, so that those who live should no longer live for themselves, but only for him who died and was raised to life for their sake.[6]—Whatever you do, whether you eat or drink, do it all for God's glory.[7]

[1]PROV. 3.9. [2]2 Cor. 9.6.—[3]1 Cor. 16.2. [4]Heb. 6.10. [5]Rom. 12.1.—[6]2 Cor. 5.14, 15.—[7]1 Cor. 10.31.

Evening

***There will be no night there.*[1]**

I, the LORD, will be your eternal light; the light of my glory will shine on you.[2]

The city has no need of the sun or the moon to shine on it, because the glory of God shines on it, and the Lamb is its lamp.[3]—They will not need lamps or sunlight, because the Lord God will be their light.[4]

You are the chosen race, the King's priests, the holy nation, God's own people, chosen to proclaim the wonderful acts of God, who called you out of darkness into his own marvellous light.[5]—With joy give thanks to the Father, who has made you fit to have your share of what God has reserved for his people in the kingdom of light. He rescued us from the power of darkness and brought us safe into the kingdom of his dear Son.[6]—You yourselves used to be in the darkness, but since you have become the Lord's people, you are in the light. So you must live like people who belong to the light.[7]

We do not belong to the night or to the darkness.[8]

The road the righteous travel is like the sunrise, getting brighter and brighter until daylight has come.[9]

[1]REV. 21.25. [2]Isa. 60.19. [3]Rev. 21.23.—[4]Rev. 22.5. [5]1 Pet. 2.9.—[6]Col. 1.12, 13.—[7]Eph. 5.8. [8]1 Thess. 5.5. [9]Prov. 4.18.

My soul will feast and be satisfied, and I will sing glad songs of praise to you. As I lie in bed, I remember you; all night long I think of you.[1]

O God, how difficult I find your thoughts; how many of them there are! If I counted them, they would be more than the grains of sand. When I awake, I am still with you.[2]—How sweet is the taste of your instructions—sweeter even than honey![3]—Your love is better than wine.[4]

What else have I in heaven but you? Since I have you, what else could I want on earth?[5]

Like an apple tree among the trees of the forest, so is my dearest compared with other men. I love to sit in its shadow, and its fruit is sweet to my taste. He brought me to his banqueting hall and raised the banner of love over me.[6]—He is majestic, like the Lebanon Mountains with their towering cedars. His mouth is sweet to kiss; everything about him enchants me. This is what my lover is like, women of Jerusalem.[7]

[1]PS. 63.5, 6. [2]Ps. 139.17, 18.—[3]Ps. 119.103.—[4]S. of S. 1.2. [5]Ps. 73.25. [6]S. of S. 2.3, 4.—[7]S. of S. 5.15, 16.

Evening

Give me again the joy that comes from your salvation.[1]

I have seen how they acted, but I will heal them. I will lead them and help them, and I will comfort those who mourn.[2]

The LORD says, "Now, let's settle the matter. You are stained red with sin, but I will wash you as clean as snow. Although your stains are deep red, you will be as white as wool."[3]—Return, all of you who have turned away from the LORD; he will heal you and make you faithful. Yes, we are coming to the LORD, because he is our God.[4]—I am listening to what the LORD God is saying; he promises peace to us, his own people, if we do not go back to our foolish ways.[5]

Praise the LORD, my soul! And do not forget how kind he is. He forgives all my sins and heals all my diseases.[6]—He gives me new strength.[7]—I praise you, LORD! You were angry with me, but now you comfort me and are angry no longer.[8]

Hold me, and I will be safe.[9]

I am the God who forgives your sins, and I do this because of who I am. I will not hold your sins against you.[10]

[1]PS. 51.12. [2]Isa. 57.18. [3]Isa. 1.18.—[4]Jer. 3.22.—[5]Ps. 85.8. [6]Ps. 103.2, 3.—[7]Ps. 23.3.—[8]Isa. 12.1. [9]Ps. 119.117. [10]Isa. 43.25.

The one who will rescue them is strong—his name is the LORD Almighty.[1]

I know how terrible your sins are and how many crimes you have committed.[2]—I have given help to a famous soldier.[3]—The LORD, the one who saves you and sets you free.[4]—Powerful to save.[5]—Able to keep you from falling.[6]—Where sin increased, God's grace increased much more.[7]

Whoever believes in the Son is not judged; but whoever does not believe has already been judged, because he has not believed in God's only Son.[8]—He is able, now and always, to save those who come to God through him.[9]

Am I too weak to save them?[10]

Who, then, can separate us from the love of Christ? I am certain that nothing can separate us from his love: neither death nor life, neither angels nor other heavenly rulers or powers, neither the present nor the future, neither the world above nor the world below—there is nothing in all creation that will ever be able to separate us from the love of God which is ours through Christ Jesus our Lord.[11]

[1]JER. 50.34. [2]Amos 5.12.—[3]Ps. 89.19.—[4]Isa. 49.26.—[5]Isa. 63.1.—[6]Jude 24.—[7]Rom. 5.20. [8]John 3.18.—[9]Heb. 7.25. [10]Isa. 50.2. [11]Rom. 8.35, 38, 39.

Evening

Are you looking for special treatment for yourself? Don't do it.[1]

Take my yoke and put it on you, and learn from me, because I am gentle and humble in spirit; and you will find rest.[2]—The attitude you should have is the one that Christ Jesus had: he always had the nature of God, but he did not think that by force he should try to become equal with God. Instead of this, of his own free will he gave up all he had, and took the nature of a servant. He beame like man and appeared in human likeness. He was humble and walked the path of obedience all the way to death—his death on the cross.[3]

Whoever does not take up his cross and follow in my steps is not fit to be my disciple.[4]—Christ himself suffered for you and left you an example, so that you would follow in his steps.[5]

Religion does make a person very rich, if he is satisfied with what he has. What did we bring into the world? Nothing! What can we take out of the world? Nothing! So then, if we have food and clothes, that should be enough for us.[6]

I have learnt to be satisfied with what I have.[7]

[1]JER. 45.5. [2]Matt. 11.29.—[3]Phil. 2.5–8. [4]Matt. 10.38.—[5]1 Pet. 2.21. [6]1 Tim. 6.6–8. [7]Phil. 4.11.

Morning

I was afraid and thought that he had driven me out of his presence. But he heard my cry, when I called to him for help.[1]

I am sinking in deep mud, and there is no solid ground; I am out in deep water, and the waves are about to drown me.[2]—Water began to close over me, and I thought death was near. From the bottom of the pit, O LORD, I cried out to you, and when I begged you to listen to my cry, you heard. You answered me and told me not to be afraid.[3]

Will the Lord always reject us? Will he never again be pleased with us? Has he stopped loving us? Does his promise no longer stand? Has God forgotten to be merciful? Has anger taken the place of his compassion? Then I said, "What hurts me most is this—that God is no longer powerful." I will remember your great deeds, LORD; I will recall the wonders you did in the past.[4]—I know that I will live to see the LORD's goodness in this present life.[5]

[1]PS. 31.22. [2]Ps. 69.2.—[3]Lam. 3.54–57. [4]Ps. 77.7–11.—[5]Ps. 27.13.

Evening

When they call to me, I will answer them; when they are in trouble, I will be with them. I will rescue them.[1]

Jabez prayed to the God of Israel, "Bless me, God, and give me much land. Be with me and keep me from anything evil that might cause me pain." And God gave him what he prayed for.[2]—"What would you like me to give you?" Solomon answered, "Give me the wisdom and knowledge I need to rule over them."[3]—God gave Solomon unusual wisdom and insight, and knowledge too great to be measured.[4]

Asa prayed to the LORD his God, "O LORD, you can help a weak army as easily as a powerful one. LORD, you are our God; no one can hope to defeat you." The LORD defeated the Sudanese army when Asa and the Judaean army attacked them.[5]

O God, it is right for us to praise you . . . because you answer prayer. People everywhere will come to you.[6]

[1]PS. 91.15. [2]1 Chr. 4.10.—[3]2 Chr. 1.7, 8, 10.—[4]1 Kgs 4.29. [5]2 Chr. 14.11, 12. [6]Ps. 65.1, 2.

Giving thanks is the sacrifice that honours me.[1]

Christ's message in all its richness must live in your hearts. Teach and instruct each other with all wisdom. Sing psalms, hymns, and sacred songs; sing to God with thanksgiving in your hearts. Everything you do or say, then, should be done in the name of the Lord Jesus, as you give thanks through him to God the Father.[2]—He bought you for a price. So use your bodies for God's glory.[3]

You are . . . the King's priests . . . chosen to proclaim the wonderful acts of God, who called you out of darkness into his own marvellous light.[4]—Come as living stones, and let yourselves be used in building the spiritual temple, where you will serve as holy priests to offer spiritual and acceptable sacrifices to God through Jesus Christ.[5]—Let us . . . always offer praise to God as our sacrifice through Jesus, which is the offering presented by lips that confess him as Lord.[6]

I will praise him for what he has done; may all who are oppressed listen and be glad! Proclaim with me the LORD's greatness; let us praise his name together![7]

[1]PS. 50.23. [2]Col. 3.16, 17.—[3]1 Cor. 6.20. [4]1 Pet. 2.9.—[5]1 Pet. 2.5.—[6]Heb. 13.15. [7]Ps. 34.2, 3.

Evening

Take me with you, and we'll run away.[1]

I have always loved you, so I continue to show you my constant love.[2]—I drew them to me with affection and love.[3]—When I am lifted up from the earth, I will draw everyone to me.[4]—There is the Lamb of God![5]—As Moses lifted up the bronze snake on a pole in the desert, in the same way the Son of Man must be lifted up, so that everyone who believes in him may have eternal life.[6]

What else have I in heaven but you? Since I have you, what else could I want on earth?[7]—We love because God first loved us.[8]

My lover speaks to me. "Come then, my love; my darling, come with me. The winter is over; the rains have stopped; in the countryside the flowers are in bloom. This is the time for singing; the song of doves is heard in the fields. Figs are beginning to ripen; the air is fragrant with blossoming vines. Come then, my love; my darling, come with me."[9]

[1]S. OF S. 1.4. [2]Jer. 31.3.—[3]Hos. 11.4.—[4]John 12.32.—[5]John 1.36.—[6]John 3.14, 15. [7]Ps. 73.25.—[8]1 John 4.19. [9]S. of S. 2.10–13.

Morning

I will send them a prophet like you from among their own people.[1]

I [Moses] stood between you and the LORD at that time to tell you what he said, because you were afraid.[2]—There is one God, and there is one who brings God and mankind together, the man Christ Jesus.[3]

Moses was a humble man, more humble than anyone else on earth.[4]—Take my yoke and put it on you, and learn from me, because I am gentle and humble in spirit; and you will find rest.[5]—The attitude you should have is the one that Christ Jesus had: he always had the nature of God, but he did not think that by force he should try to become equal with God. Instead of this, of his own free will he gave up all he had, and took the nature of a servant. He became like man and appeared in human likeness.[6]

Moses was faithful in God's house as a servant, and he spoke of the things that God would say in the future. But Christ is faithful as the Son in charge of God's house. We are his house if we keep up our courage and our confidence in what we hope for.[7]

[1]DEUT. 18.18. [2]Deut. 5.5.—[3]1 Tim. 2.5. [4]Num. 12.3.—[5]Matt. 11.29.— [6]Phil. 2.5–7. [7]Heb. 3.5, 6.

Evening

Unfailing courage.[1]

I will honour the covenant I made with you when you were young, and I will make a covenant with you that will last for ever.[2]

With one sacrifice . . . he has made perfect for ever those who are purified from sin.[3]—He is able, now and always, to save those who come to God through him, because he lives for ever to plead with God for them.[4]—I know whom I have trusted, and I am sure that he is able to keep safe until that Day what he has entrusted to me.[5]

God does not change his mind about whom he chooses and blesses.[6]—Who . . . can separate us from the love of Christ?[7]—The Lamb, who is in the centre of the throne, will be their shepherd, and he will guide them to springs of life-giving water. And God will wipe away every tear from their eyes.[8]—We will always be with the Lord. So then, encourage one another with these words.[9]

There is no safety here any more.[10]—There is no permanent city for us here on earth; we are looking for the city which is to come.[11]

[1]2 THESS. 2.16. [2]Ezek. 16.60. [3]Heb. 10.14.—[4]Heb. 7.25.—[5]2 Tim. 1.12. [6]Rom. 11.29.—[7]Rom. 8.35.—[8]Rev. 7.17.—[9]1 Thess. 4.17, 18. [10]Mic. 2.10.— [11]Heb. 13.14.

I am telling you the truth: I am the gate for the sheep.[1]

The curtain hanging in the Temple was torn in two from top to bottom.[2]—Christ died for sins once and for all, a good man on behalf of sinners, in order to lead you to God.[3]—The way into the Most Holy Place has not yet been opened as long as the outer Tent still stands.[4]

I am the gate. Whoever comes in by me will be saved; he will come in and go out and find pasture.[5]

No one goes to the Father except by me.[6]—Through Christ . . . all of us . . . are able to come in the one Spirit into the presence of the Father. So then, you . . . are not foreigners or strangers any longer; you are now fellow-citizens with God's people and members of the family of God.[7]—We have . . . complete freedom to go into the Most Holy Place by means of the death of Jesus. He opened for us a new way, a living way, through the curtain—that is, through his own body.[8]—We have peace with God through our Lord Jesus Christ. He has brought us by faith into this experience of God's grace, in which we now live. And so we boast of the hope we have of sharing God's glory![9]

[1]JOHN 10.7. [2]Matt. 27.51.—[3]1 Pet. 3.18.—[4]Heb. 9.8. [5]John 10.9. [6]John 14.6.—[7]Eph. 2.18, 19.—[8]Heb. 10.19, 20.—[9]Rom. 5.1.

Evening

Your message is like a fire burning deep within me. I try my best to hold it in, but can no longer keep it back.[1]

I preach the gospel . . . I am under orders to do so. And how terrible it would be for me if I did not preach the gospel! What pay do I get, then? It is the privilege of preaching the Good News without charging for it, without claiming my rights in my work for the gospel.[2]—They called them back in and told them that on no condition were they to speak or to teach in the name of Jesus. But Peter and John answered them, . . . "We cannot stop speaking of what we ourselves have seen and heard."[3]—We are ruled by the love of Christ.[4]

"I was afraid, so I went off and hid your money in the ground" . . . "You bad and lazy servant! . . . you should have deposited my money in the bank, and I would have received it all back with interest when I returned."[5]

Go back home to your family and tell them how much the Lord has done for you.[6]

[1]JER. 20.9. [2]1 Cor. 9.16, 18.—[3]Acts 4.18–20.—[5]Matt. 25.25–27. [6]Mark 5.19.

Do not keep for yourselves anything that was condemend to destruction.[1]

The Lord says, "You must leave them and separate yourselves from them. Have nothing to do with what is unclean."[2]—I appeal to you, my friends, as strangers and refugees in this world! Do not give in to bodily passions, which are always at war against the soul.[3]—Hate their very clothes, stained by their sinful lusts.[4]

My dear friends, we are now God's children, but it is not yet clear what we shall become. But we know that when Christ appears, we shall be like him, because we shall see him as he really is. Everyone who has this hope in Christ keeps himself pure, just as Christ is pure.[5]—God has revealed his grace for the salvation of all mankind. That grace instructs us to give up ungodly living and worldly passions, and to live self-controlled, upright, and godly lives in this world, as we wait for the blessed Day we hope for, when the glory of our great God and Saviour Jesus Christ will appear. He gave himself for us, to rescue us from all wickedness and to make us a pure people who belong to him alone and are eager to do good.[6]

[1]DEUT. 13.17. [2]2 Cor. 6.17.—[3]1 Pet. 2.11.—[4]Jude 23. [5]1 John 3.2, 3.—[6]Titus 2.11–14.

Evening

Who are you, Lord? I am Jesus.[1]

It is I. Don't be afraid![2]—When you pass through deep waters, I will be with you; your troubles will not overwhelm you. When you pass through fire, you will not be burnt; the hard trials that come will not hurt you. For I am the LORD your God, . . . who saves you.[3]

Even if I go through the deepest darkness, I will not be afraid, LORD, for you are with me. Your shepherd's rod and staff protect me.[4]—Immanuel . . . God is with us.[5]

You will name him Jesus—because he will save his people from their sins.[6]—If anyone does sin, we have someone who pleads with the Father on our behalf—Jesus Christ, the righteous one.[7]—Who . . . will condemn them? Not Christ Jesus, who died, or rather, who was raised to life and is at the right-hand side of God, pleading with him for us! Who . . . can separate us from the love of Christ? Can trouble do it, or hardship or persecution or hunger or poverty or danger or death?[8]

[1]ACTS 26.15. [2]Matt. 14.27.—[3]Isa. 43.2, 3. [4]Ps. 23.4.—[5]Matt. 1.23. [6]Matt. 1.21.—[7]1 John 2.1.—[8]Rom. 8.34, 35.

Stand firm in your life in the Lord.[1]

I follow faithfully the road he chooses, and never wander to either side.[2]

The LORD loves what is right and does not abandon his faithful people. He protects them for ever.[3]—The LORD will protect you from all danger; he will keep you safe.[4]

My righteous people . . . will believe and live; but if any of them turns back, I will not be pleased with him. We are not people who turn back and are lost. Instead, we have faith and are saved.[5]—If they had belonged to our fellowship, they would have stayed with us. But they left so that it might be clear that none of them really belonged to us.[6]

If you obey my teaching, you are really my disciples.[7]—Whoever holds out to the end will be saved.[8]—Be alert, stand firm in the faith, be brave, be strong.[9]—Keep safe what you have, so that no one will rob you of your victory prize.[10]—Those who win the victory will be clothed like this in white, and I will not remove their names from the book of the living.[11]

[1]PHIL. 4.1. [2]Job 23.11. [3]Ps. 37.28.—[4]Ps. 121.7. [5]Heb. 10.38, 39.—[6]1 John 2.19. [7]John 8.31.—[8]Matt. 24.13.—[9]1 Cor. 16.13.—[10]Rev. 3.11.—[11]Rev. 3.5.

Evening

Enoch lived in fellowship with God.[1]

Do two men start travelling together without arranging to meet?[2]

God made peace through his Son's sacrificial death on the cross . . . At one time you were far away from God and were his enemies because of the evil things you did and thought. But now, by means of the physical death of his Son, God has made you his friends, in order to bring you, holy, pure, and faultless, into his presence.[3]—In union with Christ Jesus, you who used to be far away have been brought near by the sacrificial death of Christ.[4]

We were God's enemies, but he made us his friends through the death of his Son. Now that we are God's friends, how much more will we be saved by Christ's life! But that is not all; we rejoice because of what God has done through our Lord Jesus Christ.[5]

The fellowship that we have with the Father and with his Son Jesus Christ.[6]

The grace of the Lord Jesus Christ, the love of God, and the fellowship of the Holy Spirit be with you all.[7]

[1]GEN. 5.22. [2]Amos 3.3. [3]Col. 1.20–22.—[4]Eph. 2.13. [5]Rom. 5.10, 11. [6]1 John 1.3. [7]2 Cor. 13.13.

Morning

If he is offering one of his cattle as a burnt offering, he must bring a bull without any defects. He must present it . . . so that the LORD will accept him. The man shall put his hand on its head, and it will be accepted as a sacrifice to take away his sins.[1]

Where is the lamb for the sacrifice? God himself will provide one.[2]—There is the Lamb of God, who takes away the sins of the world![3]—We are all purified from sin by the offering that he made of his own body once and for all.[4]—To give his life to redeem many people.[5]

No one takes my life away from me. I give it up of my own free will. I have the right to give it up, and I have the right to take it back.[6]—I will love them with all my heart.[7]—The Son of God, who loved me and gave his life for me.[8]

Christ was without sin, but for our sake God made him share our sin in order that in union with him we might share the righteousness of God.[9]—The free gift he gave us in his dear Son![10]

[1]LEV. 1.3, 4. [2]Gen. 22.7, 8.—[3]John 1.29.—[4]Heb. 10.10.—[5]Matt. 20.28. [6]John 10.18.—[7]Hos. 14.4.—[8]Gal. 2.20. [9]2 Cor. 5.21.—[10]Eph. 1.6.

Evening

How great is your constant love for me! You have saved me from the grave itself.[1]

Be afraid of God, who can destroy both body and soul in hell.[2]

Do not be afraid—I will save you. I have called you by name—you are mine. I alone am the LORD, the only one who can save you. I am the God who forgives your sins, and I do this because of who I am. I will not hold your sins against you.[3]—Evil men who trust in their riches and boast of their great wealth. A person can never redeem himself; he cannot pay God the price for his life, because the payment for a human life is too great.[4]—Here is the ransom to set him free.[5]—God's mercy is so abundant, and his love for us is so great, that while we were spiritually dead in our disobedience he brought us to life with Christ.[6]

Salvation is to be found through him alone; in all the world there is no one else whom God has given who can save us.[7]

[1]PS. 86.13. [2]Matt. 10.28. [3]Isa. 43.1, 11, 25.—[4]Ps. 49.6–8.—[5]Job 33.24.— [6]Eph. 2.4, 5. [7]Acts 4.12.

***The* Lord *protected me.*[1]**

We were not helped at all by our pagan worship on the hilltops. Help for Israel comes only from the Lord our God.[2]—The Lord is my protector; he is my strong fortress. My God is my protection, and with him I am safe. He protects me like a shield; he defends me and keeps me safe.[3]—Let everyone who lives in Zion shout and sing! Israel's holy God is great, and he lives among his people.[4]

His angel guards those who honour the Lord and rescues them from danger. The righteous call to the Lord, and he listens; he rescues them from all their troubles.[5]—God has always been your defence; his eternal arms are your support.[6]—Let us be bold, then, and say, "The Lord is my helper, I will not be afraid. What can anyone do to me?"[7]—The Lord alone is God; God alone is our defence. He is the God who makes me strong, who makes my pathway safe.[8]

By God's grace I am what I am.[9]

[1]PS. 18.18. [2]Jer. 3.23.—[3]Ps. 18.2.—[4]Isa. 12.6. [5]Ps. 34.7, 17.—[6]Deut. 33.27.—[7]Heb. 13.6.—[8]Ps. 18.31, 32. [9]1 Cor. 15.10.

Evening

***All of us were like sheep that were lost, each of us going his own way.*[1]**

If we say that we have no sin, we deceive ourselves, and there is no truth in us.[2]—There is no one who is righteous, no one who is wise or who worships God. All have turned away from God; they have all gone wrong; no one does what is right, not even one.[3]

You were like sheep that had lost their way, but now you have been brought back to follow the Shepherd and Keeper of your souls.[4]—I wander about like a lost sheep; so come and look for me, your servant, because I have not neglected your laws.[5]

He gives me new strength. He guides me in the right paths, as he has promised.[6]

My sheep listen to my voice; I know them, and they follow me. I give them eternal life, and they shall never die. No one can snatch them away from me.[7]

Suppose one of you has a hundred sheep and loses one of them—what does he do? He leaves the other ninety-nine sheep in the pasture and goes looking for the one that got lost until he finds it.[8]

[1]ISA. 53.6. [2]1 John 1.8.—[3]Rom. 3.10–12. [4]1 Pet. 2.25.—[5]Ps. 119.176. [6]Ps. 23.3. [7]John 10.27, 28. [8]Luke 15.4.

Morning

The Lord *blessed Sarah, as he had promised.*[1]

Trust in God at all times, my people. Tell him all your troubles, for he is our refuge.[2]—David was now in great trouble . . . but the Lord his God gave him courage.[3]—God will certainly take care of you and lead you out of this land to the land he solemnly promised to Abraham, Isaac, and Jacob.[4]—"I have seen the cruel suffering of my people in Egypt. I have heard their groans, and I have come down to set them free." He led the people out of Egypt, performing miracles and wonders in Egypt and at the Red Sea and for forty years in the desert.[5]—The Lord kept every one of the promises that he had made to the people of Israel.[6]

We can trust God to keep his promise.[7]—Whatever he promises, he does; he speaks, and it is done.[8]—Heaven and earth will pass away, but my words will never pass away.[9]—Grass withers and flowers fade, but the word of our God endures for ever.[10]

[1]GEN. 21.1. [2]Ps. 62.8.—[3]1 Sam. 30.6.—[4]Gen. 50.24.—[5]Acts 7.34, 36.—[6]Josh. 21.45. [7]Heb. 10.23.—[8]Num. 23.19.—[9]Matt. 24.35.—[10]Isa. 40.8.

Evening

All living things look hopefully to you.[1]

It is he himself who gives life and breath and everything else to everyone.[2]—He is good to everyone and has compassion on all he made.[3]—Look at the birds: they do not sow seeds, gather a harvest and put it in barns; yet your Father in heaven takes care of them![4]

God is the same Lord of all and richly blesses all who call to him.[5]

I look to the mountains; where will my help come from? My help will come from the Lord.[6]—As a servant depends on his master, as a maid depends on her mistress, so we will keep looking to you, O Lord our God.[7]

The Lord . . . always does what is right. Happy are those who put their trust in the Lord.[8]—When it happens, everyone will say, "He is our God! We have put our trust in him, and he has rescued us. He is the Lord! We have put our trust in him, and now we are happy and joyful because he has saved us."[9]—If we hope for what we do not see, we wait for it with patience.[10]

[1]PS. 145.15. [2]Acts 17.25.—[3]Ps. 145.9.—[4]Matt. 6.26. [5]Rom. 10.12. [6]Ps. 121.1, 2.—[7]Ps. 123.2. [8]Isa. 30.18.—[9]Isa. 25.9.—[10]Rom. 8.25.

You will name him Jesus—because he will save his people from their sins.[1]

You know that Christ appeared in order to take away sins.[2]—That we might die to sin and live for righteousness.[3]—He is able, now and always, to save those who come to God through him, because he lives for ever to plead with God for them.[4]

Because of our sins he was wounded, beaten because of the evil we did. We are healed by the punishment he suffered, made whole by the blows he received. The LORD made the punishment fall on him, the punishment all of us deserved.[5]—The Messiah must suffer . . . and in his name the message about repentance and the forgiveness of sins must be preached to all nations.[6]—He has appeared once and for all, to remove sin through the sacrifice of himself.[7]

God raised him to his right-hand side as Leader and Saviour, to give the people of Israel the opportunity to repent.[8]—It is through Jesus that the message about forgiveness of sins is preached to you; and that everyone who believes in him is set free from all the sins from which the Law of Moses could not set you free.[9]—Your sins are forgiven for the sake of Christ.[10]

[1]MATT. 1.21. [2]1 John 3.5.—[3]1 Pet. 2.24.—[4]Heb. 7.25. [5]Isa. 53.5, 6.—[6]Luke 24.46, 47.—[7]Heb. 9.26. [8]Acts 5.31.—[9]Acts 13.38, 39.—[10]1 John 2.12.

Evening

Our Lord Jesus Christ; rich as he was, he made himself poor for your sake, in order to make you rich by means of his poverty.[1]

It was by God's own decision that the Son has in himself the full nature of God.[2]—He reflects the brightness of God's glory and is the exact likeness of God's own being, sustaining the universe with his powerful word. After achieving forgiveness for the sins of mankind, he sat down in heaven at the right-hand side of God, the Supreme Power. The Son was made greater than the angels, just as the name that God gave him is greater than theirs.[3]—He always had the nature of God, but he did not think that by force he should try to become equal with God. Instead of this, of his own free will he gave up all he had, and took the nature of a servant.[4]

Foxes have holes, and birds have nests, but the Son of Man has nowhere to lie down and rest.[5]

Everything belongs to you: Paul, Apollos, and Peter; this world, life and death, the present and the future—all these are yours, and you belong to Christ, and Christ belongs to God.[6]

[1]2 COR. 8.9. [2]Col. 1.19.—[3]Heb. 1.3, 4.—[4]Phil. 2.6, 7. [5]Matt. 8.20. [6]1 Cor. 3.21–23.

Morning

His left hand is under my head, and his right hand caresses me.[1]

His eternal arms are your support.[2]—When [Peter] noticed the strong wind, he was afraid and started to sink down in the water. "Save me, Lord!" he cried. At once Jesus reached out and grabbed hold of him and said, "How little faith you have! Why did you doubt?"[3]—The LORD guides a man in the way he should go and protects those who please him. If they fall, they will not stay down, because the LORD will help them up.[4]

This is the tribe the LORD loves and protects; he guards them all the day long, and he dwells in their midst.[5]—Leave all your worries with him, because he cares for you.[6]—Anyone who strikes you strikes what is most precious to me.[7]

They shall never die. No one can snatch them away from me. What my Father has given me is greater than everything.[8]

[1]S. OF S. 2.6. [2]Deut. 33.27.—[3]Matt. 14.30, 31.—[4]Ps. 37.23, 24. [5]Deut. 33.12.—[6]1 Pet. 5.7.—[7]Zech. 2.8. [8]John 10.28, 29.

Evening

Who is this whose glance is like the dawn? She is beautiful and bright, as dazzling as the sun or the moon.[1]

The church of God, which he made his own through the sacrificial death of his Son.[2]

Christ loved the church and gave his life for it. He did this to dedicate the church to God by his word, after making it clean by washing it in water, in order to present the church to himself in all its beauty—pure and faultless, without spot or wrinkle or any other imperfection.[3]

A great and mysterious sight appeared in the sky. There was a woman, whose dress was the sun.[4]—The time has come for the wedding of the Lamb, and his bride has prepared herself for it. She has been given clean shining linen to wear. (The linen is the good deeds of God's people.)[5]—God puts people right through their faith in Jesus Christ. God does this to all who believe in Christ.[6]

I gave them the same glory you gave me.[7]

[1]S. OF S. 6.10. [2]Acts 20.28. [3]Eph. 5.25–27. [4]Rev. 12.1.—[5]Rev. 19.7, 8.—[6]Rom. 3.22. [7]John 17.22.

My brothers . . . there is not much time left.[1]

We are all born weak and helpless. All lead the same short, troubled life. We grow and wither as quickly as flowers; we disappear like shadows.[2]—The world and everything in it that people desire is passing away; but he who does the will of God lives for ever.[3]—As all people die because of their union with Adam, in the same way all will be raised to life because of their union with Christ. Death is destroyed, victory is complete![4]—If we live, it is for the Lord that we live, and if we die, it is for the Lord that we die. So whether we live or die, we belong to the Lord.[5]—What is life? To me, it is Christ. Death, then, will bring more.[6]

Do not lose your courage . . . because it brings with it a great reward. You need to be patient, in order to do the will of God and receive what he promises. For, as the scripture says, "Just a little while longer, and he who is coming will come; he will not delay."[7]—The night is nearly over, day is almost here. Let us stop doing the things that belong to the dark, and let us take up weapons for fighting in the light.[8]—The end of all things is near. You must be self-controlled and alert, to be able to pray.[9]

[1]1 COR. 7.29. [2]Job 14.1, 2.—[3]1 John 2.17.—[4]1 Cor. 15.22, 54.—[5]Rom. 14.8.—[6]Phil. 1.21. [7]Heb. 10.35–37.—[8]Rom. 13.12.—[9]1 Pet. 4.7.

Evening

A new name.[1]

It was at Antioch that the believers were first called Christians.[2]—Whoever says that he belongs to the Lord must turn away from wrongdoing.[3]—Those who belong to Christ Jesus have put to death their human nature with all its passions and desires.[4]—He bought you for a price. So use your bodies for God's glory.[5]

I will boast only about the cross of our Lord Jesus Christ; for by means of his cross the world is dead to me, and I am dead to the world. It does not matter at all whether or not one is circumcised; what does matter is being a new creature.[6]

Since you are God's dear children, you must try to be like him. Your life must be controlled by love, just as Christ loved us and gave his life for us as a sweet-smelling offering and sacrifice that pleases God. Since you are God's people, it is not right that any matters of sexual immorality or indecency or greed should even be mentioned among you. Since you have become the Lord's people, you are in the light. So you must live like people who belong to the light.[7]

[1]REV. 2.17. [2]Acts 11.26.—[3]2 Tim. 2.19.—[4]Gal. 5.24.—[5]1 Cor. 6.20. [6]Gal. 6.14, 15. [7]Eph. 5.1–3, 8.

There is the Lamb of God![1]

The blood of bulls and goats can never take away sins. For this reason, when Christ was about to come into the world, he said to God: "You do not want sacrifices and offerings, but you have prepared a body for me. You are not pleased with animals burnt whole on the altar or with sacrifices to take away sins. Then I said, 'Here I am, to do your will, O God, just as it is written of me in the book of the Law.' "[2]—He was treated harshly, but endured it humbly; he never said a word. Like a lamb about to be slaughtered, like a sheep about to be sheared, he never said a word.[3]

You know what was paid to set you free . . . It was not something that can be destroyed, such as silver or gold; it was the costly sacrifice of Christ, who was like a lamb without defect or flaw . . . revealed in these last days for your sake. Through him you believe in God, . . . and so your faith and hope are fixed on God.[4]

The Lamb who was killed is worthy to receive power, wealth, wisdom, and strength, honour, glory, and praise![5]

[1]JOHN 1.29. [2]Heb. 10.4–7.—[3]Isa. 53.7. [4]1 Pet. 1.18–21. [5]Rev. 5.12.

Evening

I will always put my hope in you; I will praise you more and more.[1]

I do not claim that I have already succeeded or have already become perfect.[2]—Let us go forward . . . to mature teaching and leave behind us the first lessons of the Christian message. We should not lay again the foundation of turning away from useless works and believing in God.[3]—The road the righteous travel is like the sunrise, getting brighter and brighter until daylight has come.[4]

I love the LORD, because he hears me; he listens to my prayers. He listens to me every time I call to him.[5]—I will always thank the LORD; I will never stop praising him.[6]

O God, it is right for us to praise you in Zion.[7]—Day and night they never stop singing: "Holy, holy, holy, is the Lord God Almighty."[8]—Giving thanks is the sacrifice that honours me.[9]—Be joyful always, pray at all times, be thankful in all circumstances. This is what God wants from you in your life in union with Christ Jesus.[10]—May you always be joyful in your union with the Lord. I say it again: rejoice![11]

[1]PS. 71.14. [2]Phil. 3.12.—[3]Heb. 6.1.—[4]Prov. 4.18. [5]Ps. 116.1, 2.—[6]Ps. 34.1. [7]Ps. 65.1.—[8]Rev. 4.8.—[9]Ps. 50.23.—[10]1 Thess. 5.16–18.—[11]Phil. 4.4.

Remember the great things he has done for you.[1]

Remember how the LORD your God led you on this long journey through the desert these past forty years, sending hardships to test you, so that he might know what you intended to do and whether you would obey his commands. Remember that the LORD your God corrects and punishes you just as a father disciplines his children.[2]

I know that your judgements are righteous, LORD, and that you punished me because you are faithful. My punishment was good for me, because it made me learn your commands. Before you punished me, I used to go wrong, but now I obey your word.[3]—He has punished me severely, but he has not let me die.[4]—He does not punish us as we deserve or repay us according to our sins and wrongs. As high as the sky is above the earth, so great is his love for those who honour him. He knows what we are made of; he remembers that we are dust.[5]

[1]1 SAM. 12.24. [2]Deut. 8.2, 5. [3]Ps. 119.75, 71, 67.—[4]Ps. 118.18.—[5]Ps. 103.10, 11, 14.

Evening

The blessed Day we hope for, when the glory of our great God and Saviour Jesus Christ will appear.[1]

We have this hope as an anchor for our lives. It is safe and sure, and goes through the curtain of the heavenly temple into the inner sanctuary. On our behalf Jesus has gone in there before us.[2]—He must remain in heaven until the time comes for all things to be made new.[3]—When he comes on that Day to receive glory from all his people and honour from all who believe.[4]

We know that up to the present time all of creation groans with pain, like the pain of childbirth. But it is not just creation alone which groans; we . . . also groan within ourselves, as we wait for God to make us his sons and set our whole being free.[5]—My dear friends, we are now God's children, but it is not yet clear what we shall become. But we know that when Christ appears, we shall be like him, because we shall see him as he really is.[6]—Your real life is Christ and when he appears, then you too will appear with him and share his glory![7]

Yes indeed! I am coming soon! So be it. Come, Lord Jesus![8]

[1]TITUS 2.13. [2]Heb. 6.19, 20.—[3]Acts 3.21.—[4]2 Thess. 1.10. [5]Rom. 8.22, 23.—[6]1 John 3.2.—[7]Col. 3.4. [8]Rev. 22.20.

Morning

Whoever obeys his word is the one whose love for God has really been made perfect.[1]

God has raised from death our Lord Jesus, who is the Great Shepherd of the sheep as the result of his sacrificial death, by which the eternal covenant is sealed. May the God of peace provide you with every good thing you need in order to do his will, and may he, through Jesus Christ, do in us what pleases him. And to Christ be the glory for ever and ever! Amen.[2]

If we obey God's commands, then we are sure that we know him.[3]—Whoever loves me will obey my teaching. My Father will love him, and my Father and I will come to him and live with him.[4]—Everyone who lives in union with Christ does not continue to sin; but whoever continues to sin has never seen him or known him. Let no one deceive you, my children! Whoever does what is right is righteous, just as Christ is righteous.[5]—Love is made perfect in us in order that we may have courage on Judgement Day; and we will have it because our life in this world is the same as Christ's.[6]

[1]1 JOHN 2.5. [2]Heb. 13.20, 21. [3]1 John 2.3.—[4]John 14.23.—[5]1 John 3.6, 7.—[6]1 John 4.17.

Evening

If you stay calm, you are wise.[1]

The LORD . . . passed in front of him and called out, "I the LORD, am a God who is full of compassion and pity, who is not easily angered."[2]—The Lord is not slow to do what he has promised, as some think. Instead, he is patient with you, because he does not want anyone to be destroyed, but wants all to turn away from their sins.[3]

Since you are God's dear children, you must try to be like him. Your life must be controlled by love.[4]—The Spirit produces love, joy, peace, patience, kindness, goodness, faithfulness, humility, and self-control. There is no law against such things as these.[5]—God will bless you for this, if you endure the pain of undeserved suffering because you are conscious of his will. If you endure suffering even when you have done right, God will bless you for it . . . Christ himself suffered for you and left you an example, so that you would follow in his steps . . . When he was insulted, he did not answer back with an insult; when he suffered, he did not threaten, but placed his hopes in God, the righteous Judge.[6]

If you become angry, do not let your anger lead you into sin.[7]

[1]PROV. 14.29. [2]Exod. 34.6.—[3]2 Pet. 3.9. [4]Eph. 5.1, 2.—[5]Gal. 5.22, 23.—[6]1 Pet. 2.19–21, 23. [7]Eph. 4.26.

The Spirit produces . . . peace.[1]

To be controlled by the Spirit results in life and peace.[2]

God has called you to live in peace.[3]—Peace is what I leave with you; it is my own peace that I give you. I do not give it as the world does. Do not be worried and upset; do not be afraid.[4]—May God, the source of hope, fill you with all joy and peace by means of your faith in him, so that your hope will continue to grow by the power of the Holy Spirit.[5]

I know whom I have trusted, and I am sure that he is able to keep safe until that Day what he has entrusted to me.[6]—You, LORD, give perfect peace to those who keep their purpose firm and put their trust in you.[7]

Because everyone will do what is right, there will be peace and security for ever. God's people will be free from worries, and their homes peaceful and safe.[8]—Whoever listens to me will have security. He will be safe, with no reason to be afraid.[9]

Those who love your law have perfect security.[10]

[1]GAL. 5.22. [2]Rom. 8.6. [3]1 Cor. 7.15.—[4]John 14.27.—[5]Rom. 15.13. [6]2 Tim. 1.12.—[7]Isa. 26.3. [8]Isa. 32.17, 18.—[9]Prov. 1.33. [10]Ps. 119.165.

Evening

The LORD Is Here![1]

Now God's home is with mankind! He will live with them, and they shall be his people. God himself will be with them, and he will be their God.[2]

I did not see a temple in the city, because its temple is the Lord God Almighty and the Lamb. The city has no need of the sun or the moon to shine on it, because the glory of God shines on it, and the Lamb is its lamp.[3]

When I awake, your presence will fill me with joy.[4]—What else have I in heaven but you? Since I have you, what else could I want on earth?[5]

Judah and Jerusalem will be inhabited for ever, and I, the LORD, will live on Mount Zion.[6]—The LORD said, "Sing for joy, people of Jerusalem! I am coming to live among you!"[7]—Nothing that is under God's curse will be found in the city. The throne of God and of the Lamb will be in the city, and his servants will worship him.[8]

[1]EZEK. 48.35. [2]Rev. 21.3. [3]Rev. 21.22, 23. [4]Ps. 17.15.—[5]Ps. 73.25. [6]Joel 3.20, 21.—[7]Zech. 2.10.—[8]Rev. 22.3.

The LORD *is here! He is in this place, and I didn't know it!*[1]

Where two or three come together in my name, I am there with them.[2]—I will be with you always, to the end of the age.[3]—I will go with you, and I will give you victory.[4]

Where could I go to escape from you? Where could I get away from your presence? If I went up to heaven, you would be there; if I lay down in the world of the dead, you would be there.[5]—I am a God who is everywhere and not in one place only. No one can hide where I cannot see him. Do you not know that I am everywhere in heaven and on earth?[6]

Not even all heaven is large enough to hold you, so how can this Temple that I have built be large enough?[7]—I am the high and holy God, who lives for ever. I live in a high and holy place, but I also live with people who are humble and repentant, so that I can restore their confidence and hope.[8]

[1]GEN. 28.16. [2]Matt. 18.20.—[3]Matt. 28.20.—[4]Exod. 33.14. [5]Ps. 139.7, 8.—[6]Jer. 23.23, 24. [7]1 Kgs 8.27.—[8]Isa. 57.15.

Evening

Keep yourselves safe from false gods![1]

Son . . . let my life be your example.[2]—Keep your minds fixed on things [in Heaven], not on things here on earth.[3]

Mortal man . . . these men have given their hearts to idols and are letting idols lead them into sin. Do they think I will give them an answer?[4]—You must put to death . . . the earthly desires at work in you, such as sexual immorality, indecency, lust, evil passions, and greed (for greed is a form of idolatry).[5]—Those who want to get rich fall into temptation and are caught in the trap of . . . foolish desires. For the love of money is a source of all kinds of evil. Some have been so eager to have it that they have wandered away from the faith and have broken their hearts with many sorrows. But you, man of God, avoid all these things.[6]

Even if your riches increase, don't depend on them.[7]—What you get from me is better than the finest gold, better than the purest silver.[8]

Your heart will always be where your riches are.[9]—I look at the heart.[10]

[1]1 JOHN 5.21. [2]Prov. 23.26.—[3]Col. 3.2. [4]Ezek. 14.3.—[5]Col. 3.5.—[6]1 Tim. 6.9–11. [7]Ps. 62.10.—[8]Prov. 8.19. [9]Matt. 6.21.—[10]1 Sam. 16.7.

You must be perfect—just as your Father in heaven is perfect![1]

I am the Almighty God. Obey me and always do what is right.[2]—You shall be holy and belong only to me, because I am the LORD and I am holy. I have set you apart from the other nations so that you would belong to me alone.[3]

He bought you for a price. So use your bodies for God's glory.[4]

You have been given full life in union with him. He is supreme over every spiritual ruler and authority.[5]—He gave himself for us, to rescue us from all wickedness.[6]—Do your best to be pure and faultless in God's sight and to be at peace with him.[7]

Happy are those whose lives are faultless, who live according to the law of the LORD.[8]—Whoever looks closely into the perfect law that sets people free, who keeps on paying attention to it and does not simply listen and then forget it, but puts it into practice—that person will be blessed by God in what he does.[9]—Examine me, O God, and know my mind; test me, and discover my thoughts. Find out if there is any evil in me and guide me in the everlasting way.[10]

[1]MATT. 5.48. [2]Gen. 17.1.—[3]Lev. 20.26. [4]1 Cor. 6.20. [5]Col. 2.10.—[6]Titus 2.14.—[7]2 Pet. 3.14. [8]Ps. 119.1.—[9]Jas 1.25.—[10]Ps. 139.23, 24.

Evening

Let us be completely holy by living in awe of God.[1]

My dear friends . . . let us purify ourselves from everything that makes body or soul unclean.[2]

Sincerity and truth are what you require; fill my mind with your wisdom.[3]—That grace instructs us to give up ungodly living and worldly passions, and to live self-controlled, upright, and godly lives in this world.[4]—Your light must shine before people, so that they will see the good things you do and praise your Father in heaven.[5]—I do not claim that I have already succeeded or have already become perfect.[6]

Everyone who has this hope in Christ keeps himself pure, just as Christ is pure.[7]

God is the one who has prepared us for this change, and he gave us his Spirit as the guarantee of all that he has in store for us.[8]—He did this to prepare all God's people for the work of Christian service, in order to build up the body of Christ. And so we shall all come together to that oneness in our faith and in our knowledge of the Son of God; we shall become mature people, reaching to the very height of Christ's full stature.[9]

[1]2 COR. 7.1. [2]2 Cor. 7.1. [3]Ps. 51.6.—[4]Titus 2.12.—[5]Matt. 5.16.—[6]Phil. 3.12. [7]1 John 3.3. [8]2 Cor. 5.5.—[9]Eph. 4.12, 13.

Morning

***Don't think that the LORD is too weak to save you or too deaf to hear your call for help!*[1]**

You answered me when I called to you; with your strength you strengthened me.[2]—While I was praying, Gabriel, whom I had seen in the earlier vision, came flying down to where I was. It was the time for the evening sacrifice to be offered.[3]

Don't hide yourself from me! Don't be angry with me; don't turn your servant away. You have been my help; don't leave me, don't abandon me, O God, my saviour.[4]—O LORD, don't stay away from me! Come quickly to my rescue![5]

Sovereign LORD, you made the earth and the sky by your great power and might; nothing is too difficult for you.[6]—From such terrible dangers of death he saved us, and will save us; and we have placed our hope in him that he will save us again.[7]—Will God not judge in favour of his own people who cry to him day and night for help? Will he be slow to help them? I tell you, he will judge in their favour and do it quickly.[8]

[1]ISA. 59.1. [2]Ps. 138.3.—[3]Dan. 9.21. [4]Ps. 27.9.—[5]Ps. 22.19. [6]Jer. 32.17.—[7]2 Cor. 1.10.—[8]Luke 18.7, 8.

Evening

***I have shown your glory on earth.*[1]**

My food . . . is to obey the will of the one who sent me and to finish the work he gave me to do.[2]—As long as it is day, we must keep on doing the work of him who sent me; night is coming when no one can work.[3]

"Didn't you know that I had to be in my Father's house?" But they did not understand his answer.[4]—The final result of this sickness will not be the death of Lazarus; this has happened in order to bring glory to God, and it will be the means by which the Son of God will receive glory. Didn't I tell you that you would see God's glory if you believed?[5]

Jesus grew both in body and in wisdom, gaining favour with God and men.[6]—You are my own dear Son. I am pleased with you.[7]—They were all well impressed with him and marvelled at the eloquent words that he spoke.[8]

You are worthy . . . For you were killed, and by your sacrificial death you bought for God people from every tribe, language, nation, and race. You have made them a kingdom of priests to serve our God, and they shall rule on earth.[9]

[1]JOHN 17.4. [2]John 4.34.—[3]John 9.4. [4]Luke 2.49, 50.—[5]John 11.4, 40. [6]Luke 2.52.—[7]Luke 3.22.—[8]Luke 4.22. [9]Rev. 5.9, 10.

Do not start worrying: where will my food come from? Or my drink? Or my clothes? Your Father in heaven knows that you need all these things.[1]

Honour the LORD, all his people; those who obey him have all they need. Even lions go hungry for lack of food, but those who obey the LORD lack nothing good.[2]—He does not refuse any good thing to those who do what is right. LORD Almighty, how happy are those who trust in you![3]

I would like you to be free from worry.[4]—Don't worry about anything, but in all your prayers ask God for what you need, always asking him with a thankful heart.[5]

For only a penny you can buy two sparrows, yet not one sparrow falls to the ground without your Father's consent. As for you, even the hairs of your head have all been counted. So do not be afraid; you are worth much more than many sparrows![6]—Why are you frightened? Have you still no faith?[7]—Have faith in God.[8]

[1]MATT. 6.31, 32. [2]Ps. 34.9, 10.—[3]Ps. 84.11, 12. [4]1 Cor. 7.32.—[5]Phil. 4.6. [6]Matt. 10.29–31.—[7]Mark 4.40.—[8]Mark 11.22.

Evening

God put a cloud over his people and a fire at night to give them light.[1]

As a father is kind to his children, so the LORD is kind to those who honour him. He knows what we are made of; he remembers that we are dust.[2]

The sun will not hurt you during the day, nor the moon during the night.[3]—His glory will shade the city from the heat of the day and make it a place of safety, sheltered from the rain and storm.[4]

The LORD will guard you; he is by your side to protect you. He will protect you as you come and go now and for ever.[5]—During the day the LORD went in front of them in a pillar of cloud to show them the way, and during the night he went in front of them in a pillar of fire to give them light, so that they could travel night and day. The pillar of cloud was always in front of the people during the day, and the pillar of fire at night.[6]

Jesus Christ is the same yesterday, today, and for ever.[7]

[1]PS. 105.39. [2]Ps. 103.13, 14. [3]Ps. 121.6.—[4]Isa. 4.6. [5]Ps. 121.5, 8.— [6]Exod. 13.21, 22. [7]Heb. 13.8.

Morning

Love and faithfulness will meet; righteousness and peace will embrace.[1]

The LORD, the God who saves his people.[2]

The LORD is a God who is eager to save, so he exalted his laws and teachings, and he wanted his people to honour them.[3]

God was mking all mankind his friends through Christ. God did not keep an account of their sins.[4]—God offered him, so that by his sacrificial death he should become the means by which people's sins are forgiven through their faith in him. God did this in order to demonstrate that he is righteous. In the past he was patient and overlooked people's sins; but in the present time he deals with their sins, in order to demonstrate his righteousness. In this way God shows that he himself is righteous and that he puts right everyone who believes in Jesus.[5]—Because of our sins he was wounded, beaten because of the evil we did. We are healed by the punishment he suffered, made whole by the blows he received.[6]—Who will accuse God's chosen people? God himself declares them not guilty![7]—The person who depends on his faith, not on his deeds, and who believes in the God who declares the guilty to be innocent, it is his faith that God takes into account in order to put him right with himself.[8]

[1]PS. 85.10. [2]Isa. 45.21. [3]Isa. 42.21. [4]2 Cor. 5.19.—[5]Rom. 3.25, 26.—[6]Isa. 53.5.—[7]Rom. 8.33.—[8]Rom. 4.5.

Evening

How can the dead be raised to life? What kind of body will they have?[1]

My dear friends, we are now God's children, but it is not yet clear what we shall become. But we know that when Christ appears, we shall be like him, because we shall see him as he really is.[2]—Just as we wear the likeness of the man made of earth, so we will wear the likeness of the Man from heaven.[3]

Our Saviour, the Lord Jesus Christ . . . will change our weak mortal bodies and make them like his own glorious body, using that power by which he is able to bring all things under his rule.[4]

The Lord himself stood among them and said to them, "Peace be with you." They were terrified, thinking they were seeing a ghost.[5]—He appeared to Peter and then to all twelve apostles. Then he appeared to more than five hundred of his followers at once.[6]

If the Spirit of God, who raised Jesus from death, lives in you, then he who raised Christ from death will also give life to your mortal bodies by the presence of his Spirit in you.[7]

[1]1 COR. 15.35. [2]1 John 3.2.—[3]1 Cor. 15.49. [4]Phil. 3.20, 21. [5]Luke 24.36, 37.—[6]1 Cor. 15.5, 6. [7]Rom. 8.11.

***You are going to hear the noise of battles close by and the news of battles far away; but do not be troubled.*[1]**

God is our shelter and strength, always ready to help in times of trouble. So we will not be afraid, even if the earth is shaken and mountains fall into the ocean depths; even if the seas roar and rage, and the hills are shaken by the violence.[2]—Go into your houses, my people, and shut the door behind you. Hide yourselves for a little while until God's anger is over. The LORD is coming from his heavenly dwelling-place to punish the people of the earth for their sins.[3]—In the shadow of your wings I find protection until the raging storms are over.[4]—Your life is hidden with Christ in God.[5]

He is not afraid of receiving bad news; his faith is strong, and he trusts in the LORD.[6]

I have told you this so that you will have peace by being united to me. The world will make you suffer. But be brave! I have defeated the world![7]

[1]MATT. 24.6. [2]Ps. 46.1–3.—[3]Isa. 26.20, 21.—[4]Ps. 57.1.—[5]Col. 3.3. [6]Ps. 112.7. [7]John 16.33.

Evening

***They persecute those whom you have punished.*[1]**

Things that make people fall into sin are bound to happen, but how terrible for the one who makes them happen![2]—In accordance with his own plan God had already decided that Jesus would be handed over to you; and you killed him by letting sinful men crucify him.[3]—They spat in his face and beat him; and those who slapped him said, "Prophesy for us, Messiah! Guess who hit you!"[4]—In the same way the chief priests and the teachers of the Law and the elders jeered at him. "He saved others, but he cannot save himself! Isn't he the king of Israel? If he comes down off the cross now, we will believe in him!"[5]—Indeed Herod and Pontius Pilate met together in this city with the Gentiles and the people of Israel against Jesus, your holy Servant, whom you made Messiah. They gathered to do everything that you by your power and will had already decided would happen.[6]

He endured the suffering that should have been ours, the pain that we should have borne. All the while we thought that his suffering was punishment sent by God.[7]

[1]PS. 69.26. [2]Luke 17.1.—[3]Acts 2.23.—[4]Matt. 26.67, 68.—[5]Matt. 27.41, 42.—[6]Acts 4.27, 28. [7]Isa. 53.4.

Morning

The Lord says, "It was my will that he should suffer."[1]

"Now my heart is troubled—and what shall I say? Shall I say, 'Father, do not let this hour come upon Me?' But that is why I came—so that I might go through this hour of suffering. Father, bring glory to your name!" Then a voice spoke from heaven, "I have brought glory to it, and I will do so again."[2]—"Father," he said, "if you will, take this cup of suffering away from me. Not my will, however, but your will be done." An angel from heaven appeared to him and strengthened him.[3]

He was humble and walked the path of obedience all the way to death—his death on the cross.[4]—The Father loves me because I am willing to give up my life, in order that I may receive it back again.[5]—I have come down from heaven to do not my own will but the will of him who sent me.[6]—Do you think that I will not drink the cup of suffering which my Father has given me?[7]

He who sent me is with me; he has not left me alone, because I always do what pleases him.[8]—My own dear Son, with whom I am pleased.[9]—The one I have chosen, with whom I am pleased.[10]

[1]ISA. 53.10. [2]John 12.27, 28.—[3]Luke 22.42, 43. [4]Phil. 2.8.—[5]John 10.17.—[6]John 6.38.—[7]John 18.11. [8]John 8.29.—[9]Matt. 3.17.—[10]Isa. 42.1.

Evening

They must remind the Lord of his promises and never let him forget them.[1]

You have made them a kingdom of priests to serve our God.[2]—The trumpets are to be blown by Aaron's sons, the priests. The following rule is to be observed for all time to come. When you are at war in your land, defending yourselves against an enemy who has attacked you, sound the signal for battle on these trumpets. I, the Lord your God, will help you and save you from your enemies.[3]

I did not require the people of Israel to look for me in a desolate waste.[4]—In his home in heaven God heard their prayers and accepted them.[5]—The Lord watches over the righteous and listens to their cries.[6]—Pray for one another . . . the prayer of a good person has a powerful effect.[7]

Come, Lord Jesus![8]—My God—hurry to my aid![9]—Wait for the Day of God and do your best to make it come soon.[10]

[1]ISA. 62.6. [2]Rev. 5.10.—[3]Num. 10.8, 9. [4]Isa. 45.19.—[5]2 Chr. 30.27.—[6]Ps. 34.15.—[7]Jas 5.16. [8]Rev. 22.20.—[9]Ps. 40.17.—[10]2 Pet. 3.12.

To have faith is to be sure of the things we hope for, to be certain of the things we cannot see.[1]

If our hope in Christ is good for this life only and no more, then we deserve more pity than anyone else in all the world.[2]

What no one ever saw or heard, what no one ever thought could happen, is the very thing God prepared for those who love him. It was to us that God made known his secret by means of his Spirit.[3]—You believed in Christ, and God put his stamp of ownership on you by giving you the Holy Spirit he had promised. The Spirit is the guarantee that we shall receive what God has promised his people.[4]

Jesus said to [Thomas], "Do you believe because you see me? How happy are those who believe without seeing me!"[5]—You love him, although you have not seen him, and you believe in him, although you do not now see him. So you rejoice with a great and glorious joy which words cannot express, because you are receiving the salvation of your souls, which is the purpose of your faith in him.[6]

Our life is a matter of faith, not of sight.[7]—Do not lose your courage . . . because it brings with it a great reward.[8]

[1]HEB. 11.1. [2]1 Cor. 15.19. [3]1 Cor. 2.9, 10.—[4]Eph. 1.13, 14. [5]John 20.29.— [6]1 Pet. 1.8, 9. [7]2 Cor. 5.7.—[8]Heb. 10.35.

Evening

Don't be afraid . . . it is I![1]

When I saw him, I fell down at his feet like a dead man. He placed his right hand on me and said, "Don't be afraid! I am the first and the last. I am the living one! I was dead, but now I am alive for ever and ever. I have authority over death and the world of the dead.[2]—I am the God who forgives your sins, and I do this because of who I am. I will not hold your sins against you.[3]

"There is no hope for me! I am doomed . . . with my own eyes I have seen the King, the LORD Almighty!" Then one of the creatures flew down to me, carrying a burning coal that he had taken from the altar with a pair of tongs. He touched my lips with the burning coal and said, "This has touched your lips, and now your guilt is gone, and your sins are forgiven."[4]—I have swept your sins away like a cloud. Come back to me; I am the one who saves you.[5]

If anyone does sin, we have someone who pleads with the Father on our behalf—Jesus Christ, the righteous one.[6]

[1]JOHN 6.20. [2]Rev. 1.17, 18.—[3]Isa. 43.25. [4]Isa. 6.5–7.—[5]Isa. 44.22. [6]1 John 2.1.

The Son of God appeared for this very reason, to destroy what the Devil had done.[1]

We are not fighting against human beings but against the wicked spiritual forces in the heavenly world, the rulers, authorities, and cosmic powers of this dark age.[2]—Since the children, as he calls them, are people of flesh and blood, Jesus himself became like them and shared their human nature. He did this so that through his death he might destroy the Devil.[3]—Christ freed himself from the power of the spiritual rulers and authorities; he made a public spectacle of them by leading them as captives in his victory procession.[4]—Then I heard a loud voice in heaven saying, "Now God's salvation has come! Now God has shown his power as King! Now his Messiah has shown his authority! For the one who stood before our God and accused our brothers day and night has been thrown out of heaven. Our brothers won the victory over him by the blood of the Lamb and by the truth which they proclaimed; and they were willing to give up their lives and die."[5]

Thanks be to God who gives us the victory through our Lord Jesus Christ![6]

[1]1 JOHN 3.8. [2]Eph. 6.12.—[3]Heb. 2.14.—[4]Col. 2.15.—[5]Rev. 12.10, 11. [6]1 Cor. 15.57.

Evening

Life is useless, all useless.[1]

Our life is cut short by your anger; it fades away like a whisper. Seventy years is all we have—eighty years, if we are strong; yet all they bring us is trouble and sorrow; life is soon over, and we are gone.[2]

If our hope in Christ is good for this life only and no more, then we deserve more pity than anyone else in all the world.[3]—There is no permanent city for us here on earth; we are looking for the city which is to come.[4]—I am the LORD, and I do not change.[5]—We . . . are citizens of heaven, and we eagerly wait for our Saviour, the Lord Jesus Christ, to come from heaven. He will change our weak mortal bodies and make them like his own glorious body, using that power by which he is able to bring all things under his rule.[6]—Creation was condemned to lose its purpose, not of its own will, but because God willed it to be so.[7]

Jesus Christ is the same yesterday, today, and for ever.[8]—Holy, holy, holy, is the Lord God Almighty, who was, who is, and who is to come.[9]

[1]ECCLES. 1.2. [2]Ps. 90.9, 10. [3]1 Cor. 15.19.—[4]Heb. 13.14.—[5]Mal. 3.6.— [6]Phil. 3.20, 21.—[7]Rom. 8.20. [8]Heb. 13.8.—[9]Rev. 4.8.

Come back to your right senses and stop your sinful ways.[1]

All of you are people who belong to the light, who belong to the day. So then, we should not be sleeping like the others; we should be awake and sober.[2]

The time has come for you to wake up from your sleep. For the moment when we will be saved is closer now than it was when we first believed. The night is nearly over, day is almost here. Let us stop doing the things that belong to the dark, and let us take up weapons for fighting in the light.[3]—Put on God's armour now! Then when the evil day comes, you will be able to resist the enemy's attacks; and after fighting to the end, you will still hold your ground.[4]—Give up all the evil you have been doing, and get yourselves new minds and hearts.[5]—Get rid of every filthy habit and all wicked conduct. Submit to God and accept the word that he plants in your hearts, which is able to save you.[6]—My children, remain in union with him, so that when he appears we may be full of courage and need not hide in shame from him on the Day he comes. You know that Christ is righteous; you should know, then, that everyone who does what is right is God's child.[7]

[1]1 COR. 15.34. [2]1 Thess. 5.5, 6. [3]Rom. 13.11, 12.—[4]Eph. 6.13.—[5]Ezek. 18.31.—[6]Jas 1.21.—[7]1 John 2.28, 29.

Evening

My sheep listen to my voice.[1]

Listen! I stand at the door and knock; if anyone hears my voice and opens the door, I will come into his house and eat with him, and he will eat with me.[2]

While I slept, my heart was awake. I dreamt my lover knocked at the door. I opened the door for my lover, but he had already gone. How I wanted to hear his voice! I looked for him, but couldn't find him; I called to him, but heard no answer.[3]

Speak; your servant is listening.[4]—When Jesus came to that place, he looked up and said to Zacchaeus, "Hurry down, Zacchaeus, because I must stay in your house today." Zacchaeus hurried down and welcomed him with great joy.[5]—I am listening to what the LORD God is saying; he promises peace to us, his own people, if we do not go back to our foolish ways.[6]

[1]JOHN 10.27. [2]Rev. 3.20. [3]S. of S. 5.2, 6. [4]1 Sam. 3.10.—[5]Luke 19.5, 6.—[6]Ps. 85.8.

Morning

Dear friends, let us love one another, because love comes from God. Whoever loves is a child of God and knows God.[1]

God has poured out his love into our hearts by means of the Holy Spirit, who is God's gift to us.[2]—The Spirit that God has given you does not make you slaves and cause you to be afraid; instead, the Spirit makes you God's children, and by the Spirit's power we cry out to God, "Father! my Father!" God's Spirit joins himself to our spirits to declare that we are God's children.[3]—Whoever believes in the Son of God has this testimony in his own heart. The testimony is this: God has given us eternal life, and this life has its source in his Son.[4]

God showed his love for us by sending his only Son . . . so that we might have life through him.[5]—By the sacrificial death of Christ we are set free, that is, our sins are forgiven.[6]—He did this to demonstrate for all time to come the extraordinary greatness of his grace in the love he showed us in Christ Jesus.[7]

Dear friends, if this is how God loved us, then we should love one another.[8]

[1]1 JOHN 4.7. [2]Rom. 5.5.—[3]Rom. 8.15, 16.—[4]1 John 5.10, 11. [5]1 John 4.9.—[6]Eph. 1.7.—[7]Eph. 2.7. [8]1 John 4.11.

Evening

Insults have broken my heart.[1]

Isn't he the carpenter's son?[2]—Can anything good come from Nazareth?[3]—Were we not right in saying that you are a Samaritan and have a demon in you?[4]—It is the chief of the demons who gives him the power to drive out demons.[5]—We know that this man who cured you is a sinner.[6]—He is misleading the people.[7]—This man is speaking blasphemy![8]—Look at this man! He is a glutton and a drinker, a friend of tax collectors and other outcasts![9]

A pupil should be satisfied to become like his teacher, and a slave like his master.[10]—God will bless you for this, if you endure the pain of undeserved suffering because you are conscious of his will. It was to this that God called you, for Christ himself suffered for you and left you an example, so that you would follow in his steps. He committed no sin, and no one ever heard a lie come from his lips. When he was insulted, he did not answer back with an insult; when he suffered, he did not threaten, but placed his hopes in God, the righteous Judge.[11]—Happy are you if you are insulted because you are Christ's followers.[12]

[1]PS. 69.20. [2]Matt. 13.55.—[3]John 1.46.—[4]John 8.48.—[5]Matt. 9.34.—[6]John 9.24.—[7]John 7.12.—[8]Matt. 9.3.—[9]Matt. 11.19. [10]Matt. 10.25.—[11]1 Pet. 2.19, 21–23.—[12]1 Pet. 4.14.

Lift up their hands in prayer without anger or argument.[1]

People will worship the Father as he really is, offering him the true worship that he wants. God is Spirit, and only by the power of his Spirit can people worship him as he really is.[2]—When you pray, I will answer you. When you call to me, I will respond.[3]—When you stand and pray, forgive anything you may have against anyone.[4]

No one can please God without faith, for whoever comes to God must have faith that God exists and rewards those who seek him.[5]—When you pray, you must believe and not doubt at all. Whoever doubts is like a wave in the sea that is driven and blown about by the wind. A person like that . . . must not think that he will receive anything from the Lord.[6]

If I had ignored my sins, the Lord would not have listened to me.[7]—I am writing this to you, my children, so that you will not sin; but if anyone does sin, we have someone who pleads with the Father on our behalf—Jesus Christ, the righteous one.[8]

[1]1 TIM. 2.8. [2]John 4.23, 24.—[3]Isa. 58.9.—[4]Mark 11.25. [5]Heb. 11.6.—[6]Jas 1.6–8. [7]Ps. 66.18.—[8]1 John 2.1.

Evening

My heart is pounding, my strength is gone.[1]

Hear my cry, O God; listen to my prayer! In despair and far from home I call to you! Take me to a safe refuge.[2]

His answer was: "My grace is all you need, for my power is greatest when you are weak." I am most happy, then, to be proud of my weaknesses, in order to feel the protection of Christ's power over me. For when I am weak, then I am strong.[3]

When [Peter] noticed the strong wind, he was afraid and started to sink down in the water. "Save me, Lord!" he cried. At once Jesus reached out and grabbed hold of him and said, "How little faith you have! Why did you doubt?"[4]—If you are weak in a crisis, you are weak indeed.[5]—He strengthens those who are weak and tired.[6]—God has always been your defence; his eternal arms are your support.[7]—May you be made strong with all the strength which comes from his glorious power.[8]

[1]PS. 38.10. [2]Ps. 61.1, 2. [3]2 Cor. 12.9, 10. [4]Matt. 14.30, 31.—[5]Prov. 24.10.— [6]Isa. 40.29.—[7]Deut. 33.27.—[8]Col. 1.11.

To share in his sufferings.[1]

A pupil should be satisfied to become like his teacher, and a slave like his master.[2]

We despised him and rejected him; he endured suffering and pain. No one would even look at him—we ignored him as if he were nothing.[3]—I chose you from this world, and you do not belong to it; that is why the world hates you.[4]

I had hoped for sympathy, but there was none.[5]—No one stood by me the first time I defended myself; all deserted me.[6]

Foxes have holes, and birds have nests, but the Son of Man has nowhere to lie down and rest.[7]—There is no permanent city for us here on earth; we are looking for the city which is to come.[8]

Let us run with determination the race that lies before us. Let us keep our eyes fixed on Jesus, on whom our faith depends from beginning to end. He did not give up because of the cross! On the contrary, because of the joy that was waiting for him, he thought nothing of the disgrace of dying on the cross, and he is now seated at the right-hand side of God's throne.[9]

PHIL. 3.10. [2]Matt. 10.25. [3]Isa. 53.3.—[4]John 15.19. [5]Ps. 69.20.—[6]2 Tim. 4.16. [7]Matt. 8.20.—[8]Heb. 13.14. [9]Heb. 12.1, 2.

Evening

Our brothers won the victory over him by the blood of the Lamb.[1]

Who will accuse God's chosen people? God himself declares them not guilty! Who, then, will condemn them? Not Christ Jesus, who died.[2]—Blood, which is life, takes away sins.[3]—I am the LORD. The blood on the door-posts will be a sign to mark the houses in which you live. When I see the blood, I will pass over you.[4]

There is no condemnation now for those who live in union with Christ Jesus.[5]

Who are these people dressed in white robes, and where do they come from? These are the people who have come safely through the terrible persecution. They have washed their robes and made them white with the blood of the Lamb.[6]

He loves us, and by his sacrificial death he has freed us from our sins and made us a kingdom of priests to serve his God and Father. To Jesus Christ be the glory and power for ever and ever! Amen.[7]

[1]REV. 12.11. [2]Rom. 8.33, 34.—[3]Lev. 17.11.—[4]Exod. 12.12, 13. [5]Rom. 8.1. [6]Rev. 7.13, 14. [7]Rev. 1.5, 6.

He will wipe away all tears from their eyes. There will be no more death, no more grief or crying or pain. The old things have disappeared.[1]

The Sovereign LORD will destroy death for ever! He will wipe away the tears from everyone's eyes and take away the disgrace his people have suffered throughout the world. The LORD himself has spoken![2]—No longer will the sun be your light by day or the moon be your light by night: I, the LORD, will be your eternal light . . . your days of grief will come to an end.[3]—No one who lives in our land will ever again complain of being ill, and all sins will be forgiven.[4]—There will be no weeping there, no calling for help.[5]—For ever free from sorrow and grief.[6]

The last enemy to be defeated will be death. Then the scripture will come true: "Death is destroyed; victory is complete![7]—What cannot be seen lasts for ever.[8]

[1]REV. 21.4. [2]Isa. 25.8.—[3]Isa. 60.19, 20.—[4]Isa. 33.24.—[5]Isa. 65.19.—[6]Isa. 35.10. [7]1 Cor. 15.26, 54.—[8]2 Cor. 4.18.

Evening

In our union with Christ Jesus he raised us up with him.[1]

Don't be afraid! I am the living one![2]—Father! You have given them to me, and I want them to be with me where I am.[3]

We are members of his body.[4]—He is the head of his body, the church; he is the source of the body's life. He is the first-born Son, who was raised from death.[5]—You have been given full life in union with him. He is supreme.[6]

Since the children, as he calls them, are people of flesh and blood, Jesus himself became like them and shared their human nature. He did this so that through his death he might destroy the Devil, who has the power over death, and in this way set free those who were slaves all their lives because of their fear of death.[7]

For what is mortal must be changed into what is immortal; what will die must be changed into what cannot die. So when this takes place, and the mortal has been changed into the immortal, then the scripture will come true: "Death is destroyed; victory is complete!"[8]

[1]EPH. 2.6. [2]Rev. 1.17, 18.—[3]John 17.24. [4]Eph. 5.30.—[5]Col. 1.18.—[6]Col. 2.10. [7]Heb. 2.14, 15. [8]1 Cor. 15.53, 54.

A servant of Christ Jesus.[1]

You call me Teacher and Lord, and it is right that you do so, because that is what I am.[2]—Whoever wants to serve me must follow me, so that my servant will be with me where I am. And my Father will honour anyone who serves me.[3]—Take my yoke and put it on you, and learn from me, because I am gentle and humble in spirit; and you will find rest. For the yoke I will give you is easy, and the load I will put on you is light.[4]

All those things that I might count as profit I now reckon as loss for Christ's sake.[5]—Now you have been set free from sin and are the slaves of God. Your gain is a life fully dedicated to him, and the result is eternal life.[6]

I do not call you servants any longer, because a servant does not know what his master is doing. Instead, I call you friends, because I have told you everything I have heard from my Father.[7]—You are no longer a slave but a son.[8]

Stand, then, as free people, and do not allow yourselves to become slaves again. My brothers, you were called to be free. But do not let this freedom become an excuse for letting your physical desires control you.[9]

[1]ROM. 1.1. [2]John 13.13.—[3]John 12.26.—[4]Matt. 11.29, 30. [5]Phil. 3.7.—[6]Rom. 6.22. [7]John 15.15.—[8]Gal. 4.7. [9]Gal. 5.1, 13.

Evening

I praise the LORD, *because he guides me.*[1]

He will be called "Wonderful Counsellor".[2]—I make plans and carry them out. I have understanding, and I am strong.[3]—Your word is a lamp to guide me and a light for my path.[4]—Trust in the LORD with all your heart. Never rely on what you think you know. Remember the LORD in everything you do, and he will show you the right way.[5]

LORD, I know that no one is the master of his own destiny; no person has control over his own life.[6]—If you wander off the road to the right or the left, you will hear his voice behind you saying, "Here is the road. Follow it."[7]—Ask the LORD to bless your plans, and you will be successful in carrying them out.[8]—The LORD has determined our path; how then can anyone understand the direction his own life is taking?[9]

You guide me with your instruction and at the end you will receive me with honour.[10] —This God is our God for ever and ever; he will lead us for all time to come.[11]

[1]PS. 16.7. [2]Isa. 9.6.—[3]Prov. 8.14.—[4]Ps. 119.105.—[5]Prov. 3.5, 6. [6]Jer. 10.23.—[7]Isa. 30.21.—[8]Prov. 16.3.—[9]Prov. 20.24. [10]Ps. 73.24.—[11]Ps. 48.14.

I am the Lord your God. Obey my laws and my commands.[1]

Be holy in all that you do, just as God who called you is holy.[2]—Whoever says that he remains in union with God should live just as Jesus Christ did. You know that Christ is righteous; you should know, then, that everyone who does what is right is God's child.[3]—Whether or not a man is circumcised means nothing; what matters is to obey God's commandments.[4]—Whoever breaks one commandment is guilty of breaking them all.[5]

There is nothing in us that allows us to claim that we are capable of doing this work. The capacity we have comes from God.[6]—Teach me, Lord, the meaning of your laws.[7]

Keep on working with fear and trembling to complete your salvation, because God is always at work in you to make you willing and able to obey his own purpose.[8]—May the God of peace provide you with every good thing you need in order to do his will, and may he, through Jesus Christ, do in us what pleases him.[9]

[1]EZEK. 20.19. [2]1 Pet. 1.15.—[3]1 John 2.6, 29.—[4]1 Cor. 7.19.—[5]Jas 2.10. [6]2 Cor. 3.5.—[7]Ps. 119.33. [8]Phil. 2.12, 13.—[9]Heb. 13.20, 21.

Evening

I have given the throne to one I chose from the people.[1]

It is clear that it is not the angels that he helps. Instead, as the scripture says, "He helps the descendants of Abraham." This means that he had to become like his brothers in every way.[2]—Sitting on the throne was a figure that looked like a man.[3]—The Son of Man, who came down from heaven.[4]—Look at my hands and my feet, and see that it is I myself. Feel me, and you will know, for a ghost doesn't have flesh and bones, as you can see I have.[5]

Of his own free will he gave up all he had, and took the nature of a servant. He became like man and appeared in human likeness. He was humble and walked the path of obedience all the way to death—his death on the cross. For this reason God raised him to the highest place above and gave him the name that is greater than any other name. And so, in honour of the name of Jesus all beings in heaven, on earth, and in the world below will fall on their knees.[6]—Wake up, and strengthen what you still have before it dies completely. For I find that what you have done is not yet perfect in the sight of my God.[7]

[1]PS. 89.19. [2]Heb. 2.16, 17.—[3]Ezek. 1.26.—[4]John 3.13.—[5]Luke 24.39. [6]Phil. 2.7–10.—[7]Rev. 3.2.

Just as the Father is himself the source of life, in the same way he has made his Son to be the source of life.[1]

Our Saviour, Christ Jesus . . . has ended the power of death and through the gospel has revealed immortal life.[2]—I am the resurrection and the life.[3]—Because I live, you also will live.[4]—We are all partners with Christ.[5]—They . . . received their share of the Holy Spirit.[6]—You . . . may come to share the divine nature.[7]—The first man, Adam, was created a living being; but the last Adam is the life-giving Spirit. Listen to this secret truth: we shall not all die, but when the last trumpet sounds, we shall all be changed in an instant, as quickly as the blinking of an eye. For when the trumpet sounds, the dead will be raised, never to die again, and we shall all be changed.[8]

Holy, holy, holy, is the Lord God Almighty, who was, who is, and who is to come . . . who lives for ever and ever.[9]—God, the blessed and only Ruler, the King of kings and the Lord of lords. He alone is immortal.[10]—To the eternal King . . . be honour and glory for ever and ever! Amen.[11]

[1]JOHN 5.26. [2]2 Tim. 1.10.—[3]John 11.25.—[4]John 14.19.—[5]Heb. 3.14.—[6]Heb. 6.4.—[7]2 Pet. 1.4.—[8]1 Cor. 15.45, 51, 52. [9]Rev. 4.8, 9.—[10]1 Tim. 6.15, 16.—[11]1 Tim. 1.17.

Evening

We must not be proud.[1]

[Gideon] . . . went on to say, "Let me ask one thing of you. Every one of you give me the earrings you took." (The Midianites, like other desert people, wore gold earrings.) The people answered, "We'll be glad to give them to you." They spread out a cloth, and everyone put on it the earrings that he had taken. Gideon made an idol from the gold and put it in his home town, Ophrah. All the Israelites abandoned God and went there to worship the idol.[2]

Are you looking for special treatment for yourself? Don't do it.[3]—To keep me from being puffed up with pride because of the many wonderful things I saw, I was given a painful physical ailment.[4]

Don't do anything from selfish ambition or from a cheap desire to boast, but be humble toward one another, always considering others better than yourselves.[5]—Love is patient and kind; it is not jealous or conceited or proud; love is not ill-mannered or selfish.[6]

Take my yoke and put it on you, and learn from me.[7]

[1]GAL. 5.26. [2]Judg. 8.24, 25, 27. [3]Jer. 45.5.—[4]2 Cor. 12.7. [5]Phil. 2.3.—[6]1 Cor. 13.4, 5. [7]Matt. 11.29.

Wash away all my evil and make me clean from my sin![1]

I will purify them from the sins that they have committed against me, and I will forgive their sins and their rebellion.[2]—I will sprinkle clean water on you and make you clean from all your idols and everything else that has defiled you.[3]

No one can enter the Kingdom of God unless he is born of water and the Spirit.[4]—The blood of goats and bulls and the ashes of a burnt calf are sprinkled on the people who are ritually unclean, and this purifies them by taking away their ritual impurity. Since this is true, how much more is accomplished by the blood of Christ! Through the eternal Spirit he offered himself as a perfect sacrifice to God. His blood will purify our consciences from useless rituals, so that we may serve the living God.[5]

He saved them, as he had promised, in order to show his great power.[6]—To you alone, O LORD, to you alone, and not to us, must glory be given because of your constant love and faithfulness.[7]

[1]PS. 51.2. [2]Jer. 33.8.—[3]Ezek. 36.25. [4]John 3.5.—[5]Heb. 9.13, 14. [6]Ps. 106.8.—[7]Ps. 115.1.

Evening

You have helped me in the work of the gospel.[1]

Christ is like a single body, which has many parts; it is still one body, even though it is made up of different parts. In the same way, all of us, whether Jews or Gentiles, whether slaves or free, have been baptized into the one body by the same Spirit, and we have all been given the one Spirit to drink.[2]

God is to be trusted, the God who called you to have fellowship with his Son Jesus Christ, our Lord.[3]—What we have seen and heard we announce to you also, so that you will join with us in the fellowship that we have with the Father and with his Son Jesus Christ.[4]

If we live in the light—just as he is in the light.—then we have fellowship with one another, and the blood of Jesus, his Son, purifies us from every sin.[5]—Jesus . . . looked up to heaven and said, "I pray not only for them, but also for those who believe in me because of their message. I pray that they may all be one. Father! May they be in us, just as you are in me and I am in you. May they be one."[6]

[1]PHIL. 1.5. [2]1 Cor. 12.12, 13. [3]1 Cor. 1.9.—[4]1 John 1.3. [5]1 John 1.7.— [6]John 17.1, 20, 21.

Morning

Watch yourself.[1]

Every athlete in training submits to strict discipline, in order to be crowned with a wreath that will not last; but we do it for one that will last for ever. That is why I run straight for the finishing-line; that is why I am like a boxer who does not waste his punches. I harden my body with blows and bring it under complete control, to keep myself from being disqualified after having called others to the contest.[2]—Put on all the armour that God gives you, so that you will be able to stand up against the Devil's evil tricks. For we are not fighting against human beings but against the wicked spiritual forces in the heavenly world, the rulers, authorities, and cosmic powers of this dark age.[3]

Those who belong to Christ Jesus have put to death their human nature with all its passions and desires. The Spirit has given us life; he must also control our lives.[4]—Those who are led by God's Spirit are God's sons.[5]—Practise these things and devote yourself to them, in order that your progress may be seen by all.[6]

[1] 1 TIM. 4.16. [2]1 Cor. 9.25–27.—[3]Eph. 6.11, 12. [4]Gal. 5.24, 25.—[5]Rom. 8.14.—[6]1 Tim. 4.15.

Evening

Jesus said to her, "Mary!"[1]

Do not be afraid—I will save you. I have called you by name—you are mine.[2]—The sheep hear his voice as he calls his own sheep by name, and he leads them out. And the sheep follow him, because they know his voice.[3]

I can never forget you! I have written your name on the palms of my hands.[4]

The solid foundation that God has laid cannot be shaken; and on it are written these words: "The Lord knows those who are his."[5]—We have a great High Priest who has gone into the very presence of God—Jesus the Son of God.[6]

Take two carnelian stones and engrave on them the names of the twelve sons of Jacob. Aaron will carry their names on his shoulders, so that I, the LORD, will always remember my people. Make a breast-piece . . . to use in determining God's will. Mount four rows of precious stones on it. Each is to have engraved on it the name of one of the sons of Jacob. Aaron will carry them . . . into my holy presence.[7]

[1]JOHN 20.16. [2]Isa. 43.1.—[3]John 10.3, 4. [4]Isa. 49.16. [5]2 Tim. 2.19.—[6]Heb. 4.14. [7]Exod. 28.9, 12, 15, 17, 21, 30.

Build up your strength in union with the Lord and by means of his mighty power.[1]

My grace is all you need, for my power is greatest when you are weak. I am most happy, then, to be proud of my weaknesses, in order to feel the protection of Christ's power over me. I am content with weaknesses, insults, hardships, persecutions, and difficulties for Christ's sake. For when I am weak, then I am strong.[2]—I will praise your power, Sovereign Lord; I will proclaim your goodness, yours alone.[3]—I have complete confidence in the gospel; it is God's power to save all who believe.[4]

I have the strength to face all conditions by the power that Christ gives me.[5]—I toil and struggle, using the mighty strength which Christ supplies and which is at work in me.[6]—We who have this spiritual treasure are like common clay pots, in order to show that the supreme power belongs to God, not to us.[7]

The joy that the Lord gives you will make you strong.[8]—May you be made strong with all the strength which comes from his glorious power, so that you may be able to endure everything with patience. And with joy give thanks to the Father.[9]

[1]EPH. 6.10. [2]2 Cor. 12.9, 10.—[3]Ps. 71.16.—[4]Rom. 1.16. [5]Phil. 4.13.—[6]Col. 1.29.—[7]2 Cor. 4.7. [8]Neh. 8.10.—[9]Col. 1.11.

Evening

Jesus Christ, our Lord.[1]

Jesus—because he will save his people from their sins.[2]—He was humble and walked the path of obedience all the way to death—his death on the cross. For this reason God raised him to the highest place above and gave him the name that is greater than any other name. And so, in honour of the name of Jesus all beings in heaven, on earth, and in the world below will fall on their knees.[3]

The Messiah will come.[4]—The Sovereign Lord . . . has chosen me and sent me to bring good news to the poor, to heal the broken-hearted, to announce release to captives.[5]

The last Adam is the life-giving Spirit. The second Adam came from heaven.[6]—My Lord and my God![7]—You call me Teacher and Lord, and it is right that you do so, because that is what I am. I, your Lord and Teacher, have just washed your feet. You, then, should wash one another's feet. I have set an example for you, so that you will do just what I have done for you.[8]

[1]1 COR. 1.9. [2]Matt. 1.21.—[3]Phil. 2.8–10. [4]John 4.25.—[5]Isa. 61.1. [6]1 Cor. 15.45, 47.—[7]John 20.28.—[8]John 13.13–15.

Morning

Peace is what I leave with you; it is my own peace that I give you. I do not give it as the world does.[1]

The world and everything in it that people desire is passing away.[2]—Every living man is no more than a puff of wind, no more than a shadow. All he does is for nothing; he gathers wealth, but doesn't know who will get it.[3]—What did you gain from doing the things that you are now ashamed of? The result of those things is death![4]

Martha, Martha! You are worried and troubled over so many things, but just one is needed. Mary has chosen the right thing, and it will not be taken away from her.[5]—I would like you to be free from worry.[6]

I have told you this so that you will have peace by being united to me. The world will make you suffer. But be brave! I have defeated the world![7]—May the LORD himself, who is our source of peace, give you peace at all times and in every way.[8]—May the LORD bless you and take care of you; may the LORD be kind and gracious to you; may the LORD look on you with favour and give you peace.[9]

[1]JOHN 14.17. [2]1 John 2.17.—[3]Ps. 39.5, 6.—[4]Rom. 6.21. [5]Luke 10.41, 42.—[6]1 Cor. 7.32. [7]John 16.33.—[8]2 Thess. 3.16.—[9]Num. 6.24–26.

Evening

The Spirit . . . comes to help us, weak as we are.[1]

The Helper, the Holy Spirit.[2]—Don't you know that your body is the temple of the Holy Spirit, who lives in you and who was given to you by God?[3]—God is always at work in you.[4]

We do not know how we ought to pray; the Spirit himself pleads with God for us in groans that words cannot express. And God, who sees into our hearts, knows what the thought of the Spirit is; because the Spirit pleads with God on behalf of his people and in accordance with his will.[5]

He knows what we are made of; he remembers that we are dust.[6]—He will not break off a bent reed or put out a flickering lamp.[7]

The spirit is willing, but the flesh is weak.[8]

The LORD is my shepherd; I have everything I need. He lets me rest in fields of green grass and leads me to quiet pools of fresh water.[9]

[1]ROM. 8.26. [2]John 14.26.—[3]1 Cor. 6.19.—[4]Phil. 2.13. [5]Rom. 8.26, 27. [6]Ps. 103.14.—[7]Isa. 42.3. [8]Matt. 26.41. [9]Ps. 23.1, 2.

Put [the two stones] on the shoulder-straps of the ephod to represent the twelve tribes of Israel. In this way Aaron will carry their names on his shoulders, so that I, the LORD, will always remember my people.[1]

Jesus lives on for ever, and his work as priest does not pass on to someone else. And so he is able, now and always, to save those who come to God through him, because he lives for ever to plead with God for them.[2]—Him who is able to keep you from falling, and to bring you faultless and joyful before his glorious presence.[3]

Let us . . . hold firmly to the faith we profess. For we have a great High Priest who has gone into the very presence of God—Jesus, the Son of God. Our High Priest is not one who cannot feel sympathy for our weaknesses. On the contrary, we have a High Priest who was tempted in every way that we are, but did not sin. Let us have confidence, then, and approach God's throne, where there is grace.[4]

This is the tribe the LORD loves and protects; he guards them all the day long, and he dwells in their midst.[5]

[1]EXOD. 28.12. [2]Heb. 7.24, 25.—[3]Jude 24. [4]Heb. 4.14–16. [5]Deut. 33.12.

Evening

That same night the king could not get to sleep.[1]

He keeps me awake.[2]—There is no one like the LORD our God. He bends down to see the heavens and the earth.[3]

Angels in Heaven and people on earth are under his control. No one can oppose his will or question what he does.[4]—You walked through the waves; you crossed the deep sea, but your footprints could not be seen.[5]—Men's anger only results in more praise for you; those who survive the wars will keep your festivals.[6]

The LORD keeps close watch over the whole world, to give strength to those whose hearts are loyal to him.[7]—We know that in all things God works for good with those who love him.[8]

For only a penny you can buy two sparrows, yet not one sparrow falls to the ground without your Father's consent. As for you, even the hairs of your head have all been counted.[9]

[1]ESTHER 6.1. [2]Ps. 77.4.—[3]Ps. 113.5, 6. [4]Dan. 4.35.—[5]Ps. 77.19.—[6]Ps. 76.10. [7]2 Chr. 16.9.—[8]Rom. 8.28. [9]Matt. 10.29, 30.

Do not make God's Holy Spirit sad; for the Spirit is God's mark of ownership on you, a guarantee that the Day will come when God will set you free.[1]

The love that the Spirit gives.[2]—The Helper, the Holy Spirit.[3]—He saved them from all their suffering. It was not an angel, but the LORD himself who saved them. In his love and compassion he rescued them. He had always taken care of them in the past, but they rebelled against him and made his holy spirit sad. So the LORD became their enemy and fought against them.[4]

We are sure that we live in union with God and that he lives in union with us, because he has given us his Spirit.[5]—You believed in Christ, and God put his stamps of ownership on you by giving you the Holy Spirit he had promised. The Spirit is the guarantee that we shall receive what God has promised his people, and this assures us that God will give complete freedom to those who are his.[6]—What I say is this: let the Spirit direct your lives, and you will not satisfy the desires of the human nature. For what our human nature wants is opposed to what the Spirit wants, and what the Spirit wants is opposed to what our human nature wants. These two are enemies, and this means that you cannot do what you want to do.[7]

The Spirit . . . comes to help us, weak as we are.[8]

[1]EPH. 4.30. [2]Rom. 15.30.—[3]John 14.26.—[4]Isa. 63.9, 10. [5]1 John 4.13.—[6]Eph. 1.13, 14.—[7]Gal. 5.16, 17. [8]Rom. 8.26.

Evening

I will abandon my people until they have suffered enough for their sins and come looking for me.[1]

It is because of your sins that he doesn't hear you. It is your sins that separate you from God when you try to worship him.[2]—My lover . . . had already gone. I looked for him, but couldn't find him; I called to him, but heard no answer.[3]—I punished them and abandoned them. But they were stubborn and kept on going their own way. I have seen how they acted, but I will heal them.[4]—You brought this on yourself! You deserted me, the LORD your God, while I was leading you along the way.[5]

He got up and started back to his father. He was still a long way from home when his father saw him; his heart was filled with pity, and he ran, threw his arms round his son, and kissed him.[6]—I will bring my people back to me. I will love them with all my heart; no longer am I angry with them.[7]

If we confess our sins to God, he will keep his promise and do what is right: he will forgive us our sins and purify us from all our wrongdoing.[8]

[1]HOS. 5.15. [2]Isa. 59.2.—[3]S. of S. 5.6.—[4]Isa. 57.17, 18.—[5]Jer. 2.17. [6]Luke 15.20.—[7]Hos. 14.4. [8]1 John 1.9.

How wonderful are the good things you keep for those who honour you![1]

No one has ever seen or heard of a God like you, who does such deeds for those who put their hope in him.[2]—What no one ever saw or heard, what no one ever thought could happen, is the very thing God prepared for those who love him. But it was to us that God made known his secret by means of his Spirit.[3]—You will show me the path that leads to life; your presence fills me with joy and brings me pleasure for ever.[4]

How precious, O God, is your constant love! We find protection under the shadow of your wings. We feast on the abundant food you provide; you let us drink from the river of your goodness.[5]

Spiritual exercise is valuable in every way, because it promises life both for the present and for the future.[6]

[1]PS. 31.19. [2]Isa. 64.4.—[3]1 Cor. 2.9, 10.—[4]Ps. 16.11. [5]Ps. 36.7, 8. [6]1 Tim. 4.8.

Evening

The Son of God, whose eyes blaze like fire.[1]

Who can understand the human heart? There is nothing else so deceitful; it is too sick to be healed. I, the LORD, search the minds and test the hearts of men. I treat each one according to the way he lives, according to what he does.[2]—You place our sins before you, our secret sins where you can see them.[3]—The Lord turned round and looked straight at Peter. Peter went out and wept bitterly.[4]

Jesus did not trust himself to them, because he knew them all. There was no need for anyone to tell him about them, because he himself knew what was in their hearts.[5]—He knows what we are made of; he remembers that we are dust.[6]—He will not break off a bent reed or put out a flickering lamp.[7]

The Lord knows those who are his.[8]—I am the good shepherd. I know my sheep. My sheep listen to my voice; I know them, and they follow me. I give them eternal life, and they shall never die. No one can snatch them away from me.[9]

[1]REV. 2.18. [2]Jer. 17.9, 10.—[3]Ps. 90.8.—[4]Luke 22.61, 62. [5]John 2.24, 25.—[6]Ps. 103.14.—[7]Isa. 42.3. [8]2 Tim. 2.19.—[9]John 10.14, 27, 28.

Our Lord Jesus, who is the Great Shepherd of the sheep.[1]

I am the good shepherd. I know my sheep. My sheep listen to my voice; I know them, and they follow me. I give them eternal life, and they shall never die. No one can snatch them away from me.[2]

The LORD is my shepherd; I have everything I need. He lets me rest in fields of green grass and leads me to quiet pools of fresh water. He gives me new strength. He guides me in the right paths, as he has promised.[3]

All of us were like sheep that were lost, each of us going his own way. But the LORD made the punishment fall on him, the punishment all of us deserved.[4]—I am the good shepherd, who is willing to die for the sheep.[5]—I will look for those that are lost, bring back those that wander off, bandage those that are hurt, and heal those that are sick.[6]—You were like sheep that had lost their way, but now you have been brought back to follow the Shepherd and Keeper of your souls.[7]

[1]HEB. 13.20. [2]John 10.14, 27, 28. [3]Ps. 23.1–3. [4]Isa. 53.6.—[5]John 10.11.—[6]Ezek. 34.16.—[7]1 Pet. 2.25.

Evening

The city has no need of the sun or the moon to shine on it, because the glory of God shines on it, and the Lamb is its lamp.[1]

I saw a light much brighter than the sun, coming from the sky and shining round me. "Who are you, Lord?" I asked. And the Lord answered, "I am Jesus, whom you persecute."[2]—Jesus took with him Peter and the brothers James and John and led them up a high mountain where they were alone. As they looked on, a change came over Jesus: his face was shining like the sun, and his clothes were dazzling white.[3]—No longer will the sun be your light by day or the moon be your light by night; I, the LORD, will be your eternal light; the light of my glory will shine on you. Your days of grief will come to an end. I, the LORD, will be your eternal light, more lasting than the sun and moon.[4]

The God of all grace . . . calls you to share his eternal glory in union with Christ.[5]

[1]REV. 21.23. [2]Acts 26.13, 15.—[3]Matt. 17.1, 2.—[4]Isa. 60.19, 20. [5]1 Pet. 5.10.

***The* LORD *is good; he protects his people in times of trouble; he takes care of those who turn to him.*[1]**

Give thanks to the LORD Almighty, because he is good and his love is eternal.[2]—God is our shelter and strength, always ready to help in times of trouble.[3]—You are my defender and protector. You are my God; in you I trust.[4]—Israel, how happy you are! There is no one like you, a nation saved by the LORD. The LORD himself is your shield and your sword.[5]—This God—how perfect are his deeds, how dependable his words! He is like a shield for all who seek his protection. The LORD alone is God; God alone is our defence.[6]

The person who loves God is known by him.[7]—The solid foundation that God has laid cannot be shaken; and on it are written these words: "The Lord knows those who are his" and "Whoever says that he belongs to the Lord must turn away from wrongdoing."[8]—The righteous are guided and protected by the LORD, but the evil are on the way to their doom.[9]—I know you very well and I am pleased with you.[10]

[1]NAHUM 1.7. [2]Jer. 33.11.—[3]Ps. 46.1.—[4]Ps. 91.2.—[5]Deut. 33.29.—[6]2 Sam. 22.31,32. [7]1 Cor. 8.3.—[8]2 Tim. 2.19.—[9]Ps. 1.6.—[10]Exod. 33.17.

Evening

***I would like you to be free from worry.*[1]**

He cares for you.[2]—The LORD keeps close watch over the whole world, to give strength to those whose hearts are loyal to him.[3]

Find out for yourself how good the LORD is. Happy are those who find safety with him. Even lions go hungry for lack of food, but those who obey the LORD lack nothing good.[4]—This is why I tell you not to be worried about the food and drink you need in order to stay alive, or about clothes for your body. After all, isn't life worth more than food? And isn't the body worth more than clothes? Look at the birds: they do not sow seeds, gather a harvest and put it in barns; yet your Father in heaven takes care of them! Aren't you worth much more than birds?[5]—Don't worry about anything, but in all your prayers ask God for what you need, always asking him with a thankful heart. And God's peace, which is far beyond human understanding, will keep your hearts and minds safe in union with Christ Jesus.[6]

[1]1 COR. 7.32. [2]1 Pet. 5.7.—[3]2 Chr. 16.9. [4]Ps. 34.8, 10.—[5]Matt. 6.25, 26.—[6]Phil. 4.6, 7.

Morning

We eagerly wait for our Saviour.[1]

For God has revealed his grace for the salvation of all mankind. That grace instructs us to give up ungodly living and worldly passions, and to live self-controlled, upright and godly lives in this world, as we wait for the blessed Day we hope for, when the glory of our great God and Saviour Jesus Christ will appear. He gave himself for us, to rescue us from all wickedness and to make us a pure people who belong to him alone and are eager to do good.[2]—We wait for what God has promised: new heavens and a new earth, where righteousness will be at home. And so, my friends, as you wait for that Day, do your best to be pure and faultless in God's sight and to be at peace with him.[3]

Christ . . . was offered in sacrifice once to take away the sins of many. He will appear a second time, not to deal with sin, but to save those who are waiting for him.[4]—When it happens, everyone will say, "He is our God! We have put our trust in him, and he has rescued us. He is the LORD! We have put our trust in him, and now we are happy and joyful because he has saved us."[5]

[1]PHIL. 3.20. [2]Titus 2.11–14.—[3]2 Pet. 3.13, 14. [4]Heb. 9.28.—[5]Isa. 25.9.

Evening

Run . . . in such a way as to win the prize.[1]

The lazy man stays at home; he says a lion might get him if he goes outside.[2]—Let us rid ourselves of everything that gets in the way, and of the sin which holds on to us so tightly, and let us run with determination the race that lies before us. Let us keep our eyes fixed on Jesus, on whom our faith depends from beginning to end.[3]

Let us purify ourselves from everything that makes body or soul unclean, and let us be completely holy by living in awe of God.[4]

I run straight towards the goal.[5]—I run straight for the finishing-line. I harden my body with blows and bring it under complete control, to keep myself from being disqualified.[6]

This world, as it is now, will not last much longer.[7]

We wait for what God has promised: new heavens and a new earth, where righteousness will be at home. And so, my friends, as you wait for that Day, do your best to be pure and faultless in God's sight.[8]—Have your minds ready for action. Keep alert and set your hope completely on the blessing which will be given you when Jesus Christ is revealed.[9]

[1]1 COR. 9.24. [2]Prov. 22.13.—[3]Heb. 12.1, 2. [4]2 Cor. 7.1. [5]Phil. 3.14.—[6]1 Cor. 9.26, 27. [7]1 Cor. 7.31. [8]2 Pet. 3.13, 14.—[9]1 Pet. 1.13.

The life of every living thing is in the blood, and that is why the LORD has commanded that all blood be poured out on the altar to take away the people's sins. Blood, which is life, takes away sins. [1]

There is the Lamb of God, who takes away the sin of the world![2]—The blood of the Lamb.[3]—The costly sacrifice of Christ, who was like a lamb without defect or flaw.[4]—Sins are forgiven only if blood is poured out.[5]—The blood of Jesus, his Son, purifies us from every sin.[6]

When Christ . . . entered . . . the Most Holy Place, he . . . took his own blood and obtained eternal salvation for us.[7]—We have, then, my brothers, complete freedom to go into the Most Holy Place by means of the death of Jesus. He opened for us a new way, a living way, through the curtain—that is, through his own body. So let us come near to God with a sincere heart and a sure faith.[8]

He bought you for a price. So use your bodies for God's glory.[9]

[1]LEV. 17.11. [2]John 1.29.—[3]Rev. 7.14.—[4]1 Pet. 1.19.—[5]Heb. 9.22.—[6]1 John 1.7. [7]Heb. 9.12.—[8]Heb. 10.19, 20, 22. [9]1 Cor. 6.20.

Evening

I wish I had wings, like a dove. I would fly away and find rest. [1]

After the sun had risen, God sent a hot east wind, and Jonah was about to faint from the heat of the sun beating down on his head. So he wished he were dead. "I am better off dead than alive," he said.[2]

Job broke the silence. "Why let men go on living in misery? Why give light to men in grief? They wait for death, but it never comes; they prefer a grave to any treasure."[3]—The good man suffers many troubles, but the LORD saves him from them all.[4]

Now my heart is troubled—and what shall I say? Shall I say, "Father, do not let this hour come upon me"?[5]—This means that he had to become like his brothers in every way, in order to be their faithful and merciful High Priest in his service to God, so that the people's sins would be forgiven. And now he can help those who are tempted, because he himself was tempted and suffered.[6]

[1]PS. 55.6. [2]Jonah 4.8. [3]Job 3.2, 20, 21.—[4]Ps. 34.19. [5]John 12.27.—[6]Heb. 2.17, 18.

Morning

Let us . . . do our best to receive that rest.[1]

Go in through the narrow gate, because the gate to hell is wide and the road that leads to it is easy, and there are many who travel it. But the gate to life is narrow and the way that leads to it is hard, and there are few people who find it.[2]—The Kingdom of heaven has suffered violent attacks, and violent men try to seize it.[3]—Do not work for food that goes bad; instead, work for the food that lasts for eternal life. Thsi is the food which the Son of Man will give you.[4]—Try even harder to make God's call and his choice of you a permanent experience. In this way you will be given the full right to enter the eternal Kingdom of our Lord and Saviour Jesus Christ.[5]—Run . . . in such a way as to win the prize. Every athlete in training submits to strict discipline, in order to be crowned with a wreath that will not last; but we do it for one that will last for ever.[6]

Whoever receives that rest which God promised will rest from his own work, just as God rested from his.[7]—I, the LORD, will be your eternal light; the light of my glory will shine on you.[8]

[1]HEB. 4.11. [2]Matt. 7.13, 14.—[3]Matt. 11.12.—[4]John 6.27.—[5]2 Pet. 1.10, 11.—[6]1 Cor. 9.24, 25. [7]Heb. 4.10.—[8]Isa. 60.19.

Evening

You always listen to me.[1]

Jesus looked up and said, "I thank you, Father, that you listen to me."[2]—"Father, bring glory to your name!" Then a voice spoke from heaven, "I have brought glory to it, and I will do so again."[3]—Here I am, to do your will, O God.[4]—Not my will, however, but your will be done.[5]

Our life in this world is the same as Christ's.[6]—We are sure that he hears us if we ask him for anything that is according to his will.[7]

We receive from him whatever we ask, because we obey his commands and do what pleases him.[8]

No one can please God without faith, for whoever comes to God must have faith that God exists and rewards those who seek him.[9]—He lives for ever to plead with God for them.[10]

We have someone who pleads with the Father on our behalf—Jesus Christ, the righteous one.[11]

[1]JOHN 11.42. [2]John 11.41.—[3]John 12.28.—[4]Heb. 10.7.—[5]Luke 22.42. [6]1 John 4.17.—[7]1 John 5.14. [8]1 John 3.22. [9]Heb. 11.6.—[10]Heb. 7.25. [11]1 John 2.1.

Morning

You have struggled with God and with men, and you have won; so your name will be Israel.[1]

He fought against God—he fought against an angel and won. He wept and asked for a blessing.[2]—His faith did not leave him, and he did not doubt God's promise; his faith filled him with power, and he gave praise to God.[3]

Have faith in God. I assure you that whoever tells this hill to get up and throw itself in the sea and does not doubt in his heart, but believes that what he says will happen, it will be done for him. For this reason I tell you: When you pray and ask for something, believe that you have received it, and you will be given whatever you ask for.[4]—Everything is possible for the person who has faith.[5]—How happy you are to believe that the Lord's message to you will come true![6]

Lord, make our faith greater.[7]

[1]GEN. 32.28. [2]Hos. 12.3, 4.—[3]Rom. 4.20. [4]Mark 11.22–24.—[5]Mark 9.23.—[6]Luke 1.45. [7]Luke 17.5.

Evening

My children, remain in union with him.[1]

Whoever doubts is like a wave in the sea that is driven and blown about by the wind. A person like that, unable to make up his mind and undecided in all he does, must not think that he will receive anything from the Lord.[2]

I am surprised at you! In no time at all you are deserting the one who called you by the grace of Christ, and are accepting another gospel. Actually, there is no "other gospel". But even if we or an angel from heaven should preach to you a gospel that is different from the one we preached to you, may he be condemned to hell![3]

Those of you who try to be put right with God by obeying the Law have cut yourselves off from Christ. You are outside God's grace. You were doing so well! Who made you stop obeying the truth?[4]

A branch cannot bear fruit by itself; it can do so only if it remains in the vine. In the same way you cannot bear fruit unless you remain in me. If you remain in me and my words remain in you, then you will ask for anything you wish, and you shall have it.[5]—It is he who is the "Yes" to all God's promises. This is why through Jesus Christ our "Amen" is said to the glory of God.[6]

[1]1 JOHN 2.28. [2]2 Jas 1.6–8. [3]Gal. 1.6–8. [4]Gal. 5.4, 7. [5]John 15.4, 7.—[6]2 Cor. 1.20.

The Spirit produces patience, kindness.[1]

I, the LORD, am a God who is full of compassion and pity, who is not easily angered and who shows great love and faithfulness.[2]

Live a life that measures up to the standard God set when he called you. Be always humble, gentle, and patient. Show your love by being tolerant with one another.[3]—Be kind and tender-hearted to one another, and forgive one another, as God has forgiven you through Christ.[4]—The wisdom from above is pure first of all; it is also peaceful, gentle, and friendly; it is full of compassion and produces a harvest of good deeds; it is free from prejudice and hypocrisy.[5]—Love is patient and kind.[6]

Let us not become tired of doing good; for if we do not give up, the time will come when we will reap the harvest.[7]—Be patient, then, my brothers, until the Lord comes. See how patient a farmer is as he waits for his land to produce precious crops. He waits patiently for the autumn and spring rains. You also must be patient. Keep your hopes high, for the day of the Lord's coming is near.[8]

[1]GAL. 5.22. [2]Exod. 34.6. [3]Eph. 4.1, 2.—[4]Eph. 4.32.—[5]Jas 3.17.—[6]1 Cor. 13.4. [7]Gal. 6.9.—[8]Jas 5.7, 8.

Evening

Immanuel . . . God is with us.[1]

Can you, O God, really live on earth among men and women? Not even all heaven is large enough to hold you.[2]—The Word became a human being and, full of grace and truth, lived among us. We saw his glory, the glory which he received as the Father's only Son.[3]—Great is the secret of our religion: he appeared in human form.[4]

In these last days he has spoken to us through his Son. He is the one through whom God created the universe, the one whom God has chosen to possess all things at the end.[5]

It was late that Sunday evening, and the disciples were gathered together behind locked doors. Then Jesus came and stood among them. The disciples were filled with joy at seeing the Lord. A week later the disciples were together again indoors, and Thomas was with them. [Jesus] said to Thomas, "Put your finger here, and look at my hands; then stretch out your hand and put it in my side. Stop your doubting, and believe!" Thomas answered him, "My Lord and my God!"[6]—A son is given to us! He will be called . . . "Mighty God".[7]

[1]MATT. 1.23. [2]2 Chr. 6.18.—[3]John 1.14.—[4]1 Tim. 3.16. [5]Heb. 1.2. [6]John 20.19, 20, 26–28.—[7]Isa. 9.6.

Morning

***You are to eat it quickly, for you are to be dressed for travel. It is the Passover Festival to honour me, the LORD.*[1]**

Get up and go; there is no safety here any more.[2]—There is no permanent city for us here on earth; we are looking for the city which is to come.[3]—There still remains for God's people a rest.[4]

Be ready for whatever comes, dressed for action and with your lamps lit, like servants who are waiting for their master to come back from a wedding feast. When he comes and knocks, they will open the door for him at once. How happy are those servants whose master finds them awake and ready when he returns![5]—Have your minds ready for action. Keep alert and set your hope completely on the blessing which will be given you when Jesus Christ is revealed.[6]—The one thing I do . . . is to forget what is behind me. I run straight towards the goal in order to win the prize, which is God's call through Christ Jesus to the life above.[7]

[1]EXOD. 12.11. [2]Mic. 2.10.—[3]Heb. 13.14.—[4]Heb. 4.9. [5]Luke 12.35–37.—[6]1 Pet. 1.13.—[7]Phil. 3.13–15.

Evening

***You, LORD, are all I have, and you give me all I need.*[1]**

We are his children . . . and we will also possess with Christ what God has kept for him.[2]—Everything belongs to you.[3]—My lover is mine.[4]—The Son of God, who loved me and gave his life for me.[5]

The LORD said to Aaron, "You will not receive any property that can be inherited, and no part of the land of Israel will be assigned to you. I, the LORD, am all you need."[6]

What else have I in heaven but you? Since I have you, what else could I want on earth? My mind and my body may grow weak, but God is my strength; he is all I ever need.[7]

Even if I go through the deepest darkness, I will not be afraid, LORD, for you are with me. Your shepherd's rod and staff protect me.[8]—I know whom I have trusted, and I am sure that he is able to keep safe until that Day what he has entrusted to me.[9]

O God, you are my God, and I long for you. My whole being desires you; like a dry, worn-out, and waterless land, my soul is thirsty for you.[10]

[1]PS. 16.5. [2]Rom. 8.17.—[3]1 Cor. 3.21.—[4]S. of S. 2.16.—[5]Gal. 2.20. [6]Num. 18.20. [7]Ps. 73.25, 26. [8]Ps. 23.4.—[9]2 Tim. 1.12. [10]Ps. 63.1.

The Son of Man will come at an hour when you are not expecting him. Be on your guard, then, because you do not know the day or the hour.[1]

Don't let yourselves become occupied with too much feasting and drinking and with the worries of this life, or that Day may suddenly catch you like a trap. For it will come upon all people everywhere on earth. Be on the alert and pray always that you will have the strength to go safely through all those things that will happen and to stand before the Son of Man.[2]

The Day of the Lord will come as a thief comes at night. When people say, "Everything is quiet and safe," then suddenly destruction will hit them! It will come as suddenly as the pains that come upon a woman in labour, and people will not escape. But you, brothers, are not in the darkness, and the Day should not take you by surprise like a thief. All of you are people who belong to the light, who belong to the day. We do not belong to the night or to the darkness. So then, we should not be sleeping like the others; we should be awake and sober.[3]

[1]MATT. 24.44, 25.13. [2]Luke 21.34–36. [3]1 Thess. 5.2–6.

Evening

I am the Almighty God. Obey me and always do what is right.[1]

I do not claim that I have already succeeded or have already become perfect. I keep striving to win the prize for which Christ Jesus has already won me to himself.[2]

[Enoch] spent his life in fellowship with God, and then he disappeared, because God took him away.[3]

Continue to grow in the grace and knowledge of our Lord and Saviour Jesus Christ.[4]—All of us . . . reflect the glory of the Lord with uncovered faces; and that same glory, coming from the Lord, who is the Spirit, transforms us into his likeness in an ever greater degree of glory.[5]

Jesus . . . looked up to heaven and said, "Father, . . . I do not ask you to take them out of the world, but I do ask you to keep them safe from the Evil One. I in them and you in me, so that they may be completely one."[6]

[1]GEN. 17.1. [2]Phil. 3.12–14. [3]Gen. 5.24. [4]2 Pet. 3.18.—[5]2 Cor. 3.18. [6]John 17.1, 15, 23.

Morning

***The new Temple will be more splendid than the old one, and there I will give my people prosperity and peace.*[1]**

The Temple that my son Solomon is to build must be splendid and world-famous.[2]—The dazzling light of the LORD's presence filled the Temple.[3]

"Tear down this Temple, and in three days I will build it again." The temple Jesus was speaking about was his body.[4]—Because of the far brighter glory now the glory that was so bright in the past is gone.[5]—The Word became a human being and, full of grace and truth, lived among us. We saw his glory, the glory which he received as the Father's only Son.[6]—In these last days [God] has spoken to us through his Son. He is the one through whom God created the universe, the one whom God has chosen to possess all things at the end.[7]

Glory to God in the highest heaven, and peace on earth to those with whom he is pleased![8]—Prince of Peace.[9]—Christ himself has brought us peace.[10]—God's peace, which is far beyond human understanding, will keep your hearts and minds safe in union with Christ Jesus.[11]

[1]HAG. 2.9. [2]1 Chr. 22.5.—[3]2 Chr. 7.1. [4]John 2.19, 21.—[5]2 Cor. 3.10.—[6]John 1.14.—[7]Heb. 1.1, 2. [8]Luke 2.14.—[9]Isa. 9.6.—[10]Eph. 2.14.—[11]Phil. 4.7.

Evening

***Let us take up weapons for fighting in the light.*[1]**

Take up the weapons of the Lord Jesus Christ.[2]—That I may gain Christ and be completely united with him. I no longer have a righteousness of my own, the kind that is gained by obeying the Law. I now have the righteousness that is given through faith in Christ.[3]—God puts people right through their faith in Jesus Christ. God does this to all who believe in Christ.[4]

God has clothed her with salvation and victory.[5]—I will praise your power, Sovereign LORD; I will proclaim your goodness, yours alone.[6]

You yourselves used to be in the darkness, but since you have become the Lord's people, you are in the light. So you must live like people who belong to the light. Have nothing to do with the worthless things that people do, things that belong to the darkness. Instead, bring them out to the light. When all things are brought out to the light, then their true nature is clearly revealed; for anything that is clearly revealed becomes light. Wake up, sleeper, and rise from death, and Christ will shine on you. So be careful how you live.[7]

[1]ROM. 13.12. [2]Rom. 13.14.—[3]Phil. 3.8, 9.—[4]Rom. 3.22. [5]Isa. 61.10.—[6]Ps. 71.16. [7]Eph. 5.8, 11, 13–15.

When you have done all you have been told to do, say, "We are ordinary servants; we have only done our duty." [1]

What . . . can we boast about? Nothing! And what is the reason for this? Is it that we obey the Law? No, but that we believe.[2]—Who made you superior to others? Didn't God give you everything you have? Well, then, how can you boast, as if what you have were not a gift?[3]—It is by God's grace that you have been saved through faith. It is not the result of your own efforts, but God's gift, so that no one can boast about it. God has made us what we are, and in our union with Christ Jesus he has created us for a life of good deeds, which he has already prepared for us to do.[4]

By God's grace I am what I am, and the grace that he gave me was not without effect. On the contrary, I have worked harder than any of the other apostles, although it was not really my own doing, but God's grace working with me.[5]—All things were created by him, and all things exist through him and for him.[6]—We have only given back what is yours already.[7]

Don't put me, your servant, on trial; no one is innocent in your sight.[8]

[1]LUKE 17.10. [2]Rom. 3.27.—[3]1 Cor. 4.7.—[4]Eph. 2.8–10. [5]1 Cor. 15.10.—[6]Rom. 11.36.—[7]1 Chr. 29.14. [8]Ps. 143.2.

Evening

He knows what we are made of; he remembers that we are dust. [1]

The LORD God took some soil from the ground and formed a man out of it: he breathed life-giving breath into his nostrils and the man began to live.[2]

I praise you because you are to be feared; all you do is strange and wonderful. I know it with all my heart. When my bones were being formed, carefully put together in my mother's womb, when I was growing there in secret, you knew that I was there—you saw me before I was born. The days allotted to me had all been recorded in your book, before any of them ever began.[3]

Don't we all have the same father? Didn't the same God create us all?[4]—In him we live and move and exist.[5]—As a father is kind to his children, so the LORD is kind to those who honour him.[6]

God was merciful to his people. He forgave their sin and did not destroy them. Many times he held back his anger and restrained his fury. He remembered that they were only mortal beings, like a wind that blows by and is gone.[7]

[1]PS. 103.14. [2]Gen. 2.7. [3]Ps. 139. 14–16. [4]Mal. 2.10.—[5]Acts 17.28.—[6]Ps. 103.13. [7]Ps. 78.38, 39.

In his love he will give you new life.[1]

The LORD did not love you and choose you because you outnumbered other peoples; you were the smallest nation on earth. But the LORD loved you.[2]—We love because God first loved us.[3]—You were far away from God . . . But now, by means of the physical death of his Son, God has made you his friends, in order to bring you, holy, pure and faultless, into his presence.[4]

This is what love is: it is not that we have loved God, but that he loved us and sent his Son to be the means by which our sins are forgiven.[5]—God has shown us how much he loves us—it was while we were still sinners that Christ died for us![6]

Then a voice said from heaven, "This is my own dear Son, with whom I am pleased."[7]—The Father loves me because I am willing to give up my life, in order that I may receive it back again.[8]—His Son . . . reflects the brightness of God's glory and is the exact likeness of God's own being, sustaining the universe with his powerful word. After achieving forgiveness for the sins of mankind, he sat down in heaven at the right-hand side of God, the Supreme Power.[9]

[1]ZEPH. 3.17. [2]Deut. 7.7, 8.—[3]1 John 4.19.—[4]Col. 1.21, 22. [5]1 John 4.10.—[6]Rom. 5.8. [7]Matt. 3.17.—[8]John 10.17.—[9]Heb. 1.2, 3.

Evening

A new way, a living way.[1]

Cain went away from the LORD's presence.[2]—It is because of your sins that he doesn't hear you. It is your sins that separate you from God when you try to worship him.[3]—Try to live a holy life, because no one will see the Lord without it.[4]

I am the way, the truth, and the life; no one goes to the Father except by me.[5]—Our Saviour, Christ Jesus . . . has ended the power of death and through the gospel has revealed immortal life.[6]

The way into the Most Holy Place has not yet been opened as long as the outer Tent still stands.[7]—Christ himself has brought us peace by making Jews and Gentiles one people. With his own body he broke down the wall that separated them and kept them enemies.[8]—The curtain hanging in the Temple was torn in two from top to bottom.[9]

The gate to life is narrow and the way that leads to it is hard, and there are few people who find it.[10]—You will show me the path that leads to life; your presence fills me with joy and brings me pleasure for ever.[11]

[1]HEB. 10.20. [2]Gen. 4.16.—[3]Isa. 59.2.—[4]Heb. 12.14. [5]John 14.6.—[6]2 Tim. 1.10. [7]Heb. 9.8.—[8]Eph. 2.14.—[9]Matt. 27.51. [10]Matt. 7.14.—[11]Ps. 16.11.

They should always pray and never become discouraged.[1]

Suppose one of you should go to a friend's house at midnight and say to him, "Friend, let me borrow three loaves of bread. A friend of mine who is on a journey has just come to my house, and I haven't got any food for him!" And suppose your friends should answer from inside, "Don't bother me! The door is already locked, and my children and I are in bed. I can't get up and give you anything." Well, what then? I tell you that even if he will not get up and give you the bread because you are his friend, yet he will get up and give you everything you need because you are not ashamed to keep on asking.[2]—Pray on every occasion, as the Spirit leads. For this reason keep alert and never give up; pray always for all God's people.[3]

Let me go . . . I won't, unless you bless me. You have struggled with God and with men, and you have won.[4]—Be persistent in prayer, and keep alert as you pray, giving thanks to God.[5]

Jesus went up a hill to pray and spent the whole night there praying to God.[6]

[1]LUKE 18.1. [2]Luke 11.5–8.—[3]Eph. 6.18. [4]Gen. 32.26, 28.—[5]Col. 4.2. [6]Luke 6.12.

Evening

Forgive all my sins.[1]

The LORD says, "Now, let's settle the matter. You are stained red with sin, but I will wash you as clean as snow. Although your stains are deep red, you will be as white as wool."[2]

Courage, my son! Your sins are forgiven.[3]—I am the God who forgives your sins, and I do this because of who I am. I will not hold your sins against you.[4]

The Son of Man has authority on earth to forgive sins.[5]—By the sacrificial death of Christ we are set free, that is, our sins are forgiven. How great is the grace of God![6]—It was not because of any good deeds that we ourselves had done, but because of his own mercy that he saved us, through the Holy Spirit, who gives us new birth and new life by washing us. God poured out the Holy Spirit abundantly on us through Jesus Christ our Saviour.[7]—God forgave us all our sins; he cancelled the unfavourable record of our debts with its binding rules and did away with it completely by nailing it to the cross.[8]

Praise the LORD, my soul . . . he forgives all my sins.[9]

[1]PS. 25.18. [2]Isa. 1.18. [3]Matt. 9.2.—[4]Isa. 43.25. [5]Matt. 9.6.—[6]Eph. 1.7.—[7]Titus 3.5, 6.—[8]Col. 2.13, 14. [9]Ps. 103.2, 3.

The Lord . . . made him successful in everything he did.[1]

Happy are those who obey the Lord, who live by his commands. Your work will provide for your needs; you will be happy and prosperous.[2]—Trust in the Lord and do good; live in the land and be safe. Seek your happiness in the Lord, and he will give you your heart's desire.[3]—Don't be afraid or discouraged, for I, the Lord your God, am with you wherever you go.[4]

Be concerned above everything else with the Kingdom of God and with what he requires of you, and he will provide you with all these other things.[5]

As long as . . . he served the Lord faithfully, . . . God blessed him.[6]—Make certain that you do not forget the Lord your God; do not fail to obey any of his laws that I am giving you today. You must never think that you have made yourselves wealthy by your own power and strength.[7]

The Lord your God has been with you and given you peace on all sides.[8]

[1]GEN. 39.3. [2]Ps. 128.1, 2.—[3]Ps. 37.3, 4.—[4]Josh. 1.9. [5]Matt. 6.33. [6]2 Chr. 26.5.—[7]Deut. 8.11, 17. [8]1 Chr. 22.18.

Evening

Why do you think such things?[1]

[Abraham] was then almost one hundred years old; but his faith did not weaken when he thought of his body, which was already practically dead, or of the fact that Sarah could not have children. His faith did not leave him, and he did not doubt God's promise; his faith filled him with power, and he gave praise to God.[2]

Is it easier to say to this paralysed man, "Your sins are forgiven," or to say, "Get up, pick up your mat, and walk"?[3]—Everything is possible for the person who has faith.[4]

I have been given all authority in heaven and on earth.[5]—Why are you frightened? Have you still no faith?[6]—Look at the birds . . . your Father in heaven takes care of them! Aren't you worth much more than birds?[7]—Why are you discussing among yourselves about not having any bread? Don't you remember . . . the five loaves for the five thousand men?[8]

With all his abundant wealth through Christ Jesus, my God will supply all your needs.[9]

[1]MARK 2.8. [2]Rom. 4.19, 20. [3]Mark 2.9.—[4]Mark 9.23. [5]Matt. 28.18.—[6]Mark 4.40.—[7]Matt. 6.26.—[8]Matt. 16.8, 9. [9]Phil. 4.19.

Nobody has ever talked like this man![1]

You are the most handsome of men; you are an eloquent speaker. God has always blessed you.[2]—The Sovereign LORD has taught me what to say, so that I can strengthen the weary.[3]—His mouth is sweet to kiss; everything about him enchants me. This is what my lover is like.[4]

They were all well impressed with him and marvelled at the eloquent words that he spoke.[5]—He wasn't like the teachers of the Law; instead, he taught with authority.[6]

Christ's message in all its richness must live in your hearts.[7]—Accept . . . the word of God as the sword which the Spirit gives you.[8]—The word of God is alive and active, sharper than any double-edged sword.[9]—The weapons we use in our fight are not the world's weapons but God's powerful weapons, which we use to destroy strongholds. We destroy false arguments; we pull down every proud obstacle that is raised against the knowledge of God; we take every thought captive and make it obey Christ.[10]

[1]JOHN 7.46. [2]Ps. 45.2.—[3]Isa. 50.4.—[4]S. of S. 5.16. [5]Luke 4.22.—[6]Matt. 7.29. [7]Col. 3.16.—[8]Eph. 6.17.—[9]Heb. 4.12.—[10]2 Cor. 10.4, 5.

Evening

No wicked man has been happy for long.[1]

You will bite their heel.[2]—This is your hour to act, when the power of darkness rules.[3]—Since the children, as he calls them, are people of flesh and blood, Jesus himself became like them and shared their human nature. He did this so that through his death he might destroy the Devil, who has the power over death.[4]—Christ freed himself from the power of the spiritual rulers and authorities; he made a public spectacle of them by leading them as captives in his victory procession.[5]

Be alert, be on the watch! Your enemy, the Devil, roams round like a roaring lion, looking for someone to devour. Be firm in your faith and resist him.[6]—Resist the Devil, and he will run away from you.[7]

The wicked man plots against the good man and glares at him with hate. But the Lord laughs at wicked men, because he knows they will soon be destroyed.[8]—God, our source of peace, will soon crush Satan under your feet.[9]—The Devil . . . was thrown into the lake of fire and sulphur . . . and . . . will be tormented day and night for ever and ever.[10]

[1]JOB 20.5. [2]Gen. 3.15.—[3]Luke 22.53.—[4]Heb. 2.14.—[5]Col. 2.15. [6]1 Pet. 5.8, 9.— [7]Jas 4.7. [8]Ps. 37.12, 13.—[9]Rom. 16.20.—[10]Rev. 20.10.

Morning

The younger son . . . went to a country far away, where he wasted his money in reckless living.[1]

Some of you were like that. But you have been purified from sin; you have been dedicated to God; you have been put right with God by the Lord Jesus Christ and by the Spirit of our God.[2]—All of us . . . lived according to our natural desires, doing whatever suited the wishes of our own bodies and minds. In our natural condition we, like everyone else, were destined to suffer God's anger. But God's mercy is so abundant, and his love for us is so great, that while we were spiritually dead in our disobedience he brought us to life with Christ. It is by God's grace that you have been saved. In our union with Christ Jesus he raised us up with him to rule with him in the heavenly world.[3]

This is what love is: it is not that we have loved God, but that he loved us and sent his Son to be the means by which our sins are forgiven.[4]

God has shown us how much he loves us—it was while we were still sinners that Christ died for us! We were God's enemies, but he made us his friends through the death of his Son. Now that we are God's friends, how much more will we be saved by Christ's life![5]

[1]LUKE 15.13. [2]1 Cor. 6.11.—[3]Eph. 2.3–6. [4]1 John 4.10. [5]Rom. 5.8, 10.

Evening

You must forgive one another just as the Lord has forgiven you.[1]

There were two men who owed money to a money-lender. One owed him five hundred silver coins, and the other owed him fifty. Neither of them could pay him back, so he cancelled the debts of both.[2]—I forgave you the whole amount you owed me, just because you asked me to. You should have had mercy on your fellow-servant, just as I had mercy on you.[3]

When you stand and pray, forgive anything you may have against anyone, so that your Father in heaven will forgive the wrongs you have done. If you do not forgive others, your Father in heaven will not forgive the wrongs you have done.[4]—You are the people of God . . . so then, you must clothe yourselves with compassion, kindness, humility, gentleness, and patience. Be tolerant with one another and forgive one another whenever any of you has a complaint against someone else.[5]

"If my brother keeps on sinning against me, how many times do I have to forgive him? Seven times?" "No, not seven times," answered Jesus, "but seventy times seven."[6]

Love . . . binds all things together in perfect unity.[7]

[1]COL. 3.13. [2]Luke 7.41, 42.—[3]Matt. 18.32, 33. [4]Mark 11.25, 26.—[5]Col. 3.12, 13. [6]Matt. 18.21, 22. [7]Col. 3.14.

He got up and started back to his father. He was still a long way from home when his father saw him; his heart was filled with pity, and he ran, threw his arms around his son, and kissed him.[1]

The LORD is merciful and loving, slow to become angry and full of constant love. He does not keep on rebuking; he is not angry for ever. He does not punish us as we deserve or repay us according to our sins and wrongs. As high as the sky is above the earth, so great is his love for those who honour him. As far as the east is from the west, so far does he remove our sins from us. As a father is kind to his children, so the LORD is kind to those who honour him.[2]

The Spirit makes you God's children, and by the Spirit's power we cry out to God, "Father! my Father!" God's Spirit joins himself to our spirits to declare that we are God's children.[3]—You who used to be far away have been brought near by the sacrificial death of Christ. You . . . are not foreigners or strangers any longer; you are now fellow-citizens with God's people and members of the family of God.[4]

[1]LUKE 15.20. [2]Ps. 103.8–13. [3]Rom. 8.15, 16.—[4]Eph. 2.13, 19.

Evening

Now I make all things new![1]

No one can see the Kingdom of God unless he is born again.[2]—When anyone is joined to Christ, he is a new being; the old is gone, the new has come.[3]

I will give you a new heart and a new mind. I will take away your stubborn heart of stone and give you an obedient heart.[4]—You must remove the old yeast of sin so that you will be entirely pure.[5]—The new self . . . is created in God's likeness and reveals itself in the true life that is upright and holy.[6]

You will be called by a new name, a name given by the LORD himself.[7]

I am making a new earth and new heavens. The events of the past will be completely forgotten.[8]—Since all these things will be destroyed in this way, what kind of people should you be? Your lives should be holy and dedicated to God.[9]

[1]REV. 21.5. [2]John 3.3.—[3]2 Cor. 5.17. [4]Ezek. 36.26.—[5]1 Cor. 5.7.—[6]Eph. 4.24. [7]Isa. 62.2. [8]Isa. 65.17.—[9]2 Pet. 3.11.

Everything that will not burn . . . is to be purified by passing it through fire.[1]

The LORD your God is using him to test you, to see if you love the LORD with all your heart.[2]—He will come to judge like one who refines and purifies silver. As a metal-worker refines silver and gold, so the LORD's messenger will purify the priests, so that they will bring to the LORD the right kind of offerings.[3]—The quality of each person's work will be seen when the Day of Christ exposes it. For on that Day fire will reveal everyone's work; the fire will test it and show its real quality.[4]

I will take action against you. I will purify you just as metal is refined, and will remove all your impurity.[5]—I will refine my people like metal and put them to the test.[6]

You have put us to the test, God; as silver is purified by fire, so you have tested us . . . we went through fire and flood, but now you have brought us to a place of safety.[7]

When you pass through fire, you will not be burnt; the hard trials that come will not hurt you.[8]

[1]NUM. 31.23. [2]Deut. 13.3.—[3]Mal. 3.3.—[4]1 Cor. 3.13. [5]Isa. 1.25.—[6]Jer. 9.7. [7]Ps. 66.10, 12. [8]Isa. 43.2.

Evening

We might die to sin and live for righteousness.[1]

Get rid of your old self, which made you live as you used to—the old self that was being destroyed by its deceitful desires. Your hearts and minds must be made completely new, and you must put on the new self, which is created in God's likeness and reveals itself in the true life that is upright and holy.[2]

You have died, and your life is hidden with Christ in God.[3]—Just as Christ was raised from death by the glorious power of the Father, so also we might live a new life. We know that our old being has been put to death with Christ on his cross, in order that the power of the sinful self might be destroyed, so that we should no longer be the slaves of sin. For when a person dies, he is set free from the power of sin. You are to think of yourselves as dead, so far as sin is concerned, but living in fellowship with God through Christ Jesus. Sin must no longer rule in your mortal bodies, so that you obey the desires of your natural self. Instead, give yourselves to God, as those who have been brought from death to life, and surrender your whole being to him to be used for righteous purposes.[4]

[1]1 PET. 2.24. [2]Eph. 4.22–24. [3]Col. 3.3.—[4]Rom. 6.4, 6, 7, 11–13.

Remain united to me, and I will remain united to you.[1]

I have been put to death with Christ on his cross, so that it is no longer I who live, but it is Christ who lives in me. This life that I live now, I live by faith in the Son of God, who loved me and gave his life for me.[2]

I know that good does not live in me—that is, in my human nature. For even though the desire to do good is in me, I am not able to do it. What an unhappy man I am! Who will rescue me from this body that is taking me to death? Thanks be to God, who does this through our Lord Jesus Christ![3]—If Christ lives in you, the Spirit is life for you because you have been put right with God, even though your bodies are going to die because of sin.[4]—You must . . . continue faithful on a firm and sure foundation, and must not allow yourselves to be shaken from the hope you gained when you heard the gospel.[5]

My children, remain in union with him, so that when he appears we may be full of courage and need not hide in shame from him on the Day he comes.[6]—Whoever says that he remains in union with God should live just as Jesus Christ did.[7]

[1]JOHN 15.4. [2]Gal. 2.19, 20. [3]Rom. 7.18, 24, 25.—[4]Rom. 8.10.—[5]Col. 1.23. [6]1 John 2.28.—[7]1 John 2.6.

Evening

Do you believe in the Son of Man?[1]

Tell me who he is, sir, so that I can believe in him![2]

He reflects the brightness of God's glory and is the exact likeness of God's own being.[3]—God, the blessed and only Ruler, the King of kings and the Lord of lords. He alone is immortal; he lives in the light that no one can approach. No one has ever seen him; no one can ever see him. To him be honour and eternal dominion! Amen.[4]—"I am the first and the last," says the Lord God Almighty, who is, who was, and who is to come.[5]

I believe, Lord![6]—I know whom I have trusted, and I am sure that he is able to keep safe until that Day what he has entrusted to me.[7]

I chose a valuable stone, which I am placing as the cornerstone in Zion; and whoever believes in him will never be disappointed. This stone is of great value for you that believe.[8]

[1]JOHN 9.35. [2]John 9.36. [3]Heb. 1.3.—[4]1 Tim. 6.15, 16.—[5]Rev. 1.8. [6]John 9.38.— [7]2 Tim. 1.12. [8]1 Pet. 2.6, 7.

Morning

Just as we have a share in Christ's many sufferings, so also through Christ we share in God's great help.[1]

To share in his sufferings.[2]—Be glad that you are sharing Christ's sufferings, so that you may be full of joy when his glory is revealed.[3]—If we have died with him, we shall also live with him.[4]—Since we are his children, we wil possess the blessings he keeps for his people, and we will also possess with Christ what God has kept for him; for if we share Christ's suffering, we will also share his glory.[5]

To those who were to receive what he promised, God wanted to make it very clear that he would never change his purpose; so he added his vow to the promise. There are these two things, then, that cannot change and about which God cannot lie. So we who have found safety with him are greatly encouraged to hold firmly to the hope placed before us.[6]—May our Lord Jesus Christ himself and God our Father, who loved us and in his grace gave us unfailing courage and a firm hope, encourage you and strengthen you to always do and say what is good.[7]

[1]2 COR. 1.5. [2]Phil. 3.10.—[3]1 Pet. 4.13.—[4]2 Tim. 2.11.—[5]Rom. 8.17. [6]Heb. 6.17, 18.—[7]2 Thess. 2.16, 17.

Evening

Martha, Martha! You are worried and troubled over so many things.[1]

Look at the crows: they don't sow seeds or gather a harvest. Look how the wild flowers grow: they don't work or make clothes for themselves. So don't be all upset, always concerned about what you will eat and drink. Your Father knows that you need these things.[2]

If we have food and clothes, that should be enough for us. But those who want to get rich fall into temptation and are caught in the trap of many foolish and harmful desires, which pull them down to ruin and destruction. For the love of money is a source of all kinds of evil. Some have been so eager to have it that they have wandered away from the faith and have broken their hearts with many sorrows.[3]

The worries about this life, the love for riches, and all other kinds of desires crowd in and choke the message, and they don't bear fruit.[4]

Let us rid ourselves of everything that gets in the way, and of the sin which holds on to us so tightly, and let us run with determination the race that lies before us.[5]

[1]LUKE 10.41. [2]Luke 12.24, 27, 29, 30. [3]1 Tim. 6.8–10. [4]Mark 4.19. [5]Heb. 12.1.

There are some things that the LORD our God has kept secret; but he has revealed his Law, and we and our descendants are to obey it for ever.[1]

LORD, I have given up my pride and turned away from my arrogance. I am not concerned with great matters or with subjects too difficult for me. Instead, I am content and at peace. As a child lies quietly in its mother's arms, so my heart is quiet within me.[2]

The LORD is the friend of those who obey him and he affirms his covenant with them.[3]—There is a God in heaven, who reveals mysteries.[4]—These are only hints of his power, only the whispers that we have heard.[5]

I do not call you servants any longer, because a servant does not know what his master is doing. Instead, I call you friends, because I have told you everything I have heard from my Father.[6]—If you love me, you will obey my commandments. I will ask the Father, and he will give you another Helper, who will stay with you for ever. He is the Spirit who reveals the truth about God.[7]

[1]DEUT. 29.29. [2]Ps. 131.1, 2. [3]Ps. 25.14.—[4]Dan. 2.28.—[5]Job 26.14. [6]John 15.15.—[7]John 14.15–17.

Evening

The Spirit pleads with God on behalf of his people and in accordance with his will.[1]

I am tellling you the truth: the Father will give you whatever you ask him for in my name. Until now you have not asked for anything in my name; ask and you will receive, so that your happiness may be complete.[2]—Do all this in prayer, asking for God's help. Pray on every occasion, as the Spirit leads.[3]

We have courage in God's presence, because we are sure that he hears us if we ask him for anything that is according to his will. He hears us whenever we ask him; and since we know this is true, we know also that he gives us what we ask from him.[4]—God wants you to be holy.[5]

God did not call us to live in immorality, but in holiness . . . God, who gives you his Holy Spirit.[6]

Be joyful always, pray at all times, be thankful in all circumstances. This is what God wants from you in your life in union with Christ Jesus. Do not restrain the Holy Spirit.[7]

[1]ROM. 8.27. [2]John 16.23, 24.—[3]Eph. 6.18. [4]1 John 5.14, 15.—[5]1 Thess. 4.3. [6]1 Thess. 4.7, 8. [7]1 Thess. 5.16–19.

Be careful how you live. Don't live like ignorant people, but like wise people. Make good use of every opportunity you have, because these are evil days.[1]

Make sure you obey the law that Moses commanded you: love the LORD your God, do his will, obey his commandments, be faithful to him, and serve him with all your heart and soul.[2]—Be wise in the way you act towards those who are not believers, making good use of every opportunity you have. Your speech should always be pleasant and interesting, and you should know how to give the right answer to everyone.[3]—Avoid every kind of evil.[4]

The bridegroom was late in coming, so the girls began to nod and fall asleep. It was already midnight when the cry rang out, "Here is the bridegroom! Come and meet him!" Be on your guard, then, because you do not know the day or the hour.[5]

My brothers, try even harder to make God's call and his choice of you a permanent experience; if you do so, you will never abandon your faith.[6]—How happy are those servants whose master finds them awake and ready when he returns![7]

[1]EPH. 5.15, 16. [2]Josh. 22.5.—[3]Col. 4.5, 6.—[4]1 Thess. 5.22. [5]Matt. 25.5, 6, 13. [6]2 Pet. 1.10.—[7]Luke 12.37.

Evening

Keep safe what you have, so that no one will rob you of your victory prize.[1]

If I only touch his cloak, I will get well.[2]—"Sir, if you want to, you can make me clean." "I do want to . . . Be clean!"[3]—Faith as big as a mustard seed.[4]

Do not lose your courage, then, because it brings with it a great reward.[5]—Keep on working with fear and trembling to complete your salvation, because God is always at work in you to make you willing and able to obey his own purpose.[6]

First the tender stalk appears, then the ear, and finally the ear full of corn.[7]—Let us try to know the LORD. He will come to us.[8]—The Kingdom of heaven has suffered violent attacks, and violent men try to seize it.[9]—Run . . . in such a way as to win the prize.[10]

I have done my best in the race, I have run the full distance, and I have kept the faith. And now there is waiting for me the victory prize of being put right with God, which the Lord, the righteous Judge, will give me on that Day.[11]

[1]REV. 3.11. [2]Matt. 9.21.—[3]Matt. 8.2, 3.—[4]Matt. 17.20. [5]Heb. 10.35.—[6]Phil. 2.12, 13. [7]Mark 4.28.—[8]Hos. 6.3.—[9]Matt. 11.12.—[10]1 Cor. 9.24. [11]2 Tim. 4.7, 8.

In all your prayers ask God for what you need, always asking him with a thankful heart.[1]

I love the LORD, because he hears me; he listens to my prayers. He listens to me every time I call to him.[2]

When you pray, do not use a lot of meaningless words, as the pagans do, who think that their gods will hear them because their prayers are long.[3]—The Spirit also comes to help us, weak as we are. For we do not know how we ought to pray; the Spirit himself pleads with God for us in groans that words cannot express.[4]

I want the men to pray, men who are dedicated to God and can lift up their hands in prayer without anger or argument.[5]—Pray on every occasion, as the Spirit leads. For this reason keep alert and never give up; pray always for all God's people.[6]

Whenever two of you on earth agree about anything you pray for, it will be done for you by my Father in heaven.[7]

[1]PHIL. 4.6. [2]Ps. 116.1, 2. [3]Matt. 6.7.—[4]Rom. 8.26. [5]1 Tim. 2.8.—[6]Eph. 6.18. [7]Matt. 18.19.

Evening

All your creatures, LORD, will praise you, and all your people will give you thanks.[1]

Praise the LORD, my soul! All my being, praise his holy name! Praise the LORD, my soul, and do not forget how kind he is.[2]—I will always thank the LORD; I will never stop praising him.[3]—Every day I will thank you; I will praise you for ever and ever.[4]

Your constant love is better than life itself, and so I will praise you. I will give you thanks as long as I live; I will raise my hands to you in prayer. My soul will feast and be satisfied, and I will sing glad songs of praise to you.[5]

My heart praises the Lord; my soul is glad because of God my Saviour.[6]

Our Lord and God! You are worthy to receive glory, honour, and power. For you created all things, and by your will they were given existence and life.[7]

[1]PS. 145.10. [2]Ps. 103.1, 2.—[3]Ps. 34.1.—[4]Ps. 145.2. [5]Ps. 63.3–5. [6]Luke 1.46, 47. [7]Rev. 4.11.

Put the two stone tablets inside the box and put the lid on top of it. I will meet you there.[1]

The way into the Most Holy Place has not yet been opened.[2]—Jesus again gave a loud cry and breathed his last. Then the curtain hanging in the Temple was torn in two from top to bottom.[3]

We have, my brothers, complete freedom to go into the Most Holy Place by means of the death of Jesus. He opened for us a new way, a living way, through the curtain—that is, through his own body. Let us come near to God with a sincere heart and a sure faith, with hearts that have been purified from a guilty conscience and with bodies washed with clean water.[4]—Let us have confidence, then, and approach God's throne, where there is grace. There we will receive mercy and find grace to help us just when we need it.[5]

Christ Jesus . . . sets them free. God offered him, so that by his sacrificial death he should become the means by which people's sins are forgiven through their faith in him.[6]—It is through Christ that all of us . . . are able to come in the one Spirit into the presence of the Father.[7]

[1]EXOD. 25.21, 22. [2]Heb. 9.8.—[3]Matt. 27.50, 51. [4]Heb. 10.19, 20, 22.—[5]Heb. 4.16. [6]Rom. 3.24, 25.—[7]Eph. 2.18.

Evening

Faith as big as a mustard seed.[1]

Barak replied, "I will go if you go with me, but if you don't go with me, I won't go either." That day God gave the Israelites victory over Jabin, the Cannaanite king.[2]—Gideon . . . was too afraid of his family and the people of the town to do it by day, so he did it at night. Gideon said to God, "You say that you have decided to use me to rescue Israel . . . let me make one more test . . ." God did that very thing.[3]

You have a little power; you have followed my teaching and have been faithful to me.[4]—They are disappointed because so little progress is being made.[5]

Our brothers, we must thank God at all times for you. It is right for us to do so, because your faith is growing so much and the love each of you has for the others is becoming greater.[6]—Lord, make our faith greater.[7]—I will be to the people of Israel like rain in a dry land. They will blossom like flowers; they will be firmly rooted like the trees of Lebanon.[8]

[1]MATT. 17.20. [2]Judg. 4.8, 23.—[3]Judg. 6.27, 36, 39, 40. [4]Rev. 3.8.—[5]Zech. 4.10. [6]2 Thess. 1.3.—[7]Luke 17.5.—[8]Hos. 14.5, 6.

Try to live a holy life, because no one will see the Lord without it.[1]

No one can see the Kingdom of God unless he is born again.[2]—Nothing that is impure will enter the city.[3]—How perfect you are![4]

Be holy, because I, the LORD your God, am holy.[5]—Be obedient to God, and do not allow your lives to be shaped by those desires you had when you were still ignorant. Instead, be holy in all that you do, just as God who called you is holy. The scripture says, "Be holy because I am holy." You call him Father, when you pray to God, who judges all people by the same standard, according to what each one has done; so then, spend the rest of your lives here on earth in reverence for him.[6]—Get rid of your old self, which made you live as you used to—the old self that was being destroyed by its deceitful desires. Your hearts and minds must be made completely new, and you must put on the new self, which is created in God's likeness and reveals itself in the true life that is upright and holy.[7]—Even before the world was made, God had already chosen us to be his through our union with Christ, so that we would be holy and without fault before him.[8]

[1]HEB. 12.14. [2]John 3.3.—[3]Rev. 21.27.—[4]S. of S. 4.7. [5]Lev. 19.2.—[6]1 Pet. 1.14–17.—[7]Eph. 4.22–24.—[8]Eph. 1.4.

Evening

Pure gold.[1]

Anyone who leaves home or brothers or sisters or mother or father or children or fields for me and for the gospel, will receive much more in this present age. He will receive a hundred times more houses, brothers, sisters, mothers, children and fields—and persecutions as well; and in the age to come he will receive eternal life.[2]

My dear friends, do not be surprised at the painful test you are suffering, as though something unusual were happening to you.[3]—Be glad about this, even though it may now be necessary for you to be sad for a while because of the many kinds of trials you suffer. Their purpose is to prove that your faith is genuine. Even gold, which can be destroyed, is tested by fire; and so your faith, which is much more precious than gold, must also be tested, so that it may endure. Then you will receive praise and glory and honour on the Day when Jesus Christ is revealed.[4]

After you have suffered for a little while, the God of all grace, who calls you to share his eternal glory in union with Christ, will himself perfect you and give you firmness, strength, and a sure foundation.[5]—The world will make you suffer. But be brave! I have defeated the world![6]

[1]REV. 3.18. [2]Mark 10.29, 30. [3]1 Pet. 4.12.—[4]1 Pet. 1.6, 7. [5]1 Pet. 5.10.—[6]John 16.33.

Take this baby and nurse him for me, and I will pay you.[1]

Go and work in the vineyard, and I will pay you a fair wage.[2]—I assure you that anyone who gives you a drink of water because you belong to me will certainly receive his reward.[3]—Be generous, and you will be prosperous. Help others, and you will be helped.[4]—God is not unfair. He will not forget the work you did or the love you showed for him in the help you gave and are still giving to your fellow-Christians.[5]

God will reward each one according to the work he has done.[6]

"When, Lord, did we ever see you hungry and feed you, or thirsty and give you a drink? When did we ever see you a stranger and welcome you in our homes, or naked and clothe you?" The King will reply, "I tell you, whenever you did this for one of the least important of these brothers of mine, you did it for me! Come, you that are blessed by my Father! Come and possess the kingdom which has been prepared for you ever since the creation of the world."[7]

[1]EXOD. 2.9. [2]Matt. 20.4.—[3]Mark 9.41.—[4]Prov. 11.25.—[5]Heb. 6.10. [6]1 Cor. 3.8. [7]Matt. 25.37, 38, 40, 34.

Evening

You see me, whether I am working or resting.[1]

Jacob woke up and said, "The LORD is here! He is in this place, and I didn't know it!" He was afraid and said, "What a terrifying place this is! It must be the house of God; it must be the gate that opens into heaven."[2]

The LORD keeps close watch over the whole world, to give strength to those whose hearts are loyal to him.[3]

When I lie down, I go to sleep in peace; you alone, O LORD, keep me perfectly safe.[4]

You have made the LORD your defender, the Most High your protector, and so no disaster will strike you, no violence will come near your home. God will put his angels in charge of you to protect you wherever you go.[5]—You will not be afraid when you go to bed, and you will sleep soundly through the night.[6]—The LORD provides for those he loves, while they are asleep.[7]

[1]PS. 139.3. [2]Gen. 28.16, 17. [3]2 Chr. 16.9. [4]Ps. 4.8. [5]Ps. 91.9–11.—[6]Prov. 3.24.—[7]Ps. 127.2.

Christ himself suffered for you and left you an example, so that you would follow in his steps.[1]

Even the Son of Man did not come to be served; he came to serve.[2]—If one of you wants to be first, he must be the slave of all.[3]

Jesus of Nazareth . . . went everywhere, doing good.[4]—Help to carry one another's burdens, and in this way you will obey the law of Christ.[5]

The gentleness and kindness of Christ.[6]—Be humble towards one another, always considering others better than yourselves.[7]

Forgive them, Father! They don't know what they are doing.[8]—Be kind and tender-hearted to one another, and forgive one another, as God has forgiven you through Christ.[9]

Whoever says that he remains in union with God should live just as Jesus Christ did.[10]—Let us keep our eyes fixed on Jesus, on whom our faith depends from beginning to end. He did not give up because of the cross! On the contrary, because of the joy that was waiting for him, he thought nothing of the disgrace of dying on the cross, and he is now seated at the right-hand side of God's throne.[11]

[1]1 PET. 2.21. [2]Mark 10.45.—[3]Mark 10.44. [4]Acts 10.38.—[5]Gal. 6.2. [6]2 Cor. 10.1.—[7]Phil. 2.3. [8]Luke 23.34.—[9]Eph. 4.32. [10]1 John 2.6.—[11]Heb. 12.2.

Evening

I looked for him, but couldn't find him; I called to him, but heard no answer.[1]

"What can I say, O Lord, now that Israel has retreated from the enemy?" The LORD said to Joshua, "Get up! Why are you lying on the ground like this? Israel has sinned! They have taken some of the things condemned to destruction . . . and put them with their own things."[2]

Don't think that the LORD is too weak to save you or too deaf to hear your call for help! It is because of your sins that he doesn't hear you. It is your sins that separate you from God when you try to worship him.[3]

If I had ignored my sins, the Lord would not have listened to me.[4]

My dear friends, if our conscience does not condemn us, we have courage in God's presence. We receive from him whatever we ask, because we obey his commands and do what pleases him.[5]

[1]S. OF S. 5.6. [2]Josh. 7.8, 10, 11. [3]Isa. 59.1, 2. [4]Ps. 66.18. [5]1 John 3.21, 22.

You have died, and your life is hidden with Christ in God.[1]

We have died to sin—how then can we go on living in it?[2]—I have been put to death with Christ on his cross, so that it is no longer I who live, but it is Christ who lives in me. This life that I live now, I live by faith in the Son of God, who loved me and gave his life for me.[3]—He died for all, so that those who live should no longer live for themselves, but only for him who died and was raised to life for their sake.[4]—When anyone is joined to Christ, he is a new being; the old is gone, the new has come.[5]

We live in union with the true God—in union with his Son Jesus Christ.[6]—I pray that they may all be one. Father! May they be in us, just as you are in me and I am in you.[7]—All of you are Christ's body, and each one is part of it.[8]—Because I live, you also will live.[9]

To those who win the victory I will give some of the hidden manna. I will also give each of them a white stone on which is written a new name that no one knows except the one who receives it.[10]

[1]COL. 3.3. [2]Rom. 6.2.—[3]Gal. 2.19, 20.—[4]2 Cor. 5.15.—[5]2 Cor. 5.17. [6]1 John 5.20.—[7]John 17.21.—[8]1 Cor. 12.27.—[9]John 14.19. [10]Rev. 2.17.

Evening

See how much he loved him![1]

He died for all.[2]—The greatest love a person can have for his friends is to give his life for them.[3]

He lives for ever to plead with God for them.[4]—I am going to prepare a place for you.[5]

I will come back and take you to myself, so that you will be where I am.[6]—Father! You have given them to me, and I want them to be with me where I am.[7]—He had always loved those in the world who were his own, and he loved them to the very end.[8]

We love because God first loved us.[9]—We are ruled by the love of Christ, now that we recognise that one man died for everyone, which means that all share in his death. He died for all, so that those who live should no longer live for themselves, but only for him who died and was raised to life for their sake.[10]

If you obey my commands, you will remain in my love, just as I have obeyed my Father's commands and remain in his love.[11]

[1]JOHN 11.36. [2]2 Cor. 5.15.—[3]John 15.13. [4]Heb. 7.25.—[5]John 14.2. [6]John 14.3.—[7]John 17.24.—[8]John 13.1. [9]1 John 4.19.—[10]2 Cor. 5.14, 15. [11]John 15.10.

I will ask the Father, and he will give you another Helper, who will stay with you for ever.[1]

It is better for you that I go away, because if I do not go, the Helper will not come to you.[2]

God's Spirit joins himself to our spirits to declare that we are God's children.[3]—The Spirit that God has given you does not make you slaves and cause you to be afraid; instead, the Spirit makes you God's children, and by the Spirit's power we cry out to God, "Father! my Father!"[4]—The Spirit also comes to help us, weak as we are. For we do not know how we ought to pray; the Spirit himself pleads with God for us in groans that words cannot express.[5]

May God, the source of hope, fill you with all joy and peace by means of your faith in him, so that your hope will continue to grow by the power of the Holy Spirit.[6]—Hope does not disappoint us, for God has poured out his love into our hearts by means of the Holy Spirit, who is God's gift to us.[7]

We are sure that we live in union with God and that he lives in union with us, because he has given us his Spirit.[8]

[1]JOHN 14.16, 17. [2]John 16.7. [3]Rom 8.16.—[4]Rom. 8.15.—[5]Rom 8.26. [6]Rom. 15.13.—[7]Rom. 5.5. [8]1 John 4.13.

Evening

You will have a home of your own.[1]

There still remains for God's people a rest.[2]—God's people will be free from worries, and their homes peaceful and safe.[3]—Wicked men stop their evil, and tired workmen find rest at last.[4]—They will enjoy rest from their hard work.[5]

On our behalf Jesus has gone in there before us, and has become a high priest for ever, in the priestly order of Melchizedek.[6]

Come to me, all of you who are tired from carrying heavy loads, and I will give you rest. Take my yoke and put it on you, and learn from me, because I am gentle and humble in spirit; and you will find rest. For the yoke I will give you is easy, and the load I will put on you is light.[7]—Come back and quietly trust in me. Then you will be strong and secure.[8]

The LORD is my shepherd; I have everything I need. He lets me rest in fields of green grass and leads me to quiet pools of fresh water.[9]

[1]RUTH 3.1. [2]Heb. 4.9.—[3]Isa. 32.18.—[4]Job 3.17.—[5]Rev. 14.13. [6]Heb. 6.20. [7]Matt. 11.28–30.—[8]Isa. 30.15. [9]Ps. 23.1, 2.

The LORD's Covenant Box always went ahead of them to find a place for them to camp.[1]

I am always in your care.[2]—He chose for us the land where we live.[3]—Lead me to do your will; make your way plain for me to follow.[4]

Give yourself to the LORD; trust in him, and he will help you.[5]—Remember the LORD in everything you do, and he will show you the right way.[6]—If you wander off the road to the right or the left, you will hear his voice behind you saying, "Here is the road. Follow it."[7]

The LORD is my shepherd; I have everything I need. He lets me rest in fields of green grass and leads me to quiet pools of fresh water.[8]—As a father is kind to his children, so the LORD is kind to those who honour him. He knows what we are made of; he remembers that we are dust.[9]—Your Father in heaven knows that you need all these things.[10]—Leave all your worries with him, because he cares for you.[11]

[1]NUM. 10.33. [2]Ps. 31.15.—[3]Ps. 47.4.—[4]Ps. 5.8. [5]Ps. 37.5.—[6]Prov. 3.6.—[7]Isa. 30.21. [8]Ps. 23.1, 2.—[9]Ps. 103.13, 14.—[10]Matt. 6.32.—[11]1 Pet. 5.7.

Evening

"Where do you live, Rabbi?" "Come and see," he answered.[1]

There are many rooms in my Father's house, and I am going to prepare a place for you. I would not tell you this if it were not so. And after I go and prepare a place for you, I will come back and take you to myself, so that you will be where I am.[2]—To those who win the victory I will give the right to sit beside me on my throne.[3]

I am the high and holy God, who lives for ever. I live in a high and holy place, but I also live with people who are humble and repentant, so that I can restore their confidence and hope.[4]

Listen! I stand at the door and knock; if anyone hears my voice and opens the door, I will come into his house and eat with him.[5]

I will be with you always, to the end of the age.[6]—How precious, O God, is your constant love! We find protection under the shadow of your wings.[7]

[1]JOHN 1.38, 39. [2]John 14.2, 3.—[3]Rev. 3.21. [4]Isa. 57.15. [5]Rev. 3.20. [6]Matt. 28.20.—[7]Ps. 36.7.

When Christ appears, we shall be like him, because we shall see him as he really is.[1]

Some . . . did receive him and believed in him; so he gave them the right to become God's children.[2]—In this way he has given us the very great and precious gifts he promised, so that by means of these gifts you may escape from the destructive lust that is in the world, and may come to share the divine nature.[3]

No one has ever seen or heard of a God like you, who does such deeds for those who put their hope in him.[4]

What we see now is like a dim image in a mirror; then we shall see face to face. What I know now is only partial; then it will be complete—as complete as God's knowledge of me.[5]—Christ . . . will change our weak mortal bodies and make them like his own glorious body, using that power by which he is able to bring all things under his rule.[6]—I will see you, because I have done no wrong; and when I awake, your presence will fill me with joy.[7]

[1]1 JOHN 3.2. [2]John 1.12.—[3]2 Pet. 1.4. [4]Isa. 64.4. [5]1 Cor. 13.12.—[6]Phil. 3.20, 21.—[7]Ps. 17.15.

Evening

The shepherd who works for me (the LORD Almighty)[1]

The full content of divine nature lives in Christ, in his humanity.[2]—I have given help to a famous soldier; I have given the throne to one I chose from the people.[3]—I have trampled the nations like grapes, and no one came to help me.[4]

How great is the secret of our religion: he appeared in human form.[5]—A child is born to us! A son is given to us! And he will be our ruler. He will be called, "Wonderful Counsellor," "Mighty God," "Eternal Father," "Prince of Peace."[6]

He reflects the brightness of God's glory and is the exact likeness of God's own being, sustaining the universe with his powerful word. After achieving forgiveness for the sins of mankind, he sat down in heaven at the right-hand side of God, the Supreme Power. Your kingdom, O God, will last for ever and ever! All God's angels must worship him.[7]

King of kings and Lord of lords.[8]

[1]ZECH. 13.7. [2]Col. 2.9.—[3]Ps. 89.19.—[4]Isa. 63.3. [5]1 Tim. 3.16.—[6]Isa. 9.6. [7]Heb. 1.3, 8, 6. [8]Rev. 19.16.

"Bless me, God . . . be with me and keep me from anything evil that might cause me pain." And God gave him what he prayed for.[1]

It is the LORD's blessing that makes you wealthy.[2]—If God decided to do nothing at all, no one could criticize him. If he hid his face, men would be helpless.[3]

Victory comes from the LORD—may he bless his people.[4]—How wonderful are the good things you keep for those who honour you! Everyone knows how good you are, how securely you protect those who trust you.[5]—I do not ask you to take them out of the world, but I do ask you to keep them safe from the Evil One.[6]

Ask, and you will receive; seek, and you will find; knock, and the door will be opened to you. For everyone who asks will receive, and anyone who seeks will find, and the door will be opened to him who knocks.[7]—The LORD will save his people; those who go to him for protection will be spared.[8]

[1]1 CHR. 4.10. [2]Prov. 10.22.—[3]Job 34.29. [4]Ps. 3.8.—[5]Ps. 31.19.—[6]John 17.15. [7]Matt. 7.7, 8.—[8]Ps. 34.22.

Evening

It was a night when the LORD kept watch to bring them out of Egypt.[1]

The Lord Jesus, on the night he was betrayed, took a piece of bread, gave thanks to God, broke it, and said, "This is my body, which is for you. Do this in memory of me." In the same way, after the supper he took the cup and said, "This cup is God's new covenant, sealed with my blood. Whenever you drink it, do so in memory of me."[2]

He . . . knelt down and prayed. In great anguish he prayed even more fervently; his sweat was like drops of blood falling to the ground.[3]

It was then almost noon of the day before the Passover. So they took charge of Jesus. He went out, carrying his cross, and came to "The Place of the Skull" (Golgotha). There they crucified him.[4]

Christ, our Passover lamb, has been sacrificed. Let us celebrate our Passover.[5]

[1]EXOD. 12.42. [2]1 Cor. 11.23–25. [3]Luke 22.41, 44. [4]John 19.14, 16–18. [5]1 Cor. 5.7, 8.

Who can stand against it?[1]

Who will be able to endure the day when he comes? Who will be able to survive when he appears? He will be like strong soap, like a fire that refines metal.[2]

I looked, and there was an enormous crowd—no one could count all the people! They were from every race, tribe, nation, and language, and they stood in front of the throne and of the Lamb, dressed in white robes and holding palm branches in their hands. These are the people who have come safely through the terrible persecution. They have washed their robes and made them white with the blood of the Lamb. Never again will they hunger or thirst; neither sun nor any scorching heat will burn them, because the Lamb, who is in the centre of the throne, will be their shepherd, and he will guide them to springs of life-giving water. And God will wipe away every tear from their eyes.[3]

There is no condemnation now for those who live in union with Christ Jesus.[4]—Stand, then, as free people, and do not allow yourselves to become slaves again.[5]

[1]REV. 6.17. [2]Mal. 3.2. [3]Rev. 7.9, 14, 16, 17. [4]Rom. 8.1.—[5]Gal. 5.1.

Evening

Don't put me, your servant, on trial; no one is innocent in your sight.[1]

Now, let's settle the matter. You are stained red with sin, but I will wash you as clean as snow. Although your stains are deep red, you will be as white as wool.[2]

Let them make peace with me. Yes, let them make peace with me.[3]—Make peace with God and stop treating him like an enemy.[4]

Now that we have been put right with God through faith, we have peace with God through our Lord Jesus Christ.[5]—A person is put right with God only through faith in Jesus Christ, never by doing what the Law requires.[6]—For no one is put right in God's sight by doing what the Law requires.[7]

Everyone who believes in him is set free from all the sins from which the Law of Moses could not set you free.[8]

Thanks be to God who gives us the victory through our Lord Jesus Christ![9]

[1]PS. 143.2. [2]Isa. 1.18. [3]Isa. 27.5.—[4]Job 22.21. [5]Rom. 5.1.—[6]Gal. 2.16.—[7]Rom. 3.20. [8]Acts 13.39. [9]1 Cor. 15.57.

I know there is someone in heaven who will come at last to my defence.[1]

We were God's enemies, but he made us his friends through the death of his Son. Now that we are God's friends, how much more will we be saved by Christ's life![2]—But Jesus lives on for ever, and his work as priest does not pass on to someone else. And so he is able, now and always, to save those who come to God through him, because he lives for ever to plead with God for them.[3]

Because I live, you also will live.[4]—If our hope in Christ is good for this life only and no more, then we deserve more pity than anyone else in all the world. But the truth is that Christ has been raised from death, as the guarantee that those who sleep in death will also be raised.[5]

The LORD says to his people, "I will come to Jerusalem to defend you and to save all of you that turn from your sins."[6]—For by the sacrificial death of Christ we are set free, that is, our sins are forgiven. How great is the grace of God![7]—For you know what was paid to set you free from the worthless manner of life handed down by your ancestors. It was not something that can be destroyed, such as silver or gold; it was the costly sacrifice of Christ, who was like a lamb without defect or flaw.[8]

[1]JOB 19.25. [2]Rom. 5.10.—[3]Heb. 7.24, 25. [4]John 14.19.—[5]1 Cor. 15.19, 20. [6]Isa. 59.20..—[7]Eph. 1.7.—[8]1 Pet. 1.18, 19.

Evening

The Spirit says clearly that some people will abandon the faith in later times; they will obey lying spirits and follow the teachings of demons.[1]

Be careful, then, how you listen.[2]—Christ's message in all its richness must live in your hearts.[3]—At all times carry faith as a shield; for with it you will be able to put out all the burning arrows shot by the Evil One.[4]

Those who love your law have perfect security, and there is nothing that can make them fall. How sweet is the taste of your instructions—sweeter even than honey! I gain wisdom from your laws, and so I hate all bad conduct.[5]

Your word is a lamp to guide me and a light for my path. I understand more than all my teachers, because I meditate on your instructions.[6]

Satan can disguise himself to look like an angel of light![7]—Even if we or an angel from heaven should preach to you a gospel that is different from the one we preached to you, may he be condemend to hell![8]

[1]1 TIM. 4.1. [2]Luke 8.18.—[3]Col. 3.16.—[4]Eph. 6.16. [5]Ps. 119.165, 103, 104. [6]Ps. 119.105, 99. [7]2 Cor. 11.14.—[8]Gal. 1.8.

His commands are not too hard for us.[1]

For what my Father wants is that all who see the Son and believe in him should have eternal life.[2]—We receive from him whatever we ask, because we obey his commands and do what pleases him.[3]

The yoke I will give you is easy, and the load I will put on you is light.[4]—If you love me, you will obey my commandments. Whoever accepts my commandments and obeys them is the one who loves me. My Father will love whoever loves me; I too will love him and reveal myself to him.[5]

Happy is the man who becomes wise—who gains understanding. Wisdom can make your life pleasant and lead you safely through it.[6]—Those who love your law have perfect security, and there is nothing that can make them fall.[7]—My inner being delights in the law of God.[8]

What he commands is that we believe in his Son Jesus Christ and love one another, just as Christ commanded us.[9]—If you love someone, you will never do him wrong; to love, then, is to obey the whole Law.[10]

[1]1 JOHN 5.3. [2]John 6.40.—[3]1 John 3.22. [4]Matt. 11.30.—[5]John 14.15, 21. [6]Prov. 3.13, 17.—[7]Ps. 119.165.—[8]Rom. 7.22. [9]1 John 3.23.—[10]Rom. 13.10.

Evening

Forgive the sins and errors of my youth.[1]

I have swept your sins away like a cloud. Come back to me; I am the one who saves you.[2]—I am the God who forgives your sins, and I do this because of who I am. I will not hold your sins against you.[3]—The LORD says, "Now, let's settle the matter. You are stained red with sin, but I will wash you as clean as snow. Although your stains are deep red, you will be as white as wool."[4]—I will forgive their sins and I will no longer remember their wrongs.[5]—You will trample our sins underfoot and send them to the bottom of the sea![6]

You save my life from all danger; you forgive all my sins.[7]—There is no other god like you, O LORD; you forgive the sins of your people who have survived. You do not stay angry for ever, but you take pleasure in showing us your constant love.[8]—He loves us, and by his sacrificial death he has freed us from our sins . . . To Jesus Christ be the glory and power for ever and ever! Amen.[9]

[1]PS. 25.7. [2]Isa. 44.22.—[3]Isa. 43.25.—[4]Isa. 1.18.—[5]Jer. 31.34.—[6]Mic. 7.19. [7]Isa. 38.17.—[8]Mic. 7.18.—[9]Rev. 1.5.

I rebuke and punish all whom I love.[1]

My son, pay attention when the Lord corrects you, and do not be discouraged when he rebukes you. Because the Lord corrects everyone he loves, and punishes everyone he accepts as a son.[2]—As a father corrects a son of whom he is proud.[3]—God bandages the wounds he makes; his hand hurts you, and his hand heals.[4]—Humble yourselves, then, under God's mighty hand, so that he will lift you up in his own good time.[5]—I have tested you in the fire of suffering.[6]

He takes no pleasure in causing us grief or pain.[7]—He does not punish us as we deserve or repay us according to our sins and wrongs. As high as the sky is above the earth, so great is his love for those who honour him. As far as the east is from the west, so far does he remove our sins from us. As a father is kind to his children, so the LORD is kind to those who honour him. He knows what we are made of; he remembers that we are dust.[8]

[1]REV. 3.19. [2]Heb. 12.5, 6.—[3]Prov. 3.12.—[4]Job 5.18.—[5]1 Pet. 5.6.—[6]Isa. 48.10. [7]Lam. 3.33.—[8]Ps. 103.10–14.

Evening

He is in heaven and you are on earth, so don't say any more than you have to.[1]

When you pray, do not use a lot of meaningless words, as the pagans do, who think that their gods will hear them because their prayers are long. Do not be like them. Your Father already knows what you need before you ask him.[2]

They . . . prayed to Baal until noon. They shouted, "Answer us, Baal!"[3]

Two men . . . went up to the Temple to pray: one was a Pharisee, the other a tax-collector. The Pharisee stood apart by himself and prayed, "I thank you, God, that I am not greedy, dishonest, or an adulterer, like everybody else. I thank you that I am not like that tax-collector over there." But the tax-collector stood at a distance and would not even raise his face to heaven, but beat on his breast and said, "God, have pity on me, a sinner!" "I tell you," said Jesus, "The tax-collector, and not the Pharisee, was in the right with God when he went home."[4]

Lord, teach us to pray.[5]

[1]ECCLES. 5.2. [2]Matt. 6.7, 8. [3]1 Kgs 18.26. [4]Luke 18.10, 11, 13, 14. [5]Luke 11.1.

The Spirit produces goodness.[1]

Since you are God's dear children, you must try to be like him.[2]—Love your enemies and pray for those who persecute you, so that you may become the sons of your Father in heaven. For he makes his sun to shine on bad and good people alike, and gives rain to those who do good and to those who do evil.[3]—Be merciful just as your Father is merciful.[4]

It is the light that brings a rich harvest of every kind of goodness, righteousness, and truth.[5]

When the kindness and love of God our Saviour was revealed, he saved us. It was not because of any good deeds that we ourselves had done, but because of his own mercy that he saved us, through the Holy Spirit, who gives us new birth and new life by washing us. God poured out the Holy Spirit abundantly on us through Jesus Christ our Saviour.[6]—He is good to everyone and has compassion on all he made.[7]—God, who did not even keep back his own Son, but offered him for us all! He gave us his Son—will he not also freely give us all things?[8]

[1]GAL. 5.22. [2]Eph. 5.1.—[3]Matt. 5.44, 45.—[4]Luke 6.36. [5]Eph. 5.9. [6]Titus 3.4–6.—[7]Ps. 145.9.—[8]Rom. 8.32.

Evening

The LORD has helped us all the way.[1]

When I was in danger, he saved me.[2]—Give praise to the LORD; he has heard my cry for help. The LORD protects and defends me; I trust in him. He gives me help and makes me glad; I praise him with joyful songs.[3]

It is better to trust in the LORD than to depend on man. It is better to trust in the LORD than to depend on human leaders.[4]—Happy is the man who has the God of Jacob to help him and who depends on the LORD his God.[5]—He led them by a straight road to a city where they could live.[6]—The LORD kept every one of the promises that he had made to the people of Israel.[7]

"When I sent you out that time without purse, bag, or shoes, did you lack anything?" "Not a thing," they answered.[8]—You have always been my help. In the shadow of your wings I sing for joy.[9]

[1]1 SAM. 7.12. [2]Ps. 116.6.—[3]Ps. 28.6, 7. [4]Ps. 118.8, 9.—[5]Ps. 146.5.—[6]Ps. 107.7.—[7]Josh. 21.45. [8]Luke 22.35.—[9]Ps. 63.7.

These are the Passover regulations: no foreigner shall eat the Passover meal.[1]

The priests who serve in the Jewish place of worship have no right to eat any of the sacrifice on our altar.[2]—No one can see the Kingdom of God unless he is born again.[3]—At that time you were apart from Christ. You were foreigners and did not belong to God's chosen people. You had no part in the covenants, which were based on God's promises to his people. But now, in union with Christ Jesus, you who used to be far away have been brought near by the sacrificial death of Christ.[4]

For Christ himself has brought us peace by making Jews and Gentiles one people. With his own body he broke down the wall . . . that kept them enemies. He abolished the Jewish Law . . . in order to create out of the two races one new people in union with himself, in this way making peace.[5]

So then, you Gentiles are not foreigners or strangers any longer; you are now fellow-citizens with God's people and members of the family of God.[6]

If anyone hears my voice and opens the door, I will come into his house and eat with him, and he will eat with me.[7]

[1]EXOD. 12.43. [2]Heb. 13.10.—[3]John 3.3.—[4]Eph. 2.12, 13. [5]Eph. 2.14, 15. [6]Eph. 2.19. [7]Rev. 3.20.

Evening

Jesus . . . prayed the third time, saying the same words.[1]

In his life on earth Jesus made his prayers and requests with loud cries and tears to God, who could save him from death.[2]

Let us try to know the LORD. He will come to us as surely as the day dawns.[3]—Pray at all times.[4]—Pray on every occasion, as the Spirit leads. For this reason keep alert and never give up.[5]—Don't worry about anything, but in all your prayers ask God for what you need, always asking him with a thankful heart. And God's peace, which is far beyond human understanding, will keep your hearts and minds safe in union with Christ Jesus.[6]

Yet not what I want, but what you want.[7]—We have courage in God's presence, because we are sure that he hears us if we ask him for anything that is according to his will.[8]

Seek your happiness in the LORD, and he will give you your heart's desire. Give yourself to the LORD; trust in him, and he will help you.[9]

[1]MATT. 26.44. [2]Heb. 5.7. [3]Hos. 6.3.—[4]Rom. 12.12.—[5]Eph. 6.18.—[6]Phil. 4.6, 7. [7]Matt. 26.39.—[8]1 John 5.14. [9]Ps. 37.4, 5.

Since we are his children, we will possess the blessings he keeps for his people, and we will also possess with Christ what God has kept for him.[1]

If you belong to Christ, then you are the descendants of Abraham and will receive what God has promised.[2]

See how much the Father has loved us! His love is so great that we are called God's children.[3]—You are no longer a slave but a son. And since you are his son, God will give you all that he has for his sons.[4]—God had already decided that through Jesus Christ he would make us his sons—this was his pleasure and purpose.[5]

Father! I want them to be with me where I am, so that they may see my glory, the glory you gave me.[6]

To those who win the victory, who continue to the end to do what I want . . . I will give them authority over the nations.[7]—To those who win the victory I will give the right to sit beside me on my throne, just as I have been victorious and now sit by my Father on his throne.[8]

[1]ROM. 8.17. [2]Gal. 3.29. [3]1 John 3.1.—[4]Gal. 4.7.—[5]Eph. 1.5. [6]John 17.24. [7]Rev. 2.26.—[8]Rev. 3.21.

Evening

He chose what the world looks down on and despises.[1]

These people who are talking like this are Galileans![2]

Jesus . . . saw two brothers who were fishermen . . . catching fish in the lake with a net. Jesus said to them, "Come with me."[3]—The members of the Council were amazed to see how bold Peter and John were and to learn that they were ordinary men of no education. They realized then that they had been companions of Jesus.[4]

My teaching and message were not delivered with skilful words of human wisdom, but with convincing proof of the power of God's Spirit. Your faith, then, does not rest on human wisdom but on God's power.[5]

You did not choose me; I chose you and appointed you to go and bear much fruit. Whoever remains in me, and I in him, will bear much fruit; for you can do nothing without me.[6]—We who have this spiritual treasure are like common clay pots, in order to show that the supreme power belongs to God, not to us.[7]

[1]1 COR. 1.28. [2]Acts 2.7. [3]Matt. 4.18, 19.—[4]Acts 4.13. [5]1 Cor. 2.4, 5. [6]John 15.16, 5.—[7]2 Cor. 4.7.

Sitting next to Jesus.[1]

I will comfort you . . . as a mother comforts her child.[2]—Some people brought children to Jesus for him to place his hands on them. He took the children in his arms, placed his hands on each of them, and blessed them.[3]—Jesus called his disciples to him and said, "I feel sorry for these people, because they have been with me for three days and now have nothing to eat. I don't want to send them away without feeding them, for they might faint on their way home."[4]—Our High Priest is not one who cannot feel sympathy for our weaknesses.[5]—In his love and compassion he rescued them.[6]

When I go, you will not be left all alone; I will come back to you.[7]—Can a woman forget her own baby and not love the child she bore? Even if a mother should forget her child, I will never forget you.[8]

The Lamb, who is in the centre of the throne, will be their shepherd, and he will guide them to springs of life-giving water. And God will wipe away every tear from their eyes.[9]

[1]JOHN 13.23. [2]Isa. 66.13.—[3]Mark 10.13, 16.—[4]Matt. 15.32.—[5]Heb. 4.15.— [6]Isa. 63.9. [7]John 14.18.—[8]Isa. 49.15. [9]Rev. 7.17.

Evening

Jesus Christ, the righteous one . . . is the means by which our sins are forgiven.[1]

The winged creatures are to face each other across the lid, and their outspread wings are to cover it. Put the two stone tablets inside the box and put the lid on top of it. I will meet you there and . . . I will give you all my laws for the people of Israel.[2]

Surely he is ready to save those who honour him. Love and faithfulness will meet; righteousness and peace will embrace.[3]

If you kept a record of our sins, who could escape being condemned? But you forgive us, so that we should stand in awe of you. Israel, trust in the LORD, because his love is constant and he is always willing to save. He will save his people Israel from all their sins.[4]—Everyone has sinned and is far away from God's saving presence. But by the free gift of God's grace all are put right with him through Christ Jesus, who sets them free. God offered him, so that by his sacrificial death he should become the means by which people's sins are forgiven through their faith in him. God did this in order to demonstrate that he is righteous.[5]

[1]1 JOHN 2.1, 2. [2]Exod. 25.20–22. [3]Ps. 85.9, 10. [4]Ps. 130.3, 4, 7, 8.— [5]Rom. 3.23–25.

We ourselves know and believe the love which God has for us.[1]

God's mercy is so abundant, and his love for us is so great, that while we were spiritually dead in our disobedience he brought us to life with Christ. It is by God's grace that you have been saved. In our union with Christ Jesus he raised us up with him to rule with him in the heavenly world. He did this to demonstrate for all time to come the extraordinary greatness of his grace in the love he showed us in Christ Jesus.[2]

God loved the world so much that he gave his only Son, so that everyone who believes in him may not die but have eternal life.[3]—God, who did not even keep back his own Son, but offered him for us all . . . will he not also freely give us all things?[4]—He is good to everyone and has compassion on all he made.[5]

We love because God first loved us.[6]—How happy you are to believe that the Lord's message to you will come true![7]

[1]1 JOHN 4.16. [2]Eph. 2.4–7. [3]John 3.16.—[4]Rom. 8.32.—[5]Ps. 145.9. [6]1 John 4.19.—[7]Luke 1.45.

Evening

Have the same concern for everyone.[1]

My brothers, as believers in our Lord Jesus Christ, the Lord of glory, you must never treat people in different ways according to their outward appearance. God chose the poor people of this world to be rich in faith and to possess the kingdom which he promised to those who love him.[2]

No one should be looking to his own interests, but to the interests of others.[3]—If we have food and clothes, that should be enough for us. But those who want to get rich fall into temptation and are caught in the trap of many foolish and harmful desires, which pull them down to ruin and destruction.[4]

God purposely chose what the world considers nonsense in order to shame the wise, and he chose what the world considers weak in order to shame the powerful. He chose what the world looks down on and despises, and thinks is nothing, in order to destroy what the world thinks is important. This means that no one can boast in God's presence.[5]

LORD, I have given up my pride and turned away from my arrogance.[6]

[1]ROM. 12.16. [2]Jas 2.1, 5. [3]1 Cor. 10.24.—[4]1 Tim. 6.8, 9. [5]1 Cor. 1.27–29. [6]Ps. 131.1.

Your speech should always be pleasant and interesting.[1]

An idea well-expressed is like a design of gold, set in silver. A warning given by an experienced person to someone willing to listen is more valuable than gold rings or jewellery made of the finest gold.[2]—Do not use harmful words, but only helpful words, the kind that build up and provide what is needed, so that what you say will do good to those who hear you.[3]—A good person brings good things out of his treasure of good things; a bad person brings bad things out of his treasure of bad things. Your words will be used to judge you.[4]—Wisely spoken words can heal.[5]

The people who feared the LORD spoke to one another, and the LORD listened and heard what they said. In his presence, there was written down in a book a record of those who feared the LORD and respected him.[6]

If instead of talking nonsense you proclaim a worthwhile message, you will be my prophet again.[7]—You are so rich in all you have: in faith, speech, and knowledge, in your eagerness to help . . . so we want you to be generous also in this service of love.[8]

[1]COL. 4.6. [2]Prov. 25.11, 12.—[3]Eph. 4.29.—[4]Matt. 12.35, 37.—[5]Prov. 12.18. [6]Mal. 3.16. [7]Jer. 15.19.—[8]2 Cor. 8.7.

Evening

Your constant love is my guide.[1]

The LORD is loving and merciful, slow to become angry and full of constant love.[2]—Your Father in heaven . . . makes his sun to shine on bad and good people alike, and gives rain to those who do good and to those who do evil.[3]

Since you are God's dear children, you must try to be like him. Your life must be controlled by love, just as Christ loved us and gave his life for us as a sweet-smelling offering and sacrifice that pleases God.[4]—Be kind and tender-hearted to one another, and forgive one another, as God has forgiven you through Christ.[5]—Now that by your obedience to the truth you have purified yourselves and have come to have a sincere love for your fellow-believers, love one another earnestly with all your heart.[6]

Love your enemies and do good to them; lend and expect nothing back. You will then have a great reward, and you will be sons of the Most High God. For he is good to the ungrateful and the wicked. Be merciful just as your Father is merciful.[7]

[1]PS. 26.3. [2]Ps. 145.8.—[3]Matt. 5.45. [4]Eph. 5.1, 2.—[5]Eph. 4.32.—[6]1 Pet. 1.22. [7]Luke 6.35, 36.

Then the Spirit led Jesus into the desert to be tempted by the Devil.[1]

In his life on earth Jesus made his prayers and requests with loud cries and tears to God, who could save him from death. Because he was humble and devoted, God heard him. But even though he was God's Son, he learnt through his sufferings to be obedient. When he was made perfect, he became the source of eternal salvation for all those who obey him.[2]—Our High Priest is not one who cannot feel sympathy for our weaknesses. [He] was tempted in every way that we are, but did not sin.[3]

Every test that you have experienced is the kind that normally comes to people. But God keeps his promise, and he will not allow you to be tested beyond your power to remain firm; at the time you are put to the test, he will give you the strength to endure it, and so provide you with a way out.[4]—My grace is all you need, for my power is greatest when you are weak.[5]

[1]MATT. 4.1. [2]Heb. 5.7–9.—[3]Heb. 4.15. [4]1 Cor. 10.13.—[5]2 Cor. 12.9.

Evening

The Son of Man . . . [***came***] ***to give his life to redeem many people.***[1]

The blood of goats and bulls and the ashes of a burnt calf are sprinkled on the people who are ritually unclean, and this purifies them by taking away their ritual impurity. Since this is true, how much more is accomplished by the blood of Christ! Through the eternal Spirit he offered himself as a perfect sacrifice to God. His blood will purify our consciences from useless rituals, so that we may serve the living God.[2]

Like a lamb about to be slaughtered.[3]—I know my sheep . . . and I am willing to die for them. No one takes my life away from me. I give it up of my own free will. I have the right to give it up, and I have the right to take it back.[4]

The life of every living thing is in the blood, and that is why the LORD has commanded that all blood be poured out on the altar to take away the people's sins. Blood, which is life, takes away sins.[5]—Sins are forgiven only if blood is poured out.[6]

It was while we were still sinners that Christ died for us! By his sacrificial death we are now put right with God; how much more, then, will we be saved by him from God's anger![7]

[1]MATT. 20.28. [2]Heb. 9.13, 14. [3]Isa. 53.7.—[4]John 10.15, 18. [5]Lev. 17.11.—[6]Heb. 9.22. [7]Rom. 5.8, 9.

Morning

If we confess our sins to God, he will keep his promise. He will forgive us our sins and purify us from all our wrongdoing.[1]

I recognize my faults; I am always conscious of my sins. I have sinned against you—only against you—and done what you consider evil.[2]

He got up and started back to his father. He was still a long way from home when his father saw him; his heart was filled with pity, and he ran, threw his arms round his son, and kissed him.[3]—I have swept your sins away like a cloud. Come back to me; I am the one who saves you.[4]—Your sins are forgiven for the sake of Christ.[5]—God has forgiven you through Christ.[6]—God shows that he himself is righteous and that he puts right everyone who believes in Jesus.[7]

I will sprinkle clean water on you and make you clean.[8]—You will walk with me, clothed in white, because you are worthy to do so.[9]

Jesus Christ is the one who came with the water of his baptism and the blood of his death. He came not only with the water, but with both the water and the blood.[10]

[1]1 JOHN 1.9. [2]Ps. 51.3, 4. [3]Luke 15.20.—[4]Isa. 44.22.—[5]1 John 2.12.—[6]Eph. 4.32.—[7]Rom. 3.26. [8]Ezek. 36.25.—[9]Rev. 3.4. [10]1 John 5.6.

Evening

You have nothing to do with corrupt judges.[1]

The fellowship that we have with the Father and with his Son Jesus Christ.[2]—My dear friends, we are now God's children, but it is not yet clear what we shall become. But we know that when Christ appears, we shall be like him, because we shall see him as he really is. Everyone who has this hope in Christ keeps himself pure, just as Christ is pure.[3]

The ruler of this world is coming. He has no power over me.[4]—The High Priest . . . is holy; he has no fault or sin in him; he has been set apart from sinners.[5]

We are not fighting against human beings but against the wicked spiritual forces in the heavenly world, the rulers, authorities, and cosmic powers of this dark age.[6]—The ruler of the spiritual powers in space, the spirit who now controls the people who disobey God.[7]

We know that no child of God keeps on sinning, for the Son of God keeps him safe, and the Evil One cannot harm him. We know that we belong to God even though the whole world is under the rule of the Evil One.[8]

[1]PS. 94.20. [2]1 John 1.3.—[3]1 John 3.2, 3. [4]John 14.30.—[5]Heb. 7.26. [6]Eph. 6.12.—[7]Eph. 2.2. [8]1 John 5.18, 19.

Morning

***I have taken away your sin and will give you new clothes to wear.*[1]**

Happy are those whose sins are forgiven, whose wrongs are pardoned.[2]—All of us have been sinful; even our best actions are filthy through and through.[3]—I know that good does not live in me—that is, in my human nature. For even though the desire to do good is in me, I am not able to do it.[4]

You were baptized into union with Christ, and now you are clothed . . . with the life of Christ.[5]—You have taken off the old self with its habits and have put on the new self. This is the new being which God, its Creator, is constantly renewing in his own image.[6]—I no longer have a righteousness of my own . . . gained by obeying the Law. I now have the righteousness that is given through faith in Christ.[7]

Bring the best robe and put it on him.[8]—the linen is the good deeds of God's people.[9]—Jerusalem rejoices because of what the LORD has done. She is like a bride dressed for her wedding. God has clothed her with salvation and victory.[10]

[1]ZECH. 3.4. [2]Ps. 32.1.—[3]Isa. 64.6.—[4]Rom. 7.18. [5]Gal. 3.27.—[6]Col. 3.9, 10.—[7]Phil. 3.9. [8]Luke 15.22.—[9]Rev. 19.8.—[10]Isa. 61.10.

Evening

***On that day fire will reveal everyone's work.*[1]**

You should not pass judgement on anyone before the right time comes. Final judgement must wait until the Lord comes; he will bring to light the dark secrets and expose the hidden purposes of people's minds. And then everyone will receive from God the praise he deserves.[2]

Why do you pass judgement on your brother? Why do you despise your brother? All of us will stand before God to be judged by him. Every one of us, then, will have to give an account of himself to God. Let us stop judging one another.[3]

God through Jesus Christ will judge the secret thoughts of all.[4]—Nor does the Father himself judge anyone. He has given his Son the full right to judge, so that all will honour the Son in the same way as they honour the Father.[5]

You are a great and powerful God; you are the LORD Almighty. You make wise plans and do mighty things; you see everything that people do, and you reward them according to their actions.[6]

[1]1 COR. 3.13. [2]1 Cor. 4.5. [3]Rom. 14.10, 12, 13. [4]Rom. 2.16.—[5]John 5.22, 27. [6]Jer. 32.18, 19.

Morning

No pupil is greater than his teacher.[1]

You call me Teacher and Lord, and it is right that you do so, because that is what I am.[2]

A pupil should be satisfied to become like his teacher, and a slave like his master.[3]—If they persecuted me, they will persecute you too; if they obeyed my teaching, they will obey yours too.[4]—I gave them your message, and the world hated them, because they do not belong to the world, just as I do not belong to the world.[5]

Think of what he went through; how he put up with so much hatred from sinners! So do not let yourselves become discouraged and give up. For in your struggle against sin you have not yet had to resist to the point of being killed.[6]

Let us run with determination the race that lies before us. Let us keep our eyes fixed on Jesus, on whom our faith depends from beginning to end. He did not give up because of the cross! On the contrary, because of the joy that was waiting for him, he thought nothing of the disgrace of dying on the cross, and he is now seated at the right-hand side of God's throne.[7]—Since Christ suffered physically, you too must strengthen yourselves with the same way of thinking that he had.[8]

[1]MATT. 10.24. [2]John 13.13. [3]Matt. 10.25.—[4]John 15.20.—[5]John 17.14. [6]Heb. 12.3, 4. [7]Heb. 12.1, 2.—[8]1 Pet. 4.1.

Evening

Let my life be your example.[1]

If only they would always feel like this! If only they would always honour me and obey all my commands, so that everything would go well with them and their descendants for ever.[2]

Your heart is not right in God's sight.[3]—A person becomes an enemy of God when he is controlled by his human nature; for he does not obey God's law, and in fact he cannot obey it. Those who obey their human nature cannot please God.[4]

First they gave themselves to the Lord.[5]—[Hezekiah] was successful, because everything he did . . . he did in a spirit of complete loyalty and devotion to his God.[6]

Be careful how you think; your life is shaped by your thoughts.[7]

Whatever you do, work at it with all your heart, as though you were working for the Lord.[8]—Do what God wants, as slaves of Christ. Do your work . . . cheerfully, as though you served the Lord, and not merely men.[9]

I will eagerly obey your commands, because you will give me more understanding.[10]

[1]PROV. 23.26. [2]Deut. 5.29. [3]Acts 8.21.—[4]Rom. 8.7, 8. [5]2 Cor. 8.5.—[6]2 Chr. 31.21. [7]Prov. 4.23. [8]Col. 3.23.—[9]Eph. 6.6, 7. [10]Ps. 119.32.

I will be with you to protect you and keep you safe.[1]

Can you take away a soldier's loot? Can you rescue the prisoners of a tyrant? The LORD replies, "That is just what is going to happen. The soldier's prisoners will be taken away, and the tyrant's loot will be seized. I will fight against whoever fights you. Then all mankind will know that I am the LORD, the one who saves you and sets you free. They will know that I am Israel's powerful God."[2]—Do not be afraid—I am with you! I am your God—let nothing terrify you! I will make you strong and help you; I will protect you and save you.[3]

Our High Priest is not one who cannot feel sympathy for our weaknesses . . . we have a High Priest who was tempted in every way that we are, but did not sin.[4]—Now he can help those who are tempted, because he himself was tempted and suffered.[5]—The LORD guides a man in the way he should go and protects those who please him. If they fall, they will not stay down, because the LORD will help them up.[6]

[1]JER. 15.20. [2]Isa. 49.24–26.—[3]Isa. 41.10. [4]Heb. 4.15.—[5]Heb. 2.18.—[6]Ps. 37.23, 24.

Evening

He satisfies those who are thirsty and fills the hungry with good things.[1]

You have found out for yourselves how kind the Lord is.[2]

O God, you are my God, and I long for you. My whole being desires you; like a dry, worn-out, and waterless land, my soul is thirsty for you. Let me see you in the sanctuary; let me see how mighty and glorious you are.[3]—I long to be in the LORD's Temple. With my whole being I sing for joy to the living God.[4]—I want very much to leave this life and be with Christ, which is a far better thing.[5]

When I awake, your presence will fill me with joy.[6]—Never again will they hunger or thirst; neither sun nor any scorching heat will burn them, because the Lamb, who is in the centre of the throne, will be their shepherd, and he will guide them to springs of life-giving water. And God will wipe away every tear from their eyes.[7]—We feast on the abundant food you provide; you let us drink from the river of your goodness.[8]—I will . . . satisfy all the needs of my people. I, the LORD, have spoken.[9]

[1]PS. 107.9. [2]1 Pet. 2.3. [3]Ps. 63.1, 2.—[4]Ps. 84.2.—[5]Phil. 1.23. [6]Ps. 17.15.—[7]Rev. 7.16, 17.—[8]Ps. 36.8.—[9]Jer. 31.14.

I will go with you, and I will give you victory.[1]

Be determined and confident. Do not be afraid of them. Your God, the LORD himself, will be with you. He will not fail you or abandon you. The LORD himself will lead you and be with you. He will not fail you or abandon you, so do not lose courage or be afraid.[2]—Remember that I have commanded you to be determined and confident! Don't be afraid or discouraged, for I, the LORD your God, am with you wherever you go.[3]—Remember the LORD in everything you do, and he will show you the right way.[4]

God has said, "I will never leave you; I will never abandon you." Let us be bold, then, and say, "The Lord is my helper, I will not be afraid. What can anyone do to me?"[5]—The capacity we have comes from God.[6]

Do not bring us to hard testing.[7]—LORD, I know that no one is the master of his own destiny; no person has control over his own life.[8]—I am always in your care.[9]

[1]EXOD. 33.14. [2]Deut. 31.6, 8.—[3]Josh. 1.9.—[4]Prov. 3.6. [5]Heb. 13.5, 6.—[6]2 Cor. 3.5. [7]Matt. 6.13.—[8]Jer. 10.23.—[9]Ps. 31.15.

Evening

Let us be concerned for one another, to help one another to show love and to do good.[1]

Honest words are convincing.[2]—I have tried to arouse pure thoughts in your minds by reminding you of these things.[3]

The people who feared the LORD spoke to one another, and the LORD listened and heard what they said. In his presence, there was written down in a book a record of those who feared the LORD and respected him.[4]—Whenever two of you on earth agree about anything you pray for, it will be done for you by my Father in heaven.[5]

The LORD God said, "It is not good for the man to live alone."[6]—Two are better off than one, because together they can work more effectively. If one of them falls down, the other can help him up. But if someone is alone and falls, it's just too bad, because there is no one to help him.[7]

You should decide never to do anything that would make your brother stumble or fall into sin.[8]—Help to carry one another's burdens, and in this way you will obey the law of Christ. Keep an eye on yourselves, so that you will not be tempted, too.[9]

[1]HEB. 10.24. [2]Job 6.25.—[3]2 Pet. 3.1. [4]Mal. 3.16.—[5]Matt. 18.19. [6]Gen. 2.18.—[7]Eccles. 4.9, 10. [8]Rom. 14.13.—[9]Gal. 6.2, 1.

I belong to my lover, and he desires me.[1]

I know whom I have trusted, and I am sure that he is able to keep safe until that Day what he has entrusted to me.[2]—I am certain that nothing can separate us from his love: neither death nor life, neither angels nor other heavenly rulers or powers, neither the present nor the future, neither the world above nor the world below—there is nothing in all creation that will ever be able to separate us from the love of God which is ours through Christ Jesus our Lord.[3]—I protected [those you have given me] and not one of them was lost.[4]

The LORD takes pleasure in his people.[5]—Pleased with the human race.[6]—His love for us is so great.[7]—The greatest love a person can have for his friends is to give his life for them.[8]

He bought you for a price. So use your body for God's glory.[9]—If we live, it is for the Lord that we live, and if we die, it is for the Lord that we die. So whether we live or die, we belong to the Lord.[10]

[1]S. OF S. 7.10. [2]2 Tim. 1.12.—[3]Rom. 8.38, 39.—[4]John 17.12. [5]Ps. 149.4.—[6]Prov. 8.31.—[7]Eph. 2.4.—[8]John 15.13. [9]1 Cor. 6.20.—[10]Rom. 14.8.

Evening

Search in the LORD's book.[1]

Remember these commands and cherish them. Tie them on your arms and wear them on your foreheads as a reminder.[2]—Be sure that the book of the Law is always read in your worship. Study it day and night, and make sure that you obey everything written in it. Then you will be prosperous and successful.[3]

He keeps the law of his God in his heart and never departs from it.[4]—I have obeyed your command and have not followed paths of violence.[5]—I keep your law in my heart, so that I will not sin against you.[6]

We are even more confident of the message proclaimed by the prophets. You will do well to pay attention to it, because it is like a lamp shining in a dark place until the Day dawns and the light of the morning star shines in your hearts.[7]—In order that we might have hope through the patience and encouragement which the Scriptures give us.[8]

[1]ISA. 34.16. [2]Deut. 11.18.—[3]Josh. 1.8. [4]Ps. 37.31.—[5]Ps. 17.4.—[6]Ps. 119.11. [7]2 Pet. 1.19.—[8]Rom. 15.4.

The mouth speaks what the heart is full of.[1]

Christ's message in all its richness must live in your hearts.[2]

Be careful how you think; your life is shaped by your thoughts.[3]—What you say can preserve life or destroy it.[4]—A good man's words are wise, and he is always fair. He keeps the law of his God in his heart and never departs from it.[5]—Do not use harmful words, but only helpful words, the kind that build up and provide what is needed, so that what you say will do good to those who hear you.[6]

We cannot stop speaking of what we ourselves have seen and heard.[7]—I kept on believing, even when I said, "I am completely crushed."[8]

If anyone declares publicly that he belongs to me, I will do the same for him before my Father in heaven.[9]—It is by our faith that we are put right with God; it is by our confession that we are saved.[10]

[1]MATT. 12.34. [2]Col. 3.16. [3]Prov. 4.23.—[4]Prov. 18.21.—[5]Ps. 37.30, 31.— [6]Eph. 4.29. [7]Acts 4.20.—[8]Ps. 116.10. [9]Matt. 10.32.—[10]Rom. 10.10.

Evening

I hope to see you soon, and then we will talk personally.[1]

Why don't you tear the sky apart and come down?[2]—As a deer longs for a stream of cool water, so I long for you, O God. I thirst for you, the living God; when can I go and worship in your presence?[3]—Come to me, my lover, like a gazelle, like a young stag on the mountains where spices grow.[4]

We . . . are citizens of heaven, and we eagerly wait for our Saviour, the Lord Jesus Christ, to come from heaven.[5]—We wait for the blessed Day we hope for, when the glory of our great God and Saviour Jesus Christ will appear.[6]—God our Saviour and Christ Jesus our hope.[7]—You love him, although you have not seen him.[8]

He who gives his testimony to all this says, "Yes indeed! I am coming soon!" So be it. Come, Lord Jesus![9]—When it happens, everyone will say, "He is our God! We have put our trust in him, and he has rescued us. He is the LORD! We have put our trust in him, and now we are happy and joyful because he has saved us."[10]

[1]3 JOHN 14. [2]Isa. 64.1.—[3]Ps. 42.1, 2.—[4]S. of S. 8.14. [5]Phil. 3.20.— [6]Titus 2.13.—[7]1 Tim. 1.1.—[8]1 Pet. 1.8. [9]Rev. 22.20.—[10]Isa 25.9.

May your will be done on earth as it is in heaven.[1]

Praise the LORD, you strong and mighty angels, who obey his commands, who listen to what he says. Praise the LORD, all you heavenly powers, you servants of his, who do his will![2]

I have come down from heaven not to do my own will but the will of him who sent me.[3]—How I love to do your will, my God! I keep your teaching in my heart.[4]—My Father, if this cup of suffering cannot be taken away unless I drink it, your will be done.[5]

Not everyone who calls me "Lord, Lord" will enter the Kingdom of heaven, but only those who do what my Father in heaven wants them to do.[6]—It is not by hearing the Law that people are put right with God, but by doing what the Law commands.[7]—Now that you know this truth, how happy you will be if you put it into practice![8]—The person who does not do the good he knows he should do is guilty of sin.[9]

Do not conform yourselves to the standards of this world, but let God transform you inwardly by a complete change of your mind.[10]

[1]MATT. 6.10. [2]Ps. 103.20, 21. [3]John 6.38.—[4]Ps. 40.8.—[5]Matt. 26.42. [6]Matt. 7.21.—[7]Rom. 2.13.—[8]John 13.17.—[9]Jas 4.17. [10]Rom 12.2.

Evening

You know good food when you taste it, but not wise words when you hear them.[1]

My dear friends, do not believe all who claim to have the Spirit, but test them to find out if the spirit they have comes from God. For many false prophets have gone out everywhere.[2]—Stop judging by external standards, and judge by true standards.[3]—I speak to you as sensible people; judge for yourselves what I say.[4]—Christ's message in all its richness must live in your hearts.[5]

If you have ears, then, listen to what the Spirit says to the churches![6]—Whoever has the Spirit . . . is able to judge the value of everything.[7]

Pay attention to what you hear![8]—I know what you have done; . . . and that you have tested those who say they are apostles but are not, and have found out that they are liars.[9]—Put all things to the test: keep what is good.[10]

The sheep hear his voice as he calls his own sheep by name, and he leads them out. When he has brought them out, he goes ahead of them, and the sheep follow him, because they know his voice. They will not follow someone else; instead, they will run away from such a person, because they do not know his voice.[11]

[1]JOB 34.3. [2]1 John 4.1.—[3]John 7.24.—[4]1 Cor. 10.15.—[5]Col. 3.16. [6]Rev. 2.29.— [7]1 Cor. 2.15. [8]Mark 4.24.—[9]Rev. 2.2.—[10]1 Thess. 5.21. [11]John 10.3–5.

Morning

You will be . . . a people dedicated to me alone, and you will serve me as priests.[1]

You were killed, and by your sacrificial death you bought for God people from every tribe, language, nation, and race. You have made them a kingdom of priests to serve our God.[2]—You are the chosen race, the King's priests, the holy nation, God's own people, chosen to proclaim the wonderful acts of God, who called you out of darkness into his own marvellous light.[3]

You will be known as the priests of the LORD, the servants of our God.[4]—Priests of God and of Christ.[5]

My Christian brothers, who also have been called by God! Think of Jesus, whom God sent to be the High Priest of the faith we profess.[6]—Let us, then, always offer praise to God as our sacrifice through Jesus, which is the offering presented by lips that confess him as Lord.[7]

God has made us what we are, and in our union with Christ Jesus he has created us for a life of good deeds, which he has already prepared for us to do.[8]—God's temple is holy, and you yourselves are his temple.[9]

[1]EXOD. 19.5, 6. [2]Rev. 5.9, 10.—[3]1 Pet. 2.9. [4]Isa. 61.6.—[5]Rev. 20.6. [6]Heb. 3.1.—[7]Heb. 13.15. [8]Eph. 2.10.—[9]1 Cor. 3.17.

Evening

We prayed to our God and kept men on guard against them day and night.[1]

Keep watch and pray that you will not fall into temptation.[2]—Be persistent in prayer, and keep alert as you pray, giving thanks to God.[3]—Leave all your worries with him, because he cares for you. Be alert, be on the watch! Your enemy, the Devil, roams round like a roaring lion, looking for someone to devour. Be firm in your faith and resist him.[4]

Why do you call me, "Lord, Lord," and yet you don't do what I tell you?[5]—Do not deceive yourselves by just listening to his word; instead, put it into practice.[6]

Why are you crying out for help? Tell the people to move forward.[7]

Don't worry about anything, but in all your prayers ask God for what you need, always asking him with a thankful heart. And God's peace, which is far beyond human understanding, will keep your hearts and minds safe in union with Christ Jesus.[8]

[1]NEH. 4.9. [2]Matt. 26.41.—[3]Col. 4.2.—[4]1 Pet. 5.7–9. [5]Luke 6.46.—[6]Jas 1.22. [7]Exod. 14.15. [8]Phil. 4.6, 7.

You are a loving and merciful God, always patient, always kind, and always ready to change your mind and not punish.[1]

Now LORD, I pray, show us your power and do what you promised when you said, "I, the LORD, am not easily angered, and I show great love and faithfulness and forgive sin and rebellion. Yet I will not fail to punish children and grandchildren to the third and fourth generation for the sins of their parents."[2]

Do not punish us for the sins of our ancestors. Have mercy on us now; we have lost all hope. Help us, O God, and save us; rescue us and forgive our sins for the sake of your own honour.[3]—Even though our sins accuse us, help us, LORD, as you have promised. We have turned away from you many times; we have sinned against you.[4]—We have sinned against you, LORD; we confess our own sins and the sins of our ancestors.[5]

If you kept a record of our sins, who could escape being condemned? But you forgive us, so that we should stand in awe of you.[6]

[1]JONAH 4.2. [2]Num. 14.17, 18. [3]Ps. 79.8, 9.—[4]Jer. 14.7.—[5]Jer. 14.20. [6]Ps. 130.3, 4.

Evening

Saved by the Spirit's power.[1]

Wake up, North Wind. South Wind, blow on my garden; fill the air with fragrance.[2]—See what God did with this sadness of yours: how earnest it has made you, how eager to prove your innocence! Such indignation, such alarm, such feelings, such devotion, such readiness to punish wrongdoing![3]—It is the light that brings a rich harvest of every kind of goodness, righteousness, and truth. Try to learn what pleases the Lord.[4]

The Helper, the Holy Spirit.[5]—God has poured out his love into our hearts by means of the Holy Spirit, who is God's gift to us.[6]

The Spirit produces love, joy, peace.[7]

They have been severely tested by the troubles they went through; but their joy was so great that they were extremely generous in their giving, even though they are very poor.[8]

It is one and the same Spirit who does all this; as he wishes, he gives a different gift to each person.[9]

[1]2 THESS. 2.13. [2]S. of S. 4.16.—[3]2 Cor. 7.11.—[4]Eph. 5.9, 10. [5]John 14.26.—[6]Rom. 5.5. [7]Gal. 5.22. [8]2 Cor. 8.2. [9]1 Cor. 12.11.

He calls his own sheep by name, and he leads them out.[1]

The solid foundation that God has laid cannot be shaken; and on it are written these words: "The Lord knows those who are his" and "Whoever says that he belongs to the Lord must turn away from wrongdoing."[2]—When Judgement Day comes, many will say to me, "Lord, Lord! In your name we spoke God's message, by your name we drove out many demons and performed many miracles!" Then I will say to them, "I never knew you. Get away from me, you wicked people!"[3]—The righteous are guided and protected by the LORD, but the evil are on the way to their doom.[4]

I can never forget you! I have written your name on the palms of my hands.[5]—Close your heart to every love but mine; hold no one in your arms but me.[6]—The LORD is good; he protects his people in times of trouble; he takes care of those who turn to him.[7]

I am going to prepare a place for you. And after I go and prepare a place for you, I will come back and take you to myself, so that you will be where I am.[8]

[1]JOHN 10.3. [2]2 Tim. 2.19.—[3]Matt. 7.22, 23.—[4]Ps. 1.6. [5]Isa. 49.16.—[6]S. of S. 8.6.—[7]Nahum 1.7. [8]John 14.2, 3.

Evening

She did what she could.[1]

This poor widow put in more than all the others.[2]—Anyone who gives you a drink of water because you belong to me will certainly receive his reward.[3]—If you are eager to give, God will accept your gift on the basis of what you have to give, not on what you haven't.[4]

Our love should not be just words and talk; it must be true love, which shows itself in action.[5]—Suppose there are brothers and sisters who need clothes and don't have enough to eat. What good is there in your saying to them, "God bless you! Keep warm and eat well!"—if you don't give them the necessities of life?[6]—The one who sows many seeds will have a large crop. Each one should give, then, as he has decided, not with regret or out of a sense of duty; for God loves the one who gives gladly.[7]

When you have done all you have been told to do, say, "We are ordinary servants; we have only done our duty."[8]

[1]MARK. 14.8. [2]Luke 21.3.—[3]Mark 9.41.—[4]2 Cor. 8.12. [5]1 John 3.18.—[6]Jas 2.15, 16.—[7]2 Cor. 9.6, 7. [8]Luke 17.10.

The great things the Mighty God has done for me. His name is holy.[1]

LORD, who among the gods is like you? Who is like you, wonderful in holiness? Who can work miracles and mighty acts like yours?[2]—There is no god like you, O Lord, not one has done what you have done.[3]—Who will not stand in awe of you, Lord? Who will refuse to declare your greatness? You alone are holy.[4]—May your holy name be honoured.[5]

Let us praise the Lord, the God of Israel! He has come to the help of his people and has set them free.[6]

Who is this coming from the city of Bozrah in Edom? Who is this so splendidly dressed in red, marching along in power and strength? It is the LORD, powerful to save, coming to announce his victory.[7]—I have given the throne to one I chose from the people.[8]

To him who by means of his power working in us is able to do so much more than we can ever ask for, or even think of: to God be the glory.[9]

[1]LUKE 1.49. [2]Exod. 15.11.—[3]Ps. 86.8.—[4]Rev. 15.4.—[5]Matt. 6.9. [6]Luke 1.68. [7]Isa. 63.1.—[8]Ps. 89.19. [9]Eph. 3.20, 21.

Evening

The dew on Mount Hermon[1]

Mount Sirion, that is, Mount Hermon.[2]—It is like the dew on Mount Hermon, falling on the hills of Zion. That is where the LORD has promised his blessing—life that never ends.[3]—I will be to the people of Israel like rain in a dry land. They will blossom like flowers.[4]

My teaching will fall like drops of rain and form on the erath like dew. My words will fall like showers on young plants, like gentle rain on tender grass.[5]—My word is like the snow and the rain that come down from the sky to water the earth. They make the crops grow and provide seed for sowing and food to eat. So also will be the word that I speak—it will not fail to do what I plan for it; it will do everything I send it to do.[6]

The one whom God has sent speaks God's words, because God gives him the fullness of his Spirit.[7]—Out of the fullness of his grace he has blessed us all, giving us one blessing after another.[8]—It is like the precious anointing oil running down from Aaron's head and beard, down to the collar of his robes.[9]

[1]PS. 133.3. [2]Deut. 4.48.—[3]Ps. 133.3.—[4]Hos. 14.5. [5]Deut. 32.2.—[6]Isa. 55.10, 11. [7]John 3.34.—[8]John 1.16.—[9]Ps. 133.2.

Just as I do not belong to the world, they do not belong to the world.[1]

We despised him and rejected him; he endured suffering and pain.[2]—Be glad that you are sharing Christ's sufferings, so that you may be full of joy when his glory is revealed.[3]

Jesus . . . is the High Priest that meets our needs. He is holy; he has no fault or sin in him; he has been set apart from sinners.[4]—So that you may be innocent and pure as God's perfect children, who live in a world of corrupt and sinful people.[5]

Jesus of Nazareth . . . went everywhere, doing good and healing all who were under the power of the Devil, for God was with him.[6]—As often as we have the chance, we should do good to everyone, and especially to those who belong to our family in the faith.[7]

This was the real light—the light that comes into the world and shines on all mankind.[8]—You are like light for the whole world. A city built on a hill cannot be hidden. In the same way your light must shine before people, so that they will see the good things you do and praise your Father in heaven.[9]

[1]JOHN 17.16. [2]Isa. 53.3.—[3]1 Pet. 4.13. [4]Heb. 7.26.—[5]Phil. 2.15. [6]Acts 10.38.—[7]Gal. 6.10. [8]John 1.9.—[9]Matt. 5.14, 16.

Evening

Happy people always enjoy life.[1]

The joy that the LORD gives you will make you strong.[2]—God's Kingdom is not a matter of eating and drinking, but of the righteousness, peace, and joy which the Holy Spirit gives.[3]—Be filled with the Spirit. Speak to one another with the words of psalms, hymns, and sacred songs; sing hymns and psalms to the Lord with praise in your hearts. In the name of our Lord Jesus Christ, always give thanks for everything to God the Father.[4]

Let us then, always offer praise to God as our sacrifice through Jesus, which is the offering presented by lips that confess him as Lord.[5]

Even though the fig trees have no fruit and no grapes grow on the vines, even though the olive crop fails and the fields produce no corn, even though the sheep all die and the cattle stalls are empty, I will still be joyful and glad, because the LORD God is my saviour.[6]—Although saddened, we are always glad.[7]—We also boast of our troubles.[8]

[1]PROV. 15.15. [2]Neh. 8.10.—[3]Rom. 14.17.—[4]Eph. 5.18–20. [5]Heb. 13.15. [6]Hab. 3.17, 18.—[7]2 Cor. 6.10.—[8]Rom. 5.3.

Is there any value in being circumcised?[1]

Much, indeed, in every way![2]—Keep your covenant with me, your LORD, and dedicate yourselves to me.[3]—At last, when your descendants are humbled and they have paid the penalty for their sin and rebellion, I will remember my covenant with Jacob and with Isaac and with Abraham.[4]

Christ's life of service was on behalf of the Jews, to show that God is faithful, to make his promises to their ancestors come true.[5]—In union with Christ you were circumcised, not with the circumcision that is made by men, but with the circumcision made by Christ.[6]—You were at one time spiritually dead because of your sins and because you were Gentiles without the Law. But God has now brought you to life with Christ. God forgave us all our sins.[7]

Get rid of your old self, which made you live as you used to—the old self that was being destroyed by its deceitful desires. Your hearts and minds must be made completely new, and you must put on the new self, which is created in God's likeness and reveals itself in the true life that is upright and holy.[8]

[1]ROM. 3.1. [2]Rom. 3.2.—[3]Jer. 4.4.—[4]Lev. 26.41, 42. [5]Rom. 15.8.—[6]Col. 2.11.—[7]Col. 2.13. [8]Eph. 4.22–24.

Evening

The curtain hanging in the Temple was torn in two from top to bottom.[1]

The Lord Jesus, on the night he was betrayed, took a piece of bread, gave thanks to God, broke it, and said, "This is my body, which is for you. Do this in memory of me."[2]—The bread that I will give him is my flesh, which I give so that the world may live.[3]

If you do not eat the flesh of the Son of Man and drink his blood, you will not have life in yourselves. Whoever eats my flesh and drinks my blood has eternal life. Whoever eats my flesh and drinks my blood lives in me, and I live in him. The living Father sent me, and because of him I live also. In the same way whoever eats me will live because of me. Does this make you want to give up? Suppose, then, that you should see the Son of Man go back up to the place where he was before? What gives life is God's Spirit; man's power is of no use at all.[4]

He opened for us a new way, a living way, through the curtain—that is, through his own body.[5]

[1]MATT. 27.51. [2]1 Cor. 11.23, 24.—[3]John 6.51. [4]John 6.53, 54, 56, 57, 61–63. [5]Heb. 10.20.

Because he died, sin has no power over him; and now he lives his life in fellowship with God.[1]

He . . . shared the fate of evil men.[2]—Christ also was offered in sacrifice once to take away the sins of many.[3]—Christ Himself carried our sins in His body to the cross, so that we might die to sin and live to righteousness.[4]—With one sacrifice, then, he has made perfect for ever those who are purified from sin.[5]

Jesus lives on for ever, and his work as priest does not pass on to someone else. And so he is able, now and always, to save those who come to God through him, because he lives for ever to plead with God for them.[6]—It was while we were still sinners that Christ died for us! By his sacrificial death we are now put right with God; how much more, then, will we be saved by him from God's anger![7]

Since Christ suffered physically, you too must strengthen yourselves with the same way of thinking that he had; because whoever suffers physically is no longer involved with sin. From now on, then, you must live the rest of your earthly lives controlled by God's will and not by human desires.[8]

[1]ROM. 6.10. [2]Isa. 53.12.—[3]Heb. 9.28.—[4]1 Pet. 2.24.—[5]Heb. 10.14. [6]Heb. 7.24, 25.—[7]Rom. 5.8, 9. [8]1 Pet. 4.1, 2.

Evening

Keep yourselves in the love of God.[1]

Remain united to me, and I will remain united to you. A branch cannot bear fruit by itself; it can do so only if it remains in the vine. In the same way you cannot bear fruit unless you remain in me. I am the vine, and you are the branches. Whoever remains in me, and I in him, will bear much fruit; for you can do nothing without me.[2]

The Spirit produces love.[3]

My Father's glory is shown by your bearing much fruit; and in this way you become my disciples. I love you just as the Father loves me; remain in my love. If you obey my commands, you will remain in my love, just as I have obeyed my Father's commands and remain in his love.[4]—Whoever obeys his word is the one whose love for God has really been made perfect.[5]

My commandment is this: love one another, just as I love you.[6]—God has shown us how much he loves us—it was while we were still sinners that Christ died for us![7]—God is love, and whoever lives in love lives in union with God and God lives in union with him.[8]

[1]JUDE 21. [2]John 15.4, 5. [3]Gal. 5.22. [4]John 15.8–10.—[5]1 John 2.5. [6]John. 15.12.—[7]Rom. 5.8.—[8]1 John 4.16.

Then the end will come.[1]

No one knows, however, when that day or hour will come—neither the angels in heaven, nor the Son; only the Father knows. Be on watch, be alert, fo ryou do not know when the time will come. What I say to you, then, I say to all. Watch![2]—The Lord is not slow to do what he has promised, as some think. Instead, he is patient with you, because he does not want anyone to be destroyed, but wants all to turn away from their sins.[3]—The day of the Lord's coming is near. The Judge is near, ready to appear.[4]—Yes indeed! I am coming soon![5]

Since all these things will be destroyed in this way, what kind of people should you be? Your lives whould be holy and dedicated to God.[6]

The end of all things is near. You must be self-controlled and alert, to be able to pray.[7]—Be ready for whatever comes, dressed for action and with your lamps lit, like servants who are waiting for their master to come back from a wedding feast. When he comes and knocks, they will open the door for him at once.[8]

[1]1 COR. 15.24. [2]Mark 13.32, 33, 37.—[3]2 Pet. 3.9.—[4]Jas 5.8, 9.—[5]Rev. 22.20. [6]2 Pet. 3.11. [7]1 Pet. 4.7.—[8]Luke 12.35, 36.

Evening

Pray also for us, brothers.[1]

Is there anyone who is ill? He should send for the church elders, who will pray for him and rub olive-oil on him in the name of the Lord. This prayer made in faith will heal the sick person; the Lord will restore him to health, and the sins he has committed will be forgiven. Pray for one another, so that you will be healed. The prayer of a good person has a powerful effect. Elijah was the same kind of person as we are. He prayed earnestly that there would be no rain, and no rain fell on the land for three and a half years. Once again he prayed, and the sky poured out its rain and the earth produced its crops.[2]

Pray on every occasion, as the Spirit leads. For this reason keep alert and never give up; pray always for all God's people.[3]

God knows that I remember you every time I pray.[4]—[Epaphras] always prays fervently for you, asking God to make you stand firm, as mature and fully convinced Christians, in complete obedience to God's will.[5]

[1]1 THESS. 5.25. [2]Jas 5.14–18. [3]Eph. 6.18. [4]Rom. 1.9, 10.—[5]Col. 4.12.

Be patient in your troubles.[1]

He is the LORD; he will do whatever seems best to him.[2]—Though I am innocent, all I can do is beg for mercy from God my judge.[3]—The LORD gave, and now he has taken away. May his name be praised![4]—When God sends us something good, we welcome it. How can we complain when he sends us trouble?[5]

Jesus wept.[6]—He endured suffering and pain. But he endured the suffering that should have been ours, the pain that we should have borne.[7]

The Lord corrects everyone he loves, and punishes everyone he accepts as a son. When we are punished, it seems to us at the time something to make us sad, not glad. Later, however, those who have been disciplined by such punishment reap the peaceful reward of a righteous life.[8]—May you be made strong with all the strength which comes from his glorious power, so that you may be able to endure everything with patience.[9]—The world will make you suffer. But be brave! I have defeated the world![10]

[1]ROM. 12.12. [2]1 Sam. 3.18.—[3]Job 9.15.—[4]Job 1.21.—[5]Job 2.10. [6]John 11.35.—[7]Isa. 53.3, 4. [8]Heb. 12.6, 11.—[9]Col. 1.11.—[10]John 16.33.

Evening

His faith did not leave him, and he did not doubt God's promise.[1]

Have faith in God. I assure you that whoever tells this hill to get up and throw itself in the sea and does not doubt in his heart, but believes that what he says will happen, it will be done for him. For this reason I tell you: When you pray and ask for something, believe that you have received it, and you will be given whatever you ask for.[2]—No one can please God without faith, for whoever comes to God must have faith that God exists and rewards those who seek him.[3]

It was faith that made Abraham offer his son Isaac as a sacrifice when God put Abraham to the test. Abraham was the one to whom God had made the promise, yet he was ready to offer his only son as a sacrifice. God had said to him, "It is through Isaac that you will have the descendants I promised." Abraham reckoned that God was able to raise Isaac from death.[4]—He was absolutely sure that God would be able to do what he had promised.[5]

Is anything too hard for the LORD?[6]—For God everything is possible.[7]—Make our faith greater.[8]

[1]ROM. 4.20. [2]Mark 11.22–24.—[3]Heb. 11.6. [4]Heb. 11.17–19.—[5]Rom. 4.21. [6]Gen. 18.14.—[7]Matt. 19.26.—[8]Luke 17.5.

We know that we have left death and come over into life.[1]

Whoever hears my words and believes in him who sent me has eternal life. He will not be judged, but has already passed from death to life.[2]—Whoever has the Son has this life; whoever does not have the Son of God does not have life.[3]

It is God himself who makes us, together with you, sure of our life in union with Christ; it is God himself who has set us apart, who has placed his mark of ownership upon us, and who has given us the Holy Spirit in our hearts as the guarantee of all that he has in store for us.[4]—This, then, is how we will know that we belong to the truth; this is how we will be confident in God's presence. My dear friends, if our conscience does not condemn us, we have courage in God's presence.[5]—We know that we belong to God even though the whole world is under the rule of the Evil One.[6]

You were spiritually dead because of your disobedience and sins. He brought us to life with Christ.[7]—He rescued us from the power of darkness and brought us safe into the kingdom of his dear Son.[8]

[1]1 JOHN 3.14. [2]John 5.24.—[3]1 John 5.12. [4]2 Cor. 1.21, 22.—[5]1 John 3.19, 21.— [6]1 John 5.19. [7]Eph. 2.1, 5.—[8]Col. 1.13.

Evening

You will show me the path that leads to life.[1]

Listen! I, the LORD, am giving you a choice between the way that leads to life and the way that leads to death.[2]—I will teach you what is good and right for you to do.[3]—I am the way, the truth, and the life; no one goes to the Father except by me.[4]—Come with me.[5]

What you think is the right road may lead to death.[6]—Go in through the narrow gate, because the gate to hell is wide and the road that leads to it is easy, and there are many who travel it. But the gate to life is narrow and the way that leads to it is hard, and there are few people who find it.[7]

There will be a highway there, called "The Road of Holiness". No sinner will ever travel that road; no fools will mislead those who follow it.[8]—Let us try to know the LORD.[9]

There are many rooms in my Father's house, and I am going to prepare a place for you. I would not tell you this if it were not so.[10]

[1]PS. 16.11. [2]Jer. 21.8.—[3]1 Sam. 12.23.—[4]John 14.6.—[5]Matt. 4.19. [6]Prov. 14.12.— [7]Matt. 7.13, 14. [8]Isa. 35.8.—[9]Hos. 6.3. [10]John 14.2.

It was faith that made Abraham obey when God called him to go out to a country which God had promised to give him.[1]

He chose for us the land where we live.[2]—He protected them and cared for them, as he would protect himself. Like an eagle teaching its young to fly, catching them safely on its spreading wings, the LORD kept Israel from falling. The LORD alone led his people without the help of a foreign god.[3]

I am the LORD your God, the one who wants to teach you for your own good and direct you in the way you should go.[4]—He is the greatest teacher of all.[5]

Our life is a matter of faith, not of sight.[6]—There is no permanent city for us here on earth; we are looking for the city which is to come.[7]—I appeal to you, my friends, as strangers and refugees in this world! Do not give in to bodily passions, which are always at war against the soul.[8]—Get up and go; there is no safety here any more.[9]

[1]HEB. 11.8. [2]Ps. 47.4.—[3]Deut. 32.10–12. [4]Isa. 48.17.—[5]Job 36.22. [6]2 Cor. 5.7.—[7]Heb. 13.14.—[8]1 Pet. 2.11.—[9]Mic. 2.10.

Evening

Remember what the holy God has done, and give thanks to him.[1]

Why, God does not trust even his angels; even they are not pure in his sight. And man drinks evil as if it were water; yes, man is corrupt; man is worthless.[2]—In his eyes even the moon is not bright, nor the stars pure. Then what about man, that worm? What is man worth in God's eyes?[3]

LORD, who among the gods is like you? Who is like you, wonderful in holiness?[4]—Holy, holy, holy! The LORD Almighty is holy![5]

Be holy in all that you do, just as God who called you is holy. The scripture says, "Be holy because I am holy."[6]—We may share his holiness.[7]

God's temple is holy, and you yourselves are his temple.[8]—What kind of people should you be? Your lives should be holy and dedicated to God.[9]

Do not use harmful words, but only helpful words, the kind that build up and provide what is needed, so that what you say will do good to those who hear you. And do not make God's Holy Spirit sad; for the Spirit is God's mark of ownership on you, a guarantee that the Day will come when God will set you free.[10]

[1]PS. 97.12. [2]Job 15.15, 16.—[3]Job 25.5, 6. [4]Exod. 15.11.—[5]Isa. 6.3. [6]1 Pet. 1.15, 16.—[7]Heb. 12.10. [8]1 Cor. 3.17.—[9]2 Pet. 3.11. [10]Eph. 4.29, 30.

Christ, who is the exact likeness of God.[1]

The glory of the LORD will be revealed, and all mankind will see it.[2]—No one has ever seen God. The only Son, who is the same as God and is at the Father's side, he has made him known. The Word became a human being and, full of grace and truth, lived among us. We saw his glory, the glory which he received as the Father's only Son.[3]—Whoever has seen me has seen the Father.[4]—He reflects the brightness of God's glory and is the exact likeness of God's own being.[5]—He appeared in human form.[6]

By whom we are set free, that is, our sins are forgiven. Christ is the visible likeness of the invisible God. He is the first-born Son, superior to all created things.[7]—Those whom God had already chosen he also set apart to become like his Son, so that the Son would be the first among many brothers.[8]

Just as we wear the likeness of the man made of earth, so we will wear the likeness of the Man from heaven.[9]

[1]2 COR. 4.4. [2]Isa. 40.5.—[3]John 1.18, 14.—[4]John 14.9.—[5]Heb. 1.3.—[6]1 Tim. 3.16. [7]Col. 1.14, 15.—[8]Rom. 8.29. [9]1 Cor. 15.49.

Evening

You give me strength for the battle and victory over my enemies.[1]

When I am weak, then I am strong.[2]

Asa prayed to the LORD his God, "O LORD, you can help a weak army as easily as a powerful one. Help us now, O LORD our God, because we are relying on you, and in your name we have come out to fight against this huge army. LORD, you are our God; no one can hope to defeat you."[3]—Jehoshaphat gave a shout, and the LORD God rescued him.[4]

It is better to trust in the LORD than to depend on man. It is better to trust in the LORD than to depend on human leaders.[5]—A king does not win because of his powerful army; a soldier does not triumph because of his strength. War-horses are useless for victory; their great strength cannot save.[6]

We are not fighting against human beings but against the wicked spiritual forces in the heavenly world, the rulers, authorities, and cosmic powers of this dark age. So put on God's armour now![7]

[1]PS. 18.39. [2]2 Cor. 12.10. [3]2 Chr. 14.11.—[4]2 Chr. 18.31. [5]Ps. 118.8, 9.— [6]Ps. 33.16, 17. [7]Eph. 6.12, 13.

Your life must be controlled by love.[1]

Now I give you a new commandment: love one another. As I have loved you, so you must love one another.[2]—Above everything, love one another earnestly, because love covers over many sins.[3]—Love overlooks all offences.[4]

When you stand and pray, forgive anything you may have against anyone, so that your Father in heaven will forgive the wrongs you have done.[5]—Love your enemies and do good to them; lend and expect nothing back.[6]—Don't be glad when your enemy meets disaster, and don't rejoice when he stumbles.[7]—Do not pay back evil with evil or cursing with cursing; instead, pay back with a blessing, because a blessing is what God promised to give you when he called you.[8]—Do everything possible on your part to live in peace with everybody.[9]—Be kind and tender-hearted to one another, and forgive one another, as God has forgiven you through Christ.[10]

My children, our love should not be just words and talk; it must be true love, which shows itself in action.[11]

[1]EPH. 5.2. [2]John 13.34.—[3]1 Pet. 4.8.—[4]Prov. 10.12. [5]Mark 11.25.—[6]Luke 6.35.—[7]Prov. 24.17.—[8]1 Pet. 3.9.—[9]Rom. 12.18.—[10]Eph. 4.32. [11]1 John 3.18.

Evening

In all your prayers ask God for what you need.[1]

My Father! All things are possible for you. Take this cup of suffering away from me. Yet not what I want, but what you want.[2]—I was given a painful physical ailment. Three times I prayed to the Lord about this and asked him to take it away. But his answer was: "My grace is all you need, for my power is greatest when you are weak." I am most happy, then, to be proud of my weaknesses.[3]

I bring him all my complaints; I tell him all my troubles.[4]—Hannah . . . was deeply distressed, and she cried bitterly as she prayed to the LORD. Hannah made a solemn promise: "Almighty LORD . . . See my trouble and remember me! If you give me a son, I promise that I will dedicate him to you for his whole life." The LORD answered her prayer.[5]

We do not know how we ought to pray.[6]—He chose for us the land where we live.[7]

[1]PHIL. 4.6. [2]Mark 14.36.—[3]2 Cor. 12.7–9. [4]Ps. 142.2.—[5]1 Sam. 1.9–11, 19. [6]Rom. 8.26.—[7]Ps. 47.4.

Why don't you tear the sky apart and come down?[1]

Come to me, my lover, like a gazelle, like a young stag on the mountains where spices grow.[2]—We . . . groan within ourselves, as we wait for God to make us his sons and set our whole being free.[3]—O LORD, tear the sky apart and come down; touch the mountains, and they will pour out smoke.[4]

This Jesus, who was taken from you into heaven, will come back in the same way that you saw him go to heaven.[5]—He will appear a second time, not to deal with sin, but to save those who are waiting for him.[6]—When it happens, everyone will say, "He is our God! We have put our trust in him, and he has rescued us. He is the LORD! We have put our trust in him, and now we are happy and joyful because he has saved us."[7]

He who gives his testimony to all this says, "Yes indeed! I am coming soon!" So be it. Come, Lord Jesus![8]—The blessed Day we hope for, when the glory of our great God and Saviour Jesus Christ will appear.[9]—We . . . are citizens of heaven.[10]

[1]ISA. 64.1. [2]S. of S. 8.14.—[3]Rom. 8.23.—[4]Ps. 144.5. [5]Acts 1.11.—[6]Heb. 9.28.—[7]Isa. 25.9. [8]Rev. 22.20.—[9]Titus 2.13.—[10]Phil. 3.20.

Evening

You have given me what belongs to those who honour you.[1]

No weapon will be able to hurt you; you will have an answer for all who accuse you. I will defend my servants and give them victory.[2]—His angel guards those who honour the LORD and rescues them from danger. Find out for yourself how good the LORD is. Happy are those who find safety with him. Honour the LORD, all his people; those who obey him have all they need. Even lions go hungry for lack of food, but those who obey the LORD lack nothing good.[3]—How wonderful are your gifts to me; how good they are![4]

For you who obey me, my saving power will rise on you like the sun and bring healing like the sun's rays. You will be as free and happy as calves let out of a stall.[5]—God . . . did not even keep back his own Son, but offered him for us all! He gave us his Son—will he not also freely give us all things?[6]

[1]PS. 61.5. [2]Isa. 54.17.—[3]Ps. 34.7–10.—[4]Ps. 16.6. [5]Mal. 4.2.—[6]Rom. 8.32.

Morning

Set your hearts on the things that are in heaven, where Christ sits on his throne at the right-hand side of God.[1]

Get wisdom and insight![2]—The wisdom from above.[3]—The depths of the oceans and seas say that wisdom is not found there.[4]—By our baptism . . . we were buried with him and shared his death, in order that, just as Christ was raised from death by the glorious power of the Father, so also we might live a new life. For since we have become one with him in dying as he did, in the same way we shall be one with him by being raised to life as he was.[5]

Let us rid ourselves of everything that gets in the way, and of the sin which holds on to us so tightly, and let us run with determination the race that lies before us.[6]—God . . . brought us to life with Christ. In our union with Christ Jesus he raised us up with him to rule with him in the heavenly world.[7]

Those who say such things make it clear that they are looking for a country of their own.[8]—Turn to the LORD, all you humble people of the land, who obey his commands. Do what is right, and humble yourselves before the LORD.[9]

[1]COL. 3.1. [2]Prov. 4.5.—[3]Jas 3.17.—[4]Job 28.14.—[5]Rom. 6.4, 5. [6]Heb. 12.1.—[7]Eph. 2.4–6. [8]Heb. 11.14.—[9]Zeph. 2.3.

Evening

Nicodemus, the man who had gone to see Jesus before.[1]

Peter followed from a distance.[2]—Many of the Jewish authorities believed in Jesus; but because of the Pharisees they did not talk openly, so as not to be expelled from the synagogue. They loved the approval of men rather than the approval of God.[3]—It is dangerous to be concerned with what others think of you, but if you trust the LORD, you are safe.[4]

I will never turn away anyone who comes to me.[5]—He will not break off a bent reed or put out a flickering lamp.[6]—Faith as big as a mustard seed.[7]

The Spirit that God has given us does not make us timid; instead, his Spirit fills us with power, love, and self-control. Do not be ashamed, then, of witnessing for our Lord.[8]—My children, remain in union with him, so that when he appears we may be full of courage and need not hide in shame from him on the Day he comes.[9]—If anyone declares publicly that he belongs to me, I will do the same for him before my Father in heaven.[10]

[1]JOHN 7.50. [2]Matt. 26.58.—[3]John 12.42, 43.—[4]Prov. 29.25. [5]John 6.37.—[6]Isa. 42.3.—[7]Matt. 17.20. [8]2 Tim. 1.7, 8.—[9]1 John 2.28.—[10]Matt. 10.32.

Morning

***Take your part in suffering, as a loyal soldier of Christ Jesus.*[1]**

I made him a leader and commander of nations, and through him I showed them my power.[2]—It was only right that God, who creates and preserves all things, should make Jesus perfect through suffering, in order to bring many sons to share his glory.[3]—We must pass through many troubles to enter the Kingdom of God.[4]

We are not fighting against human beings but against the wicked spiritual forces in the heavenly world, the rulers, authorities, and cosmic powers of this dark age. So put on God's armour now![5]—We do not fight from worldly motives. The weapons we use in our fight are not the world's weapons but God's powerful weapons, which we use to destroy strongholds.[6]

The God of all grace, who calls you to share his eternal glory in union with Christ, will himself perfect you and give you firmness, strength, and a sure foundation.[1]

[1]2 TIM. 2.3. [2]Isa. 55.4.—[3]Heb. 2.10.—[4]Acts 14.22. [5]Eph. 6.12, 13.—[6]2 Cor. 10.3, 4. [7]1 Pet. 5.10.

Evening

***The unity which the Spirit gives.*[1]**

There is one body and one Spirit.[2]—It is through Christ that all of us, Jews and Gentiles, are able to come in the one Spirit into the presence of the Father. So then, you Gentiles are not foreigners or strangers any longer; you are now fellow-citizens with God's people and members of the family of God. You, too, are built upon the foundation laid by the apostles and prophets, the cornerstone being Christ Jesus himself. He is the one who holds the whole building together and makes it grow into a sacred temple dedicated to the Lord. In union with him you too are being built together with all the others into a place where God lives through his Spirit.[3]

How wonderful it is, how pleasant, for God's people to live together in harmony! It is like the precious anointing oil running down from Aaron's head and beard, down to the collar of his robes.[4]

Now that by your obedience to the truth you have purified yourselves and have come to have a sincere love for your fellow-believers, love one another earnestly with all your hearts.[5]

[1]EPH. 4.3. [2]Eph. 4.4.—[3]Eph. 2.18–22. [5]1 Pet. 1.22.

The Spirit produces . . . faithfulness.[1]

It is by God's grace that you have been saved through faith. It is not the result of your own efforts, but God's gift.[2]—No one can please God without faith.[3]—Whoever believes in the Son is not judged; but whoever does not believe has already been judged, because he has not believed in God's only Son.[4]—I do have faith, but not enough. Help me to have more![5]

Whoever obeys his word is the one whose love for God has really been made perfect. This is how we can be sure that we are in union with God.[6]—Faith that works through love.[7]—Faith without actions is useless.[8]

Our life is a matter of faith, not of sight.[9]—I have been put to death with Christ on his cross, so that it is no longer I who live, but it is Christ who lives in me. This life that I live now, I live by faith in the Son of God, who loved me and gave his life for me.[10]—You love him, although you have not seen him, and you believe in him, although you do not now see him. So you rejoice with a great and glorious joy which words cannot express, because you are receiving the salvation of your souls, which is the purpose of your faith in him.[11]

[1]GAL. 5.22. [2]Eph. 2.8.—[3]Heb. 11.6.—[4]John 3.18.—[5]Mark 9.24. [6]1 John 2.5.—[7]Gal. 5.6.—[8]Jas 2.20. [9]2 Cor. 5.7.—[10]Gal. 2.19, 20.—[11]1 Pet. 1.8, 9.

Evening

The Lord is full of mercy and compassion.[1]

As a father is kind to his children, so the LORD is kind to those who honour him.[2]—The LORD . . . is kind and merciful. He never forgets his covenant.[3]

He will not let you fall; your protector is always awake. The protector of Israel never dozes or sleeps.[4]—Like an eagle teaching its young to fly, catching them safely on its spreading wings, the LORD kept Israel from falling. The LORD alone led his people without the help of a foreign god.[5]

The LORD's unfailing love and mercy still continue, fresh as the morning, as sure as the sunrise.[6]

Jesus . . . saw the large crowd, his heart was filled with pity for them, and he healed those who were ill.[7]

Even the hairs of your head have all been counted. For only a penny you can buy two sparrows, yet not one sparrow falls to the ground without your Father's consent. So do not be afraid.[8]

[1]JAS 5.11. [2]Ps. 103.13.—[3]Ps. 111.4, 5. [4]Ps. 121.3, 4.—[5]Deut. 32.11, 12. [6]Lam. 3.22, 23. [7]Matt. 14.14. [8]Matt. 10.30, 29, 31.

The Lamb that was killed.[1]

You may choose . . . a sheep . . . but it must be . . . without any defects. On the evening . . . the whole community of Israel will kill the animals. The people are to take some of the blood and put it on the door-posts and above the doors of the houses in which the animals are to be eaten. When I see the blood, I will pass over you.[2]—The sprinkled blood.[3]—Christ, our Passover lamb, has been sacrificed.[4]—In accordance with his own plan God had already decided that Jesus would be handed over to you.[5]—He saved us and called us . . . because of his own purpose and grace. He gave us this grace by means of Christ Jesus before the beginning of time.[6]

By the sacrificial death of Christ we are set free, that is, our sins are forgiven.[7]

Since Christ suffered physically, you too must strengthen yourselves with the same way of thinking that he had; because whoever suffers physically is no longer involved with sin. From now on, then, you must live the rest of your earthly lives controlled by God's will and not by human desires.[8]

[1]REV. 13.8. [2]Exod. 12.5–7, 13. [3]Heb. 12.24.—[4]1 Cor. 5.7.—[5]Acts 2.23.—[6]2 Tim. 1.9. [7]Eph. 1.7. [8]1 Pet. 4.1, 2.

Evening

I have trampled the nations like grapes, and no one came to help me.[1]

LORD, who among the gods is like you? Who is like you, wonderful in holiness? Who can work miracles and mighty acts like yours?[2]—He is astonished to see that there is no one to help the oppressed. So he will use his own power to rescue them and to win the victory.[3]—Christ himself carried our sins in his body to the cross.[4]—Becoming a curse for us.[5]

Sing a new song to the LORD; he has done wonderful things! By his own power and holy strength he has won the victory.[6]—Christ freed himself from the power of the spiritual rulers and authorities; he made a public spectacle of them by leading them as captives in his victory procession.[7]—After a life of suffering, he will again have joy; he will know that he did not suffer in vain. My devoted servant, with whom I am pleased, will bear the punishment of many and for his sake I will forgive them.[8]

I shall march, march on, with strength![9]—In all these things we have complete victory through him who loved us![10]—Our brothers won the victory . . . by the blood of the Lamb.[11]

[1]ISA. 63.3. [2]Exod. 15.11.—[3]Isa. 59.16.—[4]1 Pet. 2.24.—[5]Gal. 3.13. [6]Ps. 98.1.—[7]Col. 2.15.—[8]Isa. 53.11. [9]Judg. 5.21.—[10]Rom. 8.37.—[11]Rev. 12.11.

He shows mercy to those who honour him.[1]

How wonderful are the good things you keep for those who honour you! Everyone knows how good you are, how securely you protect those who trust you. You hide them in the safety of your presence from the plots of men; in a safe shelter you hide them from the insults of their enemies.[2]

You call him Father, when you pray to God, who judges all people by the same standard, according to what each one has done; so then, spend the rest of your lives here on earth in reverence for him.[3]—He is near to those who call to him, who call to him with sincerity. He supplies the needs of those who honour him; he hears their cries and saves them.[4]

You repented and humbled yourself before me, tearing your clothes and weeping . . . I have heard your prayer.[5]—I am pleased with those who are humble and repentant, who fear me and obey me.[6]—The LORD is near to those who are discouraged; he saves those who have lost all hope.[7]

[1]LUKE 1.50. [2]Ps. 31.19, 20. [3]1 Pet. 1.17.—[4]Ps. 145.18, 19. [5]2 Kgs 22.19.— [6]Isa. 66.2.—[7]Ps. 34.18.

Evening

I will honour those who honour me.[1]

If anyone declares publicly that he belongs to me, I will do the same for him before my Father in heaven.[2]—Whoever loves his father or mother more than me is not fit to be my disciple; whoever loves his son or daughter more than me is not fit to be my disciple. Whoever does not take up his cross and follow in my steps is not fit to be my disciple. Whoever tries to gain his own life will lose it; but whoever loses his life for my sake will gain it.[3]

Happy is the person who remains faithful under trials, because when he succeeds in passing such a test, he will receive as his reward the life which God has promised to those who love him.[4]

Don't be afraid of anything you are about to suffer. Be faithful to me, even if it means death, and I will give you life as your prize of victory.[5]

This small and temporary trouble we suffer will bring us a tremendous and eternal glory, much greater than the trouble.[6]—Praise and glory and honour on the Day when Jesus Christ is revealed.[7]

[1]1 SAM. 2.30. [2]Matt. 10.32.—[3]Matt. 10.37–39. [4]Jas 1.12. [5]Rev. 2.10. [6]2 Cor. 4.17.—[7]1 Pet. 1.7.

"It is finished!" Then he bowed his head and died.[1]

Jesus, on whom our faith depends from beginning to end.[2]—I have shown your glory on earth; I have finished the work you gave me to do.[3]—We are all purified from sin by the offering that he made of his own body once and for all. Every Jewish priest performs his services every day and offers the same sacrifices many times; but these sacrifices can never take away sins. Christ, however, offered one sacrifice for sins, an offering that is effective for ever, and then he sat down at the right-hand side of God. There he now waits until God puts his enemies as a footstool under his feet. With one sacrifice, then, he has made perfect for ever those who are purified from sin.[4]—He cancelled the unfavourable record of our debts with its binding rules and did away with it completely by nailing it to the cross.[5]

I am willing to give up my life, in order that I may receive it back again. No one takes my life away from me. I give it up of my own free will. I have the right to give it up, and I have the right to take it back.[6]—The greatest love a person can have for his friends is to give his life for them.[7]

[1]JOHN 19.30. [2]Heb. 12.2.—[3]John 17.4.—[4]Heb. 10.10–14. [5]Col. 2.14. [6]John 10.17, 18.—[7]John 15.13.

Evening

The LORD reached down from above and took hold of me; he pulled me out of the deep waters.[1]

He pulled me out of a dangerous pit, out of the deadly quicksand. He set me safely on a rock and made me secure.[2]—In the past you were spiritually dead because of your disobedience and sins. At that time you followed the world's evil way. All of us . . . lived according to our natural desires.[3]

Hear my cry, O God; listen to my prayer! In despair and far from home I call to you![4]—In my distress, O LORD, I called to you, and you answered me. From deep in the world of the dead I cried for help, and you heard me. You threw me down into the depths, to the very bottom of the sea, where the waters were all round me, and all your mighty waves rolled over me.[5]—We went through fire and flood, but now you have brought us to a place of safety.[6]

When you pass through deep waters, I will be with you; your troubles will not overwhelm you.[7]

[1]PS. 18.16. [2]Ps. 40.2.—[3]Eph. 2.1–3. [4]Ps. 61.1, 2.—[5]Jonah 2.2, 3.—[6]Ps. 66.12. [7]Isa. 43.2.

Live a new life.[1]

At one time you surrendered yourselves entirely as slaves to impurity and wickedness for wicked purposes. In the same way you must now surrender yourselves entirely as slaves of righteousness for holy purposes.[2]—My brothers, because of God's great mercy to us I appeal to you: Offer yourselves as a living sacrifice to God, dedicated to his service and pleasing to him. This is the true worship that you should offer. Do not conform yourselves to the standards of this world, but let God transform you inwardly by a complete change of your mind.[3]

When anyone is joined to Christ, he is a new being; the old is gone, the new has come.[4]—It does not matter at all whether or not one is circumcised; what does matter is being a new creature. As for those who follow this rule in their lives, may peace and mercy be with them.[5]—In the Lord's name, then, I warn you: do not continue to live like the heathen, whose thoughts are worthless. That was not what you learnt about Christ! You certainly heard about him, and as his followers you were taught the truth that is in Jesus. Put on the new self, which is created in God's likeness and reveals itself in the true life that is upright and holy.[6]

[1]ROM. 6.4. [2]Rom. 6.19.—[3]Rom. 12.1, 2. [4]2 Cor. 5.17.—[5]Gal. 6.15, 16.—[6]Eph. 4.17, 20, 21, 24.

Evening

Your will be done.[1]

LORD, I know that no one is the master of his own destiny; no person has control over his own life.[2]—Not what I want, but what you want.[3]—I am content and at peace. As a child lies quietly in its mother's arms, so my heart is quiet within me.[4]

We do not know how we ought to pray; the Spirit himself pleads with God for us in groans that words cannot express. And God, who sees into our hearts, knows what the thought of the Spirit is; because the Spirit pleads with God on behalf of his people and in accordance with his will.[5]

You don't know what you are asking for.[6]—He gave them what they asked for, but also sent a terrible disease among them.[7]—All this is an example for us, to warn us not to desire evil things, as they did.[8]

I would like you to be free from worry.[9]—You, LORD, give perfect peace to those who keep their purpose firm and put their trust in you.[10]

MATT. 26.42. [2]Jer. 10.23.—[3]Matt. 26.39.—[4]Ps. 131.2. [5]Rom. 8.26, 27. [6]Matt. 20.22.—[7]Ps. 106.15.—[8]1 Cor. 10.6. [9]1 Cor. 7.32.—[10]Isa. 26.3.

Morning

The LORD corrects those he loves.[1]

I, and I alone, am God; no other god is real. I kill and I give life, I wound and I heal, and no one can oppose what I do.[2]—[The LORD says] . . . "I alone know the plans I have for you, plans to bring you prosperity and not disaster, plans to bring about the future you hope for."[3]—"My thoughts," says the LORD, "are not like yours, and my ways are different from yours."[4]

I am going to take her into the desert again; there I will win her back with words of love.[5]—The LORD your God corrects and punishes you just as a father disciplines his children.[6]—When you are punished, it seems to us at the time something to make us sad, not glad. Later, however, those who have been disciplined by such punishment reap the peaceful reward of a righteous life.[7]—Humble yourselves, then, under God's mighty hand, so that he will lift you up in his own good time.[8]

I know that your judgements are righteous, LORD, and that you punished me because you are faithful.[9]

[1]PROV. 3.12. [2]Deut. 32.39.—[3]Jer. 29.11.—[4]Isa. 55.8. [5]Hos. 2.14.—[6]Deut. 8.5.—[7]Heb. 12.11.—[8]1 Pet. 5.6. [9]Ps. 119.75.

Evening

The world and all that is in it belong to the LORD.[1]

She would never acknowledge that I am the one who gave her the corn, the wine, the olive-oil, and all the silver and gold . . . So at harvest time I will take back my gifts of corn and wine, and will take away the wool and the linen I gave her for clothing.[2]

Everything is a gift from you, and we have only given back what is yours already. You know, O LORD, that we pass through life like exiles and strangers, as our ancestors did. Our days are like a passing shadow, and we cannot escape death. O LORD . . . all this wealth . . . came from you and all belongs to you.[3]—All things were created by him, and all things exist through him and for him. To God be the glory for ever! Amen.[4]

God . . . generously gives us everything for our enjoyment.[5]—Everything that God has created is good; nothing is to be rejected, but everything is to be received with a prayer of thanks, because the word of God and the prayer make it acceptable to God.[6]

With all his abundant wealth through Christ Jesus, my God will supply all your needs.[7]

[1]PS. 24.1. [2]Hos. 2.8, 9. [3]1 Chr. 29.14–16.—[4]Rom. 11.36. [5]1 Tim. 6.17.—[6]1 Tim. 4.4, 5. [7]Phil. 4.19.

The Helper, the Holy Spirit, whom the Father will send in my name.[1]

If only you knew what God gives and who it is that is asking you for a drink, you would ask him, and he would give you life-giving water.[2]—Bad as you are, you know how to give good things to your children. How much more, then, will the Father in heaven give the Holy Spirit to those who ask him![3]—I am telling you the truth: the Father will give you whatever you ask him for in my name. Until now you have not asked for anything in my name; ask and you will receive, so that your happiness may be complete.[4]

When . . . the Spirit comes, who reveals the truth about God, he will lead you into all the truth. He will not speak on his authority, but he will speak of what he hears, and will tell you of things to come. He will give me glory, because he will take what I say and tell it to you.[5]

They rebelled against him and made his holy spirit sad. So the LORD became their enemy and fought against them.[6]

[1]JOHN 14.26. [2]John 4.10.—[3]Luke 11.13.—[4]John 16.23, 24. [5]John 16.13, 14. [6]Isa. 63.10.

Evening

What do you think about the Messiah?[1]

Fling wide the gates, open the ancient doors, and the great king will come in. Who is this great king? The triumphant LORD—he is the great king![2]—On his robe and on his thigh was written the name: "King of kings and Lord of lords."[3]

This stone is of great value for you that believe; but for those who do not believe: "The stone which the builders rejected as worthless turned out to be the most important of all."[4]—The crucified Christ, a message that is offensive to the Jews and nonsense to the Gentiles; but for those whom God has called, both Jews and Gentiles, this message is Christ, who is the power of God and the wisdom of God.[5]

I reckon everything as complete loss for the sake of what is so much more valuable, the knowledge of Christ Jesus my Lord. For his sake I have thrown everything away; I consider it all as mere refuse, so that I may gain Christ.[6]—Lord, you know everything; you know that I love you![7]

[1]MATT. 22.42. [2]Ps. 24.9, 10.—[3]Rev. 19.16. [4]1 Pet. 2.7.—[5]1 Cor. 1.23, 24. [6]Phil. 3.8.—[7]John 21.17.

The road the righteous travel is like the sunrise, getting brighter and brighter until daylight has come.[1]

I do not claim that I have already succeeded or have already become perfect. I keep striving to win the prize for which Christ Jesus has already won me to himself.[2]—Let us try to know the LORD.[3]

Then God's people will shine like the sun in their Father's Kingdom.[4]—All of us . . . reflect the glory of the Lord with uncovered faces; and that same glory, coming from the Lord, who is the Spirit, transforms us into his likeness in an ever greater degree of glory.[5]—When what is perfect comes, then what is partial will disappear. What we see now is like a dim image in a mirror; then we shall see face to face. What I know now is only partial; then it will be complete—as complete as God's knowledge of me.[6]

My dear friends, we are now God's children, but it is not yet clear what we shall become. But we know that when Christ appears, we shall be like him, because we shall see him as he really is. Everyone who has this hope in Christ keeps himself pure, just as Christ is pure.[7]

[1]PROV. 4.18. [2]Phil. 3.12.—[3]Hos. 6.3. [4]Matt. 13.43.—[5]2 Cor. 3.18.— [6]1 Cor. 13.10, 12. [7]1 John 3.2, 3.

Evening

Everyone who calls out to the LORD for help will be saved.[1]

I will never turn away anyone who comes to me.[2]—"Remember me, Jesus, when you come as King!" Jesus said to him, "I promise you that today you will be in Paradise with me."[3]—"What do you want me to do for you?" "Sir," they answered, "we want you to give us our sight!" Jesus had pity on them and touched their eyes; at once they were able to see, and they followed him.[4]

Bad as you are, you know how to give good things to your children. How much more, then, will the Father in heaven give the Holy Spirit to those who ask him![5]—I will put my spirit in you. The Sovereign LORD says, "I will once again let the Israelites ask me for help."[6]

We have courage in God's presence, because we are sure that he hears us if we ask him for anything that is according to his will. He hears us whenever we ask him; and since we know this is true, we know also that he gives us what we ask from him.[7]

[1]ROM. 10.13. [2]John 6.37.—[3]Luke 23.42, 43.—[4]Matt. 20.32–34. [5]Luke 11.13.— [6]Ezek. 36.27, 37. [7]1 John 5.14, 15.

How beautiful you are, my love; how pefect you are![1]

Your head is already covered with wounds, and your heart and mind are sick. From head to foot there is not a healthy spot on your body. You are covered with bruises and sores and open wounds. Your wounds have not been cleaned or bandaged. No ointment has been put on them.[2]—All of us have been sinful; even our best actions are filthy through and through.[3]—I know that good does not live in me—that is, in my human nature.[4]

You have been purified from sin; you have been dedicated to God; you have been put right with God by the Lord Jesus Christ and by the Spirit of our God.[5]—The princess is in the palace—how beautiful she is![6]—"You became famous in every nation for your perfect beauty, because I was the one who made you so lovely." This is what the Sovereign LORD says.[7]

LORD our God, may your blessings be with us.[8]

They have washed their robes and made them white with the blood of the Lamb.[9]—The church . . . in all its beauty—pure and faultless, without spot or wrinkle or any other imperfection.[10]—You have been given full life in union with him.[11]

[1]S. OF S. 4.7. [2]Isa. 1.5, 6.—[3]Isa. 64.6.—[4]Rom. 7.18. [5]1 Cor. 6.11.—[6]Ps. 45.13.—[7]Ezek. 16.14. [8]Ps. 90.17. [9]Rev. 7.14.—[10]Eph. 5.27.—[11]Col. 2.10.

Evening

Cracked cisterns that can hold no water at all.[1]

[Eve] bore a son and said, "By the LORD's help I have acquired a son." So she named him Cain.[2]

They said, "Now let's build a city with a tower that reaches the sky." So the LORD scattered them.[3]—Lot chose the whole Jordan Valley for himself. [It] had plenty of water, like the Garden of the LORD. Lot . . . camped near Sodom, whose people were wicked and sinned against the LORD.[4]

I was determined to know the difference between knowledge and foolishness, wisdom and madness. But I found out that I might as well be chasing the wind. The wiser you are, the more worries you have; the more you know, the more it hurts.[5]—I accomplished great things. I built myself houses and planted vineyards. I also piled up silver and gold. Then I thought about all that I had done . . . and I realized that it didn't mean a thing. It was like chasing the wind—of no use at all.[6]

Whoever is thirsty should come to me and drink.[7]—Keep your minds fixed on things [in heaven], not on things here on earth.[8]

JER. 2.13. [2]Gen. 4.1. [3]Gen. 11.4, 8.—[4]Gen. 13.11, 10, 12, 13. [5]Eccles. 1.17, 18.—[6]Eccles. 2.4, 8, 11. [7]John 7.37.—[8]Col. 3.2.

***I do not ask you to take them out of the world, but I do ask you to keep them safe from the Evil One.*[1]**

Innocent and pure as God's perfect children, who live in a world of corrupt and sinful people. You must shine among them like stars lighting up the sky.[2]—You are like salt for all mankind. You are like light for the whole world. Your light must shine before people, so that they will see the good things you do and praise your Father in heaven.[3]

I kept you from sinning against me.[4]

The Lord is faithful, and he will strengthen you and keep you safe from the Evil One.[5]—I acted differently, because I honoured God.[6]—In order to set us free from this present evil age, Christ gave himself for our sins, in obedience to the will of our God and Father.[7]—To him who is able to keep you from falling, and to bring you faultless and joyful before his glorious presence—to the only God our Saviour, through Jesus Christ our Lord, be glory, majesty, might, and authority, from all ages past, and now, and for ever and ever! Amen.[8]

[1]JOHN 17.15. [2]Phil. 2.15.—[3]Matt. 5.13, 14, 16. [4]Gen. 20.6. [5]2 Thess. 3.3.—[6]Neh. 5.15.—[7]Gal. 1.4.—[8]Jude 24, 25.

Evening

***If you trust the Lord, you are safe.*[1]**

How great the LORD is! He rules over everything.[2]—The LORD rules over all nations; his glory is above the heavens. He raises the poor from the dust; he lifts the needy from their misery and makes them companions of princes.[3]

God's mercy is so abundant, and his love for us is so great, that while we were spiritually dead in our disobedience he brought us to life with Christ. It is by God's grace that you have been saved. In our union with Christ Jesus he raised us up with him to rule with him in the heavenly world.[4]

God . . . did not even keep back his own Son, but offered him for us all! Will he not also freely give us all things? For I am certain that nothing can separate us from his love: neither death nor life, neither angels nor other heavenly rulers or powers, neither the present nor the future, neither the world above nor the world below—there is nothing in all creation that will ever be able to separate us from the love of God which is ours through Christ Jesus our Lord.[5]

[1]PROV. 29.25. [2]Isa. 33.5.—[3]Ps. 113.4, 7, 8. [4]Eph. 2.4–6. [5]Rom. 8.32, 38, 39.

So that through his death he might destroy the Devil, who has the power over death.[1]

Our Saviour, Christ Jesus . . . has ended the power of death and through the gospel has revealed immortal life.[2]—the Sovereign LORD will destroy death for ever! He will wipe away the tears from everyone's eyes and take away the disgrace his people have suffered throughout the world. The LORD himself has spoken![3]—What will die must be changed into what cannot die. So when this takes place, and the mortal has been changed into the immortal, then the scripture will come true: "Death is destroyed; victory is complete!" "Where, Death, is your victory? Where, Death, is your power to hurt?" Death gets its power to hurt from sin, and sin gets its power from the Law. But thanks be to God who gives us the victory through our Lord Jesus Christ![4]

The Spirit that God has given us does not make us timid; instead, his Spirit fills us with power, love, and self-control.[5]—Even if I go through the deepest darkness, I will not be afraid, LORD, for you are with me. Your shepherd's rod and staff protect me.[6]

[1]HEB. 2.14. [2]2 Tim. 1.10.—[3]Isa. 25.8.—[4]1 Cor. 15.53–57. [5]2 Tim. 1.7.—[6]Ps. 23.4.

Evening

Do you know where the light comes from?[1]

God is light, and there is no darkness at all in him.[2]—While I am in the world, I am the light for the world.[3]

If . . . we say that we have fellowship with him, yet at the same time live in the darkness, we are lying both in our words and in our actions. But if we live in the light—just as he is in the light—then we have fellowship with one another, and the blood of Jesus, his Son, purifies us from every sin.[4]—The Father . . . has made you fit to have your share of what God has reserved for his people in the kingdom of light. He rescued us from the power of darkness and brought us safe into the kingdom of his dear Son, by whom we are set free, that is, our sins are forgiven.[5]

All of you are people who belong to the light, who belong to the day. We do not belong to the night or to the darkness.[6]—You are like light for the whole world. A city built on a hill cannot be hidden. In the same way your light must shine before people, so that they will see the good things you do and praise your Father in heaven.[7]

[1]JOB 38.19. [2]1 John 1.5.—[3]John 9.5. [4]1 John 1.6, 7.—[5]Col. 1.12–14. [6]1 Thess. 5.5.—[7]Matt. 5.14, 16.

The Lord . . . will not reject us for ever. He may bring us sorrow, but his love for us is sure and strong.[1]

My people, do not be afraid . . . I will come to you and save you. I will not destroy you. When I punish you, I will be fair.[2]—"For one brief moment I left you; with deep love I will take you back. I turned away angry for only a moment, but I will show you my love for ever." So says the Lord who saves you. "The mountains and hills may crumble, but my love for you will never end; I will keep for ever my promise of peace." So says the Lord who loves you.[3]—O Jerusalem, you suffering, helpless city, with no one to comfort you, I will rebuilt your foundations with precious stones.[4]

We have sinned against the Lord, so now we must endure his anger for a while. But in the end he will defend us and right the wrongs that have been done to us. He will bring us out to the light; we will live to see him save us.[5]

[1]LAM. 3.31, 32. [2]Jer. 46.27, 28.—[3]Isa. 54.7, 8, 10.—[4]Isa. 54.11. [5]Mic. 7.9.

Evening

God . . . chose what the world considers weak in order to shame the powerful.[1]

Then the Israelites cried out to the Lord, and he sent a man to free them. This was Ehud, a left-handed man. The next leader was Shamgar son of Anath. He too rescued Israel, and did so by killing six hundred Philistines with an ox-goad.[2]

The Lord ordered [Gideon], "Go with all your great strength and rescue Israel from the Midianites. I myself am sending you." Gideon replied, "But Lord, how can I rescue Israel? My clan is the weakest in the tribe of Manasseh, and I am the least important member of my family."[3]

The Lord said to Gideon, "The men you have are too many for me . . . They might think that they had won by themselves, and so give me no credit."[4]

You will succeed, not by military might or by your own strength, but by my spirit.[5]—Build up your strength in union with the Lord and by means of his mighty power.[6]

[1]1 COR. 1.27. [2]Judg. 3.15, 31. [3]Judg. 6.14, 15. [4]Judg. 7.2. [5]Zech. 4.6.—[6]Eph. 6.10.

He has prepared a city for them.[1]

After I go and prepare a place for you, I will come back and take you to myself, so that you will be where I am.[2]—Rich blessings that God keeps for his people. He keeps them for you in heaven, where they cannot decay or spoil or fade away.[3]—There is no permanent city for us here on earth; we are looking for the city which is to come.[4]

This Jesus, who was taken from you into heaven, will come back in the same way that you saw him go to heaven.[5]—Be patient, then, my brothers, until the Lord comes. See how patient a farmer is as he waits for his land to produce precious crops. He waits patiently for the autumn and spring rains. You also must be patient. Keep your hopes high, for the day of the Lord's coming is near.[6]—Just a little while longer, and he who is coming will come; he will not delay.[7]

We who are living at that time will be gathered up along with them in the clouds to meet the Lord in the air. And so we will always be with the Lord. So then, encourage one another with these words.[8]

[1]HEB. 11.16. [2]John 14.3.—[3]1 Pet. 1.4.—[4]Heb. 13.14. [5]Acts 1.11.—[6]Jas 5.7, 8.—[7]Heb. 10.37. [8]1 Thess. 4.17, 18.

Evening

He chose what the world looks down on and despises.[1]

Do not fool yourselves; people who are immoral or who worship idols or are adulterers or homosexual perverts or who steal or are greedy or are drunkards or who slander others or are thieves—none of these will possess God's Kingdom. Some of you were like that. But you have been purified from sin; you have been dedicated to God; you have been put right with God by the Lord Jesus Christ and by the Spirit of our God.[2]

In the past you were spiritually dead because of your disobedience and sins. At that time you followed the world's evil way. Actually all of us were like them and lived according to our natural desires, doing whatever suited the wishes of our own bodies and minds.[3]

Because of his own mercy . . . he saved us, through the Holy Spirit, who gives us new birth and new life by washing us. God poured out the Holy Spirit abundantly on us through Jesus Christ our Saviour.[4]

"My thoughts," says the LORD, "are not like yours, and my ways are different from yours."[5]

[1]1 COR. 1.28. [2]1 Cor. 6.9–11. [3]Eph. 2.1–3. [4]Titus 3.5, 6. [5]Isa. 55.8.

The joy that the LORD gives you will make you strong.[1]

Sing, heavens! Shout for joy, earth! Let the mountains burst into song! The LORD will comfort his people; he will have pity on his suffering people.[2]—God is my saviour; I will trust him and not be afraid. The LORD gives me power and strength; he is my saviour.[3]—The LORD protects and defends me; I trust in Him. He gives me help and makes me glad; I praise him with joyful songs.[4]—Jerusalem rejoices because of what the LORD has done. She is like a bride dressed for her wedding. God has clothed her with salvation and victory.[5]

In union with Christ Jesus, then, I can be proud of my service for God.[6]—We rejoice because of what God has done through our Lord Jesus Christ, who has now made us God's friends.[7]—I will still be joyful and glad, because the LORD God is my saviour.[8]

[1]NEH. 8.10. [2]Isa. 49.13.—[3]Isa. 12.2.—[4]Ps. 28.7.—[5]Isa. 61.10. [6]Rom. 15.17.—[7]Rom. 5.11.—[8]Hab. 3.18.

Evening

He has made an eternal covenant with me, an agreement that will not be broken.[1]

I am still full of confidence, because I know whom I have trusted, and I am sure that he is able to keep safe until that Day what he has entrusted to me.[2]

Let us give thanks to the God and Father of our Lord Jesus Christ! For in our union with Christ he has blessed us by giving us every spiritual blessing in the heavenly world. Even before the world was made, God had already chosen us to be his through our union with Christ, so that we would be holy and without fault before him. Because of his love God had already decided that through Jesus Christ he would make us his sons—this was his pleasure and purpose.[3]

We know that in all things God works for good with those who love him, those whom he has called according to his purpose. Those whom God had already chosen he also set apart to become like his Son, so that the Son would be the first among many brothers. And so those whom God set apart, he called; and those he called, he put right with himself, and he shared his glory with them.[4]

[1]2 SAM. 23.5. [2]2 Tim. 1.12. [3]Eph. 1.3–5. [4]Rom. 8.28–30.

May the God of peace provide you with every good thing you need in order to do his will.[1]

Strive for perfection; listen to my appeals; agree with one another; live in peace. And the God of love and peace will be with you.[2]

It is by God's grace that you have been saved through faith. It is not the result of your own efforts, but God's gift, so that no one can boast about it.[3]—Every good gift and every perfect present comes from heaven; it comes down from God, the Creator of the heavenly lights, who does not change or cause darkness by turning.[4]

Keep on working with fear and trembling to complete your salvation, because God is always at work in you to make you willing and able to obey his own purpose.[5]—Let God transform you inwardly by a complete change of your mind. Then you will be able to know the will of God—what is good and is pleasing to him and is perfect.[6]—Your lives will be filled with the truly good qualities which only Jesus Christ can produce, for the glory and praise of God.[7]

There is nothing in us that allows us to claim that we are capable of doing this work. The capacity we have comes from God.[8]

[1]HEB. 13.20, 21. [2]2 Cor. 13.11. [3]Eph. 2.8, 9.—[4]Jas 1.17. [5]Phil. 2.12, 13.—[6]Rom. 12.2.—[7]Phil. 1.11. [8]2 Cor. 3.5.

Evening

I am going to take her into the desert again; there I will win her back with words of love.[1]

The Lord says, "You must leave them and separate yourselves from them. Have nothing to do with what is unclean, and I will accept you. I will be your father, and you shall be my sons and daughters," says the Lord Almighty.[2]—All these promises are made to us, my dear friends. So then, let us purify ourselves from everything that makes body or soul unclean, and let us be completely holy by living in awe of God.[3]

Jesus . . . died outside the city, in order to purify the people from sin with his own blood. Let us, then, go to him outside the camp and share his shame.[4]

He said to them, "Let us go off by ourselves to some place where we will be alone and you can rest for a while."[5]—The LORD is my shepherd; I have everything I need. He lets me rest in fields of green grass and leads me to quiet pools of fresh water. He gives me new strength. He guides me in the right paths, as he has promised.[6]

[1]HOS. 2.14. [2]2 Cor. 6.17, 18.—[3]2 Cor. 7.1. [4]Heb. 13.12, 13. [5]Mark 6.31.—[6]Ps. 23.1–3.

The Temple that my son . . . is to build must be splendid.[1]

Come as living stones, and let yourselves be used in building the spiritual temple.[2]—Surely you know that you are God's temple and that God's Spirit lives in you! So if anyone destroys God's temple, God will destroy him. For God's temple is holy, and you yourselves are his temple.[3]—Don't you know that your body is the temple of the Holy Spirit, who lives in you and who was given to you by God? You do not belong to yourselves but to God; he bought you for a price. So use your bodies for God's glory.[4]—How can God's temple come to terms with pagan idols? For we are the temple of the living God! As God himself has said, "I will make my home with my people and live among them; I will be their God, and they shall be my people."[5]

You . . . are built upon the foundation laid by the apostles and prophets, the cornerstone being Christ Jesus himself. He is the one who holds the whole building together and makes it grow into a sacred temple dedicated to the Lord. In union with him you too are being built together with all the others into a place where God lives through his Spirit.[6]

[1]1 CHR. 22.5. [2]1 Pet. 2.5.—[3]1 Cor. 3.16, 17.—[4]1 Cor. 6.19, 20.—[5]2 Cor. 6.16. [6]Eph. 2.20–22.

Evening

Christ existed before all things.[1]

The Amen . . . the origin of all that God has created.[2]—He is the source . . . he is the first-born Son, who was raised from death, in order that he alone might have the first place in all things.[3]

The LORD created me first of all, the first of his works, long ago. I was made in the very beginning, at the first, before the world began. I was there when he set the sky in place, when he stretched the horizon across the ocean, when he placed the clouds in the sky, when he opened the springs of the ocean and ordered the waters of the sea to rise no further than he said. I was beside him like an architect, I was his daily source of joy, always happy in his presence.[4]—I am God and always will be.[5]

The Lamb that was killed.[6]—Jesus, on whom our faith depends from beginning to end. He did not give up because of the cross! On the contrary, because of the joy that was waiting for him, he thought nothing of the disgrace of dying on the cross, and he is now seated at the right-hand side of God's throne.[7]

[1]COL. 1.17. [2]Rev. 3.14.—[3]Col. 1.18. [4]Prov. 8.22, 23, 27–30.—[5]Isa. 43.13. [6]Rev. 13.8.—[7]Heb. 12.2.

Pray for one another, so that you will be healed.[1]

Abraham spoke again: "Please forgive my boldness in continuing to speak to you, Lord. I am only a man and have no right to say anything. But perhaps there will be only forty-five innocent people instead of fifty. Will you destroy the whole city because there are five too few?" The LORD answered, "I will not destroy the city if I find forty-five innocent people."[2]

Forgive them, Father! They don't know what they are doing.[3]—Pray for those who persecute you.[4]

I pray for them. I do not pray for the world but for those you gave me, for they belong to you. I pray not only for them, but also for those who believe in me because of their message.[5]—Help to carry one another's burdens, and in this way you will obey the law of Christ.[6]

The prayer of a good person has a powerful effect. Elijah was the same kind of person as we are. He prayed earnestly that there would be no rain, and no rain fell on the land for three and a half years.[7]

[1]JAS 5.16. [2]Gen. 18.27, 28. [3]Luke 23.34.—[4]Matt. 5.44. [5]John 17.9, 20.—[6]Gal. 6.2. [7]Jas 5.16, 17.

Evening

As for us, our life is like grass. We grow and flourish like a wild flower; then the wind blows on it, and it is gone—no one sees it again.[1]

Teach us how short our life is, so that we may become wise.[2]—Does a person gain anything if he wins the whole world but loses his life?[3]

People are no more enduring than grass. Yes, grass withers and flowers fade, but the word of our God endures for ever.[4]—The world and everything in it that people desire is passing away; but he who does the will of God lives for ever.[5]

Listen! This is the hour to receive God's favour; today is the day to be saved![6]—Those who deal in material goods [should live] as though they were not fully occupied with them. For this world, as it is now, will not last much longer.[7]—Let us be concerned for one another, to help one another to show love and to do good. Let us not give up the habit of meeting together, as some are doing. Instead, let us encourage one another all the more, since you see that the Day of the Lord is coming nearer.[8]

[1]PS. 103.15, 16. [2]Ps. 90.12.—[3]Mark 8.36. [4]Isa. 40.7, 8.—[5]1 John 2.17. [6]2 Cor. 6.2.—[7]1 Cor. 7.31.—[8]Heb. 10.24, 25.

There is no god in heaven or on earth who can do the mighty things that you have done![1]

No one in heaven is like you, LORD; none of the heavenly beings is your equal. LORD God Almighty, none is as mighty as you; in all things you are faithful, O LORD.[2]—There is no god like you, O Lord, not one has done what you have done.[3]—It was your will and purpose to do this; you have done all these great things in order to teach me. How great you are, Sovereign LORD! There is none like you; we have always known that you alone are God.[4]

What no one ever saw or heard, what no one ever thought could happen, is the very thing God prepared for those who love him. But it was to us that God made known his secret by means of his Spirit.[5]—There are some things that the LORD our God has kept secret; but he has revealed his Law, and we and our descendants are to obey it for ever.[6]

[1]DEUT. 3.24. [2]Ps. 89.6, 8.—[3]Ps. 86.8.—[4]2 Sam. 7.21, 22. [5]1 Cor. 2.9, 10.—[6]Deut. 29.29.

Evening

Whoever wants to boast must boast of what the LORD has done.[1]

The LORD says, "Wise men should not boast of their wisdom, nor strong men of their strength, nor rich men of their wealth. If anyone wants to boast, he should boast that he knows and understands me."[2]

I reckon everything as complete loss for the sake of what is so much more valuable, the knowledge of Christ Jesus my Lord. For his sake I have thrown everything away; I consider it all as mere refuse, so that I may gain Christ.[3]—I have complete confidence in the gospel; it is God's power to save all who believe.[4]—In union with Christ Jesus . . . I can be proud of my service for God.[5]

What else have I in heaven but you? Since I have you, what else could I want on earth?[6]—The LORD has filled my heart with joy . . . how joyful I am because God has helped me![7]

To you alone, O LORD, to you alone, and not to us, must glory be given because of your constant love and faithfulness.[8]

[1]1 COR. 1.31. [2]Jer. 9.23, 24. [3]Phil. 3.8.—[4]Rom. 1.16.—[5]Rom. 15.17. [6]Ps. 73.25.—[7]1 Sam. 2.1. [8]Ps. 115.1.

***Be holy in all that you do, just as God who called you is holy.*[1]**

You know that . . . we encouraged you, we comforted you, and we kept urging you to live the kind of life that pleases God, who calls you to share in his own Kingdom and glory.[2]—You are . . . chosen to proclaim the wonderful acts of God, who called you out of darkness into his own marvellous light.[3]

You yourselves used to be in the darkness, but since you have become the Lord's people, you are in the light. So you must live like people who belong to the light, for it is the light that brings a rich harvest of every kind of goodness, righteousness, and truth. Try to learn what pleases the Lord. Have nothing to do with the worthless things that people do, things that belong to the darkness. Instead, bring them out to the light.[4]—Your lives will be filled with the truly good qualities which only Jesus Christ can produce, for the glory and praise of God.[5]

Your light must shine before people, so that they will see the good things you do and praise your Father in heaven.[6]—Whatever you do, whether you eat or drink, do it all for God's glory.[7]

[1]1 PET. 1.15. [2]1 Thess. 2.11, 12.—[3]1 Pet. 2.9. [4]Eph. 5.8–11.—[5]Phil. 1.11. [6]Matt. 5.16.—[7]1 Cor. 10.31.

Evening

***You have no right to question me about my children or to tell me what I ought to do!*[1]**

I will give you a new heart and a new mind. I will take away your stubborn heart of stone and give you an obedient heart. I will put my Spirit in you and I will see to it that you follow my laws and keep all the commands I have given you. The Sovereign LORD says, "I will once again let the Israelites ask me for help."[2]

Whenever two of you on earth agree about anything you pray for, it will be done for you by my Father in heaven. For where two or three come together in my name, I am there with them.[3]

Have faith in God. I assure you that whoever tells this hill to get up and throw itself in the sea and does not doubt in his heart, but believes that what he says will happen, it will be done for him.[4]

[1]ISA. 45.11. [2]Ezek. 36.26, 27, 37. [3]Matt. 18.19, 20. [4]Mark 11.22, 23.

God is not like men, who lie; he is not a human who changes his mind.[1]

God, the Creator of the heavenly lights, who does not change or cause darkness by turning.[2]—Jesus Christ is the same yesterday, today, and for ever.[3]

His faithfulness will protect and defend you.[4]

To those who were to receive what he promised, God wanted to make it very clear that he would never change his purpose; so he added his vow to the promise. There are these two things, then, that cannot change and about which God cannot lie. So we who have found safety with him are greatly encouraged to hold firmly to the hope placed before us.[5]

God is the only God and . . . he is faithful. He will keep his covenant and show his constant love to a thousand generations of those who love him and obey his commands.[6]—With faithfulness and love he leads all who keep his covenant and obey his commands.[7]—Happy is the man who has the God of Jacob to help him and who depends on the LORD his God . . . he always keeps his promises.[8]

[1]NUM. 23.19. [2]Jas 1.17.—[3]Heb. 13.8. [4]Ps. 91.4. [5]Heb. 6.17, 18. [6]Deut. 7.9.—[7]Ps. 25.10.—[8]Ps. 146.5, 6.

Evening

If you are weak in a crisis, you are weak indeed.[1]

He strengthens those who are weak and tired.[2]—My grace is all you need, for my power is greatest when you are weak.[3]—When they call to me, I will answer them; when they are in trouble, I will be with them. I will rescue them.[4]—God has always been your defence; his eternal arms are your support. He drove out your enemies as you advanced.[5]

I had hoped for sympathy, but there was none; for comfort, but I found none.[6]

Every high priest is chosen from his fellow-men and appointed to serve God on their behalf . . . he is able to be gentle with those who are ignorant and make mistakes. In the same way, Christ . . . even though he was God's Son . . . learnt through his sufferings to be obedient. When he was made perfect, he became the source of eternal salvation for all those who obey him.[7]—He endured the suffering that should have been ours, the pain that we should have borne.[8]

[1]PROV. 24.10. [2]Isa. 40.29.—[3]2 Cor. 12.9.—[4]Ps. 91.15.—[5]Deut. 33.27. [6]Ps. 69.20. [7]Heb. 5.1, 2, 5, 8, 9.—[8]Isa. 53.4.

You are all I want, O Lord.[1]

Everything belongs to you . . . and you belong to Christ, and Christ belongs to God.[2]—Our great God and Saviour Jesus Christ . . . gave himself for us.[3]—God . . . gave him to the church as supreme Lord over all things.[4]—Christ loved the church and gave his life for it . . . in order to present the church to himself in all its beauty—pure and faultless, without spot or wrinkle or any other imperfection.[5]

I will praise him for what he has done.[6]—Jerusalem rejoices because of what the Lord has done. She is like a bride dressed for her wedding. God has clothed her with salvation and victory.[7]

What else have I in heaven but you? Since I have you, what else could I want on earth? My mind and my body may grow weak, but God is my strength; he is all I ever need.[8]—I say to the Lord, "You are my Lord. You, Lord, are all I have, and you give me all I need; my future is in your hands. How wonderful are your gifts to me; how good they are![9]

[1]PS. 119.57. [2]1 Cor. 3.21, 23.—[3]Titus 2.13, 14.—[4]Eph. 1.22.—[5]Eph. 5.25, 27. [6]Ps. 34.2.—[7]Isa. 61.10. [8]Ps. 73.25, 26.—[9]Ps. 16.2, 5, 6.

Evening

What you think is the right road may lead to death.[1]

It is foolish to follow your own opinions.[2]

Your word is a lamp to guide me and a light for my path.[3]—I have obeyed your command and have not followed paths of violence.[4]

A prophet or an interpreter of dreams may promise a miracle or a wonder, in order to lead you to worship and serve gods that you have not worshipped before . . . do not pay any attention to him. The Lord your God is using him to test you, to see if you love the Lord with all your heart. Follow the Lord and honour him; obey him and keep his commands; worship him and be faithful to him.[5]

I will teach you the way you should go; I will instruct you and advise you.[6]

[1]PROV. 14.12. [2]Prov. 28.26. [3]Ps. 119.105.—[4]Ps. 17.4. [5]Deut. 13.1–4. [6]Ps. 32.8.

 Morning

None of us lives for himself only, none of us dies for himself only.[1]

If we live, it is for the Lord that we live, and if we die, it is for the Lord that we die. So whether we live or die, we belong to the Lord.[2]—No one should be looking to his own interests, but to the interests of others.[3]—He bought you for a price. So use your bodies for God's glory.[4]

With my whole being I shall bring honour to Christ, whether I live or die. For what is life? To me, it is Christ. Death, then, will bring more. But if by continuing to live I can do more worthwhile work, then I am not sure which I should choose. I am pulled in two directions. I want very much to leave this life and be with Christ, which is a far better thing.[5]

So far as the Law is concerned . . . I am dead—killed by the Law itself—in order that I might live for God. I have been put to death with Christ on his cross, so that it is no longer I who live, but it is Christ who lives in me. This life that I live now, I live by faith in the Son of God, who loved me and gave his life for me.[6]

[1]ROM. 14.7. [2]Rom. 14.8.—[3]1 Cor. 10.24.—[4]1 Cor. 6.20. [5]Phil. 1.20–23. [6]Gal. 2.19, 20.

Evening

God gave Solomon unusual wisdom and insight, and knowledge too great to be measured.[1]

There is something here greater than Solomon![2]—"Prince of Peace."[3]

It is a difficult thing for someone to die for a righteous person. It may even be that someone might dare to die for a good person. But God has shown us how much he loves us—it was while we were still sinners that Christ died for us![4]—He always had the nature of God, but he did not think that by force he should try to become equal with God. Instead of this, of his own free will he gave up all he had, and took the nature of a servant. He became like man and appeared in human likeness. He was humble and walked the path of obedience all the way to death—his death on the cross.[5]—Christ's love . . . can never be fully known.[6]

Christ, who is the power of God and the wisdom of God.[7]—He is the key that opens all the hidden treasures of God's wisdom and knowledge.[8]—The infinite riches of Christ.[9]—God has brought you into union with Christ Jesus, and God has made Christ to be our wisdom. By him we are put right with God; we become God's holy people and are set free.[10]

[1]1 KGS 4.29. [2]Matt. 12.42.—[3]Isa. 9.6. [4]Rom. 5.7, 8.—[5]Phil. 2.6–8.—[6]Eph. 3.18, 19. [7]1 Cor. 1.24.—[8]Col. 2.3.—[9]Eph. 3.8.—[10]1 Cor. 1.30.

I have always loved you, so I continue to show you my constant love.[1]

We must thank God at all times for you, brothers, you whom the Lord loves. For God chose you as the first to be saved by the Spirit's power to make you his holy people and by your faith in the truth. God called you to this through the Good News we preached to you; he called you to possess your share of the glory of our Lord Jesus Christ.[2]—He saved us and called us to be his own people, not because of what we have done, but because of his own purpose and grace. He gave us this grace by means of Christ Jesus before the beginning of time.[3]—You saw me before I was born. The days allotted to me had all been recorded in your book, before any of them ever began.[4]

God loved the world so much that he gave his only Son, so that everyone who believes in him may not die but have eternal life.[5]

This is what love is: it is not that we have loved God, but that he loved us and sent his Son to be the means by which our sins are forgiven.[6]

[1]JER. 31.3. [2]2 Thess. 2.13, 14.—[3]2 Tim. 1.9.—[4]Ps. 139.16. [5]John 3.16. [6]1 John 4.10.

Evening

I made you and will care for you.[1]

Israel, the LORD who created you says, "Do not be afraid—I will save you. I have called you by name—you are mine. When you pass through deep waters, I will be with you; your troubles will not overwhelm you."[2]—I am your God and will take care of you until you are old and your hair is grey.[3]

Like an eagle teaching its young to fly, catching them safely on its spreading wings, the LORD kept Israel from falling. The LORD alone led his people without the help of a foreign god.[4]—He had always taken care of them in the past.[5]

Jesus Christ is the same yesterday, today, and for ever.[6]—I am certain that nothing can separate us from his love . . . neither the world above nor the world below—there is nothing in all creation that will ever be able to separate us from the love of God which is ours through Christ Jesus our Lord.[7]

Can a woman forget her own baby and not love the child she bore? Even if a mother should forget her child, I will never forget you.[8]

[1]ISA. 46.4. [2]Isa. 43.1, 2.—[3]Isa. 46.4. [4]Deut. 32.11, 12.—[5]Isa. 63.9. [6]Heb. 13.8.—[7]Rom. 8.38, 39. [8]Isa. 49.15.

Morning

I know all about their sufferings.[1]

He endured suffering and pain.[2]—Tempted in every way that we are.[3] He himself took our sickness and carried away our diseases.[4]—Jesus, tired out by the journey, sat down by the well.[5]

Jesus saw her weeping, and he saw how the people who were with her were weeping also; his heart was touched, and he was deeply moved. Jesus wept.[6]—Now he can help those who are tempted, because he himself was tempted and suffered.[7]

The LORD looked down from his holy place on high, he looked down from heaven to earth. He heard the groans of prisoners and set free those who were condemned to die.[8]—God knows every step I take; if he tests me, he will find me pure.[9]—When I am ready to give up, he knows what I should do.[10]

Anyone who strikes you strikes what is most precious to me.[11]—The LORD himself . . . saved them. In his love and compassion he rescued them.[12]

[1]EXOD. 3.7. [2]Isa. 53.3.—[3]Heb. 4.15. [4]Matt. 8.17.—[5]John 4.6. [6]John 11.33, 35.—[7]Heb. 2.18. [8]Ps. 102.19, 20.—[9]Job 23.10.—[10]Ps. 142.3. [11]Zech. 2.8.—[12]Isa. 63.9.

Evening

As long as it is day, we must keep on doing the work of him who sent me.[1]

No matter how much a lazy person may want something, he will never get it. A hard worker will get everything he wants.[2]—Help others, and you will be helped.[3]

"My food," Jesus said to them, "is to obey the will of the one who sent me and to finish the work he gave me to do. You have a saying, 'Four more months, and then the harvest.' But I tell you, take a good look at the fields; the crops are now ripe and ready to be harvested! The man who reaps the harvest is being paid and gathers the crops for eternal life; so the man who sows and the man who reaps will be glad together."[4]—The Kingdom of heaven is like this. Once there was a man who went out early in the morning to hire some men to work in his vineyard. He agreed to pay them the regular wage, a silver coin a day, and sent them to work in his vineyard.[5]

Preach the message . . . insist upon proclaiming it (whether the time is right or not).[6]—See what you can earn with this while I am gone.[7]

I have worked harder than any of the other apostles, although it was not really my own doing, but God's grace working with me.[8]

[1]JOHN 9.4. [2]Prov. 13.4.—[3]Prov. 11.25. [4]John 4.34–36.—[5]Matt. 20.1, 2. [6]2 Tim. 4.2.—[7]Luke 19.13. [8]1 Cor. 15.10.

Think of the rock from which you came, the quarry from which you were dug.[1]

I have been evil from the day I was born.[2]—No one took enough pity on you. When you were born, no one loved you. You were thrown out in an open field. Then I passed by and saw you squirming in your own blood . . . but I wouldn't let you die.[3]

He pulled me out of a dangerous pit, out of the deadly quicksand. He set me safely on a rock and made me secure. He taught me to sing a new song, a song of praise to our God.[4]

When we were still helpless, Christ died for the wicked at the time that God chose. It is a difficult thing for someone to die for a righteous person. It may even be that someone might dare to die for a good person. But God has shown us how much he loves us—it was while we were still sinners that Christ died for us![5]—God's mercy is so abundant, and his love for us is so great, that while we were spiritually dead in our disobedience he brought us to life with Christ.[6]

[1]ISA. 51.1. [2]Ps. 51.5.—[3]Ezek. 16.5, 6. [4]Ps. 40.2, 3. [5]Rom. 5.6–8.—[6]Eph. 2.4, 5.

Evening

Jerusalem rejoices because of what the LORD has done.[1]

I will always thank the LORD; I will never stop praising him. I will praise him for what he has done; may all who are oppressed listen and be glad! Proclaim with me the LORD's greatness; let us praise his name together![2]—The LORD is our protector and glorious king. He does not refuse any good thing to those who do what is right. LORD Almighty, how happy are those who trust in you![3]—Praise the LORD, my soul! All my being, praise his holy name![4]

Is anyone happy? He should sing praises.[5]—Be filled with the Spirit. Speak to one another with the words of psalms, hymns, and sacred songs; sing hymns and psalms to the Lord with praise in your hearts. Always give thanks for everything.[6]—Sing to God with thanksgiving in your hearts.[7]

About midnight Paul and Silas were praying and singing hymns to God, and the other prisoners were listening to them.[8]—May you always be joyful in your union with the Lord. I say it again: rejoice![9]

[1]ISA. 61.10. [2]Ps. 34.1–3.—[3]Ps. 84.11, 12.—[4]Ps. 103.1. [5]Jas 5.13.—
[6]Eph. 5.18–20.—[7]Col. 3.16. [8]Acts 16.25.—[9]Phil. 4.4.

Morning

Make an ornament of pure gold and engrave on it 'Dedicated to the ***LORD'.***[1]

Live a holy life, because no one will see the Lord without it.[2]—God is Spirit, and only by the power of his Spirit can people worship him as he really is.[3]—All who serve me must respect my holiness; I will reveal my glory to my people.[4]—All of us have been sinful; even our best actions are filthy through and through.[5]

This is the law of the Temple: All the area surrounding it on the top of the mountain is sacred and holy.[6]—Your Temple is holy indeed, for ever and ever.[7]

For their sake I dedicate myself to you, in order that they, too, may be truly dedicated to you.[8]—We have a great High Priest who has gone into the very presence of God—Jesus, the Son of God. Let us have confidence, then, and approach God's throne, where there is grace. There we will receive mercy and find grace to help us just when we need it.[9]

[1]EXOD. 28.36. [2]Heb. 12.14.—[3]John 4.24.—[4]Lev. 10.3.—[5]Isa. 64.6. [6]Ezek. 43.12.—[7]Ps. 93.5. [8]John 17.19.—[9]Heb. 4.14, 16.

Evening

You . . . fill my cup to the brim.[1]

Find out for yourself how good the LORD is. Happy are those who find safety with him. Honour the LORD, all his people; those who obey him have all they need. Even lions go hungry for lack of food, but those who obey the LORD lack nothing good.[2]—The LORD's unfailing love and mercy still continue, fresh as the morning, as sure as the sunrise.[3]

You, LORD, are all I have, and you give me all I need; my future is in your hands. How wonderful are your gifts to me; how good they are![4]—This world, life and death, the present and the future—all these are yours.[5]—Let us give thanks to the God and Father of our Lord Jesus Christ! For in our union with Christ he has blessed us by giving us every spiritual blessing in the heavenly world.[6]

I have learnt to be satisfied with what I have.[7]—Religion does make a person very rich, if he is satisfied with what he has.[8]—With all his abundant wealth through Christ Jesus, my God will supply all your needs.[9]

[1]PS. 23.5. [2]Ps. 34.8–10.—[3]Lam. 3.22, 23. [4]Ps. 16.5, 6.—[5]1 Cor. 3.22.—[6]Eph. 1.3. [7]Phil. 4.11.—[8]1 Tim. 6.6.—[9]Phil. 4.19.

Your word is a lamp to guide me and a light for my path.[1]

I have obeyed your command and have not followed paths of violence. I have always walked in your way and have never strayed from it.[2]

Their teaching will lead you when you travel, protect you at night, and advise you during the day. Their instructions are a shining light; their correction can teach you how to live.[3]—If you wander off the road to the right or the left, you will hear his voice behind you saying, "Here is the road. Follow it."[4]

I am the light of the world. Whoever follows me will have the light of life and will never walk in darkness.[5]—We are . . . confident of the message proclaimed by the prophets. You will do well to pay attention to it, because it is like a lamp shining in a dark place.[6]—What we see now is like a dim image in a mirror; then we shall see face to face. What I know now is only partial; then it will be complete—as complete as God's knowledge of me.[7]—They will not need lamps or sunlight, because the Lord God will be their light, and they will rule as kings for ever and ever.[8]

[1]PS. 119.105. [2]Ps. 17.4, 5. [3]Prov. 6.22, 23.—[4]Isa. 30.21. [5]John 8.12.—[6]2 Pet. 1.19.—[7]1 Cor. 13.12.—[8]Rev. 22.5.

Evening

What are you doing asleep? Get up.[1]

Get up and go; there is no safety here any more. Your sins have doomed this place to destruction.[2]—Keep your minds fixed on things [in heaven], not on things here on earth.[3]—If your riches increase, don't depend on them.[4]—Serve the LORD your God with all your heart and soul.[5]

Why are you sleeping? Get up and pray that you will not fall into temptation.[6]—Be on your guard! Don't let yourselves become occupied with too much feasting and drinking and with the worries of this life, or that Day may suddenly catch you like a trap.[7]

The bridegroom was late in coming, so the girls began to nod and fall asleep.[8]—Just a little while longer, and he who is coming will come; he will not delay.[9]—The time has come for you to wake up from your sleep. For the moment when we will be saved is closer now than it was when we first believed.[10]—Be on guard, then, because you do not know when the master of the house is coming—it might be in the evening or at midnight or before dawn or at sunrise. If he comes suddenly, he must not find you asleep.[11]

[1]JONAH 1.6. [2]Mic. 2.10.—[3]Col. 3.2.—[4]Ps. 62.10.—[5]1 Chr. 22.19. [6]Luke 22.46.—[7]Luke 21.34. [8]Matt. 25.5.—[9]Heb. 10.37.—[10]Rom. 13.11.—[11]Mark 13.35, 36.

The one who stood before our God and accused our brothers day and night has been thrown out of heaven.[1]

Our brothers won the victory over him by the blood of the Lamb and by the truth which they proclaimed.[2]—Who will accuse God's chosen people? God himself declares them not guilty! Who, then, will condemn them? Not Christ Jesus, who died, or rather, who was raised to life and is at the right-hand side of God, pleading with him for us![3]

Christ freed himself from the power of the spiritual rulers and authorities; he made a public spectacle of them.[4]—So that through his death he might destroy the Devil, who has the power over death, and in this way set free those who were slaves all their lives because of their fear of death.[5]—In all these things we have complete victory through him who loved us![6]—Put on all the armour that God gives you, so that you will be able to stand up against the Devil's evil tricks. And accept . . . the word of God as the sword which the Spirit gives you.[7]—Thanks be to God who gives us the victory through our Lord Jesus Christ![8]

[1]REV. 12.10. [2]Rev. 12.11.—[3]Rom. 8.33, 34. [4]Col. 2.15.—[5]Heb. 2.14, 15.—[6]Rom. 8.37.—[7]Eph. 6.11, 17.—[8]1 Cor. 15.57.

Evening

The tree that gives life.[1]

God has given us eternal life, and this life has its source in his Son.[2]—He gave his only Son, so that everyone who believes in him may not die but have eternal life.[3]—Just as the Father raises the dead and gives them life, in the same way the Son gives life to those he wants to. Just as the Father is himself the source of life, in the same way he has made his Son to be the source of life.[4]

To those who win the victory I will give the right to eat the fruit of the tree of life that grows in the Garden of God.[5]—On each side of the river was the tree of life, which bears fruit twelve times a year, once each month; and its leaves are for the healing of the nations.[6]

Happy is the man who becomes wise. Wisdom offers you long life. Those who become wise are happy; wisdom will give them life.[7]—God has made Christ to be our wisdom.[8]

[1]GEN. 2.9. [2]1 John 5.11.—[3]John 3.16.—[4]John 5.21, 26. [5]Rev. 2.7.—[6]Rev. 22.2. [7]Prov. 3.13, 16, 18.—[8]1 Cor. 1.30.

Trust in the LORD and you will be happy.[1]

[Abraham's] faith did not leave him, and he did not doubt God's promise; his faith filled him with power, and he gave praise to God. He was absolutely sure that God would be able to do what he had promised.[2]—The people of Judah were victorious over Israel, because they relied on the LORD, the God of their ancestors.[3]

God is our shelter and strength, always ready to help in times of trouble. So we will not be afraid, even if the earth is shaken and mountains fall into the ocean depths.[4]—It is better to trust in the LORD than to depend on man. It is better to trust in the LORD than to depend on human leaders.[5]—The LORD guides a man in the way he should go and protects those who please him. If they fall, they will not stay down, because the LORD will help them up.[6]

Find out for yourself how good the LORD is. Happy are those who find safety with him. Honour the LORD, all his people; those who obey him have all they need.[7]

[1]PROV. 16.20. [2]Rom. 4.20, 21.—[3]2 Chr. 13.18. [4]Ps. 46.1, 2.—[5]Ps. 118.8, 9.—[6]Ps. 37.23, 24. [7]Ps. 34.8, 9.

Evening

When I lie down, I go to sleep in peace; you alone, O LORD, keep me perfectly safe.[1]

You need not fear any dangers at night. He will cover you with his wings; you will be safe in his care.[2]—Just as a hen gathers her chicks under her wings.[3]—He will not let you fall; your protector is always awake. The protector of Israel never dozes or sleeps. The LORD will guard you; he is by your side to protect you.[4]

Let me live in your sanctuary all my life; let me find safety under your wings.[5]—Even darkness is not dark for you, and the night is as bright as the day. Darkness and light are the same to you.[6]

God, who did not even keep back his own Son, but offered him for us all! He gave us his Son—will he not also freely give us all things?[7]—You belong to Christ, and Christ belongs to God.[8]—I will trust him and not be afraid.[9]

[1]PS. 4.8. [2]Ps. 91.5, 4.—[3]Matt. 23.37.—[4]Ps. 121.3–5. [5]Ps. 61.4.—[6]Ps. 139.12. [7]Rom. 8.32.—[8]1 Cor. 3.23.—[9]Isa. 12.2.

***The king . . . held out to her the gold sceptre.* [*Esther*] *came up and touched the tip of it.*[1]**

When he cries out to me for help, I will answer him because I am merciful.[2]

We ourselves know and believe the love which God has for us. God is love, and whoever lives in love lives in union with God and God lives in union with him. Love is made perfect in us in order that we may have courage on Judgement Day; and we will have it because our life in this world is the same as Christ's. There is no fear in love; perfect love drives out all fear. So then, love has not been made perfect in anyone who is afraid, because fear has to do with punishment. We love because God first loved us.[3]

Let us come near to God with a sincere heart and a sure faith, with hearts that have been purified from a guilty conscience and with bodies washed with clean water.[4]—Now, in union with Christ Jesus, you . . . have been brought near by the sacrificial death of Christ.[5]—In union with Christ and through our faith in him we have the boldness to go into God's presence with all confidence.[6]—Let us have confidence, then, and approach God's throne, where there is grace. There we will receive mercy and find grace to help us just when we need it.[7]

[1]ESTHER 5.2. [2]Exod. 22.27. [3]1 John 4.16–19. [4]Heb. 10.22.—[5]Eph. 2.13.—[6]Eph. 3.12.—[7]Heb. 4.16.

Evening

***They didn't know what it was and asked each other, "What is it?"*[1]**

No one can deny how great is the secret of our religion: he appeared in human form.[2]—The bread that God gives is he who comes down from heaven and gives life to the world.[3]

Your ancestors ate manna in the desert, but they died . . . If anyone eats this bread, he will live for ever. The bread that I will give him is my flesh, which I give so that the world may live. My flesh is the real food; my blood is the real drink.[4]

The Israelites did this, some gathering more, others less. Those who gathered much did not have too much, and those who gathered less did not have too little. Every morning each one gathered as much as he needed.[5]

Do not start worrying: "Where will my food come from? or my drink? or my clothes?". Your Father in heaven knows that you need all these things. Instead, be concerned above everything else with the Kingdom of God and with what he requires of you, and he will provide you with all these other things.[6]

[1]EXOD. 16.15. [2]1 Tim. 3.16.—[3]John 6.33. [4]John 6.49, 51, 55. [5]Exod. 16.17, 18, 21. [6]Matt. 6.31–33.

Morning

After so many sins, comes the undeserved gift of "Not guilty!"[1]

You are stained red with sin, but I will wash you as clean as snow. Although your stains are deep red, you will be as white as wool.[2]—I am the God who forgives your sins, and I do this because of who I am. I will not hold your sins against you. Let us go to court; bring your accusation! Present your case to prove you are in the right![3]—I have swept your sins away like a cloud. Come back to me; I am the one who saves you.[4]

God loved the world so much that he gave his only Son, so that everyone who believes in him may not die but have eternal life.[5]—The two are not the same, because God's free gift is not like Adam's sin. It is true that many people died because of the sin of that one man. But God's grace is much greater, and so is his free gift to so many people through the grace of the one man, Jesus Christ.[6]—Some of you were like that. But you have been purified from sin; you have been dedicated to God; you have been put right with God by the Lord Jesus Christ and by the Spirit of our God.[7]

[1]ROM. 5.16. [2]Isa. 1.18.—[3]Isa. 43.25, 26.—[4]Isa. 44.22. [5]John 3.16.—[6]Rom. 5.15.—[7]1 Cor. 6.11.

Evening

See what you can earn with this while I am gone.[1]

It will be like a man who goes away from home on a journey and leaves his servants in charge, after giving to each one his own work to do and after telling the doorkeeper to keep watch.[2]—He gave to each one according to his ability: to one he gave five thousand gold coins, to another he gave two thousand, and to another he gave one thousand. Then he left on his journey.[3]

As long as it is day, we must keep on doing the work of him who sent me; night is coming when no one can work.[4]—Didn't you know that I had to be in my Father's house?[5]—Christ . . . left you an example, so that you would follow in his steps.[6]

Preach the message . . . insist upon proclaiming it (whether the time is right or not) . . . convince, reproach, and encourage, as you teach with all patience.[7]—The quality of each person's work will be seen when the Day of Christ exposes it.[8]—So then, my dear brothers, stand firm and steady. Keep busy always in your work for the Lord, since you know that nothing you do in the Lord's service is ever useless.[9]

[1]LUKE 19.13. [2]Mark 13.34.—[3]Matt. 25.15. [4]John 9.4.—[5]Luke 2.49.—[6]1 Pet. 2.21. [7]2 Tim. 4.2.—[8]1 Cor. 3.13.—[9]1 Cor. 15.58.

The Spirit produces . . . humility.[1]

Poor and humble people will once again find the happiness which the LORD, the holy God of Israel, gives.[2]—Unless you change and become like children, you will never enter the Kingdom of heaven. The greatest in the Kingdom of heaven is the one who humbles himself and becomes like this child.[3]—The ageless beauty of a gentle and quiet spirit, which is of the greatest value in God's sight.[4]—Love . . . is not . . . conceited or proud.[5]

Strive for . . . gentleness.[6]—Take my yoke and put it on you, and learn from me, because I am gentle and humble in spirit.[7]—He was treated harshly, but endured it humbly; he never said a word. Like a lamb about to be slaughtered, like a sheep about to be sheared, he never said a word.[8]—Christ himself suffered for you and left you an example, so that you would follow in his steps. He committed no sin, and no one ever heard a lie come from his lips. When he was insulted, he did not answer back with an insult . . . but placed his hopes in God, the righteous Judge.[9]

[1]GAL. 5.22, 23. [2]Isa. 29.19.—[3]Matt. 18.3, 4.—[4]1 Pet. 3, 4.—[5]1 Cor. 13.4. [6]1 Tim. 6.11.—[7]Matt. 11.29.—[8]Isa. 53.7.—[9]1 Pet. 2.21–23.

Evening

If anyone wants to come with me, he must forget self, take up his cross every day, and follow me.[1]

We are honoured and disgraced; we are insulted and praised.[2]—Everyone who wants to live a godly life in union with Christ Jesus will be persecuted.[3]

Am I trying to be popular with men? If I were still trying to do so, I would not be a servant of Christ.[4]

Happy are you if you are insulted because you are Christ's followers. If any of you suffers, it must not be because he is a murderer or a thief or a criminal or a meddler in other people's affairs. However, if you suffer because you are a Christian, don't be ashamed of it, but thank God that you bear Christ's name.[5]

You have been given the privilege of serving Christ, not only by believing in him, but also by suffering for him.[6]—One man died for everyone, which means that all share in his death. He died for all, so that those who live should no longer live for themselves, but only for him who died and was raised to life for their sake.[7]—If we continue to endure, we shall also rule with him.[8]

[1]LUKE 9.23. [2]2 Cor. 6.8.—[3]2 Tim. 3.12. [4]Gal. 1.10. [5]1 Pet. 4.14–16. [6]Phil. 1.29.—[7]2 Cor. 5.14, 15.—[8]2 Tim. 2.12.

Trust in the Lord. Have faith, do not despair. Trust in the Lord.[1]

Don't you know? Haven't you heard? The Lord is the everlasting God; he created all the world. He never grows tired or weary. He strengthens those who are weak and tired.[2]—Do not be afraid—I am with you! I am your God—let nothing terrify you! I will make you strong and help you; I will protect you and save you.[3]—The poor and the helpless have fled to you and have been safe in times of trouble. You give them shelter from storms and shade from the burning heat. Cruel men attack like a winter storm.[4]

When your faith succeeds in facing such trials, the result is the ability to endure. Make sure that your endurance carries you all the way without failing, so that you may be perfect and complete, lacking nothing.[5]—Do not lose your courage, then, because it brings with it a great reward. You need to be patient, in order to do the will of God and receive what he promises.[6]

[1]PS. 27.14. [2]Isa. 40.28, 29.—[3]Isa. 41.10.—[4]Isa. 25.4. [5]Jas 1.3, 4.—
[6]Heb. 10.35, 36.

Evening

He lets me rest in fields of green grass.[1]

"Evil men are like the restless sea, whose waves never stop rolling in. There is no safety for sinners," says the Lord.[2]

Come to me, all you you who are tired from carrying heavy loads, and I will give you rest.[3]—Be patient and wait for the Lord to act.[4]—Whoever receives that rest which God promised will rest from his own work.[5]

Do not let all kinds of strange teachings lead you from the right way. It is good to receive inner strength from God's grace.[6]—Then we shall no longer be children, carried by the waves and blown about by every shifting wind of the teaching of deceitful men, who lead others into error by the tricks they invent. Instead, by speaking the truth in a spirit of love, we must grow up in every way to Christ, who is the head.[7]

I love to sit in its shadow, and its fruit is sweet to my taste. He brought me to his banqueting hall and raised the banner of love over me.[8]

[1]PS. 23.2. [2]Isa. 57.20, 21. [3]Matt. 11.28.—[4]Ps. 37.7.—[5]Heb. 4.10. [6]Heb. 13.9.—
[7]Eph. 4.14, 15. [8]S. of S. 2.3, 4.

There must be no yeast or leavened bread anywhere in your land.[1]

To honour the LORD is to hate evil.[2]—Hate what is evil.[3]—Avoid every kind of evil.[4]—Guard against turning back from the grace of God. Let no one become like a bitter plant that grows up and causes many troubles with its poison.[5]

If I had ignored my sins, the Lord would not have listened to me.[6]

You know the saying, "A little bit of yeast makes the whole batch of dough rise." You must remove the old yeast of sin so that you will be entirely pure. Then you will be like a new batch of dough without any yeast, as indeed I know you actually are. For our Passover Festival is ready, now that Christ, our Passover lamb, has been sacrificed. Let us celebrate our Passover, then, not with bread having the old yeast of sin and wickedness, but with the bread that has no yeast, the bread of purity and truth.[7]—Everyone should examine himself first, and then eat the bread and drink from the cup.[8]

Whoever says that he belongs to the Lord must turn away from wrongdoing.[9]—Jesus . . . is the High Priest that meets our needs. He is holy; he has no fault or sin in him; he has been set apart from sinners.[10]—There is no sin in him.[11]

[1]EXOD. 13.7. [2]Prov. 8.13.—[3]Rom. 12.9.—[4]1 Thess. 5.22.—[5]Heb. 12.15. [6]Ps. 66.18. [7]1 Cor. 5.6–8.—[8]1 Cor. 11.28. [9]2 Tim. 2.19.—[10]Heb. 7.26.—[11]1 John 3.5.

Evening

The snake replied . . . "You will not die . . . you will be like God and know what is good and what is bad."[1]

I am afraid that your minds will be corrupted and that you will abandon your full and pure devotion to Christ—in the same way that Eve was deceived by the snake's clever lies.[2]

Finally, build up your strength in union with the Lord and by means of his mighty power. Put on all the armour that God gives you, so that you will be able to stand up against the Devil's evil tricks. So put on God's armour now! Then when the evil day comes, you will be able to resist the enemy's attacks; and after fighting to the end, you will still hold your ground. So stand ready, with truth as a belt tight round your waist, with righteousness as your breastplate, and as your shoes the readiness to announce the Good News of peace. At all times carry faith as a shield; for with it you will be able to put out all the burning arrows shot by the Evil One. And accept salvation as a helmet, and the word of God as the sword which the Spirit gives you.[3]—In order to keep Satan from getting the upper hand of us; for we know what his plans are.[4]

[1]GEN. 3.4, 5. [2]2 Cor. 11.3. [3]Eph. 6.10, 11, 13–17.—[4]2 Cor. 2.11.

Now be patient, Ruth.[1]

Tell him to keep alert, to stay calm, and not to be frightened or disturbed.[2]—Stop fighting, and know that I am God.[3]—Didn't I tell you that you would see God's glory if you believed?[4]—Human pride will be ended, and human arrogance will be destroyed . . . and the LORD alone will be exalted on that day.[5]

Mary . . . sat down at the feet of the Lord and listened to his teaching. "Mary has chosen the right thing, and it will not be taken away from her."[6]—Come back and quietly trust in me. Then you will be strong and secure.[7]—Think deeply about this, when you lie in silence on your beds.[8]

Be patient and wait for the LORD to act; don't be worried about those who prosper or those who succeed in their evil plans.[9]

He is not afraid of receiving bad news; his faith is strong, and he trusts in the LORD. He is not worried or afraid.[10]

Faith that is firm is also patient.[11]

[1]RUTH 3.18. [2]Isa. 7.4.—[3]Ps. 46.10.—[4]John 11.40.—[5]Isa. 2.17. [6]Luke 10.39, 42.—[7]Isa. 30.15.—[8]Ps. 4.4. [9]Ps. 37.7. [10]Ps. 112.7, 8. [11]Isa. 28.16.

Evening

You do not understand now what I am doing, but you will understand later.[1]

Remember how the LORD your God led you on this long journey through the desert these past forty years, sending hardships to test you, so that he might know what you intended to do and whether you would obey his commands.[2]

"As I passed by again, I saw that the time had come for you to fall in love. I . . . promised to love you. Yes, I made a marriage covenant with you, and you became mine." This is what the Sovereign LORD says.[3]—The Lord corrects everyone he loves.[4]

My dear friends, do not be surprised at the painful test you are suffering, as though something unusual were happening to you. Rather be glad that you are sharing Christ's sufferings, so that you may be full of joy when his glory is revealed.[5]—This small and temporary trouble we suffer will bring us a tremendous and eternal glory, much greater than the trouble. For we fix our attention, not on things that are seen, but on things that are unseen.[6]

[1]JOHN 13.7. [2]Deut. 8.2. [3]Ezek. 16.8.—[4]Heb. 12.6. [5]1 Pet. 4.12, 13.—[6]2 Cor. 4.17, 18.

Christ is like a single body, which has many parts; it is still one body.[1]

He is the head of his body, the church.[2]—Supreme Lord over all things. The church is Christ's body, the completion of him who himself completes all things everywhere.[3]—We are members of his body.[4]

You have prepared a body for me.[5]—You saw me before I was born. The days allotted to me had all been recorded in your book, before any of them ever began.[6]

They belonged to you, and you gave them to me.[7]—Even before the world was made, God had already chosen us to be his through our union with Christ.[8]—Those whom God had already chosen he also set apart to become like his Son.[9]

We must grow up in every way to Christ, who is the head. Under his control all the different parts of the body fit together, and the whole body is held together by every joint with which it is provided . . . the whole body grows and builds itself up through love.[10]

[1]1 COR. 12.12. [2]Col. 1.18.—[3]Eph. 1.22, 23.—[4]Eph. 5.30. [5]Heb. 10.5.—[6]Ps. 139.16. [7]John 17.6.—[8]Eph. 1.4.—[9]Rom. 8.29. [10]Eph. 4.15, 16.

Evening

The spring of fresh water.[1]

How precious, O God, is your constant love! We find protection under the shadow of your wings. We feast on the abundant food you provide; you let us drink from the river of your goodness. You are the source of all life.[2]

I tell you that those who worship and obey me will have plenty to eat and drink, but you will be hungry and thirsty.[3]—Whoever drinks the water that I will give him will never be thirsty again. The water that I will give him will become in him a spring which will provide him with life-giving water and give him eternal life.[4]—Jesus said this about the Spirit, which those who believed in him were going to receive.[5]

Come, everyone who is thirsty—here is water![6]—The Spirit and the Bride say, "Come!" Everyone who hears this must also say, "Come!" Come, whoever is thirsty; accept the water of life as a gift, whoever wants it.[7]

[1]JER. 2.13. [2]Ps. 36.7–9. [3]Isa. 65.13.—[4]John 4.14.—[5]John 7.39. [6]Isa. 55.1.—[7]Rev. 22.17.

Let us open our hearts to God in heaven and pray.[1]

There is no one like the LORD our God. He lives in the heights above, but he bends down to see the heavens and the earth.[2]—To you, O LORD, I offer my prayer.[3]—I lift up my hands to you in prayer; like dry ground my soul is thirsty for you. Answer me now, LORD! I have lost all hope. Don't hide yourself from me, or I will be among those who go down to the world of the dead. Remind me each morning of your constant love, for I put my trust in you. My prayers go up to you; show me the way I should go.[4]

Your constant love is better than life itself, and so I will praise you. I will give you thanks as long as I live; I will raise my hands to you in prayer.[5]—Make your servant glad, O Lord, because my prayers go up to you. You are good to us and forgiving, full of constant love for all who pray to you.[6]

If you ask me for anything in my name, I will do it.[7]

[1]LAM. 3.41. [2]Ps. 113.5, 6.—[3]Ps. 25.1.—[4]Ps. 143.6–8. [5]Ps. 63.3, 4.—[6]Ps. 86.4, 5. [7]John 14.13.

Evening

Sentry, how soon will the night be over?[1]

The time has come for you to wake up from your sleep. For the moment when we will be saved is closer now than it was when we first believed. The night is nearly over, day is almost here. Let us stop doing the things that belong to the dark, and let us take up weapons for fighting in the light.[2]

Let the fig-tree teach you a lesson. When its branches become green and tender and it starts putting out leaves, you know that summer is near. In the same way, when you see all these things, you will know that the time is near, ready to begin. Heaven and earth will pass away, but my words will never pass away.[3]

I wait eagerly for the LORD's help, and in his word I trust. I wait for the Lord more eagerly than watchmen wait for the dawn—than watchmen wait for the dawn.[4]

He who gives his testimony to all this says, "Yes indeed! I am coming soon!" So be it. Come, Lord Jesus![5]

Be on your guard, then, because you do not know the day or the hour.[6]

[1]ISA. 21.11. [2]Rom. 13.11, 12. [3]Matt. 24.32, 33, 35. [4]Ps. 130.5, 6. [5]Rev. 22.20. [6]Matt. 25.13.

Let your hope keep you joyful.[1]

What you hope for . . . is kept safe for you in heaven.[2]—If our hope in Christ is good for this life only and no more, then we deserve more pity than anyone else in all the world.[3]—We must pass through many troubles to enter the Kingdom of God.[4]—Whoever does not carry his own cross and come after me cannot be my disciple.[5]—None of you should turn back because of these persecutions. You yourselves know that such persecutions are part of God's will for us.[6]

May you always be joyful in your union with the Lord. I say it again: rejoice![7]—May God, the source of hope, fill you with all joy and peace by means of your faith in him, so that your hope will continue to grow by the power of the Holy Spirit.[8]—Let us give thanks to the God and Father of our Lord Jesus Christ! Because of his great mercy he gave us new life by raising Jesus Christ from death. This fills us with a living hope.[9]—You love him, although you have not seen him, and you believe in him, although you do not now see him. So you rejoice with a great and glorious joy which words cannot express.[10]—He has brought us by faith into this experience of God's grace, in which we now live. And so we boast of the hope we have of sharing God's glory![11]

[1]ROM. 12.12. [2]Col. 1.5.—[3]1 Cor. 15.19.—[4]Acts 14.22.—[5]Luke 14.27.—[6]1 Thess. 3.3. [7]Phil. 4.4.—[8]Rom. 15.13.—[9]1 Pet. 1.3.—[10]1 Pet. 1.8.—[11]Rom. 5.2.

Evening

I am weak and poor, O LORD, but you have not forgotten me.[1]

I alone know the plans I have for you, plans to bring you prosperity and not disaster, plans to bring about the future you hope for.[2]—"My thoughts," says the LORD, "are not like yours, and my ways are different from yours. As high as the heavens are above the earth, so high are my ways and thoughts above yours."[3]

O God, how difficult I find your thoughts; how many of them there are! If I counted them, they would be more than the grains of sand. When I awake, I am still with you.[4]—How great are your actions, LORD! How deep your thoughts![5]—You have done many things for us, O LORD our God . . . you have made many wonderful plans for us.[6]

God called you . . . few of you were . . . powerful or of high social standing.[7]—God chose the poor people of this world to be rich in faith and to possess the kingdom.[8]—We seem to have nothing, yet we really possess everything.[9]—The infinite riches of Christ.[10]

[1]PS. 40.17. [2]Jer. 29.11.—[3]Isa. 55.8, 9. [4]Ps. 139.17, 18.—[5]Ps. 92.5.—[6]Ps. 40.5. [7]1 Cor. 1.26.—[8]Jas 2.5.—[9]2 Cor. 6.10.—[10]Eph. 3.8.

You have been weighed on the scales and found to be too light. [1]

The LORD is a God who knows, and he judges all that people do.[2]—The things that are considered of great value by man are worth nothing in God's sight.[3]—I do not judge as man judges. Man looks at the outward appearance, but I look at the heart.[4]—Do not deceive yourselves; no one makes a fool of God. A person will reap exactly what he sows. If he sows in the field of his natural desires, from it he will gather the harvest of death; if he sows in the field of the Spirit, from the Spirit he will gather the harvest of eternal life.[5]

Will a person gain anything if he wins the whole world but loses his life? Of course not! There is nothing he can give to regain his life.[6]—All those things that I might count as profit I now reckon as loss for Christ's sake.[7]

Sincerity and truth are what you require.[8]—You know my heart. You have come to me at night; you have examined me completely and found no evil desire in me.[9]

[1]DAN. 5.27. [2]1 Sam. 2.3.—[3]Luke 16.15.—[4]1 Sam. 16.7.—[5]Gal. 6.7, 8. [6]Matt. 16.26.—[7]Phil. 3.7. [8]Ps. 51.6.—[9]Ps. 17.3.

Evening

Christ, first of all. [1]

A grain of wheat remains no more than a single grain unless it is dropped into the ground and dies. If it does die, then it produces many grains.[2]—If the first piece of bread is given to God, then the whole loaf is his also; and if the roots of a tree are offered to God, the branches are his also.[3]—The truth is that Christ has been raised from death, as the guarantee that those who sleep in death will also be raised.[4]—Since we have become one with him in dying as he did, in the same way we shall be one with him by being raised to life as he was.[5]—The Lord Jesus Christ . . . will change our weak mortal bodies and make them like his own glorious body, using that power by which he is able to bring all things under his rule.[6]

He is the first-born Son, who was raised from death.[7]—If the Spirit of God, who raised Jesus from death, lives in you, then he who raised Christ from death will also give life to your mortal bodies by the presence of his Spirit in you.[8]

I am the resurrection and the life. Whoever believes in me will live, even though he dies.[9]

[1]1 COR. 15.23. [2]John 12.24.—[3]Rom. 11.16.—[4]1 Cor. 15.20.—[5]Rom. 6.5.— [6]Phil. 3.20, 21. [7]Col. 1.18.—[8]Rom. 8.11. [9]John 11.25.

He has filled the hungry with good things, and sent the rich away with empty hands.[1]

You say, 'I am rich and well off, I have all I need.' But you do not know how miserable and pitiful you are! You are poor, naked, and blind. I advise you, then, to buy gold from me, pure gold, in order to be rich . . . I rebuke and punish all whom I love. Be in earnest, then, and turn from your sins.[2]

Happy are those whose greatest desire is to do what God requires; God will satisfy them fully![3]—When my people in their need look for water, when their throats are dry with thirst, then I, the LORD, will answer their prayer; I, the God of Israel, will never abandon them.[4]—I am the LORD your God . . . open your mouth, and I will feed you.[5]

Why spend money on what does not satisfy? Why spend your wages and still be hungry? Listen to me and do what I say, and you will enjoy the best food of all.[6]—I am the bread of life.[7]

[1]LUKE 1.53. [2]Rev. 3.17–19. [3]Matt. 5.6.—[4]Isa. 41.17.—[5]Ps. 81.10. [6]Isa. 55.2.—[7]John 6.35.

Evening

I had nearly lost confidence; my faith was almost gone.[1]

I said, "I am falling"; but your constant love, O LORD, held me up.[2]

"Simon, Simon! Listen! Satan has received permission to test all of you, to separate the good from the bad as a farmer separates the wheat from the chaff. But I have prayed for you, Simon, that your faith will not fail.[3]

No matter how often an honest man falls, he always gets up again.[4]—If they fall, they will not stay down, because the LORD will help them up.[5]

Our enemies have no reason to gloat over us. We have fallen, but we will rise again. We are in darkness now, but the LORD will give us light.[6]—Time after time he will save you from harm.[7]

If anyone does sin, we have someone who pleads with the Father on our behalf—Jesus Christ, the righteous one.[8]—He is able, now and always, to save those who come to God through him, because he lives for ever to plead with God for them.[9]

[1]PS. 73.2. [2]Ps. 94.18. [3]Luke 22.31, 32. [4]Prov. 24.16.—[5]Ps. 37.24. [6]Mic. 7.8.—[7]Job 5.19. [8]1 John 2.1.—[9]Heb. 7.25.

I will give them a single purpose in life: to honour me for all time, for their own good and the good of their descendants.[1]

I will give you a new heart and a new mind.[2]—Because the LORD is righteous and good, he teaches sinners the path they should follow. He leads the humble in the right way and teaches them his will. With faithfulness and love he leads all who keep his covenant and obey his commands.[3]

I pray that they may all be one. Father! May they be in us, just as you are in me and I am in you. May they be one, so that the world will believe that you sent me.[4]

I urge you, then . . . live a life that measures up to the standard God set when he called you. Be always humble, gentle, and patient. Do your best to preserve the unity which the Spirit gives by means of the peace that binds you together. There is one body and one Spirit, just as there is one hope to which God has called you. There is one Lord, one faith, one baptism; there is one God and Father of all mankind, who is Lord of all, works through all, and is in all.[5]

[1]JER. 32.39. [2]Ezek. 36.26.—[3]Ps. 25.8–10. [4]John 17.21. [5]Eph. 4.1–6.

Evening

Those who trust in the LORD for help will find their strength renewed.[1]

When I am weak, then I am strong.[2]—The LORD . . . is the source of my strength.[3]—His answer was, "My grace is all you need, for my power is greatest when you are weak." I am most happy, then, to be proud of my weaknesses, in order to feel the protection of Christ's power over me.[4]—Let them make peace with me.[5]

Leave your troubles with the LORD, and he will defend you.[6]—His arms are made strong by the power of the Mighty God of Jacob.[7]

"Let me go . . ." "I won't, unless you bless me."[8]

You are coming against me with sword, spear, and javelin, but I come against you in the name of the LORD Almighty, the God of the Israelite armies, which you have defied.[9]—Oppose those who oppose me, LORD, and fight those who fight against me! Take your shield and armour and come to my rescue.[10]

[1]ISA. 40.31. [2]2 Cor. 12.10.—[3]Isa. 49.5.—[4]2 Cor. 12.9.—[5]Isa. 27.5. [6]Ps. 55.22.—[7]Gen. 49.24. [8]Gen. 32.26. [9]1 Sam. 17.45.—[10]Ps. 35.1, 2.

Do not conform yourselves to the standards of this world, but let God transform you inwardly by a complete change of your mind.[1]

Do not follow the majority when they do wrong.[2]

Don't you know that to be the world's friend means to be God's enemy?[3]

How can right and wrong be partners? How can light and darkness live together? How can Christ and the Devil agree? What does a believer have in common with an unbeliever? How can God's temple come to terms with pagan idols?[4]—Do not love the world or anything that belongs to the world. If you love the world, you do not love the Father. The world and everything in it that people desire is passing away; but he who does the will of God lives for ever.[5]

In the past . . . you followed the world's evil way; you obeyed the ruler of the spiritual powers in space, the spirit who now controls the people who disobey God.[6]—That was not what you learnt about Christ! You certainly heard about him, and as his followers you were taught the truth that is in Jesus.[7]

[1]ROM. 12.2. [2]Exod. 23.2. [3]Jas 4.4. [4]2 Cor. 6.14–16.—[5]1 John 2.15, 17. [6]Eph. 2.1, 2.—[7]Eph. 4.20, 21.

Evening

People go out to do their work and keep working until evening.[1]

You will have to work hard and sweat to make the soil produce anything, until you go back to the soil from which you were formed.[2]—Whoever refuses to work is not allowed to eat.[3]—Make it your aim to live a quiet life, to mind your own business, and to earn your own living.[4]

Work hard at whatever you do, because there will be no action, no thought, no knowledge, no wisdom in the world of the dead—and that is where you are going.[5]—Night is coming when no one can work.[6]

Let us not become tired of doing good; for if we do not give up, the time will come when we will reap the harvest.[7]—Keep busy always in your work for the Lord, since you know that nothing you do in the Lord's service is ever useless.[8]

There still remains for God's people a rest.[9]—We put up with a whole day's work in the hot sun.[10]—He offered rest and comfort to all of you.[11]

[1]PS. 104.23. [2]Gen. 3.19.—[3]2 Thess. 3.10.—[4]1 Thess. 4.11. [5]Eccles. 9.10.—[6]John 9.4. [7]Gal. 6.9.—[8]1 Cor. 15.58. [9]Heb. 4.9.—[10]Matt. 20.12.—[11]Isa. 28.12.

Morning

I have seen how they acted, but I will heal them.[1]

I am the LORD, the one who heals you.[2]

LORD, you have examined me and you know me. You know everything I do; from far away you understand all my thoughts. You see me, whether I am working or resting; you know all my actions.[3]—You place our sins before you, our secret sins where you can see them.[4]—Everything in all creation is exposed and lies open before his eyes.[5]

The LORD says, "Now let's settle the matter. You are stained red with sin, but I will wash you as clean as snow. Although your stains are deep red, you will be as white as wool."[6]—In mercy the angel will say, "Release him! He is not to go down to the world of the dead. Here is the ransom to set him free."[7]—Because of our sins he was wounded, beaten because of the evil we did. We are healed by the punishment he suffered, made whole by the blows he received.[8]—Your faith has made you well.[9]

[1]ISA. 57.18. [2]Exod. 15.26. [3]Ps. 139.1–3.—[4]Ps. 90.8.—[5]Heb. 4.13. [6]Isa. 1.18.—[7]Job 33.24.—[8]Isa. 53.5.—[9]Mark 5.34.

Evening

It is the LORD who helps me.[1]

May the LORD answer you when you are in trouble! May the God of Jacob protect you! May he send you help from his Temple and give you aid from Mount Zion. Then we will shout for joy over your victory and celebrate your triumph by praising our God. Some trust in their war-chariots and others in their horses, but we trust in the power of the LORD our God. Such people will stumble and fall, but we will rise and stand firm.[2]

From east to west everyone will fear him and his great power. He will come like a rushing river, like a strong wind.[3]—Every test that you have experienced is the kind that normally comes to people. But God keeps his promise, and he will not allow you to be tested beyond your power to remain firm; at the time you are put to the test, he will give you the strength to endure it, and so provide you with a way out.[4]

If God is for us, who can be against us?[5]—The LORD is with me, I will not be afraid.[6]

If the God whom we serve is able to save us . . . then he will.[7]

[1]PS. 118.7. [2]Ps. 20.1, 2, 5, 7, 8. [3]Isa. 59.19.—[4]1 Cor. 10.13. [5]Rom. 8.31.—[6]Ps. 118.6. [7]Dan. 3.17.

Whoever is thirsty should come to me and drink.[1]

How I want to be there! I long to be in the LORD's Temple. With my whole being I sing for joy to the living God.[2]—O God, you are my God, and I long for you. My whole being desires you; like a dry, worn-out, and waterless land, my soul is thirsty for you. Let me see you in the sanctuary; let me see how mighty and glorious you are.[3]

Come, everyone who is thirsty—here is water! Come, you that have no money—buy corn and eat! Come! Buy wine and milk—it will cost you nothing![4]—The Spirit and the Bride say, "Come!" Everyone who hears this must also say, "Come!" Come, whoever is thirsty; accept the water of life as a gift, whoever wants it.[5]—Whoever drinks the water that I will give him will never be thirsty again. The water that I will give him will become in him a spring which will provide him with life-giving water and give him eternal life.[6]—My blood is the real drink.[7]

Eat, lovers, and drink until you are drunk with love![8]

[1]JOHN 7.37. [2]Ps. 84.2.—[3]Ps. 63.1, 2. [4]Isa. 55.1.—[5]Rev. 22.17.—[6]John 4.14.—[7]John 6.55. [8]S. of S. 5.1.

Evening

You are like salt for all mankind.[1]

Ageless beauty.[2]—Through the living and eternal word of God you have been born again as the children of a parent who is immortal, not mortal.[3]—Whoever believes in me will live, even though he dies.[4]—They are the sons of God, because they have risen from death.[5]—The immortal God.[6]

Whoever does not have the Spirit of Christ does not belong to him. But if Christ lives in you, the Spirit is life for you because you have been put right with God, even though your bodies are going to die because of sin. If the Spirit of God, who raised Jesus from death, lives in you, then he who raised Christ from death will also give life to your mortal bodies by the presence of his Spirit in you.[7]—When the body is buried, it is mortal; when raised, it will be immortal.[8]

Have the salt of friendship among yourselves, and live in peace with one another.[9]—Do not use harmful words, but only helpful words, the kind that build up and provide what is needed, so that what you say will do good to those who hear you.[10]

[1]MATT. 5:13. [2]1 Pet. 3.4.—[3]1 Pet. 1.23.—[4]John 11.25.—[5]Luke 20.36.—[6]Rom. 1.23. [7]Rom. 8.9–11.—[8]1 Cor. 15.42. [9]Mark 9.50.—[10]Eph. 4.29.

I am the one who strengthens you.[1]

Let us give thanks to the God and Father of our Lord Jesus Christ, the merciful Father, the God from whom all help comes! He helps us in all our troubles, so that we are able to help others who have all kinds of troubles, using the same help that we ourselves have received from God.[2]—As a father is kind to his children, so the LORD is kind to those who honour him. He knows what we are made of; he remembers that we are dust.[3]—I will comfort you in Jerusalem, as a mother comforts her child.[4]—Leave all your worries with him, because he cares for you.[5]

You, O Lord, are a merciful and loving God, always patient, always kind and faithful.[6]

Another Helper . . . the Spirit who reveals the truth about God.[7]—The Spirit . . . comes to help us, weak as we are.[8]

He will wipe away all tears from their eyes. There will be no more death, no more grief or crying or pain. The old things have disappeared.[9]

[1]ISA. 51.12. [2]2 Cor. 1.3, 4.—[3]Ps. 103.13, 14.—[4]Isa. 66.13.—[5]1 Pet. 5.7. [6]Ps. 86.15. [7]John 14.16, 17.—[8]Rom. 8.26. [9]Rev. 21.4.

Evening

God who called you to have fellowship with his Son.[1]

He was given honour and glory by God the Father, when the voice came to him from the Supreme Glory, saying, "This is my own dear Son, with whom I am pleased!"[2]—See how much the Father has loved us! His love is so great that we are called God's children.[3]

Since you are God's dear children, you must try to be like him.[4]—Since we are his children, we will possess the blessings he keeps for his people, and we will also possess with Christ what God has kept for him.[5]

The brightness of God's glory and . . . the exact likeness of God's own being.[6]—Your light must shine before people, so that they will see the good things you do and praise your Father in heaven.[7]

Jesus, on whom our faith depends from beginning to end . . . because of the joy that was waiting for him, he thought nothing of the disgrace of dying on the cross.[8]—I say these things in the world so that they might have my joy in their hearts in all its fullness.[9]—Just as we have a share in Christ's many sufferings, so also through Christ we share in God's great help.[10]

[1]1 COR. 1.9. [2]2 Pet. 1.17.—[3]1 John 3.1. [4]Eph. 5.1.—[5]Rom. 8.17. [6]Heb. 1.3.—[7]Matt. 5.16. [8]Heb. 12.2.—[9]John 17.13.—[10]2 Cor. 1.5.

Sin must not be your master; for you do not live under law but under God's grace.[1]

What, then? Shall we sin, because we are not under law but under God's grace? By no means![2]—As far as the Law is concerned, you . . . have died because you are part of the body of Christ; and now you belong to him who was raised from death in order that we might be useful in the service of God.[3]—This does not mean that I don't obey God's law; I am really under Christ's law.[4]—Death gets its power to hurt from sin, and sin gets its power from the Law. But thanks be to God who gives us the victory through our Lord Jesus Christ![5]

The law of the Spirit, which bring us life in union with Christ Jesus, has set me free from the law of sin and death.[6]—Everyone who sins is a slave of sin. If the Son sets you free, then you will be really free.[7]

Stand, then, as free people, and do not allow yourselves to become slaves again.[8]

[1]ROM. 6.14. [2]Rom. 6.15.—[3]Rom. 7.4.—[4]1 Cor. 9.21.—[5]1 Cor. 15.56, 57. [6]Rom. 8.2.—[7]John 8.34, 36. [8]Gal. 5.1.

Evening

A person . . . unable to make up his mind and undecided in all he does.[1]

Anyone who starts to plough and then keeps looking back is of no use to the Kingdom of God.[2]

Whoever comes to God must have faith that God exists and rewards those who seek him.[3]—When you pray, you must believe and not doubt at all. Whoever doubts is like a wave in the sea that is driven and blown about by the wind. A person like that . . . must not think that he will receive anything from the Lord.[4]—When you pray and ask for something, believe that you have received it, and you will be given whatever you ask for.[5]

We shall no longer be children, carried by the waves and blown about by every shifting wind of the teaching of deceitful men, who lead others into error by the tricks they invent. Instead, by speaking the truth in a spirit of love, we must grow up in every way to Christ, who is the head.[6]

Remain united to me.[7]—Stand firm and steady. Keep busy always in your work for the Lord, since you know that nothing you do in the Lord's service is ever useless.[8]

[1]JAS. 1.8. [2]Luke 9.62. [3]Heb. 11.6.—[4]Jas 1.6, 7.—[5]Mark 11.24. [6]Eph. 4.14, 15. [7]John 15.4.—[8]1 Cor. 15.58.

The LORD *judges your motives.*[1]

The righteous are guided and protected by the LORD, but the evil are on their way to their doom.[2]—The LORD will show us who belongs to him.[3]—Your Father, who sees what you do in private, will reward you.[4]

Examine me, O God, and know my mind; test me, and discover my thoughts. Find out if there is any evil in me and guide me in the everlasting way.[5]—There is no fear in love; perfect love drives out all fear.[6]

O Lord, you know what I long for; you hear all my groans.[7]—When I am ready to give up, he knows what I should do.[8]—God, who sees into our hearts, knows what the thought of the Spirit is; because the Spirit pleads with God on behalf of his people and in accordance with his will.[9]

The solid foundation that God has laid cannot be shaken; and on it are written these words: "The Lord knows those who are his" and "Whoever says that he belongs to the Lord must turn away from wrongdoing."[10]

[1]PROV. 21.2. [2]Ps. 1.6.—[3]Num. 16.5.—[4]Matt. 6.4. [5]Ps. 139.23, 24.—[6]1 John 4.18. [7]Ps. 38.9.—[8]Ps. 142.3.—[9]Rom. 8.27. [10]2 Tim. 2.19.

Evening

Tears may flow in the night, but joy comes in the morning.[1]

None of you should turn back because of these persecutions. You yourselves know that such persecutions are part of God's will for us. For while we were still with you, we told you beforehand that we were going to be persecuted.[2]—You will have peace by being united to me. The world will make you suffer. But be brave! I have defeated the world![3]

When I awake, your presence will fill me with joy.[4]—The night is nearly over, day is almost here.[5]—Like the sun shining on a cloudless dawn, the sun that makes the grass sparkle after rain.[6]

The Sovereign LORD will destroy death for ever! He will wipe away the tears from everyone's eyes.[7]—There will be no more death, no more grief or crying or pain. The old things have disappeared.[8]—We who are living at that time will be gathered up along with them in the clouds to meet the Lord in the air. So then, encourage one another with these words.[9]

PS. 30.5. [2]1 Thess. 3.3, 4.—[3]John 16.33. [4]Ps. 17.15.—[5]Rom. 13.12.—[6]2 Sam. 23.4. [7]Isa. 25.8.—[8]Rev. 21.4.—[9]1 Thess. 4.17, 18.

He will not break off a bent reed.[1]

My sacrifice is a humble spirit, O God; you will not reject a humble and repentant heart.[2]—He heals the broken-hearted and bandages their wounds.[3]—I am the high and holy God, who lives for ever. I live in a high and holy place, but I also live with people who are humble and repentant, so that I can restore their confidence and hope. I gave my people life, and I will not continue to accuse them or be angry with them for ever.[4]

I will look for those that are lost, bring back those that wander off, bandage those that are hurt, and heal those that are sick.[5]—Lift up your tired hands, then, and strengthen your trembling knees! Keep walking on straight paths, so that the lame foot may not be disabled, but instead be healed.[6]—God is coming to your rescue.[7]

[1]MATT. 12.20. [2]Ps. 51.17.—[3]Ps. 147.3.—[4]Isa. 57.15, 16. [5]Ezek. 34.16.—[6]Heb. 12.12, 13.—[7]Isa. 35.4.

Evening

Find out for yourself how good the Lord is. Happy are those who find safety with him.[1]

"Take it to the man in charge of the feast". They took him the water, which now had turned into wine, and he tasted it. He did not know where this wine had come from . . . He called the bridegroom and said to him, "Everyone else serves the best wine first, and after the guests have had plenty to drink, he serves the ordinary wine. But you have kept the best wine until now!"[2]

You know good food when you taste it, but not wise words when you hear them.[3]—I spoke because I believed.[4]—I know whom I have trusted.[5]—I love to sit in its shadow, and its fruit is sweet to my taste.[6]

God is kind.[7]—God, who did not even keep back his own Son, but offered him for us all . . . will he not also freely give us all things?[8]

Be like new-born babies, always thirsty for the pure spiritual milk, so that by drinking it you may grow up and be saved. As the scripture says, "You have found out for yourselves how kind the Lord is."[9]

All who find safety in you will rejoice; they can always sing for joy.[10]

[1]PS. 34.8. [2]John 2.8–10. [3]Job 34.3.—[4]2 Cor. 4.13.—[5]2 Tim. 1.12.—[6]S. of S. 2.3. [7]Rom. 2.4.—[8]Rom. 8.32. [9]1 Pet. 2.2, 3. [10]Ps. 5.11.

Open my eyes, so that I may see the wonderful truths in your law.[1]

Then he opened their minds to understand the Scriptures.[2]—The knowledge about the secrets of the Kingdom of heaven has been given to you, but not to them.[3]—Father, Lord of heaven and earth! I thank you because you have shown to the unlearned what you have hidden from the wise and learned. Yes, Father, this was how you wanted it to happen.[4]—We have not received this world's spirit; instead, we have received the Spirit sent by God, so that we may know all that God has given us.[5]—O God, how difficult I find your thoughts; how many of them there are! If I counted them, they would be more than the grains of sand.[6]—How great are God's riches! How deep are his wisdom and knowledge! Who can explain his decisions? Who can understand his ways? As the scripture says, "Who knows the mind of the Lord? Who is able to give him advice?" For all things were created by him, and all things exist through him and for him. To God be the glory for ever! Amen.[7]

[1]PS. 119.18. [2]Luke 24.45.—[3]Matt. 13.11.—[4]Matt. 11.25, 26.—[5]1 Cor. 2.12.—[6]Ps. 139.17, 18.—[7]Rom. 11.33, 34, 36.

Evening

The spring was named Hakkore [***"caller"***].[1]

If only you knew what God gives and who it is that is asking you for a drink, you would ask him, and he would give you life-giving water.[2]—"Whoever is thirsty should come to me and drink." Jesus said this about the Spirit, which those who believed in him were going to receive.[3]

Put me to the test and you will see that I will open the windows of heaven and pour out on you in abundance all kinds of good things.[4]—Bad as you are, you know how to give good things to your children. How much more, then, will the Father in heaven give the Holy Spirit to those who ask him![5]—Ask, and you will receive; seek, and you will find.[6]

To show that you are his sons, God sent the Spirit of his Son into our hearts, the Spirit who cries out, "Father, my Father."[7]—The Spirit that God has given you does not make you slaves and cause you to be afraid; instead, the Spirit makes you God's children, and by the Spirit's power we cry out to God, "Father! my Father!"[8]

[1]JUDG. 15.19. [2]John 4.10.—[3]John 7.37, 39. [4]Mal. 3.10.—[5]Luke 11.13.—[6]Luke 11.9. [7]Gal. 4.6.—[8]Rom. 8.15.

The God of all grace.[1]

In your presence I will pronounce my sacred name. I am the LORD, and I show compassion and pity on those I choose.[2]—In mercy the angel will say, "Release him! He is not to go down to the world of the dead. Here is the ransom to set him free."[3]—By the free gift of God's grace all are put right with him through Christ Jesus, who sets them free. God offered him, so that by his sacrificial death he should become the means by which people's sins are forgiven through their faith in him. God did this in order to demonstrate that he is righteous. In the past he was patient and overlooked people's sins; but in the present time he deals with their sins, in order to demonstrate his righteousness.[4]—Grace and truth came through Jesus Christ.[5]

It is by God's grace that you have been saved through faith. It is not the result of your own efforts, but God's gift.[6]—May God the Father and Christ Jesus our Lord give you grace, mercy, and peace.[7]—Each one of us has received a special gift in proportion to what Christ has given.[8]—Each one, as a good manager of God's different gifts, must use for the good of others the special gift he has received from God.[9]—The grace that God gives is even stronger.[10]

Continue to grow in the grace and knowledge of our Lord and Saviour Jesus Christ. To him be the glory, now and for ever![11]

[1]1 PET. 5.10. [2]Exod. 33.19.—[3]Job 33.24.—[4]Rom. 3.24, 25.—[5]John 1.17. [6]Eph. 2.8.—[7]1 Tim. 1.2.—[8]Eph. 4.7.—[9]1 Pet. 4.10.—[10]Jas 4.6. [11]2 Pet. 3.18.

Evening

I look to the mountains; where will my help come from? My help will come from the LORD.[1]

As the mountains surround Jerusalem, so the LORD surrounds his people now and for ever.[2]

LORD, I look up to you, up to heaven, where you rule. As a servant depends on his master, as a maid depends on her mistress, so we will keep looking to you, O LORD our God, until you have mercy on us.[3]—You have always been my help. In the shadow of your wings I sing for joy.[4]

You are our God! Punish them, for we are helpless in the face of this large army that is attacking us. We do not know what to do, but we look to you for help.[5]—I look to the LORD for help at all times, and he rescues me from danger.[6]—Our help comes from the LORD, who made heaven and earth.[7]

[1]PS. 121.1, 2. [2]Ps. 125.2. [3]Ps. 123.1, 2.—[4]Ps. 63.7. [5]2 Chr. 20.12.—[6]Ps. 25.25.—[7]Ps. 124.8.

Happy is the man who becomes wise—who gains understanding.[1]

The man who finds me finds life, and the LORD will be pleased with him.[2]

The LORD says, "Wise men should not boast of their wisdom, nor strong men of their strength . . . If anyone wants to boast, he should boast that he knows and understands me. I, the LORD, have spoken.[3]—To be wise you must first have reverence for the LORD.[4]

All those things that I might count as profit I now reckon as loss for Christ's sake. Not only those things; I reckon everything as complete loss for the sake of what is so much more valuable, the knowledge of Christ Jesus my Lord. For his sake I have thrown everything away; I consider it all as mere refuse, so that I may gain Christ.[5]—He is the key that opens all the hidden treasures of God's wisdom and knowledge.[6]—I make plans and carry them out. I have understanding, and I am strong.[7]

God has made Christ to be our wisdom. By him we are put right with God; we become God's holy people and are set free.[8]

[1]PROV. 3.13. [2]Prov. 8.35. [3]Jer. 9.23, 24.—[4]Prov. 9.10. [5]Phil. 3.7, 8.—[6]Col. 2.3.—[7]Prov. 8.14. [8]1 Cor. 1.30. [9]Prov. 11.30.

Evening

We seem poor, but we make many people rich.[1]

You know the grace of our Lord Jesus Christ; rich as he was, he made himself poor for your sake, in order to make you rich by means of his poverty.[2]—Out of the fullness of his grace he has blessed us all, giving us one blessing after another.[3]—With all his abundant wealth through Christ Jesus, my God will supply all your needs.[4]—God is able to give you more than you need, so that you will always have all you need for yourselves and more than enough for every good cause.[5]

God chose the poor people of this world to be rich in faith and to possess the kingdom which he promised to those who love him.[6]—From the human point of view few of you were wise or powerful or of high social standing. God purposely chose what the world considers nonsense in order to shame the wise, and he chose what the world considers weak in order to shame the powerful.[7]

We who have this spiritual treasure are like common clay pots, in order to show that the supreme power belongs to God, not to us.[8]

[1]2 COR. 6.10. [2]2 Cor. 8.9.—[3]John 1.16.—[4]Phil. 4.19.—[5]2 Cor. 9.8. [6]Jas 2.5.—[7]1 Cor. 1.26, 27. [8]2 Cor. 4.7.

We know that in all things God works for good with those who love him.[1]

Men's anger only results in more praise for you; those who survive the wars will keep your festivals.[2]—You plotted evil against me, but God turned it into good.[3]

Everything belongs to you: . . . this world, life and death, the present and the future—all these are yours, and you belong to Christ, and Christ belongs to God.[4]—All this is for your sake; and as God's grace reaches more and more people, they will offer to the glory of God more prayers of thanksgiving. For this reason we never become discouraged. Even though our physical being is gradually decaying, yet our spiritual being is renewed day after day. And this small and temporary trouble we suffer will bring us a tremendous and eternal glory, much greater than the trouble.[5]

My brothers, consider yourselves fortunate when all kinds of trials come your way, for you know that when your faith succeeds in facing such trials, the result is the ability to endure. Make sure that your endurance carries you all the way without failing, so that you may be perfect and complete, lacking nothing.[6]

[1]ROM. 8.28. [2]Ps. 76.10.—[3]Gen. 50.20. [4]1 Cor. 3.21–23.—[5]2 Cor. 4.15–17. [6]Jas 1.2–4.

Evening

The fellowship of the Holy Spirit be with you all.[1]

I will ask the Father, and he will give you another Helper, who will stay with you for ever. He is the Spirit who reveals the truth about God. The world cannot receive him, because it cannot see him or know him. But you know him, because he remains with you and is in you.[2]—He will not speak on his own authority. He will give me glory, because he will take what I say and tell it to you.[3]

God has poured out his love into our hearts by means of the Holy Spirit, who is God's gift to us.[4]

He who joins himself to the Lord becomes spiritually one with him. Don't you know that your body is the temple of the Holy Spirit, who lives in you and who was given to you by God? You do not belong to yourselves but to God.[5]

Do not make God's Holy Spirit sad; for the Spirit is God's mark of ownership on you, a guarantee that the Day will come when God will set you free.[6]—The Spirit also comes to help us, weak as we are. For we do not know how we ought to pray; the Spirit himself pleads with God for us.[7]

[1]2 COR. 13.13. [2]John 14.16, 17.—[3]John 16.13.14. [4]Rom. 5.5. [5]1 Cor. 6.17, 19. [6]Eph. 4.30.—[7]Rom. 8.26.

May he be pleased with my song, for my gladness comes from him.[1]

Like an apple-tree among the trees of the forest, so is my dearest compared with other men. I love to sit in its shadow, and its fruit is sweet to my taste.[2]—No one in heaven is like you, LORD; none of the heavenly beings is your equal.[3]

My lover is handsome and strong; he is one in ten thousand.[4]—One [pearl] that is unusually fine.[5]—The ruler of the kings of the world.[6]

His face is bronzed and smooth; his hair is wavy, black as a raven.[7]—Supreme Lord over all things.[8]—He is the head of his body, the church.[9]

His cheeks are as lovely as a garden that is full of herbs and spices.[10]—He could not stay hidden.[11]

His lips are like lilies, wet with liquid myrrh.[12]—Nobody has ever talked like this man![13]

He is majestic, like the Lebanon Mountains with their towering cedars.[14]—Look on your servant with kindness.[15]—Give us more blessings, O LORD. Look on us with kindness![16]

[1]PS. 104.34. [2]S. of S. 2.3.—[3]Ps. 89.6. [4]S. of S. 5.10.—[5]Matt. 13.46.—[6]Rev. 1.5. [7]S. of S. 5.11.—[8]Eph. 1.22.—[9]Col. 1.18. [10]S. of S. 5.13.—[11]Mark 7.24. [12]S. of S. 5.13.—[13]John 7.46. [14]S. of S. 5.15.—[15]Ps. 31.16.—[16]Ps. 4.6.

Evening

My Father, if it is possible, take this cup of suffering from me! Yet not what I want, but what you want.[1]

Now my heart is troubled—and what shall I say? Shall I say, 'Father, do not let this hour come upon me'? But that is why I came—so that I might go through this hour of suffering.[2]

I have come down from heaven to do not my own will but the will of him who sent me.[3]—He . . . walked the path of obedience all the way to death—his death on the cross.[4]—In his life on earth Jesus made his prayers and requests with loud cries and tears to God, who could save him from death. Because he was humble and devoted, God heard him. But even though he was God's Son, he learnt through his sufferings to be obedient.[5]

Don't you know that I could call on my Father for help, and at once he would send me more than twelve armies of angels?[6]—This is what is written: the Messiah must suffer and must rise from death three days later, and in his name the message about repentance and the forgiveness of sins must be preached to all nations, beginning in Jerusalem.[7]

[1]MATT. 26.39. [2]John 12.27. [3]John 6.38.—[4]Phil. 2.8.—[5]Heb. 5.7, 8. [6]Matt. 26.53.—[7]Luke 24.46, 47.

You did not leave us in slavery.[1]

My dear friends, do not be surprised at the painful test you are suffering, as though something unusual were happening to you.[2]—Endure what you suffer as being a father's punishment; your suffering shows that God is treating you as his sons. Was there ever a son who was not punished by his father? If you are not punished, as all his sons are, it means you are not real sons, but bastards.[3]

The LORD your God is using him to test you, to see if you love the LORD with all your heart.[4]

The LORD has made a solemn promise, and he will not abandon you, for he has decided to make you his own people.[5]—Can a woman forget her own baby and not love the child she bore? Even if a mother should forget her child, I will never forget you.[6]—Happy is the man who has the God of Jacob to help him and who depends on the LORD his God.[7]

Will God not judge in favour of his own people who cry to him day and night for help? Will he be slow to help them? I tell you, he will judge in their favour and do it quickly.[8]

[1]EZRA 9.9. [2]1 Pet. 4.12.—[3]Heb. 12.7, 8. [4]Deut. 13.3. [5]1 Sam. 12.22.—[6]Isa. 49.15.—[7]Ps. 146.5. [8]Luke 18.7, 8.

Evening

Whoever wins the victory will receive this from me: I will be his God, and he will be my son.[1]

If our hope in Christ is good for this life only and no more, then we deserve more pity than anyone else in all the world.[2]—It was a better country they longed for, the heavenly country. And so God is not ashamed for them to call him their God, because he has prepared a city for them.[3]—The rich blessings that God keeps for his people. He keeps them for you in heaven, where they cannot decay or spoil or fade away.[4]

Everything belongs to you: . . . this world, life and death, the present and the future—all these are yours.[5]—What no one ever saw or heard, what no one ever thought could happen, is the very thing God prepared for those who love him. But it was to us that God made known his secret by means of his Spirit.[6]

Be on your guard, then, so that you will not lose what we have worked for, but will receive your reward in full.[7]—Let us rid ourselves of everything that gets in the way, and of the sin which holds on to us so tightly, and let us run with determination the race that lies before us.[8]

[1]REV. 21.7. [2]1 Cor. 15.19.—[3]Heb. 11.16.—[4]1 Pet. 1.4. [5]1 Cor. 3.21, 22.—[6]1 Cor. 2.9, 10. [7]2 John 8.—[8]Heb. 12.1.

As for me, how wonderful to be near God.[1]

I love the house where you live, O LORD, the place where your glory dwells.[2]—One day spent in your Temple is better than a thousand anywhere else; I would rather stand at the gate of the house of my God than live in the homes of the wicked.[3]—Happy are those whom you choose, whom you bring to live in your sanctuary. We shall be satisfied with the good things of your house, the blessings of your sacred Temple.[4]

The LORD is good to everyone who trusts in him.[5]—The LORD is waiting to be merciful to you. He is ready to take pity on you because he always does what is right. Happy are those who put their trust in the LORD.[6]

We have, then, my brothers, complete freedom to go into the Most Holy Place by means of the death of Jesus. He opened for us a new way, a living way . . . through his own body. So let us come near to God with a sincere heart and a sure faith, with hearts that have been purified from a guilty conscience and with bodies washed with clean water.[7]

[1]PS. 73.28. [2]Ps. 26.8.—[3]Ps. 84.10.—[4]Ps. 65.4. [5]Lam. 3.25.—[6]Isa. 30.18. [7]Heb. 10.19, 20, 22.

Evening

You know the grace of our Lord Jesus Christ.[1]

The Word became a human being and, full of grace and truth, lived among us. We saw his glory, the glory which he received as the Father's only Son.[2]—You are the most handsome of men, you are an eloquent speaker.[3]—They were all well impressed with him and marvelled at the eloquent words that he spoke.[4]

Whoever believes in the Son of God has this testimony in his own heart.[5]—We speak of what we know and report what we have seen.[6]

Find out for yourself how good the LORD is. Happy are those who find safety with him.[7]—I love to sit in its shadow, and its fruit is sweet to my taste.[8]

His answer was: "My grace is all you need, for my power is greatest when you are weak."[9]—Each one of us has received a special gift in proportion to what Christ has given.[10]—Each one, as a good manager of God's different gifts, must use for the good of others the special gift he has received from God.[11]

[1]2 COR. 8.9. [2]John 1.14.—[3]Ps. 45.2.—[4]Luke 4.22. [5]1 John 5.10.—[6]John 3.11. [7]Ps. 34.8.—[8]S. of S. 2.3. [9]2 Cor. 12.9.—[10]Eph. 4.7.—[11]1 Pet. 4.10.

Make sure that your endurance carries you all the way without failing, so that you may be perfect and complete, lacking nothing.[1]

It may now be necessary for you to be sad for a while because of the many kinds of trials you suffer. Their purpose is to prove that your faith is genuine. Even gold, which can be destroyed, is tested by fire; and so your faith, which is much more precious than gold, must also be tested, so that it may endure. Then you will receive praise and glory and honour on the Day when Jesus Christ is revealed.[2]—We . . . boast of our troubles, because we know that trouble produces endurance, endurance brings God's approval, and his approval creates hope.[3]

It is best for us to wait in patience—to wait for him to save us.[4]—You knew that you still possessed something much better, which would last for ever. Do not lose your courage, then, because it brings with it a great reward. You need to be patient, in order to do the will of God and receive what he promises.[5]—May our Lord Jesus Christ himself and God our Father, who loved us and in his grace gave us unfailing courage and a firm hope, encourage you and strengthen you to always do and say what is good.[6]

[1]JAS 1.4. [2]1 Pet. 1.6, 7.—[3]Rom. 5.3, 4. [4]Lam. 3.26.—[5]Heb. 10.34–36.—[6]2 Thess. 2.16, 17.

Evening

God through Jesus Christ will judge the secret thoughts of all.[1]

You should not pass judgement on anyone before the right time comes. Final judgement must wait until the Lord comes; he will bring to light the dark secrets and expose the hidden purposes of people's minds. And then everyone will receive from God the praise he deserves.[2]—Nor does the Father himself judge anyone. He has given his Son the full right to judge . . . And he has given the Son the right to judge, because he is the Son of Man.[3]—The Son of God, whose eyes blaze like fire.[4]

They say, "God will not know; the Most High will not find out."[5]—You have done all this, and I have said nothing, so you thought that I was like you. But now I reprimand you and make the matter plain to you.[6]—Whatever is covered up will be uncovered, and every secret will be made known.[7]

O Lord, you know what I long for; you hear all my groans.[8]—Examine me and test me, LORD; judge my desires and thoughts.[9]

[1]ROM. 2.16. [2]1 Cor. 4.5.—[3]John 5.22, 27.—[4]Rev. 2.18. [5]Ps. 73.11.—[6]Ps. 50.21.—[7]Luke 12.2. [8]Ps. 38.9.—[9]Ps. 26.2.

Your God is faithful and true: he does what is right and fair.[1]

God, the righteous Judge.[2]—All of us must appear before Christ, to be judged by him. Each one will receive what he deserves, according to everything he has done, good or bad, in his bodily life.[3]—Every one of us, then, will have to give an account of himself to God.[4]—The person who sins is the one who will die.[5]

The LORD Almighty says, "Wake up, sword, and attack the shepherd who works for me! Kill him."[6]—The LORD made the punishment fall on him, the punishment all of us deserved.[7]—Love and faithfulness will meet; righteousness and peace will embrace.[8]—Mercy triumphs over judgement.[9]—Sin pays its wage—death; but God's free gift is eternal life in union with Christ Jesus our Lord.[10]

The God who saves his people . . . there is no other God.[11]—He himself is righteous and . . . he puts right everyone who believes in Jesus.[12]—By the free gift of God's grace all are put right with him through Christ Jesus, who sets them free.[13]

[1]DEUT. 32.4. [2]1 Pet. 2.23.—[3]2 Cor. 5.10.—[4]Rom. 14.12.—[5]Ezek. 18.4. [6]Zech. 13.7.—[7]Isa. 53.6.—[8]Ps. 85.10.—[9]Jas 2.13.—[10]Rom. 6.23. [11]Isa 45.21.—[12]Rom. 3.26.—[13]Rom. 3.24.

Evening

Death is destroyed; victory is complete![1]

Thanks be to God who gives us the victory through our Lord Jesus Christ![2]

Since the children . . . are people of flesh and blood, Jesus himself became like them and shared their human nature. He did this so that through his death he might destroy the Devil, who has the power over death, and in this way set free those who were slaves all their lives because of their fear of death.[3]

Since we have died with Christ, we believe that we will also live with him. For we know that Christ has been raised from death and will never die again—death will no longer rule over him. And so, because he died, sin has no power over him; and now he lives his life in fellowship with God.[4]

In the same way you are to think of yourselves as dead, so far as sin is concerned, but living in fellowship with God through Christ Jesus.[5]

In all these things we have complete victory through him who loved us![6]

[1]1 COR. 15.54. [2]1 Cor. 15.57. [3]Heb. 2.14, 15. [4]Rom. 6.8–10. [5]Rom. 6.11. [6]Rom. 8.37.

Humble yourselves . . . under God's mighty hand, so that he will lift you up in his own good time.[1]

The LORD hates everyone who is arrogant; he will never let them escape punishment.[2]

You are our Father, LORD. We are like clay, and you are like the potter. You created us, so do not be too angry with us or hold our sins against us for ever. We are your people; be merciful to us.[3]—LORD, we were like an untamed animal, but you taught us to obey. Bring us back; we are ready to return to you, the LORD our God. We turned away from you, but soon we wanted to return. After you had punished us, we hung our heads in grief. We were ashamed and disgraced, because we sinned when we were young.[4]—It is best to learn this patience in our youth.[5]

Evil does not grow in the soil, nor does trouble grow out of the ground. No indeed! Man brings trouble on himself, as surely as sparks fly up from a fire.[6]

[1]1 PET. 5.6. [2]Prov. 16.5. [3]Isa. 64.8, 9.—[4]Jer. 31.18, 19.—[5]Lam. 3.27. [6]Job 5.6, 7.

Evening

"Did God really tell you . . ."[1]

The Devil came to him and said, "If you are God's Son . . . Jesus answered, "The scripture says . . . the scripture also says . . . the scripture says . . ."[2]—Then the Devil left Jesus.[3]

The prophet from Judah answered, "I can't go home with you . . . because the LORD has commanded me not to eat or drink a thing, and not to return home the same way I came." Then the old prophet from Bethel said to him, "I, too, am a prophet just like you, and at the LORD's command an angel told me to take you home with me and offer you my hospitality." But the old prophet was lying. So the prophet from Judah went home with the old prophet and had a meal with him. "That is the prophet who disobeyed the LORD's command! And so the LORD sent the lion to attack and kill him, just as the LORD said he would."[4]—Even if we or an angel from heaven should preach to you a gospel that is different from the one we preached to you, may he be condemned to hell![5]—I keep your law in my heart, so that I will not sin against you.[6]

[1]GEN. 3.1. [2]Matt. 4.3, 4, 7, 10.—[3]Matt. 4.11. [4]1 Kgs 13.16–19, 26.—[5]Gal. 1.8.—[6]Ps. 119.11.

If they pronounce my name as a blessing upon the people of Israel, I will bless them.[1]

LORD our God, we have been ruled by others, but you alone are our LORD.[2]

All the peoples on earth will see that the LORD has chosen you to be his own people, and they will be afraid of you.[3]—The LORD has made a solemn promise, and he will not abandon you, for he has decided to make you his own people.[4]

Lord, hear us. Lord, forgive us. Lord, listen to us, and act! In order that everyone will know that you are God, do not delay! This city and these people are yours.[5]—Help us, O God, and save us; rescue us and forgive our sins for the sake of your own honour. Why should the nations ask us, "Where is your God?"[6]—The LORD is like a strong tower, where the righteous can go and be safe.[7]

[1]NUM. 6.27. [2]Isa. 26.13. [3]Deut. 28.10.—[4]1 Sam. 12.22. [5]Dan. 9.19.—[6]Ps. 79.9, 10.—[7]Prov. 18.10.

Evening

How clearly the sky reveals God's glory! How plainly it shows what he has done![1]

Ever since God created the world, his invisible qualities, both his eternal power and his divine nature, have been clearly seen; they are perceived in the things that God has made.[2]—He has always given evidence of his existence by the good things he does.[3]—Each day announces it to the following day; each night repeats it to the next. No speech or words are used, no sound is heard.[4]

When I look at the sky, which you have made, at the moon and the stars, which you set in their places—what is man, that you think of him; mere man, that you care for him?[5]

The sun has its own beauty, the moon another beauty, and the stars a different beauty; and even among stars there are different kinds of beauty. This is how it will be when the dead are raised to life.[6]—The wise leaders will shine with all the brightness of the sky. And those who have taught many people to do what is right will shine like the stars for ever.[7]

[1]PS. 19.1. [2]Rom. 1.20.—[3]Acts 14.17.—[4]Ps. 19.2, 3. [5]Ps. 8.3, 4. [6]1 Cor. 15.41, 42.—[7]Dan. 12.3.

***This is how we know what love is: Christ gave his life for us.*[1]**

His love . . . can never be fully known.[2]—The greatest love a person can have for his friends is to give his life for them.[3]—You know the grace of our Lord Jesus Christ; rich as he was, he made himself poor for your sake, in order to make you rich by means of his poverty.[4]—Dear friends, if this was how God loved us, then we should love one another.[5]—Be kind and tender-hearted to one another, and forgive one another, as God has forgiven you through Christ.[6]—Be tolerant with one another and forgive one another whenever any of you has a complaint against someone else. You must forgive one another just as the Lord has forgiven you.[7]—For even the Son of Man did not come to be served; he came to serve and to give his life to redeem many people.[8]—Christ himself suffered for you and left you an example, so that you would follow in his steps.[9]

You . . . should wash one another's feet. I have set an example for you, so that you will do just what I have done for you.[10]—We too, ought to give our lives for our brothers![11]

[1]1 JOHN 3.16. [2]Eph. 3.19.—[3]John 15.13.—[4]2 Cor. 8.9.—[5]1 John 4.11.—[6]Eph. 4.32.—[7]Col. 3.13.—[8]Mark 10.45.—[9]1 Pet. 2.21. [10]John 13.14, 15.—[11]1 John 3.16.

Evening

***What the Father does, the Son also does.*[1]**

It is the LORD who gives wisdom; from him come knowledge and understanding.[2]—I will give you such words and wisdom that none of your enemies will be able to refute or contradict what you say.[3]

Trust in the LORD. Have faith, do not despair.[4]—My grace is all you need, for my power is greatest when you are weak.[5]

Those . . . who live in the love of God the Father.[6]—He purifies people from their sins, and both he and those who are made pure all have the same Father. That is why Jesus is not ashamed to call them his brothers.[7]

Do you not know that I am everywhere in heaven and on earth?[8]—The completion of him who himself completes all things everywhere.[9]

I alone am the LORD, the only one who can save you.[10]—He really is the Saviour of the world.[11]

May God the Father and Christ Jesus our Saviour give you grace and peace.[12]

[1]JOHN 5.19. [2]Prov. 2.6.—[3]Luke 21.15. [4]Ps. 27.14.—[5]2 Cor. 12.9. [6]Jude 1.—[7]Heb. 2.11. [8]Jer. 23.24.—[9]Eph. 1.23. [10]Isa. 43.11.—[11]John 4.42. [12]Titus 1.4.

God knows every step I take; if he tests me, he will find me pure.[1]

He knows what we are made of.[2]—He takes no pleasure in causing us grief or pain.[3]

The solid foundation that God has laid cannot be shaken; and on it are written these words: "The Lord knows those who are his" and "Whoever says that he belongs to the Lord must turn away from wrongdoing." In a large house there are dishes and bowls of all kinds: some are made of silver and gold, others of wood and clay; some are for special occasions, others for ordinary use. If anyone makes himself clean from all those evil things, he will be used for special purposes, because he is dedicated and useful to his Master, ready to be used for every good deed.[4]

As a metal-worker refines silver and gold, so the LORD's messenger will purify the priests, so that they will bring to the LORD the right kind of offerings.[5]—I . . . will purify them as silver is purified . . . Then they will pray to me, and I will answer them. I will tell them that they are my people, and they will confess that I am their God.[6]

[1]JOB 23.10. [2]Ps. 103.14.—[3]Lam. 3.33. [4]2 Tim. 2.19–21. [5]Mal. 3.3.—[6]Zech. 13.9.

Evening

Teach me your ways, O LORD; make them known to me.[1]

Moses said to the LORD, . . . "You have said that you . . . are pleased with me. Now if you are, tell me your plans, so that I may serve you . . ." The LORD said, "I will go with you, and I will give you victory."[2]—He revealed his plans to Moses and let the people of Israel see his mighty deeds.[3]

He leads the humble in the right way and teaches them his will. Those who have reverence for the LORD will learn from him the path they should follow.[4]—Trust in the LORD with all your heart. Never rely on what you think you know. Remember the LORD in everything you do, and he will show you the right way.[5]

You will show me the path that leads to life; your presence fills me with joy and brings me pleasure for ever.[6]—I will teach you the way you should go; I will instruct you and advise you.[7]—The road the righteous travel is like the sunrise, getting brighter and brighter until daylight has come.[8]

[1]PS. 25.4. [2]Exod. 33.12–14.—[3]Ps. 103.7. [4]Ps. 25.9, 12.—[5]Prov. 3.5, 6. [6]Ps. 16.11.—[7]Ps. 32.8.—[8]Prov. 4.18.

The Spirit produces self-control.[1]

Every athlete in training submits to strict discipline, in order to be crowned with a wreath that will not last; but we do it for one that will last for ever. That is why I run straight for the finishing-line; that is why I am like a boxer who does not waste his punches. I harden my body with blows and bring it under complete control, to keep myself from being disqualified after having called others to the contest.[2]

Do not get drunk with wine, which will only ruin you; instead, be filled with the Spirit.[3]

If anyone wants to come with me, he must forget self, carry his cross, and follow me.[4]

We should not be sleeping like the others; we should be awake and sober. It is at night that people sleep; it is at night that they get drunk. But we belong to the day, and we should be sober.[5]—[God's] grace instructs us to give up ungodly living and worldly passions, and to live self-controlled, upright, and godly lives in this world, as we wait for the blessed Day we hope for, when the glory of our great God and Saviour Jesus Christ will appear.[6]

[1]GAL. 5.22. [2]1 Cor. 9.25–27. [3]Eph. 5.18. [4]Matt. 16.24. [5]1 Thess. 5.6–8.— [6]Titus 2.12, 13.

Evening

Grow up in every way to Christ, who is the head.[1]

First the tender stalk appears, then the ear, and finally the ear full of corn.[2]—We shall all come together to that oneness in our faith and in our knowledge of the Son of God; we shall become mature people, reaching to the very height of Christ's full stature.[3]

They make up their own standards to measure themselves by, and they judge themselves by their own standards! Whoever wants to boast must boast about what the Lord has done. For it is when the Lord thinks well of a person that he is really approved, and not when he thinks well of himself.[4]

The reality is Christ. Do not allow yourselves to be condemned by anyone who claims to be superior because of special visions and who insists on false humility and the worship of angels. For no reason at all, such a person is all puffed up by his human way of thinking and has stopped holding on to Christ, who is the head of the body. Under Christ's control the whole body is nourished and held together by its joints and ligaments, and it grows as God wants it to grow.[5]

Grow in the grace and knowledge of our Lord and Saviour Jesus Christ.[6]

[1]EPH. 4.15. [2]Mark 4.28.—[3]Eph. 4.13. [4]2 Cor. 10.12, 17, 18. [5]Col. 2.17–19. [6]2 Pet. 3.18.

Morning

The goat is to be driven off into the desert by a man appointed to do it. The goat will carry all their sins away with him into some uninhabited land.[1]

As far as the east is from the west, so far does he remove our sins from us.[2]—When that time comes, no sin will be found in Israel and no wickedness in Judah, because I will forgive those people whose lives I have spared. I, the LORD, have spoken.[3]—You will . . . send [our sins] to the bottom of the sea! There is not other god like you, O LORD; you forgive the sins of your people.[4]

All of us were like sheep that were lost, each of us going his own way. But the LORD made the punishment fall on him, the punishment all of us deserved.[5]—My devoted servant . . . will bear the punishment of many . . . And so I will give him a place of honour, a place among great and powerful men. He willingly gave his life and shared the fate of evil men. He took the place of many sinners and prayed that they might be forgiven.[6]—There is the Lamb of God, who takes away the sin of the world![7]

[1]LEV. 16.21, 22. [2]Ps. 103.12.—[3]Jer. 50.20.—[4]Mic. 7.19, 18. [5]Isa. 53.6.—[6]Isa. 53.11, 12.—[7]John 1.29.

Evening

Who made you superior to others? Didn't God give you everything you have?[1]

By God's grace I am what I am.[2]—By his own will he brought us into being through the word of truth.[3]—Everything depends, not on what man wants or does, but only on God's mercy.[4]—What, then, can we boast about? Nothing![5]—God has made Christ to be our wisdom. By him we are put right with God; we become God's holy people and are set free. Whoever wants to boast must boast of what the Lord has done.[6]

In the past you were spiritually dead because of your disobedience and sins. At that time you followed the world's evil way; you obeyed the ruler of the spiritual powers in space, the spirit who now controls the people who disobey God. Actually all of us were like them and lived according to our natural desires, doing whatever suited the wishes of our own bodies and minds. In our natural condition we, like everyone else, were destined to suffer God's anger.[7]—You have been purified from sin; you have been dedicated to God; you have been put right with God by the Lord Jesus Christ and by the Spirit of our God.[8]

[1]1 COR. 4.7. [2]1 Cor. 15.10.—[3]Jas 1.18.—[4]Rom. 9.16.—[5]Rom. 3.27.—[6]1 Cor. 1.30, 31. [7]Eph. 2.1–3.—[8]1 Cor. 6.11.

He loves us, and by his sacrificial death he has freed us from our sins.[1]

Water cannot put it out; no flood can drown it. Love is as powerful as death.[2]—The greatest love a person can have for his friends is to give his life for them.[3]

Christ himself carried our sins in his body to the cross, so that we might die to sin and live for righteousness. It is by his wounds that you have been healed.[4]—By the sacrificial death of Christ we are set free, that is, our sins are forgiven. How great is the grace of God![5]

You have been purified from sin; you have been dedicated to God; you have been put right with God by the Lord Jesus Christ and by the Spirit of our God.[6]—You are the chosen race, the King's priests, the holy nation, God's own people, chosen to proclaim the wonderful acts of God, who called you out of darkness into his own marvellous light.[7]—My brothers, because of God's great mercy to us I appeal to you: Offer yourselves as a living sacrifice to God, dedicated to his service and pleasing to him. This is the true worship that you should offer.[8]

[1]REV. 1.5. [2]S. of S. 8.7, 6.—[3]John 15.13. [4]1 Pet. 2.24.—[5]Eph. 1.7. [6]1 Cor. 6.11.—[7]1 Pet. 2.9.—[8]Rom. 12.1.

Evening

There are different ways of serving, but the same LORD is served.[1]

This is the list of those who administered the royal property: Royal storerooms: Azmaveth son of Adiel. Local storerooms: Jonathan. Farm labour: Ezri. Vineyards: Shimei.[2]

In the church God has put all in place: in the first place apostles, in the second place prophets, and in the third place teachers; then those who perform miracles, followed by those who are given the power to heal or to help others or to direct them or to speak in strange tongues. But it is one and the same Spirit who does all this; as he wishes, he gives a different gift to each person.[3]

Each one, as a good manager of God's different gifts, must use for the good of others the special gift he has received from God. Whoever preaches must preach God's messages; whoever serves must serve with the strength that God gives him, so that in all things praise may be given to God through Jesus Christ, to whom belong glory and power for ever and ever.[4]

[1]1 COR. 12.5. [2]1 Chr. 27.25–27, 31. [3]1 Cor. 12.28, 11. [4]1 Pet. 4.10, 11.

***Moses' face was shining because he had been speaking with the* Lord*; but he did not know it.*[1]**

To you alone, O Lord, to you alone, and not to us, must glory be given.[2]—When, Lord did we ever see you hungry and feed you, or thirsty and give you a drink?[3]—Be humble towards one another, always considering others better than yourselves.[4]—Put on the apron of humility.[5]

As they looked on, a change came over Jesus: his face was shining like the sun, and his clothes were dazzling white.[6]—All those sitting in the Council fixed their eyes on Stephen and saw that his face looked like the face of an angel.[7]—I gave them the same glory you gave me.[8]—All of us . . . reflect the glory of the Lord with uncovered faces; and that same glory, coming from the Lord, who is the Spirit, transforms us into his likeness in an ever greater degree of glory.[9]

You are like light for the whole world. A city built on a hill cannot be hidden. No one lights a lamp and puts it under a bowl; instead he puts it on the lampstand, where it gives light for everyone in the house.[10]

[1]EXOD. 34.29. [2]Ps. 115.1.—[3]Matt. 25.37.—[4]Phil. 2.3.—[5]1 Pet. 5.5. [6]Matt. 17.2.—[7]Acts 6.15.—[8]John 17.22.—[9]2 Cor. 3.18. [10]Matt. 5.14, 15.

Evening

***There are different abilities to perform service, but the same God gives ability to all for their particular service.*[1]**

Some soldiers from the tribe of Manasseh went over to David's side . . . They served David as officers over his troops, because they were all outstanding soldiers.[2]—The Spirit's presence is shown in some way in each person for the good of all.[3]

Issachar: 200 leaders, together with the men under their command (these leaders knew what Israel should do and the best time to do it).[4]—The Spirit gives one person a message full of wisdom, while to another person the same Spirit gives a message full of knowledge.[5]

Zebulun: 50,000 loyal and reliable men ready to fight, trained to use all kinds of weapons.[6]—A person . . . unable to make up his mind and undecided in all that he does.[7]

There is no division in the body, but all its different parts have the same concern for one another. If one part of the body suffers, all the other parts suffer with it; if one part is praised, all the other parts share its happiness.[8]

There is one Lord, one faith, one baptism.[9]

[1]1 COR. 12.6. [2]1 Chr. 12.19, 21.—[3]1 Cor. 12.7. [4]1 Chr. 12.32.—[5]1 Cor. 12.8. [6]1 Chr. 12.33.—[7]Jas 1.8. [8]1 Cor. 12.25, 26. [9]Eph. 4.5.

Morning

Call to me when trouble comes; I will save you, and you will praise me.[1]

Why am I so sad? Why am I so troubled? I will put my hope in God, and once again I will praise him, my saviour and my God.[2]—You will listen, O LORD, to the prayers of the lowly; you will give them courage.[3]—You are good to us and forgiving, full of constant love for all who pray to you.[4]

Jacob said to his family . . . "We are going to leave here and go to Bethel, where I will build an altar to the God who helped me in the time of my trouble and who has been with me everywhere I have gone."[5]

I love the LORD, because he hears me; he listens to my prayers. He listens to me every time I call to him. The danger of death was all round me; the horrors of the grave closed in on me . . . Then I called to the LORD.[6]

[1]PS. 50.15. [2]Ps. 42.11.—[3]Ps. 10.17.—[4]Ps. 86.5. [5]Gen. 35.2, 3. [6]Ps. 116.1–4.

Evening

Just a little while longer, and he who is coming will come; he will not delay.[1]

Write down clearly on clay tablets what I reveal to you, so that it can be read at a glance . . . the time is coming quickly, and what I show you will come true. It may seem slow in coming, but wait for it; it will certainly take place, and it will not be delayed.[2]

Do not forget one thing, my dear friends! There is no difference in the Lord's sight between one day and a thousand years; to him the two are the same. The Lord is not slow to do what he has promised, as some think. Instead, he is patient with you, because he does not want anyone to be destroyed, but wants all to turn away from their sins.[3]—You, O Lord, are a merciful and loving God, always patient, always kind and faithful.[4]—Why don't you tear the sky apart and come down? No one has ever seen or heard of a God like you, who does such deeds for those who put their hope in him.[5]

[1]HEB. 10.37. [2]Hab. 2.2, 3. [3]2 Pet. 3.8, 9.—[4]Ps. 86.15.—[5]Isa. 64.1, 4.

Morning

The Lord, our Almighty God, is King![1]

I know . . . that you can do everything you want.[2]—What is impossible for man is possible for God.[3]—He looks on the people of the earth as nothing; angels in heaven and people on earth are under his control. No one can oppose his will or question what he does.[4]—No one can escape from my power; no one can change what I do.[5]—My Father! All things are possible for you.[6]

"Do you believe that I can heal you?" "Yes, sir!" they answered. Then Jesus touched their eyes and said, "Let it happen, then, just as you believe!"[7]—"Sir, if you want to, you can make me clean." Jesus stretched out his hand and touched him. "I do want to," he answered. "Be clean!"[8]—"Mighty God."[9]—I have been given all authority in heaven and on earth.[10]

Some trust in their war-chariots and others in their horses, but we trust in the power of the LORD our God.[11]—Be determined and confident, and don't be afraid . . . We have more power on our side than he has on his.[12]

[1]REV. 19.6. [2]Job 42.2.—[3]Luke 18.27.—[4]Dan. 4.35.—[5]Isa. 43.13.—[6]Mark 14.36. [7]Matt. 9.28, 29.—[8]Matt. 8.2, 3.—[9]Isa. 9.6.—[10]Matt. 28.18. [11]Ps. 20.7.— [12]2 Chr. 32.7.

Evening

What did the LORD tell you?[1]

The LORD has told us what is good. What he requires of us is this: to do what is just, to show constant love, and to live in humble fellowship with our God.[2]—Obey all his laws. I am giving them to you today for your benefit.[3]

Those who depend on obeying the Law live under a curse. For the scripture says, "Whoever does not always obey everything that is written in the book of the Law is under God's curse!" Now, it is clear that no one is put right with God by means of the Law, because the scripture says, "Only the person who is put right with God through faith shall live." What, then, was the purpose of the Law? It was added in order to show what wrongdoing is, and it was meant to last until the coming of Abraham's descendant, to whom the promise was made.[4]

In the past, God spoke to our ancestors many times and in many ways through the prophets, but in these last days he has spoken to us through his Son.[5]

Speak, LORD, your servant is listening.[6]

[1]1 SAM. 3.17. [2]Mic. 6.8.—[3]Deut. 10.13. [4]Gal. 3.10, 11, 19. [5]Heb. 1.1, 2. [6]1 Sam. 3.9.

He leads the humble in the right way.[1]

Happy are those who are humble.[2]

I realized another thing, that in this world fast runners do not always win the race, and the brave do not always win the battle. Wise men do not always earn a living, intelligent men do not always get rich, and capable men do not always rise to high positions.[3]—You may make your plans, but God directs your actions.[4]

LORD, I look up to you, up to heaven, where you rule. As a servant depends on his master, as a maid depends on her mistress, so we will keep looking to you, O LORD our God.[5]—Set me free from my distress; then in the assembly of your people I will praise you.[6]

You are our God! Punish them, for we are helpless in the face of this large army that is attacking us. We do not know what to do, but we look to you for help.[7]

If any of you lacks wisdom, he should pray to God, who will give it to him; because God gives generously and graciously to all.[8]

When . . . the Spirit comes, who reveals the truth about God, he will lead you into all the truth.[9]

[1]PS. 25.9. [2]Matt. 5.5. [3]Eccles. 9.11.—[4]Prov. 16.9. [5]Ps. 123.1, 2.—[6]Ps. 142.7. [7]2 Chr. 20.12. [8]Jas 1.5. [9]John 16.13.

Evening

I ask you to bless my descendants so that they will continue to enjoy your favour.[1]

You, LORD, have blessed them, and your blessing will rest on them for ever.[2]—It is the LORD's blessing that makes you wealthy. Hard work can make you no richer.[3]

Remembering the words that the Lord Jesus himself said, "There is more happiness in giving than in receiving."[4]—When you give a feast, invite the poor, the crippled, the lame, and the blind; and you will be blessed, because they are not able to pay you back. God will repay you on the day the good people rise from death.[5]—Come, you that are blessed by my Father! Come and possess the kingdom which has been prepared for you ever since the creation of the world. I was hungry and you fed me, thirsty and you gave me a drink; I was a stranger and you received me in your homes, naked and you clothed me; I was sick and you took care of me, in prison and you visited me.[6]

Happy are those who are concerned for the poor; the LORD will help them when they are in trouble.[7]

The LORD is our protector and glorious king.[8]

[1]2 SAM. 7.29. [2]1 Chr. 17.27.—[3]Prov. 10.22. [4]Acts 20.35.—[5]Luke 14.13, 14.—[6]Matt. 25.34–36. [7]Ps. 41.1. [8]Ps. 84.11.

I will not be afraid. What can anyone do to me?[1]

Who . . . can separate us from the love of Christ? Can trouble do it, or hardship or persecution or hunger or poverty or danger or death? No, in all these things we have complete victory through him who loved us![2]

Do not be afraid of those who kill the body but cannot afterwards do anything worse. I will show you whom to fear: fear God, who, after killing, has the authority to throw into hell. Believe me, he is the one you must fear![3]

Happy are those who are persecuted because they do what God requires; the Kingdom of heaven belongs to them! Happy are you when people insult you and persecute you and tell all kinds of evil lies against you because you are my followers. Be happy and glad, for a great reward is kept for you in heaven.[4]—I reckon my own life to be worth nothing to me; I only want to complete my mission and finish the work that the Lord Jesus gave me to do.[5]—I will announce your commands to kings and I will not be ashamed.[6]

[1]HEB. 13.6. [2]Rom. 8.35, 37. [3]Luke 12.4, 5. [4]Matt. 5.10–12.— [5]Acts 20.24.— [6]Ps. 119.46.

Evening

He set me safely on a rock.[1]

That rock was Christ himself.[2]—Simon Peter answered, "You are the Messiah, the Son of the living God." [Jesus told him,] "On this rock foundation I will build my church, and not even death will ever be able to overcome it."[3]—Salvation is to be found through him alone; in all the world there is no one else whom God has given who can save us.[4]

With a sure faith . . . let us hold on firmly to the hope we profess.[5]—You must believe and not doubt at all. Whoever doubts is like a wave in the sea that is driven and blown about by the wind.[6]

Who, then, can separate us from the love of Christ? Can trouble do it, or hardship or persecution or hunger or poverty or danger or death? No, in all these things we have complete victory through him who loved us! For I am certain that nothing can separate us from his love: neither death nor life, neither angels nor other heavenly rulers or powers, neither the present nor the future, neither the world above nor the world below—there is nothing in all creation that will ever be able to separate us from the love of God which is ours through Christ Jesus our Lord.[7]

[1]PS. 40.2. [2]1 Cor. 10.4.—[3]Matt. 16.16, 18.—[4]Acts 4.12. [5]Heb. 10.22, 23.—[6]Jas 1.6. [7]Rom. 8.35, 37–39.

You are a God who forgives; you are gracious and loving . . . your mercy is great.[1]

The Lord is not slow to do what he has promised, as some think. Instead, he is patient with you, because he does not want anyone to be destroyed, but wants all to turn away from their sins.[2]—Look on our Lord's patience as the opportunity he is giving you to be saved.[3]

God was merciful to me in order that Christ Jesus might show his full patience in dealing with me, the worst of all sinners, as an example for all those who would later believe in him and receive eternal life.[4]—Everything written in the Scriptures was written to teach us, in order that we might have hope through the patience and encouragement which the Scriptures give us.[5]

Perhaps you despise his great kindness, tolerance, and patience. Surely you know that God is kind, because he is trying to lead you to repent.[6]—Let your broken heart show your sorrow; tearing your clothes is not enough. Come back to the LORD your God. He is kind and full of mercy; he is patient and keeps his promise; he is always ready to forgive and not punish.[7]

[1]NEH. 9.17. [2]2 Pet. 3.9.—[3]2 Pet. 3.15. [4]1 Tim. 1.16.—[5]Rom. 15.4. [6]Rom. 2.4.—[7]Joel 2.13.

Evening

The promises of the LORD can be trusted.[1]

How certain your promise is! How I love it![2]—The laws of the LORD are right, and those who obey them are happy. The commands of the LORD are just and give understanding to the mind.[3]—God keeps every promise he makes. He is like a shield for all who seek his protection. If you claim that he said something that he never said, he will reprimand you and show that you are a liar.[4]

I keep your law in my heart, so that I will not sin against you. I study your instructions; I examine your teachings.[5]—My brothers, fill your minds with those things that are good and that deserve praise: things that are true, noble, right, pure, lovely, and honourable.[6]—Be like new-born babies, always thirsty for the pure spiritual milk, so that by drinking it you may grow up and be saved.[7]

We are not like so many others, who handle God's message as if it were cheap merchandise; but because God has sent us, we speak with sincerity in his presence, as servants of Christ.[8]—We do not act with deceit, nor do we falsify the word of God.[9]

[1]PS. 12.6. [2]Ps. 119.140.—[3]Ps. 19.8.—[4]Prov. 30.5, 6. [5]Ps. 119.11, 15.—[6]Phil. 4.8.—[7]1 Pet. 2.2. [8]2 Cor. 2.17.—[9]2 Cor. 4.2.

***Every family in heaven and on earth.*[1]**

One God and Father of all mankind, who is Lord of all, works through all, and is in all.[2]—It is through faith that all of you are God's sons in union with Christ Jesus.[3]—This plan, which God will complete when the time is right, is to bring all creation together, everything in heaven and on earth, with Christ as head.[4]

Jesus is not ashamed to call them his brothers.[5]—Look! Here are my mother and my brothers! Whoever does what my Father in heaven wants him to do is my brother, my sister, and my mother.[6]—Go to my brothers and tell them that I am returning to him who is my Father and their Father, my God and their God.[7]

I saw underneath the altar the souls of those who had been killed because they had proclaimed God's word and has been faithful in their witnessing. Each of them was given a white robe, and they were told to rest a little while longer, until the complete number of their fellow-servants and brothers had been killed, as they had been.[8]—Only in company with us would they be made perfect.[9]

[1]EPH. 3.15. [2]Eph. 4.6.—[3]Gal. 3.26.—[4]Eph. 1.10. [5]Heb. 2.11.—[6]Matt. 12.49, 50.—[7]John 20.17. [8]Rev. 6.9, 11.—[9]Heb. 11.40.

Evening

***This . . . is how you should pray: 'Our Father in heaven.'*[1]**

[Jesus] looked up to heaven and said, "Father".[2]—My Father and their Father.[3]

It is through faith that all of you are God's sons in union with Christ Jesus.[4]—The Spirit that God has given you does not make you slaves and cause you to be afraid; instead, the Spirit makes you God's children, and by the Spirit's power we cry out to God, "Father! my Father!" God's Spirit joins himself to our spirits to declare that we are God's children.[5]

To show that you are his sons, God sent the Spirit of his Son into our hearts, the Spirit who cries out, "Father, my Father." So then, you are no longer a slave but a son.[6]

I am telling you the truth: The Father will give you whatever you ask him for in my name. Until now you have not asked for anything in my name; ask and you will receive, so that your happiness may be complete.[7]

"I will accept you. I will be your father, and you shall be my sons and daughters, says the Lord Almighty."[8]

[1]MATT. 6.9. [2]John 17.1.—[3]John 20.17. [4]Gal. 3.26.—[5]Rom. 8.15, 16. [6]Gal. 4.6, 7. [7]John 16.23, 24. [8]2 Cor. 6.17, 18.

Do not stay away from me! Trouble is near.[1]

How much longer will you forget me, LORD? For ever? How much longer will you hide yourself from me? How long must I endure trouble? How long will sorrow fill my heart day and night?[2]—Don't hide yourself from me! Don't be angry with me; don't turn your servant away. You have been my help; don't leave me, don't abandon me, O God, my saviour.[3]

When they call to me, I will answer them; when they are in trouble, I will be with them. I will rescue them and honour them.[4]—He is near to those who call to him, who call to him with sincerity. He supplies the needs of those who honour him; he hears their cries and saves them.[5]

When I go, you will not be left all alone; I will come back to you.[6]—I will be with you always, to the end of the age.[7]

God is our shelter and strength, always ready to help in times of trouble.[8]—I wait patiently for God to save me. I depend on God alone; I put my hope in him.[9]

[1]PS. 22.11. [2]Ps. 13.1, 2.—[3]Ps. 27.9. [4]Ps. 91.15.—[5]Ps. 145.18, 19. [6]John 14.18.—[7]Matt. 28.20. [8]Ps. 46.1.—[9]Ps. 62.1, 5.

Evening

May your holy name be honoured.[1]

Do not worship any other god, because I, the LORD, tolerate no rivals.[2]

LORD, who among the gods is like you? Who is like you, wonderful in holiness? Who can work miracles and mighty acts like yours?[3]—Holy, holy, holy, is the Lord God Almighty.[4]

Bow down before the Holy One when he appears.[5]—I saw the Lord. He was sitting on his throne, high and exalted, and his robe filled the whole Temple. Round him flaming creatures were standing . . . They were calling out to each other: "Holy, holy, holy! The LORD Almighty is holy! His glory fills the world." I said, "There is no hope for me! I am doomed."[6]—In the past I knew only what others had told me, but now I have seen you with my own eyes. So I am ashamed of all I have said.[7]

The blood of Jesus, his Son, purifies us from every sin.[8]—So that we may share his holiness.[9]—We have . . . my brothers, complete freedom to go into the Most Holy Place by means of the death of Jesus. So let us come near to God with a sincere heart.[10]

[1]MATT. 6.9. [2]Exod. 34.14. [3]Exod. 15.11.—[4]Rev. 4.8. [5]1 Chr. 16.29.—[6]Isa. 6.1–3, 5.—[7]Job 42.5, 6. [8]1 John 1.7.—[9]Heb. 12.10.—[10]Heb. 10.19, 22.

God was making all mankind his friends through Christ. God did not keep an account of their sins.[1]

It was by God's own decision that the Son has in himself the full nature of God. Through the Son, then, God decided to bring the whole universe back to himself.[2]—Love and faithfulness will meet; righteousness and peace will embrace.[3]

I alone know the plans I have for you, plans to bring you prosperity and not disaster.[4]—The LORD says, "Now, let's settle the matter. You are stained red with sin, but I will wash you as clean as snow. Although your stains are deep red, you will be as white as wool."[5]

There is no other god like you, O LORD; you forgive the sins of your people.[6]

Make peace with God.[7]—Keep on working with fear and trembling to complete your salvation, becasue God is always at work in you to make you willing and able to obey his own purpose.[8]—You will give us prosperity, LORD; everything that we achieve is the result of what you do.[9]

[1]2 COR. 5.19. [2]Col. 1.19, 20.—[3]Ps. 85.10. [4]Jer. 29.11.—[5]Isa. 1.18. [6]Mic. 7.18. [7]Job 22.21.—[8]Phil. 2.12, 13.—[9]Isa. 26.12.

Evening

May your kingdom come.[1]

At the time of those rulers the God of heaven will establish a kingdom that will never end. It will never be conquered, but will completely destroy all those empires, and then last for ever.[2]—A great stone broke loose from a cliff without anyone touching it.[3]—"Not by military might or by your own strength, but by my spirit."[4]—The Kingdom of God does not come in such a way as to be seen. No one will say, "Look, here it is!" or, "There it is!"; because the Kingdom of God is within you.[5]

You have been given the secret of the Kingdom of God. The Kingdom of God is like this. A man scatters seed in his field. He sleeps at night, is up and about during the day, and all the while the seeds are sprouting and growing. Yet he does not know how it happens. When the corn is ripe, the man starts cutting it with his sickle, because harvest time has come.[6]

You . . . must always be ready, because the Son of Man will come at an hour when you are not expecting him.[7]

The Spirit and the Bride say, "Come!" Everyone who hears this must also say, "Come!"[8]

[1]MATT. 6.10. [2]Dan. 2.44.—[3]Dan. 2.34.—[4]Zech. 4.6.—[5]Luke 17.20, 21. [6]Mark 4.11, 26, 27, 29. [7]Matt. 24.44. [8]Rev. 22.17.

God has heard your prayers ever since the first day you decided to humble yourself in order to gain understanding.[1]

I am the high and holy God, who lives for ever. I live in a high and holy place, but I also live with people who are humble and repentant, so that I can restore their confidence and hope.[2]—My sacrifice is a humble spirit, O God; you will not reject a humble and repentant heart.[3]—Even though you are so high above, you care for the lowly, and the proud cannot hide from you.[4]—Humble yourselves, then, under God's mighty hand, so that he will lift you up in his own good time.[5]—God resists the proud, but gives grace to the humble. So then, submit to God.[6]

You are good to us and forgiving, full of constant love for all who pray to you. Listen, LORD, to my prayer; hear my cries for help. I call to you in times of trouble, because you answer my prayers.[7]

[1]DAN. 10.12. [2]Isa. 57.15.—[3]Ps. 51.17.—[4]Ps. 138.6.—[5]1 Pet. 5.6.—[6]Jas 4.6, 7. [7]Ps. 86.5–7.

Evening

May your will be done on earth as it is in heaven.[1]

Try to find out what the Lord wants you to do.[2]

Your Father in heaven does not want any of these little ones to be lost.[3]

God wants you to be holy.[4]—From now on . . . you must live the rest of your earthly lives controlled by God's will and not by human desires.[5]—By his own will he brought us into being through the word of truth . . . so get rid of every filthy habit and all wicked conduct.[6]

Be holy because I am holy.[7]—Whoever does what God wants him to do is my brother, my sister, my mother.[8]—Anyone who hears these words of mine and obeys them is like a wise man who built his house on rock. The rain poured down, the rivers overflowed, and the wind blew hard against that house. But it did not fall, because it was built on rock.[9]—The world and everything in it that people desire is passing away; but he who does the will of God lives for ever.[10]

[1]MATT. 6.10. [2]Eph. 5.17. [3]Matt. 18.14. [4]1 Thess. 4.3.—[5]1 Pet. 4.2.—[6]Jas 1.18, 21. [7]1 Pet. 1.16.—[8]Mark 3.35.—[9]Matt. 7.24, 25.—[10]1 John 2.17.

Christ died and rose to life in order to be the Lord of the living and of the dead.[1]

The LORD says, "It was my will that he should suffer; his death was a sacrifice to bring forgiveness. And so he will see his descendants; he will live a long life, and through him my purpose will succeed. After a life of suffering, he will again have joy; he will know that he did not suffer in vain. My devoted servant, with whom I am pleased, will bear the punishment of many and for his sake I will forgive them."[2]—Was it not necessary for the Messiah to suffer these things and then to enter his glory?[3]—We recognize that one man died for everyone, which means that all share in his death. He died for all, so that those who live should no longer live for themselves, but only for him who died and was raised to life for their sake.[4]

All the people of Israel, then, are to know for sure that this Jesus, whom you crucified, is the one that God has made Lord and Messiah![5]—He had been chosen by God before the creation of the world and was revealed in these last days for your sake. Through him you believe in God.[6]

[1]ROM. 14.9. [2]Isa. 53.10, 11.—[3]Luke 24.26.—[4]2 Cor. 5.14, 15. [5]Acts 2.36.—[6]1 Pet. 1.20, 21.

Evening

Give us today the food we need.[1]

I am an old man now; I have lived a long time, but I have never seen a good man abandoned by the LORD or his children begging for food.[2]—You will have food to eat and water to drink.[3]—[Elijah] drank water from the brook, and ravens brought him bread and meat every morning and every evening.[4]

With all his abundant wealth through Christ Jesus, my God will supply all your needs.[5]—Be satisfied with what you have. For God has said, "I will never leave you; I will never abandon you."[6]

He made you go hungry, and then he gave you manna to eat, food that you and your ancestors had never eaten before. He did this to teach you that man must not depend on bread alone to sustain him, but on everything that the LORD says.[7]—"I am telling you the truth," Jesus said. "What Moses gave you was not the bread from heaven; it is my Father who gives you the real bread from heaven. For the bread that God gives is he who comes down from heaven and gives life to the world."[8]

[1]MATT. 6.11. [2]Ps. 37.25.—[3]Isa. 33.16.—[4]1 Kgs 17.6. [5]Phil. 4.19.—[6]Heb. 13.5. [7]Deut. 8.3.—[8]John 6.32, 35.

You are my refuge, O God.[1]

The LORD is my protector; he is my strong fortress. My God is my protection, and with him I am safe. He protects me like a shield; he defends me and keeps me safe. He is my saviour; he protects me and saves me from violence.[2]—The LORD protects and defends me; I trust in him. He gives me help and makes me glad; I praise him with joyful songs.[3]

From east to west everyone will fear him, and his great power. He will come like a rushing river, like a strong wind.[4]—Let us be bold, then, and say, "The Lord is my helper, I will not be afraid. What can anyone do to me?"[5]

The LORD is my light and my salvation; I will fear no one. The LORD protects me from all danger; I will never be afraid.[6]

As the mountains surround Jerusalem, so the LORD surrounds his people now and for ever.[7]—You have always been my help. In the shadow of your wings I sing for joy.[8]

You are my refuge and defence; guide me and lead me as you have promised.[9]

[1]PS. 59.9. [2]2 Sam. 22.2, 3.—[3]Ps. 28.7. [4]Isa. 59.19.—[5]Heb. 13.6. [6]Ps. 27.1. [7]Ps. 125.2.—[8]Ps. 63.7. [9]Ps. 31.3.

Evening

Forgive us the wrongs we have done, as we forgive the wrongs that others have done to us.[1]

"Lord, if my brother keeps on sinning against me, how many times do I have to forgive him? Seven times?" "No, not seven times," answered Jesus, "but seventy times seven."[2]—"You worthless slave!" he said. "I forgave you the whole amount you owed me, just because you asked me to. You should have had mercy on your fellow-servant, just as I had mercy on you." The king was very angry, and he sent the servant to jail to be punished until he should pay back the whole amount. That is how my Father in heaven will treat every one of you unless you forgive your brother from your heart.[3]—Be kind and tender-hearted to one another, and forgive one another, as God has forgiven you through Christ.[4]—God has now brought you to life with Christ. God forgave us all our sins; he cancelled the unfavourable record of our debts with its binding rules and did away with it completely by nailing it to the cross.[5]—You must forgive one another just as the Lord has forgiven you.[6]

[1]MATT. 6.12. [2]Matt. 18.21, 22.—[3]Matt. 18.32–35.—[4]Eph. 4.32.—[5]Col. 2.13, 14.—[6]Col. 3.13.

Morning

Work hard and do not be lazy. Serve the Lord with a heart full of devotion.[1]

Work hard at whatever you do, because there will be no action, no thought, no knowledge, no wisdom in the world of the dead—and that is where you are going.[2]—Whatever you do, work at it with all your heart, as though you were working for the Lord and not for men. Remember that the Lord will give you as a reward what he has kept for his people. For Christ is the real Master you serve.[3]—Remember that the Lord will reward everyone, whether slave or free, for the good work he does.[4]

As long as it is day, we must keep on doing the work of him who sent me; night is coming when no one can work.[5]—Didn't you know that I had to be in my Father's house?[6]—My devotion to your house, O God, burns in me like a fire.[7]

My brothers, try even harder to make God's call and his choice of you a permanent experience; if you do so, you will never abandon your faith.[8]—Our great desire is that each one of you keep up his eagerness to the end, so that the things you hope for will come true. We do not want you to become lazy, but to be like those who believe and are patient, and so receive what God has promised.[9]—Run . . . in such a way as to win the prize.[10]

[1]ROM. 12.11. [2]Eccles. 9.10.—[3]Col. 3.23, 24.—[4]Eph. 6.8. [5]John 9.4.—[6]Luke 2.49.—[7]John 2.17. [8]2 Pet. 1.10.—[9]Heb. 6.11.—[10]1 Cor. 9.24.

Evening

Do not bring us to hard testing, but keep us safe from the Evil One.[1]

It is foolish to follow your own opinions. Be safe, and follow the teachings of wiser people.[2]

If a person is tempted by . . . trials, he must not say, "This temptation comes from God." For God cannot be tempted by evil, and he himself tempts no one. But a person is tempted when he is drawn away and trapped by his own evil desire.[3]—The Lord says, "You must leave them and separate yourselves from them. Have nothing to do with what is unclean, and I will accept you."[4]

Lot looked round and saw that the whole Jordan Valley . . . had plenty of water, like the Garden of the LORD . . . so Lot chose the whole Jordan Valley for himself . . . and camped near Sodom, whose people were wicked and sinned against the Lord.[5]—[The Lord] rescued Lot, a good man, who was distressed by the immoral conduct of lawless people. The Lord knows how to rescue godly people from their trials.[6]—He will succeed, because the Lord is able to make him succeed.[7]

[1]MATT. 6.13. [2]Prov. 28.26. [3]Jas 1.13, 14.—[4]2 Cor. 6.17. [5]Gen. 13.10–13.—[6]2 Pet. 2.7, 9.—[7]Rom. 14.4.

***Because of you they rejoice all day long, and they praise you for your goodness.*[1]**

Only through me are victory and strength to be found; but all who hate me will suffer disgrace. I, the LORD, will rescue all the descendants of Jacob, and they will give me praise.[2]—You that are righteous, be glad and rejoice because of what the LORD has done. You that obey him, shout for joy![3]

Now God's way of putting people right with himself has been revealed. It has nothing to do with law, even though the Law of Moses and the prophets gave their witness to it. God puts people right through their faith in Jesus Christ. God does this to all who believe in Christ. In this way God shows that he himself is righteous and that he puts right everyone who believes in Jesus.[4]—You love him, although you have not seen him, and you believe in him, although you do not now see him. So you rejoice with a great and glorious joy which words cannot express.[5]

May you always be joyful in your union with the Lord. I say it again: rejoice![6]

[1]PS. 89.16. [2]Isa. 45, 24, 25.—[3]Ps. 32.11. [4]Rom. 3.21, 22, 26.—[5]1 Pet. 1.8. [6]Phil. 4.4.

Evening

***For yours is the kingdom, and the power, and the glory for ever.*[1]**

Your throne, O LORD, has been firm from the beginning, and you existed before time began.[2]

The LORD is . . . powerful.[3]—If God is for us, who can be against us?[4]—If the God whom we serve is able to save us . . . then he will.[5]—What my Father has given me is greater than everything, and no one can snatch them away from the Father's care.[6]—The Spirit who is in you is more powerful than the spirit in those who belong to the world.[7]

To you alone, O LORD, to you alone, and not to us, must glory be given.[8]—You are great and powerful, glorious, splendid, and majestic. Everything in heaven and earth is yours, and you are king, supreme ruler over all. Now, our God, we give you thanks, and we praise your glorious name. Yet my people and I cannot really give you anything, because everything is a gift from you, and we have only given back what is yours already.[9]

[1]MATT. 6.13. [2]Ps. 93.2. [3]Nahum 1.3.—[4]Rom. 8.31.—[5]Dan. 3.17.—[6]John 10.29.—[7]1 John 4.4. [8]Ps. 115.1.—[9]1 Chr. 29.11, 13, 14.

One of the soldiers . . . plunged his spear into Jesus' side, and at once blood and water poured out.[1]

This is the blood that seals the covenant which the LORD made with you.[2]—The life of every living thing is in the blood, and that is why the LORD has commanded that all blood be poured out on the altar to take away the people's sins.[3]—The blood of bulls and goats can never take away sins.[4]

Jesus said, "This is my blood which is poured out for many, my blood which seals God's covenant."[5]—When Christ . . . entered once and for all into the Most Holy Place . . . he took his own blood and obtained eternal salvation for us.[6]—Peace through his Son's sacrificial death on the cross.[7]

You know what was paid to set you free . . . It was not something that can be destroyed, such as silver or gold; it was the costly sacrifice of Christ, who was like a lamb without defect or flaw.[8]

I will sprinkle clean water on you and make you clean from all your idols.[9]—Let us come near to God with a sincere heart and a sure faith, with hearts that have been purified from a guilty conscience and with bodies washed with clean water.[10]

[1]JOHN 19.34. [2]Exod. 24.8.—[3]Lev. 17.11.—[4]Heb. 10.4. [5]Mark 14.24.—[6]Heb. 9.12.—[7]Col. 1.20. [8]1 Pet. 1.18, 19. [9]Ezek. 36.25.—[10]Heb. 10.22.

Evening

Amen.[1]

It shall be done . . . and may the LORD your God confirm it.[2]—Whoever takes an oath will swear by the name of the Faithful God.[3]

When God made his promise to Abraham, he made a vow to do what he had promised. Since there was no one greater than himself, he used his own name when he made his vow. When a person makes a vow, he uses the name of someone greater than himself, and the vow settles all arguments. To those who were to receive what he promised, God wanted to make it very clear that he would never change his purpose; so he added his vow to the promise. There are these two things, then, that cannot change and about which God cannot lie. So we who have found safety with him are greatly encouraged to hold firmly to the hope placed before us.[4]

This is the message from the Amen, the faithful and true witness.[5]—It is he who is the "Yes" to all God's promises. This is why through Jesus Christ our "Amen" is said to the glory of God.[6]

Praise the LORD, the God of Israel! He alone does these wonderful things. Praise his glorious name for ever! Amen! Amen![7]

[1]MATT. 6.13. [2]1 Kgs 1.36.—[3]Isa. 65.16. [4]Heb. 6.13, 16–18. [5]Rev. 3.14.—[6]2 Cor. 1.20. [7]Ps. 72.18, 19.

The Lord will keep you safe. He will not let you fall into a trap.[1]

Men's anger only results in more praise for you; those who survive the wars will keep your festivals.[2]—The LORD controls the mind of a king as easily as he directs the course of a stream.[3]—When you please the LORD, you can make your enemies into friends.[4]

I wait eagerly for the LORD's help, and in his word I trust. I wait for the Lord more eagerly than watchmen wait for the dawn—than watchmen wait for the dawn.[5]—I prayed to the LORD, and he answered me; he freed me from all my fears.[6]

God has always been your defence; his eternal arms are your support. He drove out your enemies as you advanced, and told you to destroy them all.[7]—I will bless the person who puts his trust in me.[8]

In view of all this, what can we say? If God is for us, who can be against us?[9]

[1]PROV. 3.26. [2]Ps. 76.10.—[3]Prov. 21.1.—[4]Prov. 16.7. [5]Ps. 130.5, 6.—[6]Ps. 34.4. [7]Deut. 33.27.—[8]Jer. 17.7. [9]Rom. 8.31.

Evening

Your life in Christ makes you strong, and his love comforts you. You have fellowship with the Spirit.[1]

We are all born weak and helpless. All lead the same short, troubled life. We grow and wither as quickly as flowers; we disappear like shadows.[2]—My mind and my body may grow weak, but God is my strength; he is all I ever need.[3]

The Father . . . will give you another Helper, who will stay with you for ever. The Holy Spirit, whom the Father will send in my name.[4]—Let us give thanks to the God and Father of our Lord Jesus Christ, the merciful Father, the God from whom all help comes! He helps us in all our troubles, so that we are able to help others who have all kinds of troubles, using the same help that we ourselves have received from God.[5]

We believe that Jesus died and rose again, and so we believe that God will take back with Jesus those who have died believing in him. And so we will always be with the Lord. So then, encourage one another with these words.[6]

[1]PHIL. 2.1. [2]Job 14.1, 2.—[3]Ps. 73.26. [4]John 14.16, 26.—[5]2 Cor. 1.3, 4. [6]1 Thess. 4.14, 17, 18.

Morning

My inner being delights in the law of God.[1]

How I love your law! I think about it all day long.[2]—You spoke to me, and I listened to every word. Your words filled my heart with joy and happiness.[3]—I love to sit in its shadow, and its fruit is sweet to my taste.[4]—I always do what God commands; I follow his will, not my own desires.[5]

How I love to do your will, my God! I keep your teaching in my heart.[6]—My food . . . is to obey the will of the one who sent me and to finish the work he gave me to do.[7]

The laws of the LORD are right, and those who obey them are happy. The commands of the LORD are just and give understanding to the mind. They are more desirable than the finest gold; they are sweeter than the purest honey.[8]—Do not deceive yourselves by just listening to his word; instead, put it into practice. Whoever listens to the word but does not put it into practice is like a man who looks in a mirror and sees himself as he is.[9]

[1]ROM. 7.22. [2]Ps. 119.97.—[3]Jer. 15.16.—[4]S. of S. 2.3.—[5]Job 23.12. [6]Ps. 40.8.—[7]John 4.34. [8]Ps. 19.8, 10.—[9]Jas 1.22, 23.

Evening

May the LORD your God accept your offering.[1]

What shall I bring to the LORD, the God of heaven, when I come to worship him? Shall I bring the best calves to burn as offerings to him? Will the LORD be pleased if I bring him thousands of sheep or endless streams of olive-oil? Shall I offer him my first-born child to pay for my sins? No, the LORD has told us what is good. What he requires of us is this: to do what is just, to show constant love, and to live in humble fellowship with our God.[2]

All of us have been sinful; even our best actions are filthy through and through.[3]—There is no one who is righteous . . . everyone has sinned and is far away from God's saving presence. But by the free gift of God's grace all are put right with him through Christ Jesus, who sets them free. God offered him, so that by his sacrificial death he should become the means by which people's sins are forgiven through their faith in him. God did this to demonstrate his righteousness. In this way God shows that he himself is righteous and that he puts right everyone who believes in Jesus.[4]

The free gift he gave us in his dear Son.[5]—You have been given full life in union with him.[6]

[1]2 SAM. 24.23. [2]Mic. 6.6–8. [3]Isa. 64.6.—[4]Rom. 3.10, 23–26. [5]Eph. 1.6.—[6]Col. 2.10.

Out of the fullness of his grace he has blessed us all, giving us one blessing after another.[1]

This is my own dear Son, with whom I am pleased.[2]—See how much the Father has loved us! His love is so great that we are called God's children.[3]

His Son . . . is the one whom God has chosen to possess all things at the end.[4]—Since we are his children, we will possess the blessings he keeps for his people, and we will also possess with Christ what God has kept for him; for if we share Christ's suffering, we will also share his glory.[5]

The Father and I are one. The Father is in me and . . . I am in the Father.[6]—My Father and their Father, my God and their God.[7]—I in them and you in me, so that they may be completely one.[8]

The church is Christ's body, the completion of him who himself completes all things everywhere.[9]

All these promises are made to us, my dear friends. So then, let us purify ourselves from everything that makes body or soul unclean, and let us be completely holy by living in awe of God.[10]

[1]JOHN 1.16. [2]Matt. 17.5.—[3]1 John 3.1. [4]Heb. 1.2.—[5]Rom. 8.17. [6]John 10.30, 38.—[7]John 20.17.—[8]John 17.23. [9]Eph. 1.23. [10]2 Cor. 7.1.

Evening

No slave is greater than his master, and no messenger is greater than the one who sent him.[1]

An argument broke out among the disciples as to which one of them should be thought of as the greatest. Jesus said to them, "The kings of the pagans have power over their people, and the rulers claim the title 'Friends of the People'. But this is not the way it is with you; rather, the greatest one among you must be like the youngest, and the leader must be like the servant. Who is greater, the one who sits down to eat or the one who serves him? The one who sits down, of course. But I am among you as one who serves."[2]—The Son of Man. who did not come to be served, but to serve and to give his life to redeem many people.[3]

[Jesus] rose from the table, took off his outer garment and tied a towel round his waist. Then he poured some water into a basin and began to wash the disciples' feet and dry them with the towel round his waist.[4]

[1]JOHN 13.16. [2]Luke 22.24–27.—[3]Matt. 20.28. [4]John 13.3–5.

Morning

I have complete confidence, O God![1]

The LORD is my light and my salvation; I will fear no one. The LORD protects me from all danger; I will never be afraid.[2]

You, LORD, give perfect peace to those who keep their purpose firm and put their trust in you.[3]—He is not afraid of receiving bad news; his faith is strong, and he trusts in the LORD. He is not worried or afraid; he is certain to see his enemies defeated.[4]

When I am afraid, O LORD Almighty, I put my trust in you.[5]—In times of trouble he will shelter me; he will keep me safe in his Temple and make me secure on a high rock. So I will triumph over my enemies around me. With shouts of joy I will offer sacrifices in his Temple; I will sing, I will praise the LORD.[6]

After you have suffered for a little while, the God of all grace, who calls you to share his eternal glory in union with Christ, will himself perfect you and give you firmness, strength, and a sure foundation. To him be the power for ever![7]

[1]PS. 108.1. [2]Ps. 27.1. [3]Isa. 26.3.—[4]Ps. 112.7, 8. [5]Ps. 56.3.—[6]Ps. 27.5, 6. [7]1 Pet. 5.10, 11.

Evening

The LORD placed his throne in heaven; he is king over all.[1]

Men cast lots to learn God's will, but God himself determines the answer.[2]—Does disaster strike a city unless the LORD sends it?[3]

I am the LORD; there is no other god. I will give you the strength you need, although you do not know me. I do this so that everyone from one end of the world to the other may know that I am the LORD and that there is no other god. I create both light and darkness; I bring both blessing and disaster. I, the LORD, do all these things.[4]

He looks on the people of the earth as nothing; angels in heaven and people on earth are under his control. No one can oppose his will or question what he does.[5]—If God is for us, who can be against us?[6]

Christ must rule until God defeats all enemies and puts them under his feet.[7]—Do not be afraid, little flock, for your Father is pleased to give you the Kingdom.[8]

[1]PS. 103.19. [2]Prov. 16.33.—[3]Amos 3.6. [4]Isa. 45.5–7. [5]Dan. 4.35.—[6]Rom. 8.31. [7]1 Cor. 15.25.—[8]Luke 12.32.

A person's true life is not made up of the things he owns, no matter how rich he may be.[1]

The little that a good man owns is worth more than the wealth of all the wicked.[2]—Better to be poor and fear the LORD than to be rich and in trouble.[3]—Religion does make a person very rich, if he is satisfied with what he has. If we have food and clothes, that should be enough for us.[4]

Let me be neither rich nor poor. So give me only as much food as I need. If I have more, I might say that I do not need you. But if I am poor, I might steal and bring disgrace on my God.[5]—Give us today the food we need.[6]

I tell you not to be worried about the food and drink you need in order to stay alive, or about clothes for your body. After all, isn't life worth more than food? And isn't the body worth more than clothes?[7]—"When I sent you out that time without purse, bag, or shoes, did you lack anything?" "Not a thing," they answered.[8]—Keep your lives free from the love of money, and be satisfied with what you have. For God has said, "I will never leave you; I will never abandon you."[9]

[1]LUKE 12.15. [2]Ps. 37.16.—[3]Prov. 15.16.—[4]1 Tim. 6.6, 8. [5]Prov. 30.8, 9.—[6]Matt. 6.11. [7]Matt. 6.25.—[8]Luke 22.35.—[9]Heb. 13.5.

Evening

What gives life is God's Spirit.[1]

The first man, Adam, was created a living being; but the last Adam is the life-giving Spirit.[2]—A person is born physically of human parents, but he is born spiritually of the Spirit.[3]—It was not because of any good deeds that we ourselves had done, but because of his own mercy that he saved us, through the Holy Spirit, who gives us new birth and new life by washing us.[4]

Whoever does not have the Spirit of Christ does not belong to him. But if Christ lives in you, the Spirit is life for you because you have been put right with God, even though your bodies are going to die because of sin. If the Spirit of God, who raised Jesus from death, lives in you, then he who raised Christ from death will also give life to your mortal bodies by the presence of his Spirit in you.[5]

It is no longer I who live, but it is Christ who lives in me. This life that I live now, I live by faith in the Son of God, who loved me and gave his life for me.[6]—Think of yourselves as dead, so far as sin is concerned, but living in fellowship with God through Christ Jesus.[7]

[1]JOHN 6.63. [2]1 Cor. 15.45.—[3]John 3.6.—[4]Titus 3.5. [5]Rom. 8.9–11. [6]Gal. 2.20.—[7]Rom. 6.11.

I thought I had been banished from your presence and would never see your holy Temple again.[1]

The people of Jerusalem said, "The LORD has abandoned us! He has forgotten us." So the LORD answers, "Can a woman forget her own baby and not love the child she bore? Even if a mother should forget her child, I will never forget you."[2]

I have forgotten what health and peace and happiness are. I have not much longer to live; my hope in the LORD is gone.[3]—Wake up, Lord! Why are you asleep? Rouse yourself! Don't reject us for ever![4]—Israel, why . . . do you complain that the LORD doesn't know your troubles or care if you suffer injustice?[5]—"I turned away angry for only a moment, but I will show you my love for ever." So says the LORD who saves you.[6]

Why am I so sad? Why am I so troubled? I will put my hope in God, and once again I will praise him, my saviour and my God.[7]—We are often troubled, but not crushed; sometimes in doubt, but never in despair; there are many enemies, but we are never without a friend; and though badly hurt at times, we are not destroyed.[8]

[1]JONAH 2.4. [2]Isa. 49.14, 15. [3]Lam. 3.17, 18.—[4]Ps. 44.23.—[5]Isa. 40.27.—[6]Isa. 54.8. [7]Ps. 43.5.—[8]2 Cor. 4.8, 9.

Evening

When my people in their need look for water, when their throats are dry with thirst, then I, the LORD, will answer their prayer.[1]

There are many who pray: "Give us more blessings, O LORD."[2]—You work and worry your way through life, and what do you have to show for it? As long as you live, everything you do brings nothing but worry and heartache. Even at night your mind can't rest. It is all useless. It had all been useless; I had been chasing the wind.[3]

They have turned away from me, the spring of fresh water, and they have dug cisterns, cracked cisterns that can hold no water at all.[4]

I will never turn away anyone who comes to me.[5]—I will give water to the thirsty land.[6]—Happy are those whose greatest desire is to do what God requires; God will satisfy them fully![7]

O God, you are my God, and I long for you. My whole being desires you; like a dry, worn-out, and waterless land, my soul is thirsty for you.[8]

[1]ISA. 41.17. [2]Ps. 4.6.—[3]Eccles. 2.22, 23, 17. [4]Jer. 2.13. [5]John 6.37.—[6]Isa. 44.3.— [7]Matt. 5.6. [8] Ps. 63.1.

I will be with you always, to the end of the age.[1]

Whenever two of you on earth agree about anything you pray for, it will be done for you by my Father in heaven. For where two or three come together in my name, I am there with them.[2]—Whoever accepts my commandments and obeys them is the one who loves me. My Father will love whoever loves me; I too will love him and reveal myself to him.[3]

"Lord, how can it be that you will reveal yourself to us and not to the world?" "Whoever loves me will obey my teaching. My Father will love him, and my Father and I will come to him and live with him."[4]

To him who is able to keep you from falling, and to bring you faultless and joyful before his glorious presence—to the only God our Saviour, through Jesus Christ our Lord, be glory, majesty, might, and authority, from all ages past, and now, and for ever and ever! Amen.[5]

[1]MATT. 28.20. [2]Matt. 18.19, 20.—[3]John 14.21. [4]John 14.22, 23. [5]Jude 24, 25.

Evening

The end of all things is near.[1]

Then I saw a great white throne and the one who sits on it. Earth and heaven fled from his presence and were seen no more.[2]—The heavens and the earth that now exist are being preserved . . . in order to be destroyed by fire. They are being kept for the day when godless people will be judged and destroyed.[3]

God is our shelter and strength, always ready to help in times of trouble. So we will not be afraid, even if the earth is shaken and mountains fall into the ocean depths; even if the seas roar and rage, and the hills are shaken by the violence.[4]—You are going to hear the noise of battles close by and the news of battles far away; but do not be troubled.[5]

God will have a house in heaven for us to live in, a home he himself has made, which will last for ever.[6]—We wait for what God has promised: new heavens and a new earth, where righteousness will be at home. And so, my friends, as you wait for that Day, do your best to be pure and faultless in God's sight and to be at peace with him.[7]

[1]1 PET. 4.7. [2]Rev. 20.11.—[3]2 Pet. 3.7. [4]Ps. 46.1–3.—[5]Matt. 24.6. [6]2 Cor. 5.1.—[7]2 Pet. 3.13, 14.

The Lord *is king.*[1]

I am the Lord; why don't you fear me? Why don't you tremble before me? I placed the sand as the boundary of the sea, a permanent boundary that it cannot cross. The sea may toss, but it cannot go beyond it; the waves may roar, but they cannot break through.[2]—Judgement does not come from the east or from the west, from the north or from the south; it is God who is the judge, condemning some and acquitting others.[3]

He controls the times and the seasons; he makes and unmakes kings; it is he who gives wisdom and understanding.[4]—You are going to hear the noise of battles close by and the news of battles far away; but do not be troubled.[5]

If God is for us, who can be against us?[6]—For only a penny you can buy two sparrows, yet not one sparrow falls to the ground without your Father's consent. As for you, even the hairs of your head have all been counted. So do not be afraid; you are worth much more than many sparrows![7]

[1]PS. 99.1. [2]Jer. 5.22.—[3]Ps. 75.6, 7. [4]Dan. 2.21.—[5]Matt. 24.6. [6]Rom. 8.31.—[7]Matt. 10.29–31.

Evening

Make sure that none of you breaks his promise.[1]

"Master, we saw a man driving out demons in your name, and we told him to stop, because he doesn't belong to our group." "Do not try to stop him," Jesus said to him . . . "because whoever is not against you is for you." "Lord, do you want us to call fire down from heaven to destroy them?" Jesus . . . rebuked them and said, "You don't know what kind of a Spirit you belong to."[2]

Eldad and Medad . . . began to shout like prophets. Then Joshua son of Nun . . . said to Moses, "Stop them, sir!" Moses answered, "Are you concerned about my interests? I wish that the Lord would give his spirit to all his people and make all of them shout like prophets!"[3]

The Spirit produces love, joy, peace, patience, kindness, goodness, faithfulness, humility, and self-control . . . Those who belong to Christ Jesus have put to death their human nature with all its passions and desires. The Spirit has given us life; he must also control our lives. We must not be proud or irritate one another or be jealous of one another.[4]

[1]MAL. 2.15. [2]Luke 9.49, 50, 54, 55. [3]Num. 11.26, 28, 29. [4]Gal. 5.22–26.

He himself took our sickness and carried away our diseases.[1]

The priest shall order two ritually clean birds to be brought, together with a piece of cedar-wood, a red cord, and a sprig of hyssop. Then the priest shall order one of the birds to be killed over a clay bowl containing fresh spring water. He shall take the other bird and dip it, together with the cedar-wood, the red cord, and the hyssop, in the blood of the bird that was killed. He shall sprinkle the blood seven times on the person who is to be purified from his skin-disease, and then he shall pronounce him clean. He shall let the live bird fly away over the open fields.[2]

There was a man who was suffering from a dreaded skin-disease. When he saw Jesus, he threw himself down and begged him, "Sir, if you want to, you can make me clean!"[3]—Jesus was filled with pity, and stretched out his hand and touched him. "I do want to," he answered. "Be clean!" At once the disease left the man, and he was clean.[4]

[1]MATT. 8.17. [2]Lev. 14.4–7. [3]Luke 5.12.—[4]Mark 1.41, 42.

Evening

When you pronounce a blessing, people are blessed.[1]

Happy are those who know they are spiritually poor; the Kingdom of heaven belongs to them!

Happy are those who mourn; God will comfort them! Happy are those who are humble; they will receive what God has promised! Happy are those whose greatest desire is to do what God requires; God will satisfy them fully! Happy are those who are merciful to others; God will be merciful to them! Happy are the pure in heart; they will see God! Happy are those who work for peace; God will call them his children! Happy are those who are persecuted because they do what God requires; the Kingdom of heaven belongs to them! Happy are you when people insult you and persecute you and tell all kinds of evil lies against you because you are my followers. Be happy and glad, for a great reward is kept for you in heaven.[2]—Happy are those who hear the word of God and obey it![3]

Happy are those who wash their robes clean and so have the right to eat the fruit from the tree of life and to go through the gates into the city.[4]

[1]NUM. 22.6. [2]Matt. 5.3–12.—[3]Luke 11.28. [4]Rev. 22.14.

He is astonished to see that there is no one to help the oppressed. So he will use his own power to rescue them.[1]

You do not want sacrifices and offerings; you do not ask for animals burnt whole on the altar or for sacrifices to take away sins. Instead, you have given me ears to hear you, and so I answered, "Here I am; your instructions for me are in the book of the Law. How I love to do your will, my God! I keep your teaching in my heart."[2]—I am willing to give up my life, in order that I may receive it back again. No one takes my life away from me. I give it up of my own free will. I have the right to give it up, and I have the right to take it back.[3]

I, the LORD, the God who saves his people. There is no other god. Turn to me now and be saved, people all over the world! I am the only God there is.[4]—In all the world there is no one else whom God has given who can save us.[5]

You know the grace of our Lord Jesus Christ; rich as he was, he made himself poor for your sake, in order to make you rich by means of his poverty.[6]

[1]ISA. 59.16. [2]Ps. 40.6–8. —[3]John 10.17, 18. [4]Isa. 45.21, 22.—[5]Acts 4.12. [6]2 Cor. 8.9.

Evening

The Enemy.[1]

Be alert, be on the watch! Your enemy, the Devil, roams round like a roaring lion, looking for someone to devour.[2]—Resist the Devil, and he will run away from you.[3]

Put on all the armour that God gives you, so that you will be able to stand up against the Devil's evil tricks. For we are not fighting against human beings but against the wicked spiritual forces in the heavenly world, the rulers, authorities, and cosmic powers of this dark age. So put on God's armour now! Then when the evil day comes, you will be able to resist the enemy's attacks; and after fighting to the end, you will still hold your ground. So stand ready, with truth as a belt tight round your waist, with righteousness as your breastplate, and as your shoes the readiness to announce the Good News of peace. At all times carry faith as a shield; for with it you will be able to put out all the burning arrows shot by the Evil One.[4]

Our enemies have no reason to gloat over us. We have fallen, but we will rise again. We are in darkness now, but the LORD will give us light.[5]

[1]LUKE 10.19. [2]1 Pet. 5.8.—[3]Jas 4.7. [4]Eph. 6.11–16. [5]Mic. 7.8.

Everything about him enchants me. [1]

May he be pleased with my song.[2]—My lover . . . is one in ten thousand.[3]—I chose a valuable stone, which I am placing as the cornerstone . . . and whoever believes in him will never be disappointed.[4]—You are the most handsome of men; you are an eloquent speaker.[5]—God raised him to the highest place above and gave him the name that is greater than any other name.[6]—It was by God's own decision that the Son has in himself the full nature of God.[7]

You love him, although you have not seen him, and you believe in him, although you do not now see him. So you rejoice with a great and glorious joy which words cannot express.[8]

I reckon everything as complete loss for the sake of what is so much more valuable, the knowledge of Christ Jesus my Lord. For his sake I have thrown everything away; I consider it all as mere refuse, so that I may gain Christ and be completely united with him. I no longer have a righteousness of my own, the kind that is gained by obeying the Law. I now have the righteousness that is given through faith in Christ, the righteousness that comes from God and is based on faith.[9]

[1]S. of S. 5.16. [2]Ps. 104.34.—[3]S. of S. 5.10.—[4]1 Pet. 2.6.—[5]Ps. 45.2.—[6]Phil. 2.9.—[7]Col. 1.19. [8]1 Pet. 1.8. [9]Phil. 3.8, 9.

Evening

The Lord his God gave [David] courage. [1]

Lord, to whom would we go? You have the words that give eternal life.[2]—I know whom I have trusted, and I am sure that he is able to keep safe until that Day what he has entrusted to me.[3]

In my trouble I called to the LORD; I called to my God for help. In his temple he heard my voice; he listened to my cry for help. When I was in trouble, they attacked me, but the LORD protected me. He helped me out of danger; he saved me because he was pleased with me.[4]

I will always thank the LORD; I will never stop praising him. I will praise him for what he has done; may all who are oppressed listen and be glad! Proclaim with me the LORD's greatness; let us praise his name together! I prayed to the LORD, and he answered me; he freed me from all my fears. Find out for yourself how good the LORD is. Happy are those who find safety with him.[5]

[1]1 SAM. 30.6. [2]John 6.68.—[3]2 Tim. 1.12. [4]Ps. 18.6, 18, 19. [5]Ps. 34.1–4, 8.

Morning

It is best for us to wait in patience—to wait for him to save us.[1]

Has God forgotten to be merciful? Has anger taken the place of his compassion?[2]—I was afraid and thought that he had driven me out of his presence. But he heard my cry, when I called to him for help.[3]

Will God not judge in favour of his own people who cry to him day and night for help? Will he be slow to help them? I tell you, he will judge in their favour and do it quickly.[4]—Trust the LORD and he will make it right.[5]—Be patient and wait for the LORD to act; don't be worried about those who prosper or those who succeed in their evil plans.[6]

You will not have to fight this battle. Just take up your positions and wait; you will see the LORD give you victory.[7]

Let us not become tired of doing good; for if we do not give up, the time will come when we will reap the harvest.[8]—See how patient a farmer is as he waits for his land to produce precious crops. He waits patiently for the autumn and spring rains.[9]

[1]LAM. 3.26. [2]Ps. 77.9.—[3]Ps. 31.22. [4]Luke 18.7, 8.—[5]Prov. 20.22.—[6]Ps. 37.7. [7]2 Chr. 20.17. [8]Gal. 6.9.—[9]Jas 5.7.

Evening

Catch the foxes, the little foxes, before they ruin our vineyard in bloom.[1]

No one can see his own errors; deliver me, LORD, from hidden faults![2]—Guard against turning back from the grace of God. Let no one become like a bitter plant that grows up and causes many troubles with its poison.[3]—You were doing so well! Who made you stop obeying the truth? How did he persuade you?[4]

I am sure that God, who began this good work in you, will carry it on until it is finished on the Day of Christ Jesus. The important thing is that your way of life should be as the gospel of Christ requires.[5]—The tongue: small as it is, it can boast about great things. Just think how large a forest can be set on fire by a tiny flame! And the tongue is like a fire. It is a world of wrong, occupying its place in our bodies and spreading evil through our whole being. It sets on fire the entire course of our existence with the fire that comes to it from hell itself. No one has ever been able to tame the tongue. It is evil and uncontrollable, full of deadly poison.[6]—Your speech should always be pleasant and interesting, and you should know how to give the right answer to everyone.[7]

[1]S. OF S. 2.15. [2]Ps. 19.12.—[3]Heb. 12.15.—[4]Gal. 5.7. [5]Phil. 1.6, 27.—[6]Jas 3.5, 6, 8.—[7]Col. 4.6.

***This message from the LORD: "You will succeed, not by military might or by your own strength, but by my spirit."*[1]**

Can anyone tell the LORD what to do? Who can teach him or give him advice?[2]

God purposely chose what the world considers nonsense in order to shame the wise, and he chose what the world considers weak in order to shame the powerful. He chose what the world looks down on and despises, and thinks is nothing, in order to destroy what the world thinks is important. This means that no one can boast in God's presence.[3]

The wind blows wherever it wishes; you hear the sound it makes, but you do not know where it comes from or where it is going. It is like that with everyone who is born of the Spirit.[4]—They did not become God's children by natural means, that is, by being born as the children of a human father; God himself was their Father.[5]

I am still with you, so do not be afraid.[6]—The battle depends on God, not on you.[7]

The LORD does not need swords or spears to save his people. He is victorious in battle.[8]

[1]ZECH. 4.6. [2]Isa. 40.13.—[3]1 Cor. 1.27–29. [4]John 3.8.—[5]John 1.13. [6]Hag. 2.5.—[7]2 Chr. 20.15. [8]1 Sam. 17.47.

Evening

***Do what you said you would.*[1]**

Keep your promise to me, your servant—the promise you make to those who obey you. Then I can answer those who insult me because I trust in your word. Remember your promise to me, your servant; it has given me hope. During my brief earthly life I compose songs about your commands.[2]

The law that you gave means more to me than all the money in the world. Your word, O LORD, will last for ever; it is eternal in heaven. Your faithfulness endures through all the ages.[3]

To those who were to receive what he promised, God wanted to make it very clear that he would never change his purpose; so he added his vow to the promise. There are these two things, then, that cannot change and about which God cannot lie. So we who have found safety with him are greatly encouraged to hold firmly to the hope placed before us. We have this hope as an anchor for our lives. It is safe and sure, and goes through the curtain of the heavenly temple into the inner sanctuary. On our behalf Jesus has gone in there before us.[4]

The very great and precious gifts he promised.[5]

[1]2 SAM. 7.25. [2]Ps. 119.38, 42, 49, 54. [3]Ps. 119.72, 89, 90. [4]Heb. 6.17–20. [5]2 Pet. 1.4.

The man who listens to me will be happy—the man who stays at my door every day, waiting at the entrance to my home.[1]

As a servant depends on his master, as a maid depends on her mistress, so we will keep looking to you, O LORD our God, until you have mercy on us.[2]

For all time to come, this burnt-offering is to be offered in my presence at the entrance of the Tent of my presence. That is where I will meet my people and speak to you.[3]—In every place that I set aside for you to worship me, I will come to you and bless you.[4]

Where two or three come together in my name, I am there with them.[5]

The time is coming and is already here, when by the power of God's Spirit people will worship the Father as he really is, offering him the true worship that he wants. God is Spirit, and only by the power of his Spirit can people worship him as he really is.[6]

Pray on every occasion, as the Spirit leads.[7]—Pray at all times.[8]

[1]PROV. 8.34. [2]Ps. 123.2. [3]Exod. 29.42.—[4]Exod. 20.24. [5]Matt. 18.20. [6]John 4.23, 24. [7]Eph. 6.18.—[8]1 Thess. 5.17.

Evening

He will be called "Wonderful Counsellor".[1]

The spirit of the LORD will give him wisdom, and the knowledge and skill to rule his people. He will know the LORD's will and have reverence for him, and find pleasure in obeying him.[2]

Listen! Wisdom is calling out. Reason is making herself heard. "I appeal to you, mankind; I call to everyone on earth. Are you immature? Learn to be mature. Are you foolish? Learn to have sense. Listen to my excellent words; all I tell you is right. I make plans and carry them out. I have understanding, and I am strong."[3]

All this wisdom comes from the LORD Almighty. The plans God makes are wise, and they always succeed![4]—If any of you lacks wisdom, he should pray to God, who will give it to him; because God gives generously and graciously to all.[5]—Trust in the LORD with all your heart. Never rely on what you think you know. Remember the LORD in everything you do, and he will show you the right way.[6]

[1]ISA. 9.6. [2]Isa. 11.2, 3. [3]Prov. 8.1, 4–6, 14. [4]Isa. 28.29.—[5]Jas 1.5.—[6]Prov. 3.5, 6.

At all times make it your aim to do good.[1]

It was to this that God called you, for Christ himself suffered for you and left you an example, so that you would follow in his steps. He committed no sin, and no one ever heard a lie come from his lips. When he was insulted, he did not answer back with an insult; when he suffered, he did not threaten, but placed his hopes in God, the righteous Judge.[2]—Think of what he went through; how he put up with so much hatred from sinners! So do not let yourselves become discouraged and give up.[3]

Let us rid ourselves of everything that gets in the way, and of the sin which holds on to us so tightly, and let us run wth determination the race that lies before us. Let us keep our eyes fixed on Jesus, on whom our faith depends from beginning to end. He did not give up because of the cross! On the contrary, because of the joy that was waiting for him, he thought nothing of the disgrace of dying on the cross, and he is now seated at the right-hand side of God's throne.[4]

In conclusion, my brothers, fill your minds with those things that are good and that deserve praise: things that are true, noble, right, pure, lovely, and honourable.[5]

[1]1 THESS. 5.15. [2]1 Pet. 2.21–23.—[3]Heb. 12.3. [4]Heb. 12.1, 2. [5]Phil. 4.8.

Evening

Mighty God.[1]

You are the most handsome of men; you are an eloquent speaker. God has always blessed you. Buckle on your sword, mighty king; you are glorious and majestic. Ride on in majesty to victory. The kingdom that God has given you will last for ever and ever. You rule over your people with justice.[2]—In a vision long ago you said to your faithful servants, "I have given help to a famous soldier."[3]—The LORD Almighty says . . . "The shepherd who works for me!"[4]

God is my saviour; I will trust him and not be afraid. The LORD gives me power and strength; he is my saviour.[5]—Thanks be to God! For in union with Christ we are always led by God as prisoners in Christ's victory procession.[6]

To him who is able to keep you from falling, and to bring you faultless and joyful before his glorious presence—to the only God our Saviour, through Jesus Christ our Lord, be glory, majesty, might, and authority, from all ages past, and now, and for ever and ever![7]

[1]ISA. 9.6. [2]Ps. 45.2–4, 6.—[3]Ps. 89.19.—[4]Zech. 13.7. [5]Isa. 12.2.—[6]2 Cor. 2.14. [7]Jude 24, 25.

The LORD's ways are right, and righteous people live by following them, but sinners stumble and fall because they ignore them.[1]

This stone is of great value for you that believe; but for those who do not believe . . . "This is the stone that will make people stumble, the rock that will make them fall."[2]—The LORD protects honest people, but destroys those who do wrong.[3]

Listen . . . if you have ears![4]—May those who are wise think about these things; may they consider the LORD's constant love.[5]—The eyes are like a lamp for the body. If your eyes are sound, your whole body will be full of light; but if your eyes are no good, your body will be in darkness.[6]—Whoever is willing to do what God wants will know whether what I teach comes from God or whether I speak on my own authority.[7]—The person who has something will be given more, so that he will have more than enough.[8]

He who comes from God listens to God's words. You, however, are not from God, and that is why you will not listen.[9]—You are not willing to come to me in order to have life.[10]—My sheep listen to my voice; I know them, and they follow me.[11]

[1]HOS. 14.9. [2]1 Pet. 2.7, 8.—[3]Prov. 10.29. [4]Matt. 11.15.—[5]Ps. 107.43.—[6]Matt. 6.22.—[7]John 7.17.—[8]Matt. 13.12. [9]John 8.47.—[10]John 5.40.—[11]John 10.27.

Evening

Eternal Father.[1]

Israel, remember this! The LORD—and the LORD alone—is our God.[2]

The Father and I are one. The Father is in me and . . . I am in the Father.[3]—If you knew me, you would know my Father also.[4]—Philip said to him, "Lord, show us the Father; that is all we need." Jesus answered, "For a long time I have been with you all; yet you do not know me, Philip? Whoever has seen me has seen the Father."[5]—Here I am with the children that God has given me.[6]—After a life of suffering, he will again have joy.[7]—"I am the first and the last," says the Lord God Almighty, who is, who was, and who is to come.[8]

Before Abraham was born, 'I Am.'[9]—God said, "I am who I am. This is what you must say to them: 'The one who is called I AM has sent me to you.' "[10]

About the Son . . . God said: "Your kingdom, O God, will last for ever and ever!"[11]—Christ existed before all things, and in union with him all things have their proper place.[12]

[1]ISA. 9.6. [2]Deut. 6.4. [3]John 10.30, 38.—[4]John 8.19.—[5]John 14.8, 9.—[6]Heb. 2.13.—[7]Isa. 53.11.—[8]Rev. 1.8. [9]John 8.58.—[10]Exod. 3.14. [11]Heb. 1.8.—[12]Col. 1.17.

It may now be necessary for you to be sad for a while because of the many kinds of trials you suffer.[1]

My dear friends, do not be surprised at the painful test you are suffering, as though something unusual were happening to you. Rather be glad that you are sharing Christ's sufferings, so that you may be full of joy when his glory is revealed.[2]—The encouraging words which God speaks to you as his sons . . . "My son, pay attention when the Lord corrects you, and do not be discouraged when he rebukes you."[3]—When we are punished, it seems to us at the time something to make us sad, not glad. Later, however, those who have been disciplined by such punishment reap the peaceful reward of a righteous life.[4]

Our High Priest is not one who cannot feel sympathy for our weaknesses. On the contrary, [he] . . . was tempted in every way that we are, but did not sin.[5]—Now he can help those who are tempted, because he himself was tempted and suffered.[6]—God keeps his promise, and he will not allow you to be tested beyond your power to remain firm.[7]

[1]1 PET. 1.6. [2]1 Pet. 4.12, 13.—[3]Heb, 12,5,—[4]Heb. 12.11. [5]Heb. 4.15.— [6]Heb. 2.18.—[7]1 Cor. 10.13.

Evening

Prince of Peace.[1]

He will rule over your people with justice and govern the oppressed with righteousness. May the land enjoy prosperity; may it experience righteousness. May the king be like rain on the fields, like showers falling on the land. May righteousness flourish in his lifetime, and may prosperity last as long as the moon gives light.[2]—Glory to God . . . and peace on earth to those with whom he is pleased![3]

Our God is merciful and tender. He will cause the bright dawn of salvation to rise on us and to shine from heaven on all those who live in the dark shadow of death, to guide our steps into the path of peace.[4]

I have told you this so that you will have peace by being united to me. The world will make you suffer. But be brave! I have defeated the world![5]—Peace is what I leave with you; it is my own peace that I give you. I do not give it as the world does.[6]—God's peace, which is far beyond human understanding, will keep your hearts and minds safe in union with Christ Jesus.[7]

[1]ISA. 9.6. [2]Ps. 72.2, 3, 6, 7.—[3]Luke 2.14. [4]Luke 1.78, 79. [5]John 16.33.— [6]John 14.27.—[7]Phil. 4.7.

Take the finest spices . . . and make a sacred anointing oil.[1]

It must not be poured on ordinary men, and you must not use the same formula to make any mixture like it. It is holy, and you must treat it as holy.[2]—One Spirit.[3]—There are different kinds of spiritual gifts, but the same Spirit gives them.[4]

Your God . . . has poured out more happiness on you than on any other king.[5]—Jesus of Nazareth . . . God poured out on him the Holy Spirit and power.[6]—God gives him the fullness of his Spirit.[7]

Out of the fullness of his grace he has blessed us all.[8]—His Spirit teaches you about everything, and what he teaches is true, not false. Obey the Spirit's teaching, then, and remain in union with Christ.[9]—It is God himself who has set us apart, who has placed his mark of ownership upon us, and who has given us the Holy Spirit in our hearts as the guarantee of all that he has in store for us.[10]

The Spirit produces love, joy, peace, patience, kindness, goodness, faithfulness, humility, and self-control. There is no law against such things as these.[11]

[1]EXOD. 30.23, 25. [2]Exod. 30.32.—[3]Eph. 4.4.—[4]1 Cor. 12.4. [5]Ps. 45.7.—[6]Acts 10.38.—[7]John 3.34. [8]John 1.16.—[9]1 John 2.27.—[10]2 Cor. 1.21, 22. [11]Gal. 5.22, 23.

Evening

This world, as it is now, will not last much longer.[1]

Methuselah . . . died at the age of 969.[2]

The Christian who is poor must be glad when God lifts him up, and the rich Christian must be glad when God brings him down. For the rich will pass away like the flower of a wild plant. The sun rises with its blazing heat and burns the plant; its flower falls off, and its beauty is destroyed. In the same way the rich man will be destroyed while he goes about his business.[3]—You don't even know what your life tomorrow will be! You are like a puff of smoke, which appears for a moment and then disappears.[4]

LORD, how long will I live? When will I die? Tell me how soon my life will end.[5]—When people say, "Everything is quiet and safe," then suddenly destruction will hit them! It will come as suddenly as the pains that come upon a woman in labour, and people will not escape. But you, brothers, are not in the darkness, and the Day should not take you by surprise like a thief.[6]

[1]1 COR. 7.31. [2]Gen. 5.25, 27. [3]Jas 1.9–11.—[4]Jas 4.14. [5]Ps. 39.4.—[6]1 Thess. 5.3, 4.

Morning

Your real life is Christ and when he appears, then you too will appear with him and share his glory![1]

I am the resurrection and the life. Whoever believes in me will live, even though he dies.[2]—God has given us eternal life, and this life has its source in his Son. Whoever has the Son has this life; whoever does not have the Son of God does not have life.[3]

There will be the shout of command, the archangel's voice, the sound of God's trumpet, and the Lord himself will come down from heaven. Those who have died believing in Christ will rise to life first; then we who are living at that time will be gathered up along with them in the clouds to meet the Lord in the air. And so we will always be with the Lord. So then, encourage one another with these words.[4]—When Christ appears, we shall be like him, because we shall see him as he really is.[5]—When buried, it is ugly and weak; when raised, it will be beautiful and strong.[6]

After I go and prepare a place for you, I will come back and take you to myself, so that you will be where I am.[7]

[1]COL. 3.4. [2]John 11.25.—[3]1 John 5.11, 12. [4]1 Thess. 4.16–18.—[5]1 John 3.2.—[6]1 Cor. 15.43. [7]John 14.3.

Evening

Teach me to live according to your truth.[1]

When . . . the Spirit comes, who reveals the truth about God, he will lead you into all the truth.[2]—You have had the Holy Spirit poured out on you by Christ, and so all of you know the truth.[3]

Listen to what the LORD is teaching you! Don't listen to mediums—what they tell you will do you no good.[4]—All Scripture is inspired by God and is useful for teaching the truth, rebuking error, correcting faults, and giving instruction for right living, so that the person who serves God may be fully qualified and equipped to do every kind of good deed.[5]—The Holy Scriptures . . . are able to give you the wisdom that leads to salvation through faith in Christ Jesus.[6]

I will teach you the way you should go; I will instruct you and advise you.[7]—The eyes are like a lamp for the body. If your eyes are sound, your whole body will be full of light.[8]—Whoever is willing to do what God wants will know whether what I teach comes from God.[9]—No fools will mislead those who follow [that road].[10]

[1]PS. 25.5. [2]John 16.13.—[3]1 John 2.20. [4]Isa. 8.20.—[5]2 Tim. 3.16, 17.—[6]2 Tim. 3.15. [7]Ps. 32.8.—[8]Matt. 6.22.—[9]John 7.17.—[10]Isa. 35.8.

Morning

They must thank the LORD for his constant love, for the wonderful things he did for them.[1]

Find out for yourself how good the LORD is. Happy are those who find safety with him.[2]—How wonderful are the good things you keep for those who honour you![3]

They are the people I made for myself, and they will sing my praises![4]—God had already decided that through Jesus Christ he would make us his sons—this was his pleasure and purpose. Let us praise God for his glorious grace, for the free gift he gave us in his dear Son! Let us, then, who were the first to hope in Christ, praise God's glory![5]

How good and beautiful [his] land will be![6]—He is good to everyone and has compassion on all he made. All your creatures, LORD, will praise you, and all your people will give you thanks. They will speak of the glory of your royal power and tell of your might, so that everyone will know your mighty deeds and the glorious majesty of your kingdom.[7]

[1]PS. 107.8. [2]Ps. 34.8.—[3]Ps. 31.19. [4]Isa. 43.21.—[5]Eph. 1.5, 6, 12. [6]Zech. 9.17.—[7]Ps. 145.9–12.

Evening

We call them happy because they endured.[1]

We also boast of our troubles, because we know that trouble produces endurance, endurance brings God's approval, and his approval creates hope. This hope does not disappoint us, for God has poured out his love into our hearts by means of the Holy Spirit, who is God's gift to us.[2]—When we are punished, it seems to us at the time something to make us sad, not glad. Later, however, those who have been disciplined by such punishment reap the peaceful reward of a righteous life.[3]—My brothers, consider yourselves fortunate when all kinds of trials come your way, for you know that when your faith succeeds in facing such trials, the result is the ability to endure. Make sure that your endurance carries you all the way without failing, so that you may be perfect and complete, lacking nothing.[4]—Happy is the person who remains faithful under trials, because when he succeeds in passing such a test, he will receive as his reward the life which God has promised to those who love him.[5]—I am most happy . . . to be proud of my weaknesses, in order to feel the protection of Christ's power over me. For when I am weak, then I am strong.[6]

[1]JAS 5.11. [2]Rom. 5.3–5.—[3]Heb. 12.11.—[4]Jas 1.2–4.—[5]Jas 1.12.—[6]2 Cor. 12.9, 10.

We belong to the day, and we should be sober. We must wear faith and love as a breastplate, and our hope of salvation as a helmet.[1]

Have your minds ready for action. Keep alert and set your hope completely on the blessing which will be given you when Jesus Christ is revealed.[2]—Stand ready, with truth as a belt tight round your waist, with righteousness as your breastplate. At all times carry faith as a shield; for with it you will be able to put out all the burning arrows shot by the Evil One. And accept salvation as a helmet, and the word of God as the sword which the Spirit gives you.[3]

The Sovereign LORD will destroy death for ever! He will wipe away the tears from everyone's eyes and take away the disgrace his people have suffered throughout the world. The LORD himself has spoken! When it happens, everyone will say, "He is our God! We have put our trust in him, and he has rescued us. He is the LORD! We have put our trust in him, and now we are happy and joyful because he has saved us."[4]

To have faith is to be sure of the things we hope for, to be certain of the things we cannot see.[5]

[1]1 THESS. 5.8. [2]1 Pet. 1.13.—[3]Eph. 6.14, 16, 17. [4]Isa. 25.8, 9. [5]Heb. 11.1.

Evening

The Israelites looked like two small flocks of goats compared with the Syrians, who spread out over the countryside.[1]

This is what the LORD says: "Because the Syrians say that I am a god of the hills and not of the plains, I will give you victory over their huge army, and you and your people will know that I am the LORD." For seven days the Syrians and the Israelites stayed in their camps, facing each other. On the seventh day they started fighting, and the Israelites killed a hundred thousand Syrians.[2]—You belong to God, my children, and have defeated the false prophets, because the Spirit who is in you is more powerful than the spirit in those who belong to the world.[3]

Do not be afraid—I am with you! I am your God—let nothing terrify you! I will make you strong and help you; I will protect you and save you.[4]

They will not defeat you, for I will be with you to protect you. I, the LORD, have spoken.[5]

[1]1 KGS 20.27. [2]1 Kgs 20.28, 29.—[3]1 John 4.4. [4]Isa. 41.10. [5]Jer. 1.19.

I have given help to a famous soldier; I have given the throne to one I chose from the people.[1]

I alone am the LORD, the only one who can save you.[2]—There is one God, and there is one who brings God and mankind together, the man Christ Jesus.[3]—In all the world there is no one else whom God has given who can save us.[4]

Mighty God.[5]—Of his own free will he gave up all he had, and took the nature of a servant. He became like man and appeared in human likeness. He was humble and walked the path of obedience all the way to death—his death on the cross. For this reason God raised him to the highest place above and gave him the name that is greater than any other name.[6]—We do see Jesus, who for a little while was made lower than the angels, so that through God's grace he should die for everyone. We see him now crowned with glory and honour because of the death he suffered.[7]—Since the children . . . are people of flesh and blood, Jesus himself became like them and shared their human nature.[8]

[1]PS. 89.19. [2]Isa. 43.11.—[3]1 Tim. 2.5.—[4]Acts 4.12. [5]Isa. 9.6.—[6]Phil. 2.7–9.—[7]Heb. 2.9.—[8]Heb. 2.14.

Evening

Gather my faithful people to me, those who made a covenant with me by offering a sacrifice.[1]

Christ also was offered in sacrifice once to take away the sins of many. He will appear a second time, not to deal with sin, but to save those who are waiting for him.[2]—Christ is the one who arranges a new covenant, so that those who have been called by God may receive the eternal blessings that God has promised.[3]

Father! You have given them to me, and I want them to be with me where I am.[4]—He will send the angels out to the four corners of the earth to gather God's chosen people from one end of the world to the other.[5]—Even if you are scattered to the farthest corners of the earth, the LORD your God will gather you together and bring you back.[6]

Those who have died believing in Christ will rise to life first; then we who are living at that time will be gathered up along with them in the clouds to meet the Lord in the air. And so we will always be with the Lord.[7]

[1]PS. 50.5. [2]Heb. 9.28.—[3]Heb. 9.15. [4]John 17.24.—[5]Mark 13.27.—[6]Deut. 30.4. [7]1 Thess. 4.16, 17.

Your lives will produce all kinds of good deeds, and you will grow in your knowledge of God.[1]

My brothers, because of God's great mercy to us I appeal to you: Offer yourselves as a living sacrifice to God, dedicated to his service and pleasing to him. This is the true worship that you should offer. Do not conform yourselves to the standards of this world, but let God transform you inwardly by a complete change of your mind. Then you will be able to know the will of God—what is good and is pleasing to him and is perfect.[2]—At one time you surrendered yourselves entirely as slaves to impurity and wickedness for wicked purposes. In the same way you must now surrender yourselves entirely as slaves of righteousness for holy purposes.[3]—It does not matter at all whether or not one is circumcised; what does matter is being a new creature. As for those who follow this rule in their lives, may peace and mercy be with them.[4]

My Father's glory is shown by your bearing much fruit; and in this way you become my disciples.[5]—You did not choose me; I chose you and appointed you to go and bear much fruit, the kind of fruit that endures.[6]

[1]COL. 1.10. [2]Rom. 12.1, 2.—[3]Rom. 6.19.—[4]Gal. 6.15, 16. [5]John 15.8.—[6]John 15.16.

Evening

I was looking for him, but couldn't find him.[1]

Return to the LORD your God, people of Israel. Your sin has made you stumble and fall. Return to the LORD, and let this prayer be your offering to him: "Forgive all our sins and accept our prayer, and we will praise you as we have promised."[2]

If a person is tempted by . . . trials, he must not say, "This temptation comes from God." But a person is tempted when he is drawn away and trapped by his own evil desire. Do not be deceived, my dear brothers! Every good gift and every perfect present comes from heaven; it comes down from God, the Creator of the heavenly lights, who does not change or cause darkness by turning.[3]

Trust in the LORD. Have faith, do not despair. Trust in the LORD.[4]—It is best for us to wait in patience—to wait for him to save us.[5]—Will God not judge in favour of his own people who cry to him day and night for help? Will he be slow to help them?[6]

I wait patiently for God to save me; I depend on him alone. I depend on God alone; I put my hope in him.[7]

[1]S. OF S. 3.1. [2]Hos. 14.1, 2. [3]Jas 1.13, 14, 16, 17. [4]Ps. 27.14.—[5]Lam. 3.26.—[6]Luke. 18.7. [7]Ps. 62.1, 5.

He led them safely, and they were not afraid.[1]

I walk the way of righteousness; I follow the paths of justice.[2]

I will send an angel ahead of you to protect you as you travel and to bring you to the place which I have prepared.[3]—It was not an angel, but the LORD himself who saved them. In his love and compassion he rescued them. He had always taken care of them in the past.[4]

Your people did not conquer the land with their swords; they did not win it by their own power; it was by your power and your strength, by the assurance of your presence, which showed that you loved them.[5]—He led his people and brought honour to his name.[6]

LORD, I have so many enemies! Lead me to do your will; make your way plain for me to follow.[7]—Send your light and your truth; may they lead me and bring me back to Zion, your sacred hill, and to your Temple, where you live. Then I will go to your altar, O God; you are the source of my happiness. I will play my harp and sing praise to you, O God, my God.[8]

[1]PS. 78.53. [2]Prov. 8.20. [3]Exod. 23.20.—[4]Isa. 63.9. [5]Ps. 44.3.—[6]Isa. 63.14. [7]Ps. 5.8.—[8]Ps. 43.3, 4.

Evening

You have been purified . . . you have been dedicated . . . you have been put right with God.[1]

The blood of Jesus, his Son, purifies us from every sin.[2]—We are healed by the punishment he suffered, made whole by the blows he received.[3]

Christ loved the church and gave his life for it. He did this to dedicate the church to God by his word, after making it clean by washing it in water, in order to present the church to himself in all its beauty—pure and faultless, without spot or wrinkle or any other imperfection.[4]—She has been given clean shining linen to wear. (The linen is the good deeds of God's people.)[5]—Let us come near to God with a sincere heart and a sure faith, with hearts that have been purified from a guilty conscience and with bodies washed with clean water.[6]

Who will accuse God's chosen people? God himself declared them not guilty![7]—Happy are those whose sins are forgiven . . . Happy is the man whom the LORD does not accuse of doing wrong and who is free from all deceit.[8]

[1]1 COR. 6.11. [2]1 John 1.7.—[3]Isa. 53.5. [4]Eph. 5.25–27.—[5]Rev. 19.8.—[6]Heb. 10.22. [7]Rom. 8.33.—[8]Ps. 32.1, 2.

The sadness that is used by God brings a change of heart that leads to salvation—and there is no regret in that![1]

Peter remembered what Jesus had told him: "Before the cock crows, you will say three times that you do not know me." He went out and wept bitterly.[2]—If we confess our sins to God, he will keep his promise and do what is right: he will forgive us our sins and purify us from all our wrongdoing.[3]—The blood of Jesus, his Son, purifies us from every sin.[4]

My sins have caught up with me, and I can no longer see; they are more than the hairs of my head, and I have lost my courage. Save me, LORD! Help me now![5]

Trust in your God and return to him. Be loyal and just, and wait patiently for your God to act.[6]

My sacrifice is a humble spirit, O God; you will not reject a humble and repentant heart.[7]—He heals the broken-hearted.[8]—The LORD has told us what is good. What he requires of us is this: to do what is just, to show constant love, and to live in humble fellowship with our God.[9]

[1]2 COR. 7.10. [2]Matt. 26.75.—[3]1 John 1.9.—[4]1 John 1.7. [5]Ps. 40.12, 13. [6]Hos. 12.6. [7]Ps. 51.17.—[8]Ps. 147.3.—[9]Mic. 6.8.

Evening

"Find out if everything is all right." She told Gehazi that everything was all right.[1]

In the same spirit of faith, we also speak because we believe.[2]

Although punished, we are not killed; although saddened, we are always glad; we seem poor, but we make many people rich; we seem to have nothing, yet we really possess everything.[3]

We are often troubled, but not crushed; sometimes in doubt, but never in despair; there are many enemies, but we are never without a friend; and though badly hurt at times, we are not destroyed. At all times we carry in our mortal bodies the death of Jesus, so that his life may also be seen in our bodies. For this reason we never become discouraged. Even though our physical being is gradually decaying, yet our spiritual being is renewed day after day. And this small and temporary trouble we suffer will bring us a tremendous and eternal glory, much greater than the trouble. For we fix our attention, not on things that are seen, but on things that are unseen.[4]

My dear friend, I pray that everything may go well with you and that you may be in good health—as I know you are well in spirit.[5]

[1]2 KGS 4.26. [2]2 Cor. 4.13. [3]2 Cor. 6.9, 10. [4]2 Cor. 4.8–10, 16–18. [5]3 John 2.

Christ loved the church and gave his life for it. He did this to dedicate the church to God by his word, after making it clean by washing it in water.[1]

Your life must be controlled by love, just as Chirst loved us and gave his life for us as a sweet-smelling offering and sacrifice that pleases God.[2]

For through the living and eternal word of God you have been born again as the children of a parent who is immortal, not mortal.[3]—Dedicate them to yourself by means of the truth; your word is truth.[4]—No one can enter the Kingdom of God unless he is born of water and the Spirit.[5]—It was not because of any good deeds that we ourselves had done, but because of his own mercy that he saved us, through the Holy Spirit, who gives us new birth and new life by washing us.[6]—Your promise gave me life.[7]

The law of the LORD is perfect; it gives new strength. The commands of the LORD are trustworthy, giving wisdom to those who lack it. The laws of the LORD are right, and those who obey them are happy. The commands of the LORD are just and give understanding to the mind.[8]

[1]EPH. 5.25, 26. [2]Eph. 5.2. [3]1 Pet. 1.23.—[4]John 17.17.—[5]John 3.5.—[6]Titus 3.5.— [7]Ps. 119.50. [8]Ps. 19.7, 8.

Evening

It is through Christ that all of us . . . are able to come in the one Spirit into the presence of the Father.[1]

I in them and you in me, so that they may be completely one.[2]

I will do whatever you ask for in my name, so that the Father's glory will be shown through the Son. If you ask me for anything in my name, I will do it. I will ask the Father, and he will give you another Helper, who will stay with you for ever. He is the Spirit who reveals the truth about God. The world cannot receive him, because it cannot see him or know him. But you know him, because he remains with you and is in you.[3]—There is one body and one Spirit, just as there is one hope to which God has called you. There is one Lord, one faith, one baptism; there is one God and Father of all mankind, who is Lord of all, works through all, and is in all.[4]—When you pray, say this: "Father."[5]

We have, then, my brothers, complete freedom to go into the Most Holy Place by means of the death of Jesus. He opened for us a new way, a living way . . . So let us come near to God.[6]

[1]EPH. 2.18. [2]John 17.23. [3]John 14.13, 14, 16, 17.—[4]Eph. 4.4–6.—[5]Luke 11.2. [6]Heb. 10.19, 20, 22.

You are my saviour and my God—hurry to my aid![1]

The LORD guides a man in the way he should go and protects those who please him. If they fall, they will not stay down, because the LORD will help them up.[2]—Reverence for the LORD gives confidence and security to a man and his family.[3]—Why should you fear mortal man, who is no more enduring than grass? Have you forgotten the LORD who made you?[4]

I will be with you to protect you.[5]—Be determined and confident. Do not be afraid of them. Your God, the LORD himself, will be with you. He will not fail you or abandon you.[6]

I will sing about your strength; every morning I will sing aloud of your constant love. You have been a refuge for me, a shelter in my time of trouble.[7]—You are my hiding place; you will save me from trouble. I sing aloud of your salvation, because you protect me.[8]

[1]PS. 40.17. [2]Ps. 37.23, 24.—[3]Prov. 14.16.—[4]Isa. 51.12, 13. [5]Jer. 1.8.—[6]Deut. 31.6. [7]Ps. 59.16.—[8]Ps. 32.7.

Evening

How will you manage in the jungle by the Jordan?[1]

It was harvest time, and the river was in flood.[2]

While the people walked across on dry ground, the priests carrying the LORD's Covenant Box stood on dry ground in the middle of the Jordan until all the people had crossed over.[3]

We . . . see Jesus, who for a little while was made lower than the angels, so that through God's grace he should die for everyone. We see him now crowned with glory and honour because of the death he suffered.[4]

Even though I go through the deepest darkness, I will not be afraid, LORD, for you are with me. Your shepherd's rod and staff protect me.[5]—When you pass through deep waters, I will be with you; your troubles will not overwhelm you.[6]

Don't be afraid! I am the first and the last. I am the living one! I was dead, but now I am alive for ever and ever. I have authority over death and the world of the dead.[7]

[1]JER. 12.5. [2]Josh. 3.15. [3]Josh. 3.17. [4]Heb. 2.9. [5]Ps. 23.4.—[6]Isa. 43.2. [7]Rev. 1.17, 18.

God is to be trusted, the God who called you to have fellowship with his Son Jesus Christ, our Lord.[1]

Let us hold on firmly to the hope we profess, because we can trust God to keep his promise.[2]—As God himself has said, "I will make my home with my people and live among them; I will be their God, and they shall be my people."[3]—The fellowship that we have with the Father and with his Son Jesus Christ.[4]—Rather be glad that you are sharing Christ's sufferings so that you may be full of joy when his glory is revealed.[5]

I pray that Christ will make his home in your hearts through faith. I pray that you may have your roots and foundation in love, so that you, together with all God's people, may have the power to understand how broad and long, how high and deep, is Christ's love. Yes, may you come to know his love—although it can never be fully known—and so be completely filled with the very nature of God.[6]

If anyone declares that Jesus is the Son of God, he lives in union with God and God lives in union with him.[7]—Whoever obeys God's commands lives in union with God and God lives in union with him.[8]

[1]1 COR. 1.9. [2]Heb. 10.23.—[3]2 Cor. 6.16.—[4]1 John 1.3.—[5]1 Pet. 4.13. [6]Eph. 3.17–19. [7]1 John 4.15.—[8]1 John 3.24.

Evening

God has made us what we are.[1]

They quarried fine large stones for the foundation of the Temple.[2]—The stones with which the Temple was built had been prepared at the quarry, so that there was no noise made by hammers, axes, or any other iron tools as the Temple was being built.[3]

Come as living stones, and let yourselves be used in building the spiritual temple.[4]—Built upon the foundation laid by the apostles and prophets, the cornerstone being Christ Jesus himself. He is the one who holds the whole building together and makes it grow into a sacred temple dedicated to the Lord. In union with him you too are being built together with all the others into a place where God lives through his Spirit.[5]—At one time you were not God's people, but now you are his people.[6]

You are also God's building.[7]—When anyone is joined to Christ, he is a new being; the old is gone, the new has come.[8]—God is the one who has prepared us for this change, and he gave us his Spirit as the guarantee of all that he has in store for us.[9]

[1]EPH. 2.10. [2]1 Kgs 5.17..—[3]1 Kgs 6.7. [4]1 Pet. 2.5.—[5]Eph. 2.20–22.—[6]1 Pet. 2.10. [7]1 Cor. 3.9.—[8]2 Cor. 5.17.—[9]2 Cor. 5.5.

Dedicate them to yourself by means of the truth; your word is truth.[1]

You have been made clean already by the teaching I have given you.[2]—Christ's message in all its richness must live in your hearts.[3]

How can a young man keep his life pure? By obeying your commands. With all my heart I try to serve you; keep me from disobeying your commandments.[4]

You will become wise, and your knowledge will give you pleasure. Your insight and understanding will protect you.[5]

I follow faithfully the road he chooses, and never wander to either side. I always do what God commands; I follow his will, not my own desires.[6]—I understand more than all my teachers, because I meditate on your instructions.[7]—If you obey my teaching, you are really my disciples; you will know the truth, and the truth will set you free.[8]

[1]JOHN 17.17. [2]John 15.3.—[3]Col. 3.16. [4]Ps. 119.9, 10. [5]Prov. 2.10, 11. [6]Job 23.11, 12.—[7]Ps. 119.99.—[8]John 8.31, 32.

Evening

Fellow-citizens with God's people.[1]

You have come to Mount Zion and to the city of the living God, the heavenly Jerusalem, with its thousands of angels. You have come to the joyful gathering of God's first-born sons, whose names are written in heaven. You have come to God, who is the judge of all mankind, and to the spirits of good people made perfect.[2]

It was in faith that all these persons died. They did not receive the things God had promised, but from a long way off they saw them and welcomed them, and admitted openly that they were foreigners and refugees on earth.[3]—We . . . are citizens of heaven, and we eagerly wait for our Saviour, the Lord Jesus Christ, to come from heaven. He will change our weak mortal bodies and make them like his own glorious body, using that power by which he is able to bring all things under his rule.[4]—The Father . . . rescued us from the power of darkness and brought us safe into the kingdom of his dear Son.[5]

I appeal to you . . . as strangers and refugees in this world! Do not give in to bodily passions, which are always at war against the soul.[6]

[1]EPH. 2.19. [2]Heb. 12.22, 23. [3]Heb. 11.13.—[4]Phil. 3.20, 21.—[5]Col. 1.12, 13. [6]1 Pet. 2.11.

How deep are your thoughts![1]

We have always prayed for you . . . we ask God to fill you with the knowledge of his will, with all the wisdom and understanding that his Spirit gives.[2]—I pray that you may have your roots and foundation in love, so that you, together with all God's people, may have the power to understand how broad and long, how high and deep, is Christ's love. Yes, may you come to know his love—although it can never be fully known—and so be completely filled with the very nature of God.[3]

How great are God's riches! How deep are his wisdom and knowledge! Who can explain his decisions? Who can understand his ways?[4]—"My thoughts," says the LORD, "are not like yours, and my ways are different from yours. As high as the heavens are above the earth, so high are my ways and thoughts above yours."[5]—You have done many things for us, O LORD our God; there is no one like you! You have made many wonderful plans for us. I could never speak of them all—their number is so great![6]

[1]PS. 92.5. [2]Col. 1.9.—[3]Eph. 3.17–19. [4]Rom. 11.33.—[5]Isa. 55.8, 9.—[6]Ps. 40.5.

Evening

A person will reap exactly what he sows.[1]

I have seen people plough fields of evil and sow wickedness like seed; now they harvest wickedness and evil.[2]—When they sow the wind, they will reap a storm![3]—If he sows in the field of his natural desires, from it he will gather the harvest of death.[4]

If you do what is right, you are certain to be rewarded.[5]—If he sows in the field of the Spirit, from the Spirit he will gather the harvest of eternal life. So let us not become tired of doing good; for if we do not give up, the time will come when we will reap the harvest. So then, as often as we have the chance, we should do good to everyone, and especially to those who belong to our family in the faith.[6]

Some people spend their money freely and still grow richer. Others are cautious, and yet grow poorer. Be generous, and you will be prosperous. Help others, and you will be helped.[7]—Remember that the person who sows few seeds will have a small crop; the one who sows many seeds will have a large crop.[8]

[1]GAL. 6.7. [2]Job 4.8.—[3]Hos. 8.7.—[4]Gal. 6.8. [5]Prov. 11.18.—[6]Gal. 6.8–10. [7]Prov. 11.24, 25.—[8]2 Cor. 9.6.

Morning

He took them away with a cruel wind from the east.[1]

Let the LORD himself be the one to punish us, for he is merciful.[2]—I will come to you and save you. I will not let you go unpunished; but when I punish you, I will be fair.[3]—He does not keep on rebuking; he is not angry for ever. He does not punish us as we deserve or repay us according to our sins and wrongs. He knows what we are made of; he remembers that we are dust.[4]—I will be merciful to them, as a father is merciful to the son who serves him.[5]

God keeps his promise, and he will not allow you to be tested beyond your power to remain firm; at the time you are put to the test, he will give you the strength to endure it, and so provide you with a way out.[6]—Satan has received permission to test all of you, to separate the good from the bad, as a farmer separates the wheat from the chaff. But I have prayed for you . . . that your faith will not fail.[7]

The poor and the helpless have fled to you and have been safe in times of trouble. You give them shelter from storms and shade from the burning heat.[8]

[1]ISA. 27.8. [2]2 Sam. 24.14.—[3]Jer. 30.11.—[4]Ps. 103.9, 10, 14.—[5]Mal. 3.17. [6]1 Cor. 10.13.—[7]Luke 22.31, 32. [8]Isa. 25.4.

Evening

I couldn't believe it until I had come and seen it all for myself. But I didn't hear even half of it.[1]

On Judgement Day the Queen of Sheba will stand up and accuse you, because she travelled all the way from her country to listen to King Solomon's wise teaching; and I assure you that there is something here greater than Solomon![2]—We saw his glory, the glory which he received as the Father's only Son.[3]

My teaching and message were . . . delivered . . . with convincing proof of the power of God's Spirit. Your faith, then, does not rest on human wisdom but on God's power. As the scripture says, "What no one ever saw or heard, what no one ever thought could happen, is the very thing God prepared for those who love him." But it was to us that God made known his secret by means of his Spirit. The Spirit searches everything, even the hidden depths of God's purposes.[4]

You will see a king ruling in splendour.[5]—We shall see him as he really is.[6]—While still in this body I will see God.[7]—Your presence will fill me with joy.[8]

[1]1 KGS 10.7. [2]Matt. 12.42.—[3]John 1.14. [4]1 Cor. 2.4, 5, 9, 10. [5]Isa. 33.17.— [6]1 John 3.2.—[7]Job 19.26.—[8]Ps. 17.15.

You will know the false prophets by what they do.[1]

Let no one deceive you, my children! Whoever does what is right is righteous, just as Christ is righteous.[2]—No spring of water pours out sweet water and bitter water from the same opening. A fig-tree, my brothers, cannot bear olives; a grapevine cannot bear figs, nor can a salty spring produce sweet water. Is there anyone among you who is wise and understanding? He is to prove it by his good life, by his good deeds performed with humility and wisdom.[3]—Your conduct among the heathen should be so good that when they accuse you of being evildoers, they will have to recognize your good deeds and so praise God on the Day of his coming.[4]

To have good fruit you must have a healthy tree; if you have a poor tree, you will have bad fruit. A tree is known by the kind of fruit it bears.[5]—A good person brings good things out of his treasure of good things; a bad person brings bad things out of his treasure of bad things.[6]

Is there anything I failed to do for [my vineyard]?[7]

[1]MATT. 7.20. [2]1 John 3.7.—[3]Jas 3.11–13.—[4]1 Pet. 2.12. [5]Matt. 12.33.—[6]Matt. 12.35. [7]Isa. 5.4.

Evening

To make my city glorious.[1]

The LORD says, "Heaven is my throne, and the earth is my footstool."[2]

Can you, O God, really live on earth among men and women? Not even all heaven is large enough to hold you, so how can this Temple that I have built be large enough?[3]

"Before long I will shake heaven and earth, land and sea. I will overthrow all the nations, and their treasures will be brought here, and the Temple will be filled with wealth. The new Temple will be more splendid than the old one." The LORD Almighty has spoken.[4]

Then I saw a new heaven and a new earth. The first heaven and the first earth disappeared, and the sea vanished. I heard a loud voice speaking from the throne: "Now God's home is with mankind! He will live with them, and they shall be his people. God himself will be with them, and he will be their God.[5]

[1]ISA. 60.13. [2]Isa. 66.1. [3]2 Chr. 6.18. [4]Hag. 2.6, 7, 9. [5]Rev. 21.1, 3.

***We are in darkness now, but the* LORD *will give us light.*[1]**

When you pass through deep waters, I will be with you; your troubles will not overwhelm you. When you pass through fire, you will not be burnt; the hard trials that come will not hurt you. For I am the LORD your God, the holy God of Israel, who saves you.[2]—I will lead my blind people by roads they have never travelled. I will turn their darkness into light and make rough country smooth before them. These are my promises, and I will keep them without fail.[3]

Even if I go through the deepest darkness, I will not be afraid, LORD, for you are with me. Your shepherd's rod and staff protect me.[4]—When I am afraid, O LORD Almighty, I put my trust in you. I trust in God and am not afraid; I praise him for what he has promised. What can a mere human being do to me?[5]—The LORD is my light and my salvation; I will fear no one. The LORD protects me from all danger; I will never be afraid.[6]

[1]MIC. 7.8. [2]Isa. 43.2, 3.—[3]Isa. 42.16. [4]Ps. 23.4.—[5]Ps. 56.3, 4.—[6]Ps. 27.1.

Evening

***There is one God, and there is one who brings God and mankind together, the man Christ Jesus.*[1]**

Israel, remember this! The LORD—and the LORD alone—is our God.[2]—A go-between is not needed when only one person is involved; and God is one.[3]

We have sinned as our ancestors did; we have been wicked and evil. Our ancestors in Egypt did not understand God's wonderful acts; they forgot the many times he showed them his love . . . When God said that he would destroy his people, his chosen servant, Moses, stood up against God and prevented his anger from destroying them.[4]

My Christian brothers, who also have been called by God! Think of Jesus, whom God sent to be the High Priest of the faith we profess. He was faithful to God, who chose him to do this work, just as Moses was faithful in his work in God's house.[5]

The covenant which [Jesus] arranged between God and his people is a better one, because it is based on promises of better things. "I will forgive their sins and will no longer remember their wrongs."[6]

[1]1 TIM. 2.5. [2]Deut. 6.4.—[3]Gal. 3.20. [4]Ps. 106.6, 7, 23. [5]Heb. 3.1, 2. [6]Heb. 8.6, 12.

I will never turn away anyone who comes to me.[1]

When he cries out to me for help, I will answer him because I am merciful.[2]—I will not completely abandon or destroy them. That would put an end to my covenant with them, and I am the LORD their God.[3]—I will honour the covenant I made with you when you were young, and I will make a covenant with you that will last for ever.[4]

The LORD says, "Now, let's settle the matter. You are stained red with sin, but I will wash you as clean as snow. Although your stains are deep red, you will be as white as wool."[5]—Let the wicked leave their way of life and change their way of thinking. Let them turn to the LORD, our God; he is merciful and quick to forgive.[6]—"Remember me, Jesus, when you come as King!" Jesus said to him, "I promise you that today you will be in Paradise with me."[7]

He will not break off a bent reed or put out a flickering lamp.[8]

[1]JOHN 6.37. [2]Exod. 22.27.—[3]Lev. 26.44.—[4]Ezek. 16.60. [5]Isa. 1.18.—[6]Isa. 55.7.—[7]Luke 23.42, 43. [8]Isa. 42.3.

Evening

His dear Son.[1]

Then a voice said from heaven, "This is my own dear Son, with whom I am pleased."[2]—Here is my servant, whom I strengthen—the one I have chosen, with whom I am pleased.[3]—The only Son, who is the same as God and is at the Father's side.[4]

God showed his love for us by sending his only Son into the world, so that we might have life through him. This is what love is: it is not that we have loved God, but that he loved us and sent his Son to be the means by which our sins are forgiven. And we ourselves know and believe the love which God has for us. God is love.[5]

I gave them the same glory you gave me, so that they may be one, just as you and I are one; I in them and you in me, so that they may be completely one, in order that the world may know that you sent me and that you love them as you love me.[6]—See how much the Father has loved us! His love is so great that we are called God's children.[7]

[1]COL. 1.13. [2]Matt. 3.17.—[3]Isa. 42.1.—[4]John 1.18. [5]1 John 4.9, 10, 16. [6]John 17.22–24.—[7]1 John 3.1.

Pray in the power of the Holy Spirit.[1]

God is Spirit, and only by the power of his Spirit can people worship him as he really is.[2]—All of us . . . are able to come in the one Spirit into the presence of the Father.[3]

My Father, if it is possible, take this cup of suffering from me! Yet not what I want, but what you want.[4]

The Spirit . . . comes to help us, weak as we are. For we do not know how we ought to pray; the Spirit himself pleads with God for us in groans that words cannot express. And God, who sees into our hearts, knows what the thought of the Spirit is; because the Spirit pleads with God on behalf of his people and in accordance with his will.[5]—We have courage in God's presence, because we are sure that he hears us if we ask him for anything that is according to his will.[6]—When . . . the Spirit comes, who reveals the truth about God, he will lead you into all the truth.[7]

Pray on every occasion, as the Spirit leads. For this reason keep alert and never give up; pray always for all God's people.[8]

[1]JUDE 20. [2]John 4.24.—[3]Eph. 2.18. [4]Matt. 26.39. [5]Rom. 8.26, 27.—[6]1 John 5.14.—[7]John 16.13. [8]Eph. 6.18.

Evening

There is hope for a tree that has been cut down; it can come back to life and sprout.[1]

He will not break off a bent reed.[2]—He gives me new strength.[3]

The sadness that is used by God brings a change of heart that leads to salvation—and there is no regret in that! But sadness that is merely human causes death.[4]—When we are punished, it seems to us at the time something to make us sad, not glad. Later, however, those who have been disciplined by such punishment reap the peaceful reward of a righteous life.[5]

Before you punished me, I used to go wrong, but now I obey your word.[6]—Even after everything that has happened to us in punishment for our sins and wrongs, we know that you, our God, have punished us less than we deserve and have allowed us to survive.[7]

Our enemies have no reason to gloat over us. We have fallen, but we will rise again. We are in darkness now, but the LORD will give us light. He will bring us out to the light; we will live to see him save us.[8]

[1]JOB 14.7. [2]Isa. 42.3.—[3]Ps. 23.3. [4]2 Cor. 7.10.—[5]Heb. 12.11. [6]Ps. 119.67.—[7]Ezra 9.13. [8]Mic. 7.8, 9.

Whoever listens to me will have security. He will be safe, with no reason to be afraid.[1]

O Lord, you have always been our home.[2]—Whoever goes to the LORD for safety, whoever remains under the protection of the Almighty.[3]—His faithfulness will protect and defend you.[4]

Your life is hidden with Christ in God.[5]—Anyone who strikes you strikes what is most precious to me.[6]—Don't be afraid! Stand your ground, and you will see what the LORD will do to save you today. The LORD will fight for you, and there is no need for you to do anything.[7]—God is our shelter and strength, always ready to help in times of trouble.[8]

Jesus spoke to them at once. "Courage!" he said. "It is I. Don't be afraid!"[9]—Why are you alarmed? Why are these doubts coming up in your minds? Look at my hands and my feet, and see that it is I myself. Feel me, and you will know, for a ghost doesn't have flesh and bones, as you can see I have.[10]—I know whom I have trusted, and I am sure that he is able to keep safe until that Day what he has entrusted to me.[11]

[1]PROV. 1.33. [2]Ps. 90.1.—[3]Ps. 91.1.—[4]Ps. 91.4. [5]Col. 3.3.—[6]Zech. 2.8.—[7]Exod. 14.13, 14.—[8]Ps. 46.1. [9]Matt. 14.27.—[10]Luke 24.38, 39.—[11]2 Tim. 1.12.

Evening

My kingdom does not belong to this world.[1]

Christ . . . offered one sacrifice for sins, an offering that is effective for ever, and then he sat down at the right-hand side of God. There he now waits until God puts his enemies as a footstool under his feet.[2]—From this time on you will see the Son of Man sitting on the right of the Almighty and coming on the clouds of heaven![3]

Christ must rule until God defeats all enemies and puts them under his feet.[4]

Thanks be to God who gives us the victory through our Lord Jesus Christ![5]—He raised Christ from death and seated him at his right side in the heavenly world . . . above all heavenly rulers, authorities, powers, and lords; he has a title superior to all titles of authority in this world and in the next. God put all things under Christ's feet and gave him to the church as supreme Lord over all things. The church is Christ's body, the completion of him who himself completes all things everywhere.[6]—His appearing will be brought about at the right time by God, the blessed and only Ruler, the King of kings and the Lord of lords.[7]

[1]JOHN 18.36. [2]Heb. 10.12, 13.—[3]Matt. 26.64. [4]1 Cor. 15.25. [5]1 Cor. 15.57.—[6]Eph. 1.20–23.—[7]1 Tim. 6.15.

My mother and brothers are those who hear the word of God and obey it.[1]

He purifies people from their sins, and both he and those who are made pure all have the same Father. That is why Jesus is not ashamed to call them his brothers. He says to God, "I will tell my brothers what you have done; I will praise you in their meeting."[2]—When we are in union with Christ Jesus, neither circumcision nor the lack of it makes any difference at all; what matters is faith that works through love.[3]—You are my friends if you do what I command you.[4]—How happy are those who hear the word of God and obey it![5]

Not everyone who calls me 'Lord, Lord' will enter the Kingdom of heaven, but only those who do what my Father in heaven wants them to do.[6]—My food . . . is to obey the will of the one who sent me.[7]

If . . . we say that we have fellowship with him, yet at the same time live in the darkness, we are lying both in our words and in our actions.[8]—Whoever obeys his word is the one whose love for God has really been made perfect. This is how we can be sure that we are in union with God.[9]

[1]LUKE 8.21. [2]Heb. 2.11, 12.—[3]Gal. 5.6.—[4]John 15.14.—[5]Luke 11.28. [6]Matt. 7.21.—[7]John 4.34. [8]1 John 1.6.—[9]1 John 2.5.

Evening

Elijah, what are you doing here?[1]

God knows every step I take.[2]—LORD, you have examined me and you know me. You know everything I do; from far away you understand all my thoughts. You see me, whether I am working or resting; you know all my actions. Where could I go to escape from you? Where could I get away from your presence? If I flew away beyond the east or lived in the farthest place in the west, you would be there to lead me, you would be there to help me.[3]

Elijah was the same kind of person as we are.[4]—It is dangerous to be concerned with what others think of you, but if you trust the LORD, you are safe.[5]—If they fall, they will not stay down, because the LORD will help them up.[6]—No matter how often an honest man falls, he always gets up again.[7]

Let us not become tired of doing good; for if we do not give up, the time will come when we will reap the harvest.[8]—As a father is kind to his children, so the LORD is kind to those who honour him.[9]

[1]1 KGS 19.19. [2]Job 23.10.—[3]Ps. 139.1–3, 7, 9, 10. [4]Jas 5.17.—[5]Prov. 29.25.—[6]Ps. 37.24.—[7]Prov. 24.16. [8]Gal. 6.9.—[9]Ps. 103.13, 14.

You were set free from sin and became the slaves of righteousness.[1]

You cannot serve both God and money.[2]—When you were the slaves of sin, you were free from righteousness. What did you gain from doing the things that you are now ashamed of? The result of those things is death! But now you have been set free from sin and are the slaves of God. Your gain is a life fully dedicated to him, and the result is eternal life.[3]

Christ has brought the Law to an end, so that everyone who believes is put right with God.[4]

Whoever wants to serve me must follow me, so that my servant will be with me where I am. And my Father will honour anyone who serves me.[5]—Take my yoke and put it on you, and learn from me, because I am gentle and humble in spirit; and you will find rest. For the yoke I will give you is easy, and the load I will put on you is light.[6]

LORD our God, we have been ruled by others, but you alone are our LORD.[7]—I will eagerly obey your commands, because you will give me more understanding.[8]

[1]ROM. 6.18. [2]Matt. 6.24.—[3]Rom. 6.20–22. [4]Rom. 10.4. [5]John 12.26.—[6]Matt. 11.29, 30. [7]Isa. 26.13.—[8]Ps. 119.32.

Evening

Whoever calls out to the Lord for help will be saved.[1]

Following the disgusting practices of the nations whom the LORD had driven out of the land as his people advanced, Manasseh sinned against the LORD. He built altars for the worship of Baal. In the two courtyards of the Temple he built altars for the worship of the stars. He sacrificed his son as a burnt-offering. He practised divination and magic and consulted fortune-tellers and mediums. He sinned greatly against the LORD and stirred up his anger.[2]—In his suffering he became humble, turned to the LORD his God, and begged him for help. God accepted Manasseh's prayer and answered it.[3]

The LORD says, "Now, let's settle the matter. You are stained red with sin, but I will wash you as clean as snow. Although your stains are deep red, you will be as white as wool.[4]—The Lord . . . is patient with you, because he does not want anyone to be destroyed, but wants all to turn away from their sins.[5]

[1]ACTS 2.21. [2]2 Kgs 21.2, 3, 5, 6.—[3]2 Chr. 33.12, 13. [4]Isa. 1.18.—[5]2 Pet. 3.9.

The Lord *is pleased with you.*[1]

The Lord who created you says, "Do not be afraid—I will save you. I have called you by name—you are mine."[2]—Can a woman forget her own baby and not love the child she bore? Even if a mother should forget her child, I will never forget you . . . I can never forget you! I have written your name on the palms of my hands.[3]

The Lord guides a man in the way he should go and protects those who please him.[4]—Pleased with the human race.[5]—He takes pleasure in those who honour him, in those who trust in his constant love.[6]—"They will be my people," says the Lord Almighty. "On the day when I act, they will be my very own. I will be merciful to them, as a father is merciful to the son who serves him."[7]

At one time you were far away from God and were his enemies because of the evil things you did and thought. But now, by means of the physical death of his Son, God has made you his friends, in order to bring you, holy, pure, and faultless, into his presence.[8]

[1]ISA. 62.4. [2]Isa. 43.1.—[3]Isa. 49.15, 16. [4]Ps. 37.23.—[5]Prov. 8.31.—[6]Ps. 147.11.—[7]Mal. 3.17. [8]Col. 1.21, 22.

Evening

Sadness that is merely human causes death.[1]

When Ahithophel saw that his advice had not been followed, he saddled his donkey and went back to his own city. After putting his affairs in order, he hanged himself. He was buried in the family grave.[2]—If you lose [your will to live], your last hope is gone.[3]

Is there no medicine in Gilead? Are there no doctors there? Why, then, have my people not been healed?[4]—The Sovereign Lord has filled me with his spirit. He has chosen me and sent me to bring good news to the poor, to heal the broken-hearted . . . to comfort all who mourn, to give to those who mourn in Zion joy and gladness instead of grief, a song of praise instead of sorrow.[5]—Come to me, all of you who are tired from carrying heavy loads, and I will give you rest. Take my yoke and put it on you, and learn from me, because I am gentle and humble in spirit; and you will find rest.[6]

Philip . . . told him the Good News about Jesus.[7]—He heals the broken-hearted and bandages their wounds.[8]

[1]2 COR. 7.10. [2]2 Sam. 17.23.—[3]Prov. 18.14. [4]Jer. 8.22.—[5]Isa. 61.1–3.—[6]Matt. 11.28, 29. [7]Acts 8.35.—[8]Ps. 147.3.

I gave them the same glory you gave me.[1]

I saw the Lord. He was sitting on his throne, high and exalted, and his robe filled the whole Temple. Round him flaming creatures were standing. They were calling out to each other: "Holy, holy, holy! The LORD Almighty is holy! His glory fills the world."[2]—Isaiah said this because he saw Jesus' glory and spoke about him.[3]—Sitting on the throne was a figure that looked like a man. It shone all over with a bright light that had in it all the colours of the rainbow. This was the dazzling light that shows the presence of the LORD.[4]

"Please, let me see the dazzling light of your presence." [The LORD answered,] "I will not let you see my face, because no one can see me and stay alive."[5]—No one has ever seen God. The only Son, who is the same as God and is at the Father's side, he has made him known.[6]—The God who said, "Out of darkness the light shall shine!" is the same God who made his light shine in our hearts, to bring us the knowledge of God's glory shining in the face of Christ.[7]

[1]JOHN 17.22. [2]Isa. 6.1–3.—[3]John 12.41.—[4]Ezek. 1.26, 28. [5]Exod. 33.18, 20.—[6]John 1.18.—[7]2 Cor. 4.6.

Evening

When sinners tempt you, my son, don't give in.[1]

She took some of the fruit and ate it. Then she gave some to her husband, and he also ate it.[2]—Remember how Achan son of Zerah refused to obey the command about the things condemned to destruction; the whole community of Israel was punished for that. Achan was not the only one who died because of his sin.[3]

Do not follow the majority when they do wrong.[4]

Go in through the narrow gate, because the gate to hell is wide and the road that leads to it is easy, and there are many who travel it.[5]

None of us lives for himself only.[6]—My brothers, you were called to be free. But do not let this freedom become an excuse for letting your physical desires control you. Instead, let love make you serve one another.[7]—Be careful . . . not to let your freedom of action make those who are weak in the faith fall into sin. In this way you will be sinning against Christ by sinning against your Christian brothers and wounding their weak conscience.[8]

All of us were like sheep that were lost, each of us going his own way. But the LORD made the punishment fall on him, the punishment all of us deserved.[9]

[1]PROV. 1.10. [2]Gen. 3.6.—[3]Josh. 22.20. [4]Exod. 23.2. [5]Matt. 7.13. [6]Rom. 14.7.—[7]Gal. 5.13.—[8]1 Cor. 8.9, 12. [9]Isa. 53.6.

As the body without the spirit is dead, so also faith without actions is dead.[1]

Not everyone who calls me 'Lord, Lord' will enter the Kingdom of heaven, but only those who do what my Father in heaven wants them to do.[2]—Try to live a holy life, because no one will see the Lord without it.[3]—Do your best to add goodness to your faith; to your goodness add knowledge; to your knowledge add self-control; to your self-control add endurance; to your endurance add godliness; to your godliness add brotherly affection and love. These are the qualities you need, and if you have them in abundance, they will make you active and effective in your knowledge of our Lord Jesus Christ. But whoever does not have them is so short-sighted that he cannot see and has forgotten that he has been purified from his past sins. So then, my brothers, try even harder to make God's call and his choice of you a permanent experience; if you do so, you will never abandon your faith.[4]

It is by God's grace that you have been saved through faith. It is not the result of your own efforts, but God's gift, so that no one can boast about it.[5]

[1]JAS 2.26. [2]Matt. 7.21.—[3]Heb. 12.14.—[4]2 Pet. 1.5–10. [5]Eph. 2.8.

Evening

Since the children . . . are people of flesh and blood, Jesus himself became like them and shared their human nature . . . and in this way set free those who were slaves all their lives because of their fear of death.[1]

Where, Death, is your victory? Where, Death, is your power to hurt? Thanks be to God who gives us the victory through our Lord Jesus Christ![2]—For this reason we never become discouraged. Even though our physical being is gradually decaying, yet our spiritual being is renewed day after day.[3]

We know that when this tent we live in—our body here on earth—is torn down, God will have a house in heaven for us to live in, a home he himself has made, which will last for ever. So we are always full of courage. We know that as long as we are at home in the body we are away from the Lord's home. We are full of courage and would much prefer to leave our home in the body and be at home with the Lord.[4]

Do not be worried and upset . . . believe in God and believe also in me. There are many rooms in my Father's house, and I am going to prepare a place for you. I would not tell you this if it were not so.[5]

[1]HEB. 2.14, 15. [2]1 Cor. 15.55, 57.—[3]2 Cor. 4.16. [4]2 Cor. 5.1, 6, 8. [5]John 14.1–3.

We shall be satisfied with the good things of your house.[1]

I have asked the LORD for one thing; one thing only do I want: to live in the LORD's house all my life, to marvel there at his goodness, and to ask for his guidance.[2]

Happy are those whose greatest desire is to do what God requires; God will satisfy them fully![3]—He has filled the hungry with good things, and sent the rich away with empty hands.[4]

He satisfies those who are thirsty and fills the hungry with good things.[5]—I am the bread of life . . . he who comes to me will never be hungry; he who believes in me will never be thirsty.[6]

How precious, O God, is your constant love! We find protection under the shadow of your wings. We feast on the abundant food you provide; you let us drink from the river of your goodness. You are the source of all life, and because of your light we see the light.[7]

[1]PS. 65.4. [2]Ps. 27.4. [3]Matt. 5.6.—[4]Luke 1.53. [5]Ps. 107.9.—[6]John 6.35. [7]Ps. 36.7–9.

Evening

Do you believe now?[1]

My brothers, what good is it for someone to say that he has faith if his actions do not prove it? Can that faith save him? Faith, if it is alone and includes no actions . . . is dead.[2]

It was faith that made Abraham offer his son Isaac as a sacrifice when God put Abraham to the test. Abraham was the one to whom God had made the promise, yet he was ready to offer his only son as a sacrifice. Abraham reckoned that God was able to raise Isaac from death.[3]—How was our ancestor Abraham put right with God? It was through his actions, when he offered his son Isaac on the altar. You see, then, that it is by his actions that a person is put right with God, and not by his faith alone.[4]

Whoever looks closely into the perfect law that sets people free, who keeps on paying attention to it and does not simply listen and then forget it, but puts it into practice—that person will be blessed by God in what he does.[5]

You will know the false prophets by what they do. Not everyone who calls me 'Lord, Lord' will enter the Kingdom of heaven, but only those who do what my Father in heaven wants them to do.[6]—Now that you know this truth, how happy you will be if you put it into practice![7]

[1]JOHN 16.31. [2]Jas 2.14, 17. [3]Heb. 11.17, 19.—[4]Jas 2.21, 24. [5]Jas 1.25. [6]Matt. 7.20, 21.—[7]John 13.17.

May the Lord himself, who is our source of peace, give you peace at all times and in every way. The Lord be with you all.[1]

Peace be yours from God, who is, who was, and who is to come.[2]—God's peace, which is far beyond human understanding, will keep your hearts and minds safe in union with Christ Jesus.[3]

The Lord himself stood among them and said to them, "Peace be with you."[4]—Peace is what I leave with you; it is my own peace that I give you. I do not give it as the world does. Do not be worried and upset; do not be afraid.[5]

The Helper . . . the Spirit, who reveals the truth about God.[6]—The Spirit produces love, joy, peace.[7]—God's Spirit joins himself to our spirits to declare that we are God's children.[8]

The LORD said, "I will go with you, and I will give you victory." Moses replied, "If you do not go with us, don't make us leave this place. How will anyone know that you are pleased with your people and with me if you do not go with us?"[9]

[1]2 THESS. 3.16. [2]Rev. 1.4.—[3]Phil. 4.7. [4]Luke 24.36.—[5]John 14.27. [6]John 15.26.—[7]Gal. 5.22.—[8]Rom. 8.16. [9]Exod. 33.14–16.

Evening

We . . . boast of our troubles.[1]

If our hope in Christ is good for this life only and no more, then we deserve more pity than anyone else in all the world.[2]

My dear friends, do not be surprised at the painful test you are suffering, as though something unusual were happening to you. Rather be glad that you are sharing Christ's sufferings, so that you may be full of joy when his glory is revealed.[3]—Although saddened, we are always glad.[4]

May you always be joyful in your union with the Lord. I say it again: rejoice![5]—As the apostles left the Council, they were happy, because God had considered them worthy to suffer disgrace for the sake of Jesus.[6]

May God, the source of hope, fill you with all joy and peace by means of your faith in him.[7]

Even though the fig-trees have no fruit and no grapes grow on the vines, even though the olive-crop fails and the fields produce no corn, even though the sheep all die and the cattle-stalls are empty, I will still be joyful and glad, because the LORD God is my Saviour.[8]

[1]ROM. 5.3. [2]1 Cor. 15.19. [3]1 Pet. 4.12, 13.—[4]2 Cor. 6.10. [5]Phil. 4.4.—[6]Acts 5.41. [7]Rom. 15.13. [8]Hab. 3.17, 18.

Like a shelter from the wind and a place to hide from storms.[1]

He had to become like his brothers in every way.[2]—The LORD Almighty says, ". . . the shepherd who works for me!"[3]—The Father and I are one.[4]

Whoever goes to the LORD for safety . . . remains under the protection of the Almighty.[5]—His glory will shade the city from the heat of the day and make it a place of safety, sheltered from the rain and storm.[6]—The LORD will guard you; he is by your side to protect you. The sun will not hurt you during the day, nor the moon during the night.[7]

In despair and far from home I call to you! Take me to a safe refuge.[8]—You are my hiding place; you will save me from trouble.[9]—The poor and the helpless have fled to you and have been safe in times of trouble. You give them shelter from storms and shade from the burning heat.[10]

[1]ISA. 32.2. [2]Heb. 2.17.—[3]Zech. 13.7.—[4]John 10.30. [5]Ps. 91.1.—[6]Isa. 4.6.—[7]Ps. 121.5, 6. [8]Ps. 61.2.—[9]Ps. 32.7.—[10]Isa. 25.4.

Evening

I am making a new earth and new heavens.[1]

We wait for what God has promised: new heavens and a new earth, where righteousness will be at home.[2]

Just as the new earth and the new heavens will endure by my power, so your descendants and your name will endure.[3]

Then I saw a new heaven and a new earth. The first heaven and the first earth disappeared, and the sea vanished. And I saw the Holy City, the new Jerusalem, coming down out of heaven from God, prepared and ready, like a bride dressed to meet her husband. I heard a loud voice speaking from the throne: "Now God's home is with mankind! He will live with them, and they shall be his people. God himself will be with them, and he will be their God. He will wipe away all tears from their eyes. There will be no more death, no more grief or crying or pain. The old things have disappeared." Then the one who sits on the throne said, "And now I make all things new!"[4]

[1]ISA. 65.17. [2]2 Pet. 3.13. [3]Isa. 66.22. [4]Rev. 21.1–5.

Morning

***You have had the Holy Spirit poured out on you by Christ, and so all of you know the truth.*[1]**

You know about Jesus of Nazareth and how God poured out on him the Holy Spirit and power.[2]—It was by God's own decision that the Son has in himself the full nature of God.[3]—Out of the fullness of his grace he has blessed us all, giving us one blessing after another.[4]

You welcome me as an honoured guest.[5]—Christ has poured out his Spirit on you. As long as his Spirit remains in you, you do not need anyone to teach you. For his Spirit teaches you about everything, and what he teaches is true, not false. Obey the Spirit's teaching, then, and remain in union with Christ.[6]

The Helper, the Holy Spirit, whom the Father will send in my name, will teach you everything and make you remember all that I have told you.[7]

The Spirit also comes to help us, weak as we are. For we do not know how we ought to pray; the Spirit himself pleads with God for us in groans that words cannot express.[8]

[1]1 JOHN 2.20. [2]Acts 10.38.—[3]Col. 1.19.—[4]John 1.16. [5]Ps. 23.5.—[6]1 John 2.27. [7]John 14.26. [8]Rom. 8.26.

Evening

***With hearts that have been purified from a guilty conscience.*[1]**

The blood of goats and bulls and the ashes of a burnt calf are sprinkled on the people who are ritually unclean, and this purifies them by taking away their ritual impurity. Since this is true, how much more is accomplished by the blood of Christ! Through the eternal Spirit he offered himself as a perfect sacrifice to God. His blood will purify our consciences from useless rituals, so that we may serve the living God.[2]—The sprinkled blood that promises much better things than does the blood of Abel.[3]

By the sacrificial death of Christ we are set free, that is, our sins are forgiven. How great is the grace of God, which he gave to us in such large measure![4]

First, Moses proclaimed to the people all the commandments as set forth in the Law. Then he took the blood of bulls and goats, mixed it with water, and sprinkled it on the book of the Law and all the people, using a sprig of hyssop and some red wool. In the same way Moses also sprinkled the blood on the Covenant Tent and over all the things used in worship. Indeed, according to the Law almost everything is purified by blood, and sins are forgiven only if blood is poured out.[5]

[1]HEB. 10.22. [2]Heb. 9.13, 14.—[3]Heb. 12.24. [4]Eph. 1.7. [5]Heb. 9.19, 21, 22.

I would turn to God and present my case to him.[1]

Is anything too hard for the LORD?[2]—Give yourself to the LORD; trust in him, and he will help you.[3]—Don't worry about anything, but in all your prayers ask God for what you need, always asking him with a thankful heart.[4]—Leave all your worries with him, because he cares for you.[5]

King Hezekiah took the letter from the messengers and read it. Then he went to the Temple, placed the letter there in the presence of the LORD, and prayed.[6]

Even before they finish praying to me, I will answer their prayers.[7]—The prayer of a good person has a powerful effect.[8]

I love the LORD, because he hears me; he listens to my prayers. He listens to me every time I call to him.[9]

[1]JOB 5.8. [2]Gen. 18.14.—[3]Ps. 37.5.—[4]Phil. 4.6.—[5]1 Pet. 5.7. [6]Isa. 37.14, 15. [7]Isa. 65.24.—[8]Jas 5.16. [9]Ps. 116.1, 2.

Evening

With bodies washed with clean water.[1]

Make a bronze basin with a bronze base. Place it between the Tent and the altar, and put water in it. Aaron and his sons are to use the water to wash their hands and feet before they go into the Tent . . . Then they will not be killed. They must wash their hands and feet, so that they will not die.[2]—Your body is the temple of the Holy Spirit, who lives in you.[3]—If anyone destroys God's temple, God will destroy him. For God's temple is holy, and you yourselves are his temple.[4]

Even after my skin is eaten by disease, while still in this body I will see God. I will see him with my own eyes, and he will not be a stranger.[5]—Nothing that is impure will enter the city.[6]—Your eyes are too holy to look at evil, and you cannot stand the sight of people doing wrong.[7]—My brothers, because of God's great mercy to us I appeal to you: Offer yourselves as a living sacrifice to God, dedicated to his service and pleasing to him. This is the true worship that you should offer.[8]

[1]HEB. 10.22. [2]Exod. 30.18–21.—[3]1 Cor. 6.19.—[4]1 Cor. 3.17. [5]Job 19.26, 27.— [6]Rev. 21.27.—[7]Hab. 1.13.—[8]Rom. 12.1.

Morning

Where can wisdom be found?[1]

If any of you lacks wisdom, he should pray to God, who will give it to him; because God gives generously and graciously to all. But when you pray, you must believe and not doubt at all.[2]—Trust in the LORD with all your heart. Never rely on what you think you know. Remember the LORD in everything you do, and he will show you the right way.[3]—The only God.[4]—Never let yourself think that you are wiser than you are; simply obey the LORD and refuse to do wrong.[5]

"Sovereign LORD, I don't know how to speak; I am too young." But the LORD said to me, "Do not say that you are too young, but go to the people I send you to, and tell them everything I command you to say. Do not be afraid of them, for I will be with you to protect you. I, the LORD, have spoken!"[6]

The Father will give you whatever you ask him for in my name. Until now you have not asked for anything in my name; ask and you will receive, so that your happiness may be complete.[7]—If you believe, you will receive whatever you ask for in prayer.[8]

[1]JOB 28.12. [2]Jas 1.5, 6.—[3]Prov. 3.5, 6.—[4]1 Tim. 1.17.—[5]Prov. 3.7. [6]Jer. 1.6–8. [7]John 16.23, 24.—[8]Matt. 21.22.

Evening

I am tired of living.[1]

I wish I had wings, like a dove. I would fly away and find rest. I would quickly find myself a shelter from the raging wind and the storm.[2]

Now we sigh, so great is our desire that our home which comes from heaven should be put on over us . . . While we live in this earthly tent, we groan with a feeling of oppression; it is not that we want to get rid of our earthly body, but that we want to have the heavenly one put on over us, so that what is mortal will be transformed by life.[3]—I want very much to leave this life and be with Christ, which is a far better thing.[4]

Let us run with determination the race that lies before us. Let us keep our eyes fixed on Jesus, on whom our faith depends from beginning to end. He did not give up because of the cross! On the contrary, because of the joy that was waiting for him, he thought nothing of the disgrace of dying on the cross, and he is now seated at the right-hand side of God's throne. Think of what he went through; how he put up with so much hatred from sinners! So do not let yourselves become discouraged and give up.[5]

Do not be worried and upset; do not be afraid.[6]

[1]JOB 7.16. [2]Ps. 55.6, 8. [3]2 Cor. 5.2, 4.—[4]Phil. 1.23. [5]Heb. 12.1–3. [6]John 14.27.

My punishment was good for me, because it made me learn your commands.[1]

Even though he was God's Son, he learnt through his sufferings to be obedient.[2]—If we share Christ's suffering, we will also share his glory. I consider that what we suffer at this present time cannot be compared at all with the glory that is going to be revealed to us.[3]

God knows every step I take; if he tests me, he will find me pure. I follow faithfully the road he chooses, and never wander to either side.[4]

Remember how the LORD your God led you on this long journey through the desert these past forty years, sending hardships to test you, so that he might know what you intended to do and whether you would obey his commands. Remember that the LORD your God corrects and punishes you just as a father disciplines his children. So then, do as the LORD has commanded you: live according to his laws and obey him.[5]

[1]PS. 119.71. [2]Heb. 5.8.—[3]Rom. 8.17, 18. [4]Job 23.10, 11. [5]Deut. 8.2, 5, 6.

Evening

A man does not triumph by his own strength.[1]

David answered, "You are coming against me with sword, spear, and javelin, but I come against you in the name of the LORD Almighty, the God of the Israelite armies, which you have defied." He put his hand into his bag and took out a stone, which he slung at Goliath. And so, without a sword, David defeated and killed Goliath with a sling and a stone![2]

A king does not win because of his powerful army; a soldier does not triumph because of his strength. The LORD watches over those who obey him, those who trust in his constant love.[3]—All riches and wealth come from you; you rule everything by your strength and power; and you are able to make anyone great and strong.[4]

I am most happy . . . to be proud of my weaknesses, in order to feel the protection of Christ's power over me. I am content with weaknesses, insults, hardships, persecutions, and difficulties for Christ's sake. For when I am weak, then I am strong.[5]

[1]1 SAM. 2.9. [2]1 Sam. 17.45, 49, 50. [3]Ps. 33.16, 18.—[4]1 Chr. 29.12.
[5]2 Cor. 12.9, 10.

God is always at work in you.[1]

There is nothing in us that allows us to claim that we are capable of doing this work. The capacity we have comes from God.[2]—No one can have anything unless God gives it to him.[3]—No one can come to me unless the Father who sent me draws him to me; and I will raise him to life on the last day.[4]—I will give them a single purpose in life: to honour me for all time.[5]

Do not be deceived, my dear brothers! Every good gift and every perfect present comes from heaven; it comes down from God, the Creator of the heavenly lights, who does not change or cause darkness by turning. By his own will he brought us into being through the word of truth, so that we should have first place among all his creatures.[6]

God has made us what we are, and in our union with Christ Jesus he has created us for a life of good deeds, which he has already prepared for us to do.[7]

You will give us prosperity, LORD; everything that we achieve is the result of what you do.[8]

[1]PHIL. 2.13. [2]2 Cor. 3.5.—[3]John 3.27.—[4]John 6.44.—[5]Jer. 32.39. [6]Jas 1.16–18. [7]Eph. 2.10. [8]Isa. 26.12.

Evening

The spirit is willing, but the flesh is weak.[1]

We follow your will and put our hope in you; you are all that we desire. At night I long for you with all my heart.[2]

I know that good does not live in me—that is, in my human nature. For even though the desire to do good is in me, I am not able to do it. My inner being delights in the law of God. But I see a different law at work in my body—a law that fights against the law which my mind approves of. It makes me a prisoner to the law of sin which is at work in my body.[3]—What our human nature wants is opposed to what the Spirit wants, and what the Spirit wants is opposed to what our human nature wants. These two are enemies, and this means that you cannot do what you want to do.[4]

I have the strength to face all conditions by the power that Christ gives me.[5]—The capacity we have comes from God.[6]—My grace is all you need.[7]

[1]MATT. 26.41. [2]Isa. 26.8, 9. [3]Rom. 7.18, 22, 23.—[4]Gal. 5.17. [5]Phil. 4.13.— [6]2 Cor. 3.5.—[7]2 Cor. 12.9.

Christ was without sin, but for our sake God made him share our sin in order that in union with him we might share the righteousness of God.[1]

The LORD made the punishment fall on him.[2]—Christ himself carried our sins in his body to the cross, so that we might die to sin and live for righteousness. It is by his wounds that you have been healed.[3]—Just as all people were made sinners as the result of the disobedience of one man, in the same way they will all be put right with God as the result of the obedience of the one man.[4]

When the kindness and love of God our Saviour was revealed, he saved us. It was not because of any good deeds that we ourselves had done, but because of his own mercy that he saved us, through the Holy Spirit, who gives us new birth and new life by washing us. God poured out the Holy Spirit abundantly on us through Jesus Christ our Saviour, so that by his grace we might be put right with God and come into possession of the eternal life we hope for.[5]—There is no condemnation now for those who live in union with Christ Jesus.[6]

'The LORD Our Salvation.'[7]

[1]2 COR. 5.21. [2]Isa. 53.6.—[3]1 Pet. 2.24.—[4]Rom. 5.19. [5]Titus 3.4–7.—[6]Rom. 8.1. [7]Jer. 23.6.

Evening

I will be to the people of Israel like rain in a dry land.[1]

The gentleness and kindness of Christ.[2]

He will not break off a bent reed or put out a flickering lamp.[3]

"The Spirit of the Lord is upon me, because he has chosen me to bring good news to the poor. He has sent me to proclaim liberty to the captives and recovery of sight to the blind; to set free the oppressed and announce that the time has come when the Lord will save his people." He said to them, "This passage of scripture has come true today, as you heard it being read." They were all well impressed with him and marvelled at the eloquent words that he spoke.[4]

The Lord turned round and looked straight at Peter, and Peter remembered that the Lord had said to him, "Before the cock crows tonight, you will say three times that you do not know me." Peter went out and wept bitterly.[5]

He will take care of his flock like a shepherd; he will gather the lambs together and carry them in his arms.[6]

[1]HOS. 14.5. [2]2 Cor. 10.1. [3]Isa. 42.3. [4]Luke 4.18, 19, 21, 22. [5]Luke 22.61, 62. [6]Isa. 40.11.

Let love make you serve one another.[1]

My brothers, if anyone is caught in any kind of wrongdoing, those of you who are spiritual should set him right; but you must do it in a gentle way. And keep an eye on yourselves, so that you will not be tempted, too. Help to carry one another's burdens, and in this way you will obey the law of Christ.[2]

My brothers, if one of you wanders away from the truth and another one brings him back again, remember this: whoever turns a sinner back from his wrong way will save that sinner's soul from death and bring about the forgiveness of many sins.[3]—Now that by your obedience to the truth you have purified yourselves and have come to have a sincere love for your fellow-believers, love one another earnestly with all your heart.[4]—Be under obligation to no one—the only obligation you have is to love one another. Whoever does this has obeyed the Law.[5]—Love one another warmly as Christian brothers, and be eager to show respect for one another.[6]—All of you must put on the apron of humility, to serve one another; for the scripture says, "God resists the proud, but shows favour to the humble."[7]

We who are strong in the faith ought to help the weak to carry their burdens. We should not please ourselves.[8]

[1]GAL. 5.13. [2]Gal. 6.1, 2. [3]Jas 5.19, 20.—[4]1 Pet. 1.22.—[5]Rom. 13.8.—[6]Rom. 12.10.—[7]1 Pet. 5.5. [8]Rom. 15.1.

Evening

Our bodies will return to the dust of the earth.[1]

When the body is buried, it is mortal. When buried, it is ugly and weak. When buried, it is a physical body.[2]—The first Adam, made of earth, came from the earth.[3]

You were made from soil, and you will become soil again.[4]—Some men stay healthy till the day they die; they die happy and at ease. Others have no happiness at all; they live and die with bitter hearts. But all alike die and are buried; they all are covered with worms.[5]

I feel completely secure.[6]—Even after my skin is eaten by disease, while still in this body I will see God.[7]—The Lord Jesus Christ . . . will change our weak mortal bodies and make them like his own glorious body, using that power by which he is able to bring all things under his rule.[8]

LORD, how long will I live? When will I die? Tell me how soon my life will end.[9]—Teach us how short our life is, so that we may become wise.[10]

[1]ECCLES. 12.7. [2]1 Cor. 15.42–44.—[3]1 Cor. 15.47. [4]Gen. 3.19.—[5]Job 21.23, 25, 26. [6]Ps. 16.9.—[7]Job 19.26.—[8]Phil. 3.20, 21. [9]Ps. 39.4.—[10]Ps. 90.12.

Do what is right and fair; that pleases the Lord more than bringing him sacrifices.[1]

The Lord has told us what is good. What he requires of us is this: to do what is just, to show constant love, and to live in humble fellowship with our God.[2]—Which does the Lord prefer: obedience or offerings and sacrifices? It is better to obey him than to sacrifice the best sheep to him.[3]—Man must love God with all his heart and with all his mind and with all his strength; and he must love his neighbour as he loves himself. It is more important to obey these two commandments than to offer animals and other sacrifices to God.[4]

Trust in your God and return to him. Be loyal and just, and wait patiently for your God to act.[5]—Mary . . . sat down at the feet of the Lord and listened to his teaching. "Mary has chosen the right thing, and it will not be taken away from her."[6]

God is always at work in you to make you willing and able to obey his own purpose.[7]

[1]PROV. 21.3. [2]Mic. 6.8.—[3]1 Sam. 15.22.—[4]Mark 12.33. [5]Hos. 12.6.—[6]Luke 10.39, 42. [7]Phil. 2.13.

Evening

The breath of life will go back to God, who gave it to us.[1]

The Lord God took some soil from the ground and formed a man out of it; he breathed life-giving breath into his nostrils and the man began to live.[2]—It is the spirit of Almighty God that comes to men and gives them wisdom.[3]—The first man, Adam, was created a living being.[4]

As long as we are at home in the body we are away from the Lord's home. We are full of courage and would much prefer to leave our home in the body and be at home with the Lord.[5]—With Christ, which is a far better thing.[6]—Our brothers, we want you to know the truth about those who have died, so that you will not be sad, as are those who have no hope. We believe that Jesus died and rose again, and so we believe that God will take back with Jesus those who have died believing in him.[7]

I am going to prepare a place for you. And after I go and prepare a place for you, I will come back and take you to myself, so that you will be where I am.[8]

[1]ECCLES. 12.7. [2]Gen. 2.7.—[3]Job 32.8.—[4]1 Cor. 15.45. [5]2 Cor. 5.6, 8.—[6]Phil. 1.23.—[7]1 Thess. 4.13, 14. [8]John 14.2, 3.

No one can snatch them away from the Father's care.[1]

I know whom I have trusted, and I am sure that he is able to keep safe until that Day what he has entrusted to me.[2]—The Lord will rescue me from all evil and take me safely into his heavenly Kingdom.[3]—We have complete victory through him who loved us! For I am certain that nothing can separate us from his love: neither death nor life, neither angels nor other heavenly rulers or powers, neither the present nor the future, neither the world above nor the world below—there is nothing in all creation that will ever be able to separate us from the love of God which is ours through Christ Jesus our Lord.[4]—Your life is hidden with Christ in God.[5]

God chose the poor people of this world to be rich in faith and to possess the kingdom which he promised to those who love him.[6]

May our Lord Jesus Christ himself and God our Father, who loved us and in his grace gave us unfailing courage and a firm hope, encourage you and strengthen you to always do and say what is good.[7]

[1]JOHN 10.29. [2]2 Tim. 1.12.—[3]2 Tim. 4.18.—[4]Rom. 8.37–39.—[5]Col. 3.3. [6]Jas 2.5. [7]2 Thess. 2.16, 17.

Evening

The perfect law that sets people free.[1]

You will know the truth, and the truth will set you free. I am telling you the truth: everyone who sins is a slave of sin. If the Son sets you free, then you will be really free.[2]

Stand . . . as free people, and do not allow yourselves to become slaves again. As for you, my brothers, you were called to be free. But do not let this freedom become an excuse for letting your physical desires control you. Instead, let love make you serve one another. For the whole Law is summed up in one commandment: "Love your neighbour as you love yourself."[3]—You were set free from sin and became the slaves of righteousness.[4]—A married woman, for example, is bound by the law to her husband as long as he lives; but if he dies, then she is free from the law that bound her to him.[5]

The law of the Spirit, which brings us life in union with Christ Jesus, has set me free from the law of sin and death.[6]—I will live in perfect freedom, because I try to obey your teachings.[7]

[1]JAS 1.25. [2]John 8.32, 34, 36. [3]Gal. 5.1, 13, 14.—[4]Rom. 6.18.—[5]Rom. 7.2. [6]Rom. 8.2.—[7]Ps. 119.45.

Do not let what you regard as good get a bad name.[1]

Avoid every kind of evil.[2]—Our purpose is to do what is right, not only in the sight of the Lord, but also in the sight of man.[3]—God wants you to silence the ignorant talk of foolish people by the good things you do.[4]

If any of you suffers, it must not be because he is a murderer or a thief or a criminal or a meddler in other people's affairs. However, if you suffer because you are a Christian, don't be ashamed of it, but thank God that you bear Christ's name.[5]

My brothers, you were called to be free. But do not let this freedom become an excuse for letting your physical desires control you. Instead, let love make you serve one another.[6]—Be careful . . . not to let your freedom of action make those who are weak in the faith fall into sin.[7]—If anyone should cause one of these little ones to lose his faith in me, it would be better for that person to have a large millstone tied round his neck and be drowned in the deep sea.[8]—Whenever you did this for one of the least important of these brothers of mine, you did it for me![9]

[1]ROM. 14.16. [2]1 Thess. 5.22.—[3]2 Cor. 8.21.—[4]1 Pet. 2.15. [5]1 Pet. 4.15, 16. [6]Gal. 5.13.—[7]1 Cor. 8.9.—[8]Matt. 18.6.—[9]Matt. 25.40.

Evening

Wake up, sleeper, and rise from death, and Christ will shine on you.[1]

The time has come for you to wake up from your sleep. For the moment when we will be saved is closer now than it was when we first believed.[2]—We should not be sleeping like the others; we should be awake and sober. We must wear faith and love as a breastplate, and our hope of salvation as a helmet.[3]

Arise, Jerusalem, and shine like the sun; the glory of the LORD is shining on you! Other nations will be covered by darkness, but on you the light of the LORD will shine; the brightness of his presence will be with you.[4]

Have your minds ready for action. Keep alert and set your hope completely on the blessing which will be given you when Jesus Christ is revealed.[5]—Be ready for whatever comes, dressed for action and with your lamps lit, like servants who are waiting for their master.[6]

[1]EPH. 5.14. [2]Rom. 13.11.—[3]1 Thess. 5.6–8. [4]Isa. 60.1, 2. [5]1 Pet. 1.13.— [6]Luke 12.35, 36.

***The* L*ORD* . . . *is with you.*[1]**

Do not be afraid—I am with you! I am your God—let nothing terrify you! I will make you strong and help you; I will protect you and save you.[2]—Give strength to hands that are tired and to knees that tremble with weakness. Tell everyone who is discouraged, "Be strong and don't be afraid! God is coming to your rescue, coming to punish your enemies."[3]—The LORD your God is with you; his power gives you victory. The LORD will take delight in you, and in his love he will give you new life. He will sing and be joyful over you.[4]—Trust in the LORD. Have faith, do not despair. Trust in the LORD.[5]

I heard a loud voice speaking from the throne: "Now God's home is with mankind! He will live with them, and they shall be his people. God himself will be with them, and he will be their God. He will wipe away all tears from their eyes. There will be no more death, no more grief or crying or pain."[6]

[1]ZEPH. 3.15. [2]Isa. 41.10.—[3]Isa. 35.3, 4.—[4]Zeph. 3.17.—[5]Ps. 27.14. [6]Rev. 21.3, 4.

Evening

***Why are you crying out for help? Tell the people to move forward.*[1]**

Be strong and courageous! Let's fight hard for our people and for the cities of our God. And may the LORD's will be done.[2]—We prayed to our God and kept men on guard against them day and night.[3]

Not everyone who calls me 'Lord, Lord' will enter the Kingdom of heaven, but only those who do what my Father in heaven wants them to do.[4]—Whoever is willing to do what God wants will know whether what I teach comes from God.[5]—Let us try to know the LORD.[6]

Keep watch and pray that you will not fall into temptation.[7]—Be alert, stand firm in the faith, be brave, be strong.[8]—Work hard and do not be lazy. Serve the Lord with a heart full of devotion.[9]

Give strength to hands that are tired and to knees that tremble with weakness. Tell everyone who is discouraged, "Be strong and don't be afraid!"[10]

[1]EXOD. 14.15. [2]1 Chr. 19.13.—[3]Neh. 4.9. [4]Matt. 7.21.—[5]John 7.17.—[6]Hos. 6.3. [7]Matt. 26.41.—[8]1 Cor. 16.13.—[9]Rom. 12.11. [10]Isa. 35.3, 4.

Be strong through the grace that is ours in union with Christ Jesus.[1]

May you be made strong with all the strength which comes from his glorious power.[2]—Since you have accepted Christ Jesus as Lord, live in union with him. Keep your roots deep in him, build your lives on him, and become stronger in your faith as you were taught. And be filled with thanksgiving.[3]—They will be like trees that the LORD himself has planted. They will all do what is right, and God will be praised for what he has done.[4]—You . . . are built upon the foundation laid by the apostles and prophets, the cornerstone being Christ Jesus himself. He is the one who holds the whole building together and makes it grow into a sacred temple dedicated to the Lord. In union with him you too are being built together with all the others into a place where God lives through his Spirit.[5]

I commend you to the care of God and to the message of his grace, which is able to build you up and give you the blessings God has for all his people.[6]—Your lives will be filled with the truly good qualities which only Jesus Christ can produce, for the glory and praise of God.[7]

Run your best in the race of faith.[8]—Don't be afraid of your enemies.[9]

[1]2 TIM. 2.1. [2]Col. 1.11.—[3]Col. 2.6, 7.—[4]Isa. 61.3.—[5]Eph. 2.20–22. [6]Acts 20.32.—[7]Phil. 1.11. [8]1 Tim. 6.12.—[9]Phil. 1.28.

Evening

You yourself, O Lord, reward everyone according to his deeds.[1]

God has already placed Jesus Christ as the one and only foundation, and no other foundation can be laid. If what was built on the foundation survives the fire, the builder will receive a reward. But if anyone's work is burnt up, then he will lose it; but he himself will be saved, as if he had escaped through the fire.[2]—All of us must appear before Christ, to be judged by him. Each one will receive what he deserves, according to everything he has done, good or bad, in his bodily life.[3]

When you help a needy person, do it in such a way that even your closest friend will not know about it. Then it will be a private matter. And your Father, who sees what you do in private, will reward you.[4]—After a long time the master of those servants came back and settled accounts with them.[5]

There is nothing in us that allows us to claim that we are capable of doing this work. The capacity we have comes from God.[6]—You will give us prosperity, LORD; everything that we achieve is the result of what you do.[7]

[1]PS. 62.12. [2]1 Cor. 3.11, 14, 15.—[3]2 Cor. 5.10. [4]Matt. 6.3, 4.—[5]Matt. 25.19. [6]2 Cor. 3.5.—[7]Isa. 26.12.

Offer him glorious praise![1]

They are the people I made for myself, and they will sing my praises![2]—I will purify them from the sins that they have committed against me, and I will forgive their sins and their rebellion. Jerusalem will be a source of joy, honour, and pride to me; and every nation in the world will fear and tremble when they hear about the good things that I do.[3]—Let us, then, always offer praise to God as our sacrifice through Jesus, which is the offering presented by lips that confess him as Lord.[4]

I will praise you with all my heart, O Lord my God; I will proclaim your greatness for ever. How great is your constant love for me! You have saved me from the grave itself.[5]—LORD, who among the gods is like you? Who is like you, wonderful in holiness? Who can work miracles and mighty acts like yours?[6]—I will praise God with a song; I will proclaim his greatness by giving him thanks.[7]—[They were] . . . singing the song of Moses, the servant of God, and the song of the Lamb; "Lord God Almighty, how great and wonderful are your deeds!"[8]

[1]PS. 66.2. [2]Isa. 43.21.—[3]Jer. 33.8, 9.—[4]Heb. 13.15. [5]Ps. 86.12, 13.—[6]Exod. 15.11.—[7]Ps. 69.30.—[8]Rev. 15.3.

Evening

We, like everyone else, were destined to suffer God's anger.[1]

We ourselves were once foolish, disobedient, and wrong. We were slaves to passions and pleasures of all kinds. We spent our lives in malice and envy; others hated us and we hated them.[2]—Do not be surprised because I tell you that you must all be born again.[3]

I spoke foolishly, LORD. What can I answer? I will not try to say anything else.[4]—"Did you notice my servant Job?" the LORD asked [Satan]. "There is no one on earth as faithful and good as he is. He worships me and is careful not to do anything evil."[5]

I have been evil from the day I was born; from the time I was conceived, I have been sinful.[6]—This is what God said about [David]: 'I have found that David son of Jesse is the kind of man I like, a man who will do all I want him to do.'[7]

In the past I spoke evil of him and persecuted and insulted him. But God was merciful to me.[8]

A person is born physically of human parents, but he is born spiritually of the Spirit.[9]

[1]EPH. 2.3. [2]Titus 3.3.—[3]John 3.7. [4]Job 40.3, 4.—[5]Job 1.8. [6]Ps. 51.5.—[7]Acts 13.22. [8]1 Tim. 1.13. [9]John 3.6.

Help to carry one another's burdens, and in this way you will obey the law of Christ.[1]

Look out for one another's interests, not just for your own. The attitude you should have is the one that Christ Jesus had: He . . . took the nature of a servant.[2]—Even the Son of Man did not come to be served; he came to serve and to give his life to redeem many people.[3]—He died for all, so that those who live should no longer live for themselves, but only for him who died and was raised to life for their sake.[4]

Jesus saw her weeping, and he saw how the people who were with her were weeping also; his heart was touched, and he was deeply moved. Jesus wept.[5]—Be happy with those who are happy, weep with those who weep.[6]

You must all have the same attitude and the same feelings; love one another as brothers, and be kind and humble with one another. Do not pay back evil with evil or cursing with cursing; instead, pay back with a blessing, because a blessing is what God promised to give you when he called you.[7]

[1]GAL. 6.2. [2]Phil. 2.4, 5, 7.—[3]Mark 10.45.—[4]2 Cor. 5.15. [5]John 11.33, 35.—[6]Rom. 12.15. [7]1 Pet. 3.8, 9.

Evening

Son, go and work in the vineyard today.[1]

You are no longer a slave but a son. And since you are his son, God will give you all that he has for his sons.[2]

You are to think of yourselves as dead, so far as sin is concerned, but living in fellowship with God through Christ Jesus. Sin must no longer rule in your mortal bodies, so that you obey the desires of your natural self. Nor must you surrender any part of yourselves to sin to be used for wicked purposes. Instead, give yourselves to God, as those who have been brought from death to life, and surrender your whole being to him to be used for righteous purposes.[3]—Be obedient to God, and do not allow your lives to be shaped by those desires you had when you were still ignorant. Instead, be holy in all that you do, just as God who called you is holy. The scripture says, "Be holy because I am holy."[4]—Dedicated and useful to his Master, ready to be used for every good deed.[5]

So then, my dear brothers, stand firm and steady. Keep busy always in your work for the Lord, since you know that nothing you do in the Lord's service is ever useless.[6]

[1]MATT. 21.28. [2]Gal. 4.7. [3]Rom. 6.11–13.—[4]1 Pet. 1.14, 15.—[5]2 Tim. 2.21. [6]1 Cor. 15.58.

He had always loved those in the world who were his own, and he loved them to the very end.[1]

I pray for them. I do not pray for the world but for those you gave me, for they belong to you. All I have is yours, and all you have is mine; and my glory is shown through them. I do not ask you to take them out of the world, but I do ask you to keep them safe from the Evil One. Just as I do not belong to the world, they do not belong to the world.[2]

I love you just as the Father loves me; remain in my love.[3]—The greatest love a person can have for his friends is to give his life for them. And you are my friends if you do what I command you.[4]—Now I give you a new commandment: love one another. As I have loved you, so you must love one another.[5]

God, who began this good work in you, will carry it on until it is finished on the Day of Christ Jesus.[6]—Christ loved the church and gave his life for it. He did this to dedicate the church to God by his word, after making it clean by washing it in water.[7]

[1]JOHN 13.1. [2]John 17.9, 10, 15, 16. [3]John 15.9.—[4]John 15.13, 14.—[5]John 13.34. [6]Phil. 1.6.—[7]Eph. 5.25, 26.

Evening

The hidden depths of God's purposes.[1]

I do not call you servants any longer, because a servant does not know what his master is doing. Instead, I call you friends, because I have told you everything I have heard from my Father.[2]—The knowledge about the secrets of the Kingdom of heaven has been given to you.[3]

We have not received this world's spirit; instead we have received the Spirit sent by God, so that we may know all that God has given us.[4]

For this reason I fall on my knees before the Father, from whom every family in heaven and on earth receives its true name. I ask God from the wealth of his glory to give you power through his Spirit to be strong in your inner selves. I pray that you may have your roots and foundation in love, so that you, together with all God's people, may have the power to understand how broad and long, how high and deep, is Christ's love. Yes, may you come to know his love—although it can never be fully known—and so be completely filled with the very nature of God.[5]

[1]1 COR. 2.10. [2]John 15.15.—[3]Matt. 13.11. [4]1 Cor. 2.12. [5]Eph. 3.14–19.

Keep us alive, and we will praise you.[1]

What gives life is God's Spirit.[2]—The Spirit also comes to help us, weak as we are. For we do not know how we ought to pray; the Spirit himself pleads with God for us in groans that words cannot express. And God, who sees into our hearts, knows what the thought of the Spirit is; because the Spirit pleads with God on behalf of his people and in accordance with his will.[3]—Pray on every occasion, as the Spirit leads. For this reason keep alert and never give up.[4]

I will never neglect your instructions, because by them you have kept me alive.[5]—The words I have spoken to you bring God's life-giving Spirit.[6]—The written law brings death, but the Spirit gives life.[7]—If you remain in me and my words remain in you, then you will ask for anything you wish, and you shall have it.[8]—We have courage in God's presence, because we are sure that he hears us if we ask him for anything that is according to his will.[9]

No one can confess "Jesus is Lord," unless he is guided by the Holy Spirit.[10]

[1]PS. 80.18. [2]John 6.63.—[3]Rom. 8.26, 27.—[4]Eph. 6.18. [5]Ps. 119.93.—[6]John 6.63.—[7]2 Cor. 3.6.—[8]John 15.7.—[9]1 John 5.14. [10]1 Cor. 12.3.

Evening

Have nothing to do with the worthless things that people do, things that belong to the darkness. Instead, bring them out to the light.[1]

Do not be fooled. "Bad companions ruin good character."[2]

You know the saying, "A little bit of yeast makes the whole batch of dough rise." You must remove the old yeast of sin. In the letter that I wrote you I told you not to associate with immoral people. Now I did not mean pagans who are immoral or greedy or are thieves or who worship idols. To avoid them you would have to get out of the world completely. What I meant was that you should not associate with a person who calls himself a brother but is immoral or greedy or worships idols or is a slanderer or a drunkard or a thief. Don't even sit down to eat with such a person.[3]—So that you may be innocent and pure as God's perfect children, who live in a world of corrupt and sinful people. You must shine among them like stars lighting up the sky.[4]

In a large house there are dishes and bowls of all kinds: some are made of silver and gold, others of wood and clay; some are for special occasions, others for ordinary use.[5]

[1]EPH. 5.11. [2]1 Cor. 15.33. [3]1 Cor. 5.6, 7, 9–11.—[4]Phil. 2.15. [5]2 Tim. 2.20.

Let us have confidence . . . and approach God's throne, where there is grace. There we will receive mercy and find grace to help us just when we need it.[1]

Don't worry about anything, but in all your prayers ask God for what you need, always asking him with a thankful heart. And God's peace, which is far beyond human understanding, will keep your hearts and minds safe in union with Christ Jesus.[2]—The Spirit that God has given you does not make you slaves and cause you to be afraid; instead, the Spirit makes you God's children, and by the Spirit's power we cry out to God, "Father! my Father!"[3]

I did not require the people of Israel to look for me in a desolate waste.[4]—We have, then, my brothers, complete freedom to go into the Most Holy Place by means of the death of Jesus. He opened for us a new way, a living way, through the curtain—that is, through his own body. We have a great priest in charge of the house of God. So let us come near to God with a sincere heart and a sure faith, with hearts that have been purified from a guilty conscience and with bodies washed with clean water.[5]—Let us be bold, then, and say, "The Lord is my helper, I will not be afraid. What can anyone do to me?"[6]

[1]HEB. 4.16. [2]Phil. 4.6, 7.—[3]Rom. 8.15. [4]Isa. 45.19.—[5]Heb. 10.19–22.—[6]Heb. 13.6.

Evening

You will know the truth, and the truth will set you free.[1]

Where the Spirit of the Lord is present, there is freedom.[2]—The law of the Spirit, which brings us life in union with Christ Jesus, has set me free from the law of sin and death.[3]—If the Son sets you free, then you will be really free.[4]

My brothers, we are not the children of a slave-woman but of a free woman.[5]—We know that a person is put right with God only through faith in Jesus Christ, never by doing what the Law requires. We, too, have believed in Christ Jesus in order to be put right with God through our faith in Christ, and not by doing what the Law requires. For no one is put right with God by doing what the Law requires.[6]

Whoever looks closely into the perfect law that sets people free, who keeps on paying attention to it and does not simply listen and then forget it, but puts it into practice—that person will be blessed by God in what he does.[7]—Stand, then, as free people, and do not allow yourselves to become slaves again.[8]

[1]JOHN 8.32. [2]2 Cor. 3.17.—[3]Rom. 8.2.—[4]John 8.36. [5]Gal. 4.31.—[6]Gal. 2.16. [7]Jas 1.25.—[8]Gal. 5.1.

Light shines in the darkness for good men.[1]

All of you that honour the LORD and obey the words of his servant, the path you walk may be dark indeed, but trust in the LORD, rely on your God.[2]—If they fall, they will not stay down, because the LORD will help them up.[3]—Their instructions are a shining light; their correction can teach you how to live.[4]

Our enemies have no reason to gloat over us. We have fallen, but we will rise again. We are in darkness now, but the LORD will give us light. We have sinned against the LORD, so now we must endure his anger for a while. But in the end he will defend us and right the wrongs that have been done to us. He will bring us out to the light; we will live to see him save us.[5]

The eyes are like a lamp for the body. If your eyes are sound, your whole body will be full of light; but if your eyes are no good, your body will be in darkness. So if the light in you is darkness, how terribly dark it will be![6]

[1]PS. 112.4. [2]Isa. 50.10.—[3]Ps. 37.24.—[4]Prov. 6.23. [5]Mic. 7.8, 9. [6]Matt. 6.22, 23.

Evening

He will take care of his flock like a shepherd; he will gather the lambs together and carry them in his arms; he will gently lead their mothers.[1]

I feel sorry for these people, because they have been with me for three days and now have nothing to eat. I don't want to send them away without feeding them, for they might faint on their way home.[2]—Our High Priest is not one who cannot feel sympathy for our weaknesses.[3]

Some people brought children to Jesus . . . he took the children in his arms, placed his hands on each of them, and blessed them.[4]

I wander about like a lost sheep; so come and look for me, your servant, because I have not neglected your laws.[5]—The Son of Man came to seek and to save the lost.[6]—You were like sheep that had lost their way, but now you have been brought back to follow the Shepherd and Keeper of your souls.[7]

Do not be afraid, little flock, for your Father is pleased to give you the Kingdom.[8]—I myself will be the shepherd of my sheep, and I will find them a place to rest. I, the Sovereign LORD, have spoken.[9]

[1]ISA. 40.11. [2]Matt. 15.32.—[3]Heb. 4.15. [4]Mark 10.13, 16. [5]Ps. 119.176.—[6]Luke 19.10.—[7]1 Pet. 2.25. [8]Luke 12.32.—[9]Ezek. 34.15.

Even before the world was made, God had already chosen us to be his through our union with Christ.[1]

So that we would be holy and without fault before him.[2]

God chose you as the first to be saved by the Spirit's power to make you his holy people and by your faith in the truth . . . he called you to possess your share of the glory of our Lord Jesus Christ.[3]—Those whom God had already chosen he also set apart to become like his Son, so that the Son would be the first among many brothers. And so those whom God set apart, he called; and those he called, he put right with himself, and he shared his glory with them.[4]—You were chosen according to the purpose of God the Father and were made a holy people by his Spirit, to obey Jesus Christ and be purified by his blood.[5]

I will give you a new heart and a new mind. I will take away your stubborn heart of stone and give you an obedient heart.[6]—God did not call us to live in immorality, but in holiness.[7]

[1]EPH. 1.4. [2]Eph. 1.4. [3]2 Thess. 2.13, 14.—[4]Rom. 8.29, 30.—[5]1 Pet. 1.2. [6]Ezek. 36.26.—[7]1 Thess. 4.7.

Evening

That can't happen—not even if the* Lord *himself were to send grain at once![1]

Have faith in God.[2]—No one can please God without faith.[3]—For God everything is possible.[4]

Am I too weak to save them?[5]

"My thoughts," says the Lord, "are not like yours, and my ways are different from yours. As high as the heavens are above the earth, so high are my ways and thoughts above yours."[6]—Put me to the test and you will see that I will open the windows of heaven and pour out on you in abundance all kinds of good things.[7]

Don't think that the Lord is too weak to save you or too deaf to hear your call for help![8]—O Lord, you can help a weak army as easily as a powerful one.[9]

We should rely, not on ourselves, but only on God, who raises the dead.[10]

[1]2 KGS 7.2. [2]Mark 11.22.—[3]Heb. 11.6.—[4]Matt. 19.26. [5]Isa. 50.2. [6]Isa. 55.8, 9.—[7]Mal. 3.10. [8]Isa. 59.1.—[9]2 Chr. 14.11. [10]2 Cor. 1.9.

Your days of grief will come to an end.[1]

The world will make you suffer.[2]—We know that up to the present time all of creation groans with pain, like the pain of childbirth. But it is not just creation alone which groans; we who have the Spirit as the first of God's gifts also groan within ourselves, as we wait for God to make us his sons and set our whole being free.[3]—While we live in this earthly tent, we groan with a feeling of oppression; it is not that we want to get rid of our earthly body, but that we want to have the heavenly one put on over us, so that what is mortal will be transformed by life.[4]

These are the people who have come safely through the terrible persecution. They have washed their robes and made them white with the blood of the Lamb. That is why they stand before God's throne and serve him day and night in his temple. He who sits on the throne will protect them with his presence. Never again will they hunger or thirst; neither sun nor any scorching heat will burn them, because the Lamb, who is in the centre of the throne, will be their shepherd, and he will guide them to springs of life-giving water. And God will wipe away every tear from their eyes.[5]

[1]ISA. 60.20. [2]John 16.33.—[3]Rom. 8.22, 23.—[4]2 Cor. 5.4. [5]Rev. 7.14–17.

Evening

Teacher, don't you care that we are about to die?[1]

He is good to everyone and has compassion on all he made.[2]

All the animals, birds, and fish will live in fear of you. They are all placed under your power. Now you can eat them, as well as green plants; I give them all to you for food.[3]—As long as the world exists, there will be a time for planting and a time for harvest. There will always be cold and heat, summer and winter, day and night.[4]

The LORD is good; he protects his people in times of trouble; he takes care of those who turn to him.[5]—God heard the boy crying, and from heaven the angel of God spoke to Hagar, "What are you troubled about, Hagar? Don't be afraid. God has heard the boy crying." Then God opened her eyes, and she saw a well. She went and filled the leather bag with water and gave some to the boy.[6]

Do not start worrying: "Where will my food come from? or my drink? or my clothes?" Your Father in heaven knows that you need all these things.[7]—Place their hope . . . in God, who generously gives us everything for our enjoyment.[8]

[1]MARK 4.38. [2]Ps. 145.9. [3]Gen. 9.2, 3.—[4]Gen. 8.22. [5]Nahum 1.7.—[6]Gen. 21.17, 19. [7]Matt. 6.31, 32.—[8]1 Tim. 6.17.

Morning

You put your faith into practice.[1]

What God wants you to do is to believe in the one he sent.[2]

So it is with faith; if it is alone and includes no actions, then it is dead.[3]—Faith . . . works through love.[4]—If he sows in the field of his natural desires, from it he will gather the harvest of death; if he sows in the field of the Spirit, from the Spirit he will gather the harvest of eternal life.[5]—God has made us what we are, and in our union with Christ Jesus he has created us for a life of good deeds, which he has already prepared for us to do.[6]—He gave himself for us, to rescue us from all wickedness and to make us a pure people who belong to him alone and are eager to do good.[7]

Our brothers, we must thank God at all times for you. It is right for us to do so, because your faith is growing so much and the love each of you has for the others is becoming greater. That is why we always pray for you. We ask our God to make you worthy of the life he has called you to live. May he fulfil by his power all your desire for goodness and complete your work of faith.[8]—God is always at work in you to make you willing and able to obey his own purpose.[9]

[1]1 THESS. 1.3. [2]John 6.29. [3]Jas 2.17.—[4]Gal. 5.6.—[5]Gal. 6.8.—[6]Eph. 2.10.—[7] Titus 2.14. [8]2 Thess. 1.3, 11.—[9]Phil. 2.13.

Evening

He promised to come, didn't he? Where is he?[1]

Enoch, the sixth direct descendant from Adam . . . prophesied this about them: "The Lord will come with many thousands of his holy angels to bring judgement on all."[2]—Look, he is coming on the clouds! Everyone will see him, including those who pierced him. All peoples on earth will mourn over him.[3]

There will be the shout of command, the archangel's voice, the sound of God's trumpet, and the Lord himself will come down from heaven. Those who have died believing in Christ will rise to life first; then we who are living at that time will be gathered up along with them in the clouds to meet the Lord in the air. And so we will always be with the Lord.[4]

God has revealed his grace for the salvation of all mankind. That grace instructs us to give up ungodly living and worldly passions, and to live self-controlled, upright, and godly lives in this world, as we wait for the blessed Day we hope for, when the glory of our great God and Saviour Jesus Christ will appear.[5]

[1]2 PET. 3.4. [2]Jude 14, 15.—[3]Rev. 1.7. [4]1 Thess. 4.16, 17. [5]Titus 2.11–13.

If the enemies of my people want my protection, let them make peace with me.[1]

I alone know the plans I have for you, plans to bring you prosperity and not disaster.[2]—"There is no safety for sinners," says the LORD.[3]

Now, in union with Christ Jesus, you who used to be far away have been brought near by the sacrificial death of Christ. For Christ himself has brought us peace.[4]

It was by God's own decision that the Son has in himself the full nature of God. Through the Son, then, God decided to bring the whole universe back to himself.[5]—Christ Jesus . . . God offered him, so that by his sacrificial death he should become the means by which people's sins are forgiven through their faith in him. In this way God shows that he himself is righteous and that he puts right everyone who believes in Jesus.[6]—If we confess our sins to God, he will keep his promise and do what is right: he will forgive us our sins and purify us from all our wrongdoing.[7]

Trust in the LORD for ever; he will always protect us.[8]

[1]ISA. 27.5. [2]Jer. 29.11.—[3]Isa. 48.22. [4]Eph. 2.13, 14. [5]Col. 1.19, 20.—[6]Rom. 3.24–26.—[7]1 John 1.9. [8]Isa. 26.4.

Evening

God has given us eternal life, and this life has its source in his Son.[1]

Just as the Father is himself the source of life, in the same way he has made his Son to be the source of life. Just as the Father raises the dead and gives them life, in the same way the Son gives life to those he wants to.[2]

I am the resurrection and the life. Whoever believes in me will live, even though he dies; and whoever lives and believes in me will never die.[3]—I am the good shepherd, who is willing to die for the sheep. I am willing to give up my life, in order that I may receive it back again. No one takes my life away from me. I give it up of my own free will. I have the right to give it up, and I have the right to take it back. This is what my Father has commanded me to do.[4]

No one goes to the Father except by me.[5]—Whoever has the Son has [eternal] life; whoever does not have the Son of God does not have life.[6]—You have died, and your life is hidden with Christ in God. Your real life is Christ and when he appears, then you too will appear with him and share his glory![7]

[1]1 JOHN 5.11. [2]John 5.26, 21. [3]John 11.25, 26.—[4]John 10.11, 17, 18. [5]John 14.6.—[6]1 John 5.12.—[7]Col. 3.3.

If you live according to your human nature, you are going to die; but if by the Spirit you put to death your sinful actions, you will live.[1]

What human nature does is quite plain. It shows itself in immoral, filthy, and indecent actions; . . . and . . . other things like these. I warn you now as I have before: those who do these things will not possess the Kingdom of God. But the Spirit produces love, joy, peace, patience, kindness, goodness, faithfulness, humility, and self-control. There is no law against such things as these. And those who belong to Christ Jesus have put to death their human nature with all its passions and desires. The Spirit has given us life; he must also control our lives.[2]

God has revealed his grace for the salvation of all mankind. That grace instructs us to give up ungodly living and worldly passions, and to live self-controlled, upright, and godly lives in this world, as we wait for the blessed Day we hope for, when the glory of our great God and Saviour Jesus Christ will appear. He gave himself for us, to rescue us from all wickedness.[3]

[1]ROM. 8.13. [2]Gal. 5.19, 21–25. [3]Titus 2.11–14.

Evening

The Philistine commanders . . . asked, "What are these Hebrews doing here?"[1]

Happy are you if you are insulted because you are Christ's followers; this means that the glorious Spirit, the Spirit of God, is resting on you. If any of you suffers, it must not be because he is a murderer or a thief or a criminal or a meddler in other people's affairs.[2]

Do not let what you regard as good get a bad name.[3]—Your conduct among the heathen should be . . . good.[4]

Do not try to work together as equals with unbelievers, for it cannot be done. How can right and wrong be partners? How can light and darkness live together? For we are the temple of the living God! And so the Lord says, "You must leave them and separate yourselves from them. Have nothing to do with what is unclean."[5]

You are the chosen race, the King's priests, the holy nation, God's own people, chosen to proclaim the wonderful acts of God, who called you out of darkness into his own marvellous light.[6]

[1]1 SAM. 29.3. [2]1 Pet. 4.14, 15. [3]Rom. 14.16.—[4]1 Pet. 2.12. [5]2 Cor. 6.14, 16, 17. [6]1 Pet. 2.9.

The kindness and love of God our Saviour was revealed.[1]

I continue to show you my constant love.[2]

God showed his love for us by sending his only Son into the world, so that we might have life through him. This is what love is: it is not that we have loved God, but that he loved us and sent his Son to be the means by which our sins are forgiven.[3]

When the right time finally came, God sent his own Son. He came as the son of a human mother and lived under the Jewish Law, to redeem those who were under the Law, so that we might become God's sons.[4]—The Word became a human being and, full of grace and truth, lived among us. We saw his glory, the glory which he received as the Father's only Son.[5]—How great is the secret of our religion: he appeared in human form.[6]

Since the children . . . are people of flesh and blood, Jesus himself became like them and shared their human nature. He did this so that through his death he might destroy the Devil, who has the power over death.[7]

[1]TITUS 3.4. [2]Jer. 31.3. [3]1 John 4.9, 10. [4]Gal. 4.4, 5.—[5]John 1.14.—[6]1 Tim. 3.16. [7]Heb. 2.14.

Evening

Let us thank God for his priceless gift![1]

Sing to the LORD, all the world! Worship the LORD with joy; come before him with happy songs! Enter the temple gates with thanksgiving, go into its courts with praise. Give thanks to him and praise him.[2]—A child is born to us! A son is given to us! And he will be our ruler. He will be called, "Wonderful Counsellor," "Mighty God," "Eternal Father," "Prince of Peace."[3]

God, who did not even keep back his own Son, but offered him for us all![4]—The only one left to send was the man's own dear son . . . he sent his son.[5]

They must thank the LORD for his constant love, for the wonderful things he did for them.[6]—Praise the LORD, my soul! All my being, praise his holy name![7]

My heart praises the Lord; my soul is glad because of God my Saviour.[8]

[1]2 COR. 9.15. [2]Ps. 100.1, 2, 4.—[3]Isa. 9.6, 7. [4]Rom. 8.32.—[5]Mark 12.6. [6]Ps. 107.21.—[7]Ps. 103.1. [8]Luke 1.46, 47.

Morning

***Stand firm and steady. Keep busy always in your work for the Lord.*[1]**

You know that nothing you do in the Lord's service is ever useless.[2]—Since you have accepted Christ Jesus as Lord, live in union with him. Keep your roots deep in him, build your lives on him, and become stronger in your faith, as you were taught. And be filled with thanksgiving.[3]—Whoever holds out to the end will be saved.[4]—The seeds that fell in good soil stand for those who hear the message and retain it in a good and obedient heart, and they persist until they bear fruit.[5]

You stand firm in the faith.[6]

As long as it is day, we must keep on doing the work of him who sent me; night is coming when no one can work.[7]

If he sows in the field of his natural desires, from it he will gather the harvest of death; if he sows in the field of the Spirit, from the Spirit he will gather the harvest of eternal life. So let us not become tired of doing good; for if we do not give up, the time will come when we will reap the harvest. So then, as often as we have the chance, we should do good to everyone, and especially to those who belong to our family in the faith.[8]

[1]1 COR. 15.58. [2]1 Cor. 15.58.—[3]Col. 2.6, 7.—[4]Matt. 24.13.—[5]Luke 8.15. [6]2 Cor. 1.24. [7]John 9.4. [8]Gal. 6.8–10.

Evening

***He is able . . . to save those who come to God through him.*[1]**

I am the way, the truth and the life; no one goes to the Father except by me.[2]—Salvation is to be found through him alone; in all the world there is no one else whom God has given who can save us.[3]

My sheep listen to my voice; I know them, and they follow me. I give them eternal life, and they shall never die. No one can snatch them away from me.[4]

God, who began this good work in you, will carry it on until it is finished on the Day of Christ Jesus.[5]

Is anything too hard for the LORD?[6]

To him who is able to keep you from falling, and to bring you faultless and joyful before his glorious presence—to the only God our Saviour, through Jesus Christ our Lord, be glory, majesty, might, and authority, from all ages past, and now, and for ever and ever! Amen.[7]

[1]HEB. 7.25. [2]John 14.6.—[3]Acts 4.12. [4]John 10.27, 28. [5]Phil. 1.6. [6]Gen. 18.14. [7]Jude 24, 25.

We fix our attention, not on things that are seen . . . what can be seen lasts only for a time, but what cannot be seen lasts for ever.[1]

There is no permanent city for us here on earth.[2]—You knew that you still possessed something much better, which would last for ever.[3]

Do not be afraid, little flock, for your Father is pleased to give you the Kingdom.[4]

It may now be necessary for you to be sad for a while because of the many kinds of trials you suffer.[5]—In the grave wicked men stop their evil, and tired workmen find rest at last.[6]

While we live in this earthly tent, we groan with a feeling of oppression.[7]—He will wipe away all tears from their eyes. There will be no more death, no more grief or crying or pain. The old things have disappeared.[8]

What we suffer at this present time cannot be compared at all with the glory that is going to be revealed to us.[9]—This small and temporary trouble we suffer will bring us a tremendous and eternal glory, much greater than the trouble.[10]

[1]2 COR. 4.18. [2]Heb. 13.14.—[3]Heb. 10.34. [4]Luke 12.32. [5]1 Pet. 1.6.—[6]Job 3.17. [7]2 Cor. 5.4.—[8]Rev. 21.4. [9]Rom. 8.18.—[10]2 Cor. 4.17.

Evening

Christ himself has brought us peace.[1]

God was making all mankind his friends through Christ. God did not keep an account of their sins, and he has given us the message which tells how he makes them his friends.[2]—God made peace through his Son's sacrificial death on the cross and so brought back to himself all things, both on earth and in heaven. At one time you were far away from God and were his enemies because of the evil things you did and thought. But now, by means of the physical death of his Son, God has made you his friends, in order to bring you, holy, pure, and faultless, into his presence.[3]—He cancelled the unfavourable record of our debts with its binding rules and did away with it completely by nailing it to the cross.[4]—He abolished the Jewish Law with its commandments and rules, in order to create out of the two races one new people in union with himself, in this way making peace.[5]

Peace is what I leave with you; it is my own peace that I give you. I do not give it as the world does. Do not be worried and upset; do not be afraid.[6]

[1]EPH. 2.14. [2]2 Cor. 5.19, 21.—[3]Col. 1.20–22.—[4]Col. 2.14.—[5]Eph. 2.15. [6]John 14.27.

Your sins are forgiven.[1]

I will forgive their sins and I will no longer remember their wrongs.[2]—God is the only one who can forgive sins![3]

I am the God who forgives your sins, and I do this because of who I am. I will not hold your sins against you.[4]—Happy are those whose sins are forgiven, whose wrongs are pardoned. Happy is the man whom the LORD does not accuse of doing wrong.[5]—There is no other god like you, O LORD; you forgive the sins of your people.[6]

God has forgiven you through Christ.[7]—The blood of Jesus, his Son, purifies us from every sin. If we say that we have no sin, we deceive ourselves, and there is no truth in us. But if we confess our sins to God, he will keep his promise and do what is right: he will forgive us our sins and purify us from all our wrongdoing.[8]

As far as the east is from the west, so far does he remove our sins from us.[9]—Sin must not be your master; for you do not live under law but under God's grace. You were set free from sin and became the slaves of righteousness.[10]

[1]MARK 2.5. [2]Jer. 31.34.—[3]Mark 2.7. [4]Isa. 43.25.—[5]Ps. 32.1, 2.—[6]Mic. 7.18. [7]Eph. 4.32.—[8]1 John 1.7–9. [9]Ps. 103.12.—[10]Rom. 6.14, 18.

Evening

Sir, we want to see Jesus.[1]

We follow your will and put our hope in you; you are all that we desire.[2]

He is near to those who call to him, who call to him with sincerity.[3]

Where two or three come together in my name, I am there with them.[4]—You will not be left all alone; I will come back to you.[5]—I will be with you always, to the end of the age.[6]

Let us run with determination the race that lies before us. Let us keep our eyes fixed on Jesus, on whom our faith depends from beginning to end.[7]

What we see now is like a dim image in a mirror; then we shall see face to face.[8]—I want very much to leave this life and be with Christ, which is a far better thing.[9]

My dear friends, we are now God's children, but it is not yet clear what we shall become. But we know that when Christ appears, we shall be like him, because we shall see him as he really is. Everyone who has this hope in Christ keeps himself pure, just as Christ is pure.[10]

[1]JOHN 12.21. [2]Isa. 26.8. [3]Ps. 145.18. [4]Matt. 18.20.—[5]John 14.18.—[6]Matt. 28.20. [7]Heb. 12.1, 2. [8]1 Cor. 13.12.—[9]Phil. 1.23. [10]1 John 3.2, 3.

Try to find out what the Lord wants you to do.[1]

God wants you to be holy.[2]—Make peace with God . . . if you do, then he will bless you.[3]—Eternal life means knowing you, the only true God, and knowing Jesus Christ, whom you sent.[4]

We know that the Son of God has come and has given us understanding, so that we know the true God. We live in union with the true God—in union with his Son Jesus Christ.[5]

We have always prayed for you . . . We ask God to fill you with the knowledge of his will, with all the wisdom and understanding that his Spirit gives.[6]—[I] ask the God of our Lord Jesus Christ, the glorious Father, to give you the Spirit who will make you wise and reveal God to you, so that you will know him. I ask that your minds may be opened to see his light, so that you will know what is the hope to which he has called you, how rich are the wonderful blessings he promises his people, and how very great is his power at work in us who believe.[7]

[1]EPH. 5.17. [2]1 Thess. 4.3.—[3]Job 22.21.—[4]John 17.3. [5]1 John 5.20. [6]Col. 1.9.—[7]Eph. 1.17–19.

Evening

Come near to God, and he will come near to you.[1]

[Enoch] . . . spent his life in fellowship with God.[2]—Do two men start travelling together without arranging to meet?[3]—As for me, how wonderful to be near God![4]

"The LORD is with you as long as you are with him. If you look for him, he will let you find him, but if you turn away, he will abandon you." When trouble came, they turned to the LORD, the God of Israel. They searched for him, and found him.[5]

I alone know the plans I have for you, plans to bring you prosperity and not disaster, plans to bring about the future you hope for. Then you will call to me. You will come and pray to me, and I will answer you. You will seek me, and you will find me because you will seek me with all your heart.[6]

We have, then, my brothers, complete freedom to go into the Most Holy Place by means of the death of Jesus. He opened for us a new way, a living way . . . We have a great priest in charge of the house of God. So let us come near to God with a sincere heart and a sure faith.[7]

[1]JAS 4.8. [2]Gen. 5.24.—[3]Amos 3.3.—[4]Ps. 73.28. [5]2 Chr. 15.2, 4. [6]Jer. 29.11–13. [7]Heb. 10.19–22.

Faultless on the Day of our Lord Jesus Christ.[1]

At one time you were far away from God and were his enemies because of the evil things you did and thought. But now, by means of the physical death of his Son, God has made you his friends, in order to bring you, holy, pure, and faultless, into his presence. You must, of course, continue faithful on a firm and sure foundation, and must not allow yourselves to be shaken from the hope you gained when you heard the gospel.[2]—So that you may be innocent and pure as God's perfect children, who live in a world of corrupt and sinful people. You must shine among them like stars lighting up the sky.[3]

So, my friends, as you wait for that Day, do your best to be pure and faultless in God's sight and to be at peace with him.[4]—Then you will be free from all impurity and blame on the Day of Christ.[5]

To him who is able to keep you from falling, and to bring you faultless and joyful before his glorious presence—to the only God our Saviour, through Jesus Christ our Lord, be glory, majesty, might, and authority, from all ages past, and now, and for ever and ever![6]

[1]1 COR. 1.8. [2]Col. 1.21–23.—[3]Phil. 2.15. [4]2 Pet. 3.14.—[5]Phil. 1.10. [6]Jude 24, 25.

Evening

He protects the lives of his faithful people.[1]

If . . . we say that we have fellowship with him, yet at the same time live in the darkness, we are lying both in our words and in our actions. But if we live in the light—just as he is in the light—then we have fellowship with one another, and the blood of Jesus, his Son, purifies us from every sin.[2]—Anyone who has had a bath is completely clean and does not have to wash himself, except for his feet.[3]

I have taught you wisdom and the right way to live. Nothing will stand in your way if you walk wisely, and you will not stumble when you run. Do not go where evil men go. Do not follow the example of the wicked. Don't do it! Keep away from evil! Refuse it and go on your way. Look straight ahead with honest confidence; don't hang your head in shame. Plan carefully what you do, and whatever you do will turn out right. Avoid evil and walk straight ahead. Don't go one step off the right way.[4]

The Lord will rescue me from all evil and take me safely into his heavenly Kingdom. To him be the glory for ever and ever! Amen.[5]

[1]1 SAM. 2.9. [2]1 John 1.6, 7.—[3]John 13.10. [4]Prov. 4.11, 12, 14, 15, 25–27. [5]2 Tim. 4.18.

He brought you safely all the way to this place, just as a father would carry his son.[1]

I carried you as an eagle carries her young on her wings, and brought you here to me.[2]—In his love and compassion he rescued them. He had always taken care of them in the past.[3]—Like an eagle teaching its young to fly, catching them safely on its spreading wings, the LORD kept Israel from falling. The LORD alone led his people.[4]

I am your God and will take care of you until you are old and your hair is grey. I made you and will care for you; I will give you help and rescue you.[5]—This God is our God for ever and ever; he will lead us for all time to come.[6]

Leave your troubles with the LORD, and he will defend you; he never lets honest men be defeated.[7]—I tell you not to be worried about the food and drink you need in order to stay alive, or about clothes for your body. Your Father in heaven knows that you need all these things.[8]

The LORD has helped us all the way.[9]

[1]DEUT. 1.31. [2]Exod. 19.4.—[3]Isa. 63.9.—[4]Deut. 32.11, 12. [5]Isa. 46.4.—[6]Ps. 48.14. [7]Ps. 55.22.—[8]Matt. 6.25, 32. [9]1 Sam. 7.12.

Evening

There is still much land to be taken.[1]

I do not claim that I have already succeeded or have already become perfect. I keep striving to win the prize for which Christ Jesus has already won me to himself.[2]

You must be perfect.[3]—Do your best to add goodness to your faith; to your goodness add knowledge; to your knowledge add self-control; to your self-control add endurance; to your endurance add godliness; to your godliness add brotherly affection; and to your brotherly affection add love.[4]

I pray that your love will keep on growing more and more, together with true knowledge and perfect judgement.[5]

What no one ever saw or heard, what no one ever thought could happen, is the very thing God prepared for those who love him. But it was to us that God made known his secret by means of his Spirit.[6]

There still remains for God's people a rest.[7]—Once again you will see a king ruling in splendour over a land that stretches in all directions.[8]

[1]JOSH. 13.1. [2]Phil. 3.12. [3]Matt. 5.48.—[4]2 Pet. 1.5–7. [5]Phil. 1.9. [6]1 Cor. 2.9, 10. [7]Heb. 4.9.—[8]Isa. 33.17.

For special occasions

In their trouble they called to the LORD, and he saved them from their distress. They must thank the LORD for his constant love, for the wonderful things he did for them.[1]

There were ten men who were healed; where are the other nine?[2]—Do not forget how kind he is.[3]—God, who helped me in the time of my trouble.[4]

I prayed to the LORD, and he answered me; he freed me from all my fears.[5]—I love the LORD, because he hears me; he listens to my prayers. He listens to me every time I call to him.[6]—The LORD protects and defends me; I trust in him. He gives me help and makes me glad; I praise him with joyful songs.[7]

Call to me when trouble comes; I will save you, and you will praise me. Giving thanks is the sacrifice that honours me.[8]

In the name of our Lord Jesus Christ, always give thanks for everything to God the Father.[9]

[1]PS. 107.19, 21. [2]Luke 17.17.—[3]Ps. 103.2.—[4]Gen. 35.3. [5]Ps. 34.4.—[6]Ps. 116.1, 2.—[7]Ps. 28.7. [8]Ps. 50.15, 23. [9]Eph. 5.20.

Evening

No one who waits for my help will be disappointed.[1]

Didn't I tell you that you would see God's glory if you believed?[2]

"Daniel, servant of the living God! Was the God you serve so loyally able to save you?" He had not been hurt at all, for he trusted God.[3]

I asked him . . . and he gave me what I asked for. The LORD has filled my heart with joy.[4]—Come and listen, all who honour God, and I will tell you what he has done for me. I praise God, because he did not reject my prayer or keep back his constant love from me.[5]—I praise you and honour you, God of my ancestors. You have given me wisdom and strength; you have answered my prayer.[6]—You rule over the powerful sea; you calm its angry waves.[7]

He calmed the raging storm, and the waves became quiet. They were glad because of the calm, and he brought them safe to the port they wanted. They must thank the LORD for his constant love, for the wonderful things he did for them.[8]—Happy are those who find safety with him.[9]

[1]ISA. 49.23. [2]John 11.40. [3]Dan. 6.20, 23. [4]1 Sam. 1.27; 2.1.—[5]Ps. 66.16, 20.—[6]Dan. 2.23.—[7]Ps. 89.9. [8]Ps. 107.29–31.—[9]Ps. 34.8.

May the LORD bless you and take care of you.[1]

May the LORD, who made heaven and earth, bless you![2]—God our Father.[3]—God, who generously gives us everything for our enjoyment.[4]

Your Father in heaven knows that you need all these things.[5]—For the Father himself loves you.[6]

He does not refuse any good thing to those who do what is right.[7]—He provides help and protection for righteous, honest men.[8]—Happy are those who follow his commands, who obey him with all their heart.[9]

He will not let you fall; your protector is always awake. The protector of Israel never dozes or sleeps.[10]—The LORD will keep you safe. He will not let you fall into a trap.[11]—You, LORD, give perfect peace to those who keep their purpose firm and put their trust in you.[12]

May the Lord himself, who is our source of peace, give you peace at all times and in every way.[13]

[1]NUM. 6.24. [2]Ps. 134.3.—[3]2 Thess. 2.16.—[4]1 Tim. 6.17. [5]Matt. 6.32.—[6]John 16.27. [7]Ps. 84.11.—[8]Prov. 2.7.—[9]Ps. 119.2. [10]Ps. 121.3, 4.—[11]Prov. 3.26.—[12]Isa. 26.3. [13]2 Thess. 3.16.

Evening

I the LORD your God, am with you wherever you go.[1]

I have given you and all my people the entire land that you will be marching over. No one will be able to defeat you as long as you live. I will be with you as I was with Moses. I will always be with you; I will never abandon you.[2]—The land that you are about to enter is a land of mountains and valleys, a land watered by rain. The LORD your God takes care of this land and watches over it throughout the year.[3]—We are partners working together for God, and you are God's field.[4]—In our union which Christ Jesus he has created us for a life of good deeds, which he has already prepared for us to do.[5]

How wonderful are the good things you keep for those who honour you! You hide them in the safety of your presence from the plots of men; in a safe shelter you hide them from the insults of their enemies.[6]—Whoever goes to the LORD for safety, whoever remains under the protection of the Almighty.[7]

[1]JOSH. 1.9. [2]Josh. 1.3, 5.—[3]Deut. 11.11, 12.—[4]1 Cor. 3.9.—[5]Eph. 2.10. [6]Ps. 31.19, 20.—[7]Ps. 91.1.

Jesus and his disciples had also been invited to the wedding.[1]

Marriage is to be honoured by all.[2]—The LORD God said, "It is not good for the man to live alone."[3]—Everything that God has created is good; nothing is to be rejected, but everything is to be received with a prayer of thanks, because the word of God and the prayer make it acceptable to God.[4]

It is the LORD's blessing that makes you wealthy. Hard work can make you no richer.[5]—God, who generously gives us everything for our enjoyment.[6]—He . . . blesses me with love and mercy. He fills my life with good things.[7]

Christ loved the church and gave his life for it.[8]—You do not belong to yourselves.[9]

My brothers . . . there is not much time left, and from now on married men should live as though they were not married; . . . those who laugh, as though they were not happy; . . . those who deal in material goods, as though they were not fully occupied with them. For this world, as it is now, will not last much longer.[10]—Keep your minds fixed on things [in heaven], not on things here on earth.[11]

[1]JOHN 2.2. [2]Heb. 13.4.—[3]Gen. 2.18.—[4]1 Tim. 4.4, 5. [5]Prov. 10.22.—[6]1 Tim. 6.17.—[7]Ps. 103.4, 5. [8]Eph. 5.25.—[9]1 Cor. 6.19. [10]1 Cor. 7.29, 31.—[11]Col. 3.2.

Evening

I will live a pure life in my house.[1]

As for my family and me, we will serve the LORD.[2]

Be concerned above everything else with the Kingdom of God and with what he requires of you, and he will provide you with all these other things.[3]—No servant can be the slave of two masters. You cannot serve both God and money.[4]

They also will receive, together with you, God's gift of life. Do this so that nothing will interfere with your prayers.[5]—Two are better off than one . . . if one of them falls down, the other can help him up.[6]—Let us be concerned for one another, to help one another to show love and to do good.[7]

Husbands, love your wives.[8]—In order to train the younger women to love their husbands.[9]—Love is not . . . irritable.[10]—Be kind to one another, and forgive one another, as God has forgiven you through Christ.[11]

The capacity we have comes from God.[12]—I am the LORD your God; I strengthen you and say, 'Do not be afraid; I will help you.'[13]

[1]PS. 101.2. [2]Josh. 24.15. [3]Matt. 6.33.—[4]Luke 16.13. [5]1 Pet. 3.7.—[6]Eccles. 4.9, 10.—[7]Heb. 10.24. [8]Col. 3.19.—[9]Titus 2.4.—[10]1 Cor. 13.5.—[11]Eph. 4.32. [12]2 Cor. 3.5.—[13]Isa. 41.13.

We do not know what to do, but we look to you for help.[1]

My sins, O God, are not hidden from you; you know how foolish I have been.[2]—You are my God; teach me to do your will.[3]—LORD . . . lead me to do your will; make your way plain for me to follow.[4]—I am always in your care.[5]

If any of you lacks wisdom, he should pray to God, who will give it to him; because God gives generously and graciously to all. But when you pray, you must believe and not doubt at all.[6]—All of you that honour the LORD and obey the words of his servant, the path you walk may be dark indeed, but trust in the LORD, rely on your God.[7]

Whenever I am anxious and worried, you comfort me and make me glad.[8]—Why am I so sad? Why am I so troubled? I will put my hope in God.[9]

Jesus said to his disciples, "Why are you frightened? Have you still no faith?"[10]—To have faith is to be . . . certain of the things we cannot see.[11]

[1]2 CHR. 20.12. [2]Ps. 69.5.—[3]Ps. 143.10.—[4]Ps. 5.8.—[5]Ps. 31.15. [6]Jas 1.5, 6.—[7]Isa. 50.10. [8]Ps. 94.19.—[9]Ps. 42.5. [10]Mark 4.40.—[11]Heb. 11.1.

Evening

Do not be afraid; I will help you.[1]

Come to me, all of you who are tired from carrying heavy loads, and I will give you rest.[2]—It is he who is the "Yes" to all God's promises. This is why through Jesus Christ our "Amen" is said to the glory of God.[3]

When they call to me, I will answer them; when they are in trouble, I will be with them.[4]—I made you and will care for you; I will give you help and rescue you.[5]—I will be with you.[6]

Don't worry about anything, but in all your prayers ask God for what you need, always asking him with a thankful heart. And God's peace, which is far beyond human understanding, will keep your hearts and minds safe in union with Christ Jesus.[7]

I will teach you the way you should go; I will instruct you and advise you.[8]—I will never leave you; I will never abandon you.[9]—I will be with you always, to the end of the age.[10]

Don't be afraid! I am the first and the last.[11]

[1]ISA. 41.13. [2]Matt. 11.28.—[3]2 Cor. 1.20. [4]Ps. 91.15.—[5]Isa. 46.4.—[6]Isa. 43.2. [7]Phil. 4.6, 7. [8]Ps. 32.8.—[9]Heb. 13.5.—[10]Matt. 28.20. [11]Rev. 1.17.

Save me, O God! The waves are about to drown me.[1]

My Father, if it is possible, take this cup of suffering from me! Yet not what I want, but what you want.[2]—In great anguish.[3]—Jesus wept.[4]

He endured the suffering that should have been ours, the pain that we should have borne.[5]—Our High Priest is not one who cannot feel sympathy for our weaknesses. On the contrary, we have a High Priest who was tempted in every way that we are, but did not sin. Let us have confidence, then, and approach God's throne, where there is grace.[6]

He cares for you.[7]—I have called you by name—you are mine. When you pass through deep waters, I will be with you: your troubles will not overwhelm you.[8]—I will never leave you; I will never abandon you.[9]

What if God kills me? I am going to state my case to him.[10]—My mind and my body may grow weak, but God is my strength; he is all I ever need.[11]

[1]PS. 69.1, 2. [2]Matt. 26.39.—[3]Luke 22.44.—[4]John 11.35. [5]Isa. 53.4.—[6]Heb. 4.15, 16. [7]1 Pet. 5.7.—[8]Isa. 43.1, 2.—[9]Heb. 13.5. [10]Job 13.15.—[11]Ps. 73.26.

Evening

I am the one who strengthens you.[1]

The LORD's unfailing love and mercy still continue. He takes no pleasure in causing us grief or pain.[2]—You do not understand now what I am doing, but you will understand later.[3]—These are only hints of his power, only the whispers that we have heard.[4]

The LORD is full of mercy and compassion.[5]—The merciful Father, the God from whom all help comes! He helps us in all our troubles, so that we are able to help others who have all kinds of troubles, using the same help that we ourselves have received from God.[6]

He has . . . sent me . . . to heal the broken-hearted.[7]—He endured suffering and pain.[8]—You will not be left all alone.[9]

Another Helper . . . he is the spirit who reveals the truth about God.[10]

God has always been your defence; his eternal arms are your support.[11]—I will comfort you . . . as a mother comforts her child.[12]

[1]ISA. 51.12. [2]Lam. 3.22, 23.—[3]John 13.7.—[4]Job 26.14. [5]Jas 5.11.—[6]2 Cor, 1.3, 4. [7]Isa. 61.1.—[8]Isa. 53.3.—[9]John 14.18. [10]John 14.16, 17. [11]Deut. 33.27.—[12]Isa. 66.13.

Lord, your dear friend is ill.[1]

He endured the suffering that should have been ours, the pain that we should have borne.[2]—He himself took our sickness and carried away our diseases.[3]—God was merciful to his people.[4]—As a father is kind to his children, so the LORD is kind to those who honour him. He knows what we are made of.[5]

Who, then, can separate us from the love of Christ? Can trouble do it, or hardship?[6]—The LORD corrects everyone he loves. When we are punished, it seems to us at the time something to make us sad, not glad. Later, however, those who have been disciplined by such punishment reap the peaceful reward of a righteous life.[7]—We know that in all things God works for good with those who love him.[8]

His answer was, "My grace is all you need, for my power is greatest when you are weak." I am most happy, then, to be proud of my weaknesses, in order to feel the protection of Christ's power over me.[9]

[1]JOHN 11.3. [2]Isa. 53.4.—[3]Matt. 8.17.—[4]Ps. 78.38.—[5]Ps. 103.13, 14. [6]Rom. 8.35.—[7]Heb. 12.6, 11.—[8]Rom. 8.28. [9]2 Cor. 12.9.

Evening

I am worn out, O LORD; have pity on me! Give me strength; I am completely exhausted.[1]

In despair and far from home I call to you! Take me to a safe refuge.[2]—He strengthens those who are weak and tired.[3]—The LORD protects me from all danger; I will never be afraid.[4]

Do not stay away from me! Trouble is near.[5]—You are near to me, LORD.[6]—When I begged you to listen to my cry, you heard. You answered me and told me not to be afraid.[7]—Always ready to help.[8]

LORD, rescue me from all this trouble.[9]—He will not break off a bent reed.[10]—Even if I go through the deepest darkness, I will not be afraid, LORD, for you are with me.[11]—His eternal arms are your support.[12]

May your Lord Jesus Christ himself and God our Father, who loved us and in his grace gave us unfailing courage and a firm hope, encourage you.[13]

[1]PS. 6.2. [2]Ps. 61.2.—[3]Isa. 40.29.—[4]Ps. 27.1. [5]Ps. 22.11.—[6]Ps. 119.151.—[7]Lam. 3.56, 57.—[8]Ps. 46.1. [9]Isa. 38.14.—[10]Matt. 12.20.—[11]Ps. 23.4.—[12]Deut. 33.27. [13]2 Thess. 2.16, 17.

Father! You have given them to me and I want them to be with me where I am.[1]

A man dies and never returns; he is forgotten by all who knew him.[2]

As long as we are at home in the body we are away from the Lord's home. We . . . would much prefer to leave our home in the body and be at home with the Lord.[3]—I am pulled in two directions. I want very much to leave this life and be with Christ, which is a far better thing.[4]—Whether we live or die, we belong to the Lord.[5]

You . . . possessed something much better, which would last for ever.[6]—It is not yet clear what we shall become. But we know that when Christ appears, we shall be like him, because we shall see him as he really is.[7]—What we see now is like a dim image in a mirror; then we shall see face to face.[8]—I will see you, because I have done no wrong; and when I awake, your presence will find me with joy.[9]

So we will always be with the Lord. So then encourage one another with these words.[10]

[1]JOHN 17.24. [2]Job 7.10. [3]2 Cor. 5.6, 8.—[4]Phil. 1.23.—[5]Rom. 14.8. [6]Heb. 10.34.—[7]1 John 3.2.—[8]1 Cor. 13.12.—[9]Ps. 17.15. [10]1 Thess. 4.17, 18.

Evening

Those who have died believing in [***Jesus***].[1]

"Our friend Lazarus has fallen asleep." Jesus meant that Lazarus had died.[2]—The LORD provides for those he loves, while they are asleep.[3]

Christ Jesus . . . has ended the power of death.[4]—He did this so that through his death he might . . . set free those who were slaves all their lives because of their fear of death.[5]—Through God's grace he should die for everyone.[6]

Death is destroyed; victory is complete! Where, Death, is your victory? Where, Death, is your power to hurt? Death gets its power to hurt from sin, and sin gets its power from the Law. But thanks be to God who gives us the victory through our Lord Jesus Christ! So then, my dear brothers, stand firm and steady. Keep busy always in your work for the Lord, since you know that nothing you do in the Lord's service is ever useless.[7]

[1]1 THESS. 4.14. [2]John 11.11, 13.—[3]Ps. 127.2. [4]2 Tim. 1.10.—[5]Heb. 2.14, 15.—[6]Heb. 2.9. [7]1 Cor. 15.54–58.

***When God sends us something good, we welcome it. How can we complain when he sends us trouble?*[1]**

He is not afraid of receiving bad news; his faith is strong, and he trusts in the LORD.[2]—You do not understand now what I am doing, but you will understand later.[3]—We know that in all things God works for good with those who love him, those whom he has called according to his purpose.[4]

A messenger came running to Job, "We were ploughing the fields with the oxen," he said, "and the donkeys were in a nearby pasture. Suddenly the Sabeans attacked and stole them all . . ." Another servant came and said, "Lightning struck the sheep and the shepherds and killed them all . . ." Another servant came and said, "Your children were having a feast at the home of your eldest son, when a storm swept in from the desert. It blew the house down and killed them all. I am the only one who escaped to tell you."[5]

He is the LORD; he will do whatever seems best to him.[6]

[1]JOB 2.10. [2]Ps.112.7.—[3]John 13.7.—[4]Rom. 8.28. [5]Job 1.14–16, 18, 19. [6]1 Sam. 3.18.

Evening

***Have you asked God to show you your faults?*[1]**

A messenger reported to David, "The Israelites are pledging their loyalty to Absalom." So David said . . . "We must get away at once if we want to escape from Absalom."[2]—The king said to Zadok, "Take the Covenant Box back to the city. If the LORD is pleased with me, some day he will let me come back to see it and the place where it stays. But if he isn't pleased with me—well, then, let him do to me what he wishes." David went on up to the Mount of Olives weeping.[3]

Tears may flow in the night, but joy comes in the morning.[4]—I will make a lasting covenant with you and give you the blessings I promised to David.[5]

The LORD blessed the last part of Job's life even more than he had blessed the first.[6]—My dear friends, do not be surprised at the painful test you are suffering, as though something unusual were happening to you. Rather be glad that you are sharing Christ's sufferings.[7]

[1]JOB 34.32. [2]2 Sam. 15.13, 14.—[3]2 Sam. 15.25, 26, 30. [4]Ps. 30.5.—[5]Isa. 55.3. [6]Job 48.12.—[7]1 Pet. 4.12, 13.

Mizpah.[1]

May the LORD keep an eye on us while we are separated from each other.[2] Keep on praying for us . . . I beg you even more earnestly to pray that God will send me back to you soon.[3]—As for us, brothers, when we were separated from you for a little while—not in our thoughts, of course, but only in body—how we missed you and how hard we tried to see you again! We wanted to return to you. I myself tried to go back more than once, but Satan would not let us.[4]

Who, then, can separate us from the love of Christ? For I am certain that nothing can separate us from his love: neither death nor life, neither angels nor other heavenly rulers or powers, neither the present nor the future, neither the world above nor the world below—there is nothing in all creation that will ever be able to separate us from the love of God which is ours through Christ Jesus our Lord.[5]

God has said, "I will never leave you; I will never abandon you." Let us be bold, then, and say, "The Lord is my helper, I will not be afraid. What can anyone do to me?"[6]—I will be with you always, to the end of the age.[7]

[1]GEN. 31.49. [2]Gen. 31.49. [3]Heb. 13.18, 19.—[4]1 Thess. 2.17, 18. [5]Rom. 8.35, 38, 39. [6]Heb. 13.5, 6.—[7]Matt. 28.20.

Evening

When I go, you will not be left all alone; I will come back to you.[1]

Hearing good news from a distant land is like a drink of cold water when you are dry and thirsty.[2]

They left Egypt and went back home to their father Jacob in Canaan. "Joseph is still alive!" they told him. "He is the ruler of all Egypt!" Jacob was stunned and could not believe them. But when they told him all that Joseph had said to them, and when he saw the wagons which Joseph had sent to take him to Egypt, he recovered from the shock. "My son Joseph is still alive!" he said. "This is all I could ask for! I must go and see him before I die."[3]

"I have gone about among all of you, preaching the Kingdom of God. And now I know that none of you will ever see me again . . ." When Paul finished, he knelt down with them and prayed. They were all crying as they hugged him and kissed him goodbye. They were especially sad because he had said that they would never see him again. And so they went with him to the ship.[4]

[1]JOHN 14.18. [2]Prov. 25.25. [3]Gen. 45.25–28. [4]Acts 20.25, 36, 38.

I will see you again.[1]

Jacob said to Joseph, "I never expected to see you again, and now God has even let me see your children."[2]

When the LORD brought us back to Jerusalem, it was like a dream! How we laughed, how we sang for joy! Then the other nations said about us, "The LORD did great things for them." Indeed he did great things for us; how happy we were! Those who wept as they went out carrying the seed will come back singing for joy, as they bring in the harvest.[3]

When they arrived . . . they gathered the people of the church together and told them about all that God had done with them and how he had opened the way for the Gentiles to believe.[4]

I am going to prepare a place for you. And after I go and prepare a place for you, I will come back and take you to myself, so that you will be where I am.[5]—Just a little while longer, and he who is coming will come; he will not delay.[6]

[1]JOHN 16.22. [2]Gen. 48.11. [3]Ps. 126.1–3, 6. [4]Acts 14.27. [5]John 14.2, 3.—[6]Heb. 10.37.

Evening

For ever free from sorrow and grief.[1]

Jacob saw Esau coming with his four hundred men. Esau ran to meet him, threw his arms round him, and kissed him. They were both crying. Jacob said, ". . . if I have gained your favour, accept my gift. To see your face is for me like seeing the face of God, now that you have been so friendly to me."[2]

Joseph told his brothers who he was . . . He said, "I am your brother Joseph, whom you sold into Egypt. Now do not be upset or blame yourselves because you sold me here. It was really God who sent me ahead of you to save people's lives . . . Tell my father how powerful I am here in Egypt . . . Then hurry and bring him here."[3]

Peter was kept in jail, but the people of the church were praying earnestly to God for him . . . He explained to them how the Lord had brought him our of prison.[4]

[1]ISA. 35.10. [2]Gen. 33.1, 4, 10. [3]Gen. 45.1, 4, 5, 13. [4]Acts 12.5, 17.

I am the LORD, the one who heals you.[1]

I will not die; instead, I will live and proclaim what the LORD has done. He has punished me severely, but he has not let me die.[2]

Praise the LORD, my soul, and do not forget how kind he is. He forgives all my sins and heals all my diseases.[3]—About this time King Hezekiah fell ill and almost died. Hezekiah . . . prayed: "Remember, LORD, that I have served you faithfully and loyally, and that I have always tried to do what you wanted me to." And he began to cry bitterly. Then the LORD commanded Isaiah to go back to Hezekiah and say to him, "I, the LORD, the God of your ancestor David, have heard your prayer and seen your tears; I will let you live fifteen years longer."[4]

A man suffering from a dreaded skin disease came to him, knelt down before him, and said, "Sir, if you want to, you can make me clean." Jesus stretched out his hand and touched him. "I do want to," he answered. "Be clean!" At once the man was healed of his disease.[5]

[1]EXOD. 15.26. [2]Ps. 118.17, 18. [3]Ps. 103.2, 3.—[4]Isa. 38.1–5. [5]Matt. 8.2, 3.

Evening

This prayer made in faith will heal the sick person.[1]

The final result of this illness will not be the death of Lazarus; this has happened in order to bring glory to God.[2]—God knows every step I take; if he tests me, he will find me pure.[3]

I have thought it is necessary to send you our brother Epaphroditus, who has worked and fought by my side and who has served as your messenger in helping me. He is anxious to see you all and is very upset because you had heard that he was ill. Indeed he was ill and almost died. But God had pity on him and not only on him but on me, too, and spared me an even greater sorrow . . . Show respect to all such people as he, because he risked his life and nearly died for the sake of the work of Christ, in order to give me the help that you yourselves could not give.[4]

His answer was: "My grace is all you need, for my power is greatest when you are weak." I am most happy, then, to be proud of my weaknesses, in order to feel the protection of Christ's power over me.[5]

[1]JAS 5.15. [2]John 11.4.—[3]Job 23.10. [4]Phil. 2.25–27, 29, 30. [5]2 Cor. 12.9.

Be patient and wait for the Lord to act.[1]

Let us go off by ourselves to some place where we will be alone and you can rest for a while.[2]—They came to Elim, where there were twelve springs and seventy palm-trees; there they camped by the water.[3]

He lay down under the tree and fell asleep. Suddenly an angel touched him and said, "Wake up and eat." He looked round, and saw a loaf of bread and a jar of water near his head. He ate and drank, and lay down again. The Lord's angel returned and woke him up a second time, saying, "Get up and eat, or the journey will be too much for you." Elijah got up, ate and drank, and the food gave him enough strength to walk forty days to Sinai, the holy mountain.[4]

The Lord is my shepherd; I have everything I need. He lets me rest in fields of green grass and leads me to quiet pools of fresh water. He gives me new strength.[5]

[1]PS. 37.7. [2]Mark 6.31.—[3]Exod. 15.27. [4]1 Kgs 19.5–8. [5]Ps. 23.1–3.

Evening

The Lord will guard you: he is by your side to protect you.[1]

Don't you know? Haven't you heard? The Lord is the everlasting God; he created all the world. He never grows tired or weary. No one understands his thoughts. He strengthens those who are weak and tired. Even those who are young and grow weak; young men can fall exhausted. But those who trust in the Lord for help will find their strength renewed. They will rise on wings like eagles; they will run and not get weary; they will walk and not grow weak.[2]

I stay young and strong like an eagle. As a father is kind to his children, so the Lord is kind to those who honour him. He knows what we are made of; he remembers that we are dust.[3]

We who have this spiritual treasure are like common clay pots, in order to show that the supreme power belongs to God, not to us. And this small and temporary trouble we suffer will bring us a tremendous and eternal glory, much greater than the trouble.[4]

[1]PS. 121.5. [2]Isa. 40.28–31. [3]Ps. 103.5, 13, 14. [4]2 Cor. 4.7, 17.

When trouble comes, just remember:[1]

If you are weak in a crisis, you are weak indeed.[2]—I have tested you in the fire of suffering, as silver is refined in a furnace.[3]—We must pass through many troubles to enter the Kingdom of God.[4]

Even though the fig-trees have no fruit and no grapes grow on the vines, even though the olive-crop fails and the fields produce no corn, even though the sheep all die and the cattle-stalls are empty, I will still be joyful and glad, because the LORD God is my Saviour.[5]

Let us give thanks to the God and Father of our Lord Jesus Christ, the merciful Father, the God from whom all help comes! He helps us in all our troubles, so that we are able to help others who have all kinds of troubles, using the same help that we ourselves have received from God.[6]

We also boast of our troubles.[7]—I have learnt to be satisfied with what I have.[8]—Your sadness will turn into gladness.[9]

[1]ECCLES. 7.14. [2]Prov. 24.10.—[3]Isa. 48.10.—[4]Acts 14.22. [5]Hab. 3.17, 18. [6]2 Cor. 1.3, 4. [7]Rom. 5.3.—[8]Phil. 4.11.—[9]John 16.20.

Evening

Trouble produces endurance.[1]

Why am I so sad? Why am I so troubled? I will put my hope in God, and once again I will praise him, my saviour and my God.[2]

I was jealous of the proud when I saw that things go well for the wicked. I tried to think this problem through, but it was too difficult for me until I went into your Temple. Then I understood what will happen to the wicked.[3]—Leave your troubles with the LORD, and he will defend you.[4]

No one stood by me the first time I defended myself; all deserted me. May God not count it against them! But the Lord stayed with me and gave me strength . . . and I was rescued from being sentenced to death.[5]

If it were an enemy that mocked me, I could endure it . . . But it is you, my companion, my colleague and close friend. We had intimate talks with each other and worshipped together in the Temple.[6]—Without fail, he brings justice to his people.[7]

[1]ROM. 5.3. [2]Ps. 42.5. [3]Ps. 73.3, 16, 17.—[4]Ps. 55.22. [5]2 Tim. 4.16, 17. [6]Ps. 55.12–14.—[7]Zeph. 3.5.

Morning

When things are going well for you, be glad.[1]

The LORD was with Joseph and made him successful.[2]—How great is the LORD! He is pleased with the success of his servant.[3]

Happy are those who reject the advice of evil men, who do not follow the example of sinners or join those who have no use for God. Instead, they find joy in obeying the Law of the LORD, and they study it day and night. They are like trees that grow beside a stream, that bear fruit at the right time, and whose leaves do not dry up. They succeed in everything they do.[4]

Be sure that the book of the Law is always read in your worship. Study it day and night, and make sure that you obey everything written in it. Then you will be prosperous and successful.[5]

The LORD was with him, and he was successful in everything he did.[6]—He was successful, because everything he did . . . he did in a spirit of complete loyalty and devotion to his God.[7]

[1]ECCLES. 7.14. [2]Gen. 39.2.—[3]Ps. 35.27. [4]Ps. 1.1–3. [5]Josh. 1.8. [6]2 Kgs. 18.7.—[7]2 Chr. 31.21.

Evening

If God is for us, who can be against us?[1]

My dear friend, I pray that everything may go well with you and that you may be in good health—as I know you are well in spirit.[2]

Every Sunday each of you must put aside some money, in proportion to what he has earned.[3]—Bring the full amount of your tithes to the Temple, so that there will be plenty of food there. Put me to the test and you will see that I will open the windows of Heaven and pour out on you in abundance all kinds of good things.[4]

All riches and wealth come from you; you rule everything by your strength and power.[5]—So Solomon succeeded his father David on the throne which the LORD had established. He was a successful king.[6]—Be concerned above everything else with the Kingdom of God and with what he requires of you, and he will provide you with all these other things.[7]

Do not store up riches for yourselves here on earth, where moths and rust destroy, and robbers break in and steal. Instead, store up riches for yourselves in heaven . . . For your heart will always be where your riches are.[8]

[1]ROM. 8.31. [2]3 John 2. [3]1 Cor. 16.2.—[4]Mal. 3.10. [5]1 Chr. 29.12.—[6]1 Chr. 29.23.—[7]Matt. 6.33. [8]Matt. 6.19–21.

If your riches increase, don't depend on them.[1]

Remember that it is the LORD your God who gives you the power to become rich.[2]—It is the LORD's blessing that makes you wealthy. Hard work can make you no richer.[3]—"Rich men [should not boast] of their wealth. If anyone wants to boast, he should boast that he knows and understands me . . . I, the LORD, have spoken."[4]

Your money can be gone in a flash, as if it had grown wings and flown away like an eagle.[5]—Command those who are rich in the things of this life not to be proud, but to place their hope, not in such an uncertain thing as riches, but in God, who generously gives us everything for our enjoyment.[6]—I will also give you what you have not asked for: all your life you will have wealth and honour, more than that of any other king.[7]—Wealth is not permanent.[8]

Let me be neither rich nor poor. So give me only as much food as I need.[9]—Honour the LORD by making him an offering from the best of all that your land produces. If you do, your barns will be filled with grain, and you will have too much wine to be able to store it all.[10]

[1]PS. 62.10. [2]Deut. 8.18.—[3]Prov. 10.22.—[4]Jer. 9.23, 24. [5]Prov. 23.5.—[6]1 Tim. 6.17.—[7]1 Kgs 3.13.—[8]Prov. 27.24. [9]Prov. 30.8.—[10]Prov. 3.9, 10.

Evening

Do whatever he tells you.[1]

You can do nothing without me.[2]—When he finished speaking, he said to Simon, "Push the boat out further to the deep water, and you and your partners let down your nets for a catch." "Master," Simon answered, "we worked hard all night long and caught nothing. But if you say so, I will let down the nets." They let them down and caught such a large number of fish that the nets were about to break. So they motioned to their partners in the other boat to come and help them. They came and filled both boats so full of fish that the boats were about to sink. When Simon Peter saw what had happened, he fell on his knees before Jesus and said, "Go away from me, Lord! I am a sinful man!"[3]

My dear brothers, stand firm and steady. Keep busy always in your work for the Lord, since you know that nothing you do in the Lord's service is ever useless.[4]

[1]JOHN 2.5. [2]John 15.5.—[3]Luke 5.4–9. [4]1 Cor. 15.58.

Morning

I asked him for this child, and he gave me what I asked for.[1]

Children are a gift from the LORD; they are a real blessing.[2]

Little children will take care of them.[3]—Teach a child how he should live, and he will remember it all his life.[4]—I have chosen him in order that he may command his sons and his descendants to obey me and to do what is right and just.[5]—Your sons will be like young olive-trees round your table.[6]—He took a child and made him stand in front of them. He put his arms round him and said to them, "Whoever welcomes in my name one of these children, welcomes me; and whoever welcomes me, welcomes not only me but also the one who sent me."[7]

Jesus . . . said . . . "Let the children come to me, and do not stop them, because the Kingdom of God belongs to such as these."[8]

See that you don't despise any of these little ones. Their angels in Heaven, I tell you, are always in the presence of my father in heaven.[9]

[1]1 SAM 1.27. [2]Ps. 127.3. [3]Isa. 11.6.—[4]Prov. 22.6.—[5]Gen. 18.19.—[6]Ps. 128.3.—[7]Mark 9.36, 37. [8]Mark 10.14. [9]Matt. 18.10.

Evening

Let us thank God for his priceless gift![1]

God showed his love for us by sending his only Son into the world, so that we might have life through him.[2]

She gave birth to her first son, wrapped him in strips of cloth and laid him in a manger—there was no room for them to stay in the inn.[3]

Then there were some shepherds in that part of the country who were spending the night in the fields, taking care of their flocks. An angel of the Lord appeared to them, and the glory of the Lord shone over them. They were terribly afraid, but the angel said to them, "Don't be afraid! I am here with good news for you, which will bring great joy to all the people. This very day in David's town your Saviour was born—Christ the Lord! And this is what will prove it to you: you will find a baby wrapped in strips of cloth and lying in a manger."[4]

Suddenly a great army of heaven's angels appeared with the angel, singing praises go God: "Glory to God in the highest heaven, and peace on earth to those with whom he is pleased!"[5]

[1]2 COR. 9.15. [2]1 John 4.9. [3]Luke 2.7. [4]Luke 2.8–12. [5]Luke 2.13, 14.

You shall set the fiftieth year apart.[1]

And proclaim the freedom to all the inhabitants of the land. During this year all property that has been sold shall be restored to the original owner or his descendants, and anyone who has been sold as a slave shall return to his family.[2]

You will know the truth, and the truth will set you free. If the Son sets you free, then you will be really free.[3]—Remember how the LORD your God led you.[4]—He found them wandering through the desert, a desolate, wind-swept wilderness. He protected them and cared for them, as he would protect himself.[5]

Happy is the man who has the God of Jacob to help him and who depends on the LORD his God.[6]—He keeps me from the grave and blesses me with love and mercy.[7]

I will sing to the LORD all my life; as long as I live I will sing praises to my God. May he be pleased with my song, for my gladness comes from him.[8]

[1]LEV. 25.10. [2]Lev. 25.10. [3]John 8.32, 36.—[4]Deut. 8.2.—[5]Deut. 32.10. [6]Ps. 146.5.—[7]Ps. 103.4. [8]Ps. 104.33, 34.

Evening

You shall set the fiftieth year apart.[1]

The whole year shall be sacred for you . . . In this year all property that has been sold shall be restored to its original owner. Your land must not be sold on a permanent basis . . . it belongs to God.[2]—Send a man to blow a trumpet throughout the land.[3]

May you always be joyful in your union with the Lord. I say it again: rejoice![4]—Christ has set us free! Stand, then, as free people, and do not allow yourselves to become slaves again.[5]

Jesus Christ is the same yesterday, today, and for ever.[6]— I will proclaim your greatness, my God and king; I will thank you for ever and ever. Every day I will thank you . . . The LORD is great and is to be highly praised; his greatness is beyond understanding. What you have done will be praised from one generation to the next; they will proclaim your mighty acts. They will tell about all your goodness and sing about your kindness.[7]

Praise the LORD! Praise him for the mighty things he has done. Praise his supreme greatness.[8]

[1]LEV. 25.10. [2]Lev. 25.12, 13, 23.—[3]Lev. 25.9. [4]Phil. 4.4.—[5]Gal. 5.1. [6]Heb. 13.8.—[7]Ps. 145.1–4, 7. [8]Ps. 150.1, 2.

Old men have wisdom . . . old men have insight.[1]

Seventy years is all we have—eighty years if we are strong; yet all they bring us is trouble and sorrow; life is soon over, and we are gone. Our life . . . fades away like a whisper.[2]—I am your God and will take care of you until you are old and your hair is grey. I made you and will care for you; I will give you help and rescue you.[3]

We . . . respect the grey hair of age.[4]—Happy is the man who becomes wise—who gains understanding. There is more profit in it than there is in silver; it is worth more to you than gold. Wisdom is more valuable than jewels; nothing you could want can compare with it. Wisdom offers you long life, as well as wealth and honour.[5]

Ever since you were a child, you have known the Holy Scriptures, which are able to give you the wisdom that leads to salvation through faith in Christ Jesus.[6]

[1]JOB 12.12. [2]Ps. 90.10, 9.—[3]Isa. 46.4. [4]Prov. 20.29.—[5]Prov. 3.13–16. [6]2 Tim. 3.15.

Evening

[***They***] ***still bear fruit in old age.***[1]

Whoever goes to the LORD for safety, whoever remains under the protection of the Almighty . . . I will reward them with long life; I will save them.[2]

Respect your father and your mother, so that you may live a long time in the land that I am giving you.[3]

Show respect for old people and honour them. Reverently obey me; I am the Lord.[4]—Love the LORD your God, obey him and be faithful to him, and then you and your descendants will live long.[5]—Use true and honest weights and measures, so that you may live a long time in the land.[6]

Trust in the LORD with all your heart. Never rely on what you think you know. Remember the LORD in everything you do, and he will show you the right way.[7]—The road the righteous travel is like the sunrise, getting brighter and brighter until daylight has come.[8]

[1]PS. 92.14. [2]Ps. 91.1, 16. [3]Exod. 20.12. [4]Lev. 19.32.—[5]Deut. 30.20.—[6]Deut. 25.15. [7]Prov. 3.5, 6.—[8]Prov. 4.18.

You guide me with your instruction and at the end you will receive me with honour.[1]

Faithful to your promise, you led the people you had rescued; by your strength you guided them to your sacred land. You bring them in and plant them on your mountain, the place that you, LORD, have chosen for your home, the Temple that you yourself have built.[2]

The LORD your God has given you all the good things that he promised. Every promise he made has been kept; not one has failed.[3]

God, who has led me to this very day.[4]—Your presence fills me with joy and brings me pleasure for ever.[5]—I know that your goodness and love will be with me all my life; and your house will be my home as long as I live.[6]

Now, Lord, you have kept your promise, and you may let your servant go in peace. With my own eyes I have seen your salvation.[7]

[1]PS. 73.24. [2]Exod. 15.13, 17. [3]Josh. 23.14. [4]Gen. 48.15.—[5]Ps. 16.11.—[6]Ps. 23.6. [7]Luke 2.29, 30.

Evening

There are many rooms in my Father's house.[1]

Teach us how short our life is, so that we may become wise.[2]—In this way you will be given the full right to enter the eternal Kingdom of our Lord and Saviour Jesus Christ.[3]—By the sacrificial death of Christ we are set free, that is, our sins are forgiven.[4]

For our gifts of knowledge and of inspired messages are only partial; but when what is perfect comes, then what is partial will disappear. What we see now is like a dim image in a mirror; then we shall see face to face. What I know now is only partial; then it will be complete—as complete as God's knowledge of me.[5]—He will wipe away all tears from their eyes. There will be no more death, no more grief or crying or pain. The old things have disappeared.[6]

You will see a king ruling in splendour.[7]—Listen to this secret truth: we shall not all die, but . . . we shall all be changed.[8]—We shall be like him, because we shall see him as he really is.[9]

[1]JOHN 14.2. [2]Ps. 90.12.—[3]2 Pet. 1.11.—[4]Eph. 1.7. [5]1 Cor. 13.9, 10, 12.— [6]Rev. 21.4. [7]Isa. 33.17.—[8]1 Cor. 15.51.—[9]1 John 3.2.